Excellent Dr Stanley

THE LIFE OF DEAN STANLEY OF WESTMINSTER

FOR CHARLOTTE, HARRIET, GEORGE
AND HENRY

There's a wideness in God's mercy,
Like the wideness of the sea;
There's a kindness in his justice,
Which is more than liberty.

F. W. FABER, 1814–63

Contents

Illustrations	ix
Acknowledgements	xi
Family Trees	xiii
Preface	1
Introduction: Thomas Arnold's Biographer	3

PART ONE: ALDERLEY AND RUGBY 1815–1834

1	'In Possession of a Good Fortune' 1815–1828	25
2	'Under the Boughs of a Mighty Oak' 1829–1834	45

PART TWO: OXFORD 1834–1851

3	'Trailing Clouds of Glory' 1834–1837	71
4	'From the Dust of Creeds Outworn' 1838–1842	103
5	'O for … the Sound of a Voice that is Still!' 1842–1851	129

PART THREE: CANTERBURY AND OXFORD 1851–1863

6	'Treading the Pilgrim's Ground' 1851–1858	169
7	'The Rays of Regal Bounty Shine' 1858–1863	198

PART FOUR: WESTMINSTER 1864–1881

8	'That Temple of … Reconciliation' 1864–1870	243
9	'To Dust and Ashes Turned' 1870–1876	267
10	'Of Slowly Ebbing Powers' 1876–1881	303

APPENDICES

I Stanley's eyewitness account of the Coronation of Queen
   Victoria, 28 June 1838   333
II Extract from 'The Murder of Becket', *Historical Memorials
   of Canterbury,* 1855   335
III Stanley's account of David and Goliath, *Lectures on the
    History of the Jewish Church,* ii, 1865   340
IV Address delivered in Rugby Chapel on 12 June 1874,
   thirty-two years after the death of Arnold   342

Source Notes   346
Select Bibliography   380
Index   389

© John Witheridge 2013

The right of John Witheridge to be identified as the author of this work has been asserted by him in accordance with the Copyright, Designs and Patents Act, 1988

First published in Great Britain 2013
by Michael Russell (Publishing) Ltd
Wilby Hall, Wilby, Norwich NR16 2JP

Typeset in Sabon by Waveney Typesetters
Wymondham, Norfolk
Printed and bound in Great Britain
by MPG Books Group, Bodmin and King's Lynn

All rights reserved

ISBN 978–0–85955–323–0

Excellent Dr Stanley

THE LIFE OF DEAN STANLEY OF WESTMINSTER

John Witheridge

MICHAEL RUSSELL

Illustrations

Between pages 176 and 177:

1a   Stanley's father as Bishop of Norwich
1b   Stanley's mother, Kitty, the year after her marriage
1c   Kitty Stanley, when she was living at Canterbury
1d   Mary Stanley, after the Crimean War
2a   The church and rectory at Alderley
2b   Stanley as a pupil at Rugby
2c   Thomas Arnold by Thomas Phillips, RA (*National Portrait Gallery*)
3   Ackermann print of Rugby School
4a   The sixth form schoolroom at Rugby
4b   Charles Vaughan, Headmaster of Harrow, by George Richmond (*Keepers and Governors of Harrow School*)
4c   Balliol College, the front quadrangle, 1810
5a   Queen Victoria's Coronation, 28 June 1838 (*HM the Queen*)
5b   University College, Oxford, from the High Street
6a   John Henry Newman, 1847, two years after his conversion to Rome
6b   Stanley as fellow and tutor of University College, by Eden Eddis, 1851 (*Master and Fellows, University College, Oxford*)
6c   Canterbury Cathedral in Stanley's time
7a   The opening of the Great Exhibition, 1 May 1851 (*HM the Queen*)
7b   Archibald Campbell Tait as Headmaster of Rugby
7c   Benjamin Jowett by George Richmond, 1850 (*Master and Fellows, Balliol College, Oxford*)
8a   The Duke of Wellington's funeral procession, 18 November 1852 (*English Heritage*)
8b   R. D. Hampden by H. W. Pickersgill (*Governing Body, Christ Church, Oxford*)
8c   Dean Liddell by George Richmond, 1858 (*Governing Body, Christ Church, Oxford*)

Between pages 304 and 305:

9   Portrait of Stanley by Lowes Cato Dickinson (*National Portrait Gallery*)
10 The Great Quadrangle (Tom Quad) at Christ Church, with Wren's Tom Tower
11 Lewis Carroll's photograph of Stanley at Christ Church (*National Portrait Gallery*)
12a The Prince of Wales's wedding, with Queen Victoria (and bust of Prince Albert)
12b Lady Augusta Stanley by George Richmond
12c Some Oxford liberals associated with *Essays and Reviews* (*Bodleian Libraries, University of Oxford* [G.A. Oxon. 4° 414, no. 430] *and Hymns Ancient and Modern Ltd*)
13a Westminster Abbey and St Margaret's Church, 1753 (*City of London, London Metropolitan Archives*)
13b Stanley at his standing-desk in the Deanery at Westminster
13c The entrance to the Deanery
14 Portrait of Stanley by G. F. Watts, RA, 1866–7 (*University of Oxford*)
15 Portrait of Stanley by Heinrich von Angeli (*Dean and Chapter of Westminster*)
16 'Philosophic Belief', *Vanity Fair*, September 1872

Acknowledgements

LORD STANLEY of Alderley not only authorised this biography but lent books and documents and took an interest in its writing. I am grateful too to the Governing Body of Charterhouse, and especially to the then chairman, John Walker-Haworth, for granting me a sabbatical, part of which I spent researching in Oxford as a guest of his college. Thanks are due to the Master and Fellows of Pembroke for their hospitality.

I owe much to my friends and colleagues, Tony Bennett, Emily Fox and Jim Freeman, for advice on matters American, French and classical. Helen Pinkney generously devoted her skills to reproducing the illustrations. Five expert friends read and commented on every draft chapter: D. R. Thorpe, who has done much to help me answer Virginia Woolf's vexed question, 'My God, how does one write a Biography?'; Zoë Green, who has reminded me that a biographer should be a novelist as well as an historian; and Robin Darwall-Smith, Robert Fox and Simon Heffer, whose detailed knowledge has been astonishing, and advice invaluable.

Librarians and archivists have proved invariably welcoming and helpful. I am indebted to archivists Jenny Youatt at Alderley parish church, Louise Martin at the Cheshire Record Office, Rusty MacLean at Rugby, John Jones and Anna Sander at Balliol, Judith Curthoys at Christ Church, Barry Orford at Pusey House, Cressida Williams at Canterbury Cathedral, Pamela Clark at Windsor Castle, and Tony Trowles at Westminster Abbey. I am grateful to librarians at the Bodleian, the British Library, Lambeth Palace, the London Library, and Gladstone's library at St Deiniol's, Hawarden.

Acknowledgement is readily made to those who have kindly given me permission to quote from documents in their possession or care. First and foremost, Her Majesty Queen Elizabeth II; also Cheshire Archives and Local Studies; the Headmaster and Governing Body of Rugby School; at Oxford, the Bodleian Library, the Masters and Fellows of Balliol and University Colleges, the Governing Body of Christ Church, and the Principal and Chapter of Pusey House; and the Deans and Chapters of Westminster and Canterbury Cathedral.

My secretaries are heroines: Helen Laurie, who, in addition to all her other work, has helped me with research; and Sue Cook, who has faithfully typed every word, and at least seven times. My publisher, Michael Russell, has also been extraordinarily patient during seven years of gestation.

Most important, I am, in everything, most thankful to Sarah: *sine qua non*.

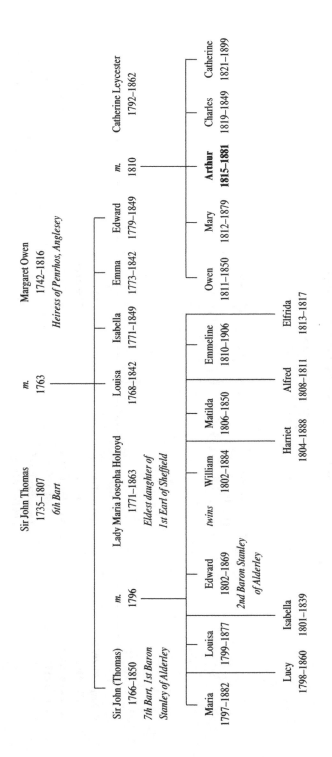

The Leycesters of Toft
1751–1798

The Revd Oswald
1751–1848

(1)   *m.*   Mary Johnson
d. 1812

Catherine ('Kitty')
1792–1862
m. Edward Stanley
1779–1849

Edward Penrhyn
1794–1861
m. Lady Charlotte Stanley
1801–1853
Eldest daughter of
13th Earl of Derby

Charles
1796–1820

Maria
1798–1870
m. Augustus Hare
1792–1834
adopted Augustus J. C. Hare,
1834–1903, son of Francis Hare

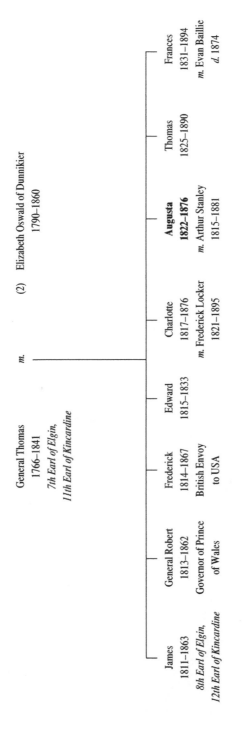

Preface

ARTHUR STANLEY was an eminent Victorian. Born in the year of Waterloo, he was named Arthur after the Duke of Wellington. His father was rector of Alderley in Cheshire, until Lord Melbourne appointed him Bishop of Norwich in 1837. Arthur was sent to Rugby (George Arthur in *Tom Brown's Schooldays?*) where Thomas Arnold was the new headmaster. Arnold and Stanley became devoted to each other, and Arnold exercised a powerful influence on the rest of Stanley's life. He won Rugby's first scholarship to Balliol, where he and Benjamin Jowett, Balliol's future master, became lifelong friends, and where Archibald Campbell Tait, later Archbishop of Canterbury, was his tutor. Stanley flirted briefly with the High Church Oxford Movement but rejected it on the liberal, Broad Church (he was the first to use that phrase) principles he had learnt from home and from Arnold, and which were to become fundamental to his life and work.

Snubbed by Balliol for his liberalism, Stanley became instead a fellow and tutor of University College, Oxford, where he wrote Arnold's biography and established Arnold's reputation as a headmaster. In 1851 Stanley was appointed a canon of Canterbury, returning seven years later to Oxford as Regius Professor of Ecclesiastical History and a canon of Christ Church. In 1863 Queen Victoria's 'excellent Dr Stanley' married Lady Augusta Bruce, her favourite lady-in-waiting and daughter of the Earl of Elgin (of the Parthenon marbles). The following month he was installed as Dean of Westminster. He made the Abbey the national temple and shrine we take for granted today.

Stanley was present at most of the landmark Victorian events: the Coronation, the opening of the Great Exhibition, the funerals of the Duke of Wellington and the Prince Consort, the marriage of the Prince of Wales. A list of his friends and acquaintances reads like a Victorian *Who's Who*. He met Gladstone as a boy, and his companions at Rugby included the poet Arthur Clough. Before Stanley went up to Oxford he was coached by Julius Hare (to whom he was related by marriage), and when he arrived he encountered Keble, Newman and Pusey. Later at

Christ Church he taught the Prince of Wales, and among his colleagues were Lewis Carroll and Alice's father, Dean Liddell. His circle at Westminster included Disraeli, Carlyle, Tennyson, Lyell, Browning, Dickens, Matthew Arnold, Kingsley, and even occasionally the Queen herself. Indeed Stanley's royal connections were considerable. Before Westminster he had been chaplain to both Queen Victoria and Prince Albert, and he officiated at the wedding in St Petersburg of Prince Alfred to Princess Marie of Russia.

His championing of liberal theology drew Stanley into an important and often painful role in the many controversies of the Victorian Church: subscription to the articles of religion, the Oxford Movement, the degradation of Ward, the Gorham judgment, *Essays and Reviews*, ritualism, and the rows over Bishops Hampden and Colenso.

A tireless traveller and travel-writer with a passion for historic sites, Stanley was a knowledgeable visitor to Egypt and the Holy Land, and escorted the Prince of Wales there in 1862. He was also a prolific author of articles and books, the most popular of which were his *Life and Correspondence of Thomas Arnold* and *Sinai and Palestine*. He died in office in 1881 and was buried with Lady Augusta in Henry VII's Chapel in the Abbey (his ancestor, Sir Thomas Stanley, was the King's stepfather). Matthew Arnold lamented Stanley's death in his poem 'Westminster Abbey':

> Ay me! 'Tis deaf, that ear
> Which joyed my voice to hear;
> Yet would I not disturb thee from thy tomb,
> Thus sleeping in thine Abbey's friendly shade,
> And the rough waves of life for ever laid!
> I would not break thy rest, nor change thy doom.
> Even as my father, thou –
> Even as that loved, that well-recorded friend –
> Hast thy commission done; ye both may now
> Wait for the leaven to work, the let to end.

This Victorian elegy immortalises the extraordinary relationship between Arthur Stanley and Thomas Arnold, the poet's father. Stanley's veneration of Arnold, and the profound and enduring effect Arnold had on him, are the leitmotifs of this biography.

Introduction

THOMAS ARNOLD'S BIOGRAPHER

ARTHUR STANLEY'S biography of Thomas Arnold stands near the heart of his achievements. Both men's reputations were created by Stanley's *Life*. It was once regarded as among the best biographies in the English language. It made Stanley a household name and linked him indelibly with Arnold.

The two volumes of *Life and Correspondence* were published in 1844, only two years after Arnold's sudden and premature death. Stanley was twenty-eight. His first book won immediate acclaim, running through a remarkable four editions in its first year alone. It was one of those occasional books that strikes exactly the right chord and attracts an unexpected popularity. 'No biography which has been written since,' said Benjamin Jowett nearly forty years later, 'and not more than one or two which preceded it, have ever produced an equal impression on the English-speaking world.'[1]

Stanley was the obvious choice for Mrs Arnold when it came to commissioning a memoir of her husband. She knew how fond Dr Arnold had been of young Arthur Stanley, and how highly he regarded his abilities as a scholar. More important, she knew the extent of Stanley's devotion to his headmaster, his admiration for what he had achieved at Rugby, and his sympathy for Arnold's ideas and opinions. Indeed few pupils can have felt a greater love and reverence for their teacher, or disciples for their master. Arnold's and Stanley's lives were already closely linked, giving power to the biography which in turn established a bond between them as inseparable as that between Johnson and Boswell.

A special one-volume edition was published in 1901 and presented to all candidates for the new teachers' certificate. The preface[a] praises the book 'as a classic, and as the most solid and enduring contribution to educational literature produced in England in the nineteenth century'.[2]

---

[a] The author was Sir Joshua Fitch, chief inspector of training colleges, 1885–94.

Popular at first because of interest in Arnold's religious and political opinions, Stanley's biography introduced the public to his work at Rugby, and it is this, his then lesser known but greater achievement, for which Arnold became renowned. The book had a considerable influence on subsequent generations of schoolmasters, and did much to fulfil the famous prediction of the Provost of Oriel that 'if Mr. Arnold were elected to the headmastership of Rugby, he would change the face of education all through the public schools of England.'[3] Among Stanley's closest friends was Charles Vaughan, Headmaster of Harrow until the threat of scandal cut short a promising career.[4] They had been companions at Rugby, and Vaughan married Stanley's younger sister. In his sermon at Stanley's funeral, Vaughan explained: 'It was quite possible so to have written the life of Arnold as that it should become the quarrel of a year, and then the oblivion of a century. It was the genius of Arthur Stanley which created the posthumous influence of Arnold.'[5]

Stanley's *Life* not only secured his and Arnold's reputations, it also set the trend for a new style of biography. All those two or three commemorative tomes of eulogy, laboriously supported by scores of letters, look back to Stanley. The earnestness of Victorian biography, and its emphasis on moral stature and public good, also take their cue from the *Life of Arnold*. The result is easily criticised, and it is true that many of these biographies depict not human portraits but moral heroes, ethical types, men (in Virginia Woolf's image) 'like the wax figures now preserved in Westminster Abbey, that were carried in funeral processions through the street – effigies that have only a smooth superficial likeness to the body in the coffin'.[6] But these represent perversions, or at best poor imitations, of Stanley's prototype.

* * *

The biography of Arnold has had its critics, not least from the Bloomsbury set, with their contempt for all things Victorian. In a lecture on English biography, Harold Nicolson drew a distinction between 'pure' and 'impure' biography. 'Pure' biography, he argued, is objective, historically accurate and well-constructed. 'Impure' biography, on the other hand, is sullied by extraneous subjective elements like the desire to illustrate a theory or celebrate the dead. In Nicolson's view, hagiography, the writing of the lives of saints, with all its 'impure' wonder and devotion, 'returned in stately triumph with Dean Stanley's *Life*'.[7] 'The complete rejection of truthful representation, the bag-and-baggage return to hagiography, cannot be dated earlier than 1844, the year in which Stanley published his egregious *Life of Arnold*.'[8] For Nicolson, Stanley's *Life* is too admiring, and his subject too earnest and exemplary, for it to be anything but bad biography.

Lytton Strachey's censures of Stanley's biography were implied and more subtle than this, but no less disdainful. In his preface to *Eminent Victorians* he accused biography of having 'fallen on evil times in England ...

> With us, the most delicate and humane of all the branches of the art of writing has been relegated to the journeymen of letters; we do not reflect that it is perhaps as difficult to write a good life as to live one. Those two volumes, with which is it our custom to commemorate the dead – who does not know them, with their ill-digested masses of material, their slipshod style, their tone of tedious panegyric, their lamentable lack of selection, of detachment, of design?[9]

Nonetheless, Strachey's biographical sketch of Dr Arnold has Stanley's *Life and Correspondence* at the head of a short bibliography. Strachey admits in the preface that, despite his rejection of what he calls 'Standard Biographies', he remains 'indebted, in more ways than one, to such works'.[10] However, his own caustic chapter on Arnold could not be more different. Stanley's volumes are plundered for facts, but his admirable subject is lampooned as a tyrannical and sanctimonious prig.

The anti-Victorian bias of these Bloomsbury critics is clear on every page. Nonetheless, the criticisms they make of Stanley's *Life* – that it is idolising, moralising and eulogising, let alone badly written – need to be addressed. Are they fair to Stanley, or are they reading back into this pioneering work that of his less successful imitators? In any case, is devotion to the subject necessarily a bad trait in a biographer? Is an emphasis on moral authority a mistake if it is indeed a person's cardinal characteristic? And is a biography at fault if it does commend and commemorate its subject, and hold him up as an exemplar?

Furthermore, how accurate and reliable is Stanley's depiction of Arnold? This is the fundamental question the biographer of Stanley must answer at the outset because Stanley knew himself to be deeply influenced by Arnold. What exactly was that influence? Was it the influence of Arnold as he was, or was it instead the influence of Stanley's idealised and distorted understanding of a man he adored? These are difficult questions to answer because Stanley's biography remains our most complete source of information. Nonetheless, we need to be sure of our understanding of Arnold in order to assess whether the profound effect he had on Stanley was caused by the man himself, or by Stanley's image of him. If the latter, we may have to conclude that Stanley's own life and work were modelled on a misunderstanding.

* * *

It is certainly true that Stanley was captivated by Arnold from the start. By every account, Arnold was a man of strong and compelling character, 'the secret of his power consisting not so much in the novelty of his ideas and methods as in his commanding and magnetic personality, and the intensity and earnestness with which he impressed his views'.[11] His preaching in Rugby's chapel made a very deep impression, even on the youngest boys. Here is Thomas Hughes's vivid description in *Tom Brown's Schooldays*:

> – the oak pulpit standing out by itself above the School seats; the tall, gallant form, the kindling eye, the voice, now soft as the low notes of a flute, now clear and stirring as the call of the light-infantry bugle, of him who stood there Sunday after Sunday, witnessing and pleading for his Lord, the King of righteousness and love and glory, with whose spirit he was filled, and in whose power he spoke; the long lines of young faces, rising tier above tier down the whole length of the chapel, from the little boy's who had just left his mother to the young man's who was going out next week into the great world, rejoicing in his strength …
>
> But what was it, after all, which seized and held these three hundred boys, dragging them out of themselves, willing or unwilling, for twenty minutes, on Sunday afternoons? … We couldn't enter into half that we heard; we hadn't the knowledge of our own hearts or the knowledge of one another, and little enough of the faith, hope, and love needed to that end. But we listened, as all boys in their better moods will listen … to a man whom we felt to be, with all his heart and soul and strength, striving against whatever was mean and unmanly and unrighteous in our little world.[12]

According to Stanley's friend Vaughan, Arnold's sermons were the 'joy and pride of [Stanley's] week'. As Arnold climbed into the pulpit the two boys 'used to nudge each other with delight', and 'the sermon ended, Stanley hastened back to his study … and there he wrote down from loving memory the thing heard.' 'They who have not seen his face as he drank in one of those brief, manly, original, often heart-stirring, School Sermons, have not seen that face at its most beautiful, most rapturous, and most inspired.'[13]

It was, however, not until he entered the sixth form that Stanley really fell under Arnold's spell. For his last three years Stanley was taught every day by Arnold, and served under him as a praepostor, or prefect, charged with running the school. Stanley thrilled to Arnold's teaching, and delighted in the conviction that he was sharing in Arnold's moral purpose. By the end of his time at school he confessed (to Vaughan) to an idolatrous affection:

> Most sincerely must I thank God for His goodness in placing me here to live with Arnold. Yet I always feel that the happiness is a dangerous one, and that loving him and admiring him as I do to the very verge of all love and admiration that can be paid to man, I fear I have passed the limit, and made him my idol ...[14]

Ten years later, when Stanley was putting the finishing touches to the biography, idolatry had been reduced to what he now referred to as 'the almost filial relation in which I stood towards him'.[15] This is a more respectable description of his feelings, certainly, and one better suited to an author's preface, but does it do justice to the true depth and intensity of Stanley's affections?

Arnold died eight years after Stanley had left Rugby, and the shock was traumatic. It seemed 'as though the solid earth had passed away beneath my feet'.[16] Stanley took to his bed, prostrated by what he described as 'this dreadful calamity – the greatest that ever has – almost the greatest that ever can befall me'.[17] 'I loved him too much,' he told his sister Mary, 'it is both just as to the past, and good as to the future, that he should be taken away from me.'[18]

*   *   *

That Stanley was deeply attached to Arnold there is no doubt. It is, of course, why Mrs Arnold asked him to write her husband's *Life*. But biographies written under the supervising eyes of widows are, as Virginia Woolf explained, prone to dishonesty:

> The widow and the friends were hard taskmasters. Suppose, for example, that the man of genius was immoral, ill-tempered, and threw the boots at the maid's head. The widow would say: 'Still I loved him – he was the father of my children; and the public, who

love his books, must on no account be disillusioned. Cover up; omit.' The biographer obeyed.[19]

It is unthinkable that Arnold would have thrown his boots at the servants but it is chiefly Stanley's biography that makes us assume that this is so. On the other hand, Stanley does show Arnold to be bad-tempered at times, and there is no evidence that Mrs Arnold objected.

Stanley's preface makes plain his determination to control his bias and to be as detached and disinterested as he can. 'It was given to him to write, not indeed the first immortal biography, but the first of a new order of biographies, in which it is the one aim of the writer to stand aside out of the life of his subject.'[20] Stanley explains first that he has drawn on a variety of sources, and 'although, in its present shape, the responsibility of arranging and executing it has fallen upon one person, yet it should still be clearly understood how largely I have availed myself of the aid of others.'[21] Secondly, Stanley explains that the many letters he includes are an essential and integral part of the biography, and are there 'to give in his own words and in his own manner what (Arnold) felt and thought on the subjects of most interest to him'.[22] Over 300 letters are reproduced and they comprise nearly two-thirds of the book. The rest, the narrative, 'has been to state so much as would enable the reader to enter upon the Letters with a correct understanding of their writer ... In all cases where it was possible, his opinions and plans have been given in his own words.'[23]

By allowing Arnold to speak for himself Stanley imposes discipline on his own feelings and opinions. In this sense the *Life* contains more autobiography than biography, and Stanley concludes his preface by admitting to the subjective dangers of which he is only too aware, and which the incorporation of Arnold's correspondence, and the views of others who knew him, was designed to combat:

> It will be obvious that to have mixed up any judgment of my own, either of praise or censure, with the facts or statements contained in this work would have been wholly irrelevant. The only question that I have allowed myself to ask in each particular act or opinion ... has been not whether I approved or disapproved of it, but whether it was characteristic of him.[24]

Stanley strives in the biography to be objective, authentic and (in Nicolson's sense) 'pure'. The prose is generally concise, detailed and matter-of-fact – a style that indicates Stanley's resolve to remain impartial.

He is largely successful in this, and arguably it is Nicolson's criticisms that are subjective, and symptomatic of his own Bloomsbury bias. Most commentators have taken a more complimentary view of Stanley's remarkable achievement in writing what is a classic biography. To Edward Mack, for instance, 'Stanley's biography of his master is a great book because it combines the reverent idealisation of the disciple with the powerful realism and objectivity of a mature individual.'[25]

In his study of Victorian biography, A. O. J. Cockshut argues that Stanley's detachment is most apparent and effective in 'the finest and best-remembered scene in Stanley's book – the death scene. Its power, which is considerable, is a restrained power. Though writing so near the event, Stanley avoided strong expressions of grief or loss.'[26] We know from his correspondence how devastating Arnold's sudden death was to Stanley, and it may have been fortunate that he had not been at Rugby when Arnold collapsed. He had to rely not on his own impressions but on others', especially Mrs Arnold's[b] and his schoolfriend William Lake's (he happened to be staying with the Arnolds). Stanley manages to describe Arnold's last days calmly and dispassionately, making his account all the more moving. He skilfully weaves the shock of a sudden, unexpected and premature death into a narrative which makes this tragic end seem a great destiny fulfilled:

> The last week of the long summer half-year had now arrived – his fourteenth year at Rugby was drawing to its close ... On the 5th of June the last and farewell sermon was preached in the chapel, before the final dispersion of the boys for the holidays ... The school business was now completely over ... One more act, the last before he retired that night, remains to be recorded – the last entry in his Diary, which was not known or seen till the next morning, when it was discovered by those to whom every word bore a weight and meaning, which he who wrote it had but little anticipated.
>
> Saturday evening, June 11th. – The day after to-morrow is my birthday, if I am permitted to live to see it – my forty-seventh birthday since my birth. How large a portion of my life on earth is already passed. And then – what is to follow this life?[27]

Before his *Life of Arnold* Stanley had no experience of writing biography, and would have seen himself as no more than one of Strachey's

---

[b] Mrs Arnold wrote a detailed account of her husband's final days in a black notebook (Rugby School archives); Stanley had this to hand when he wrote his final chapter.

journeymen of letters. With the death scene, Stanley's biography transcends the memoir he set out to write, and the fusion here of detachment and feeling, detail and explanation, puts him in the company of the best biographers:

> All sensitively-written death scenes are a product of a tension between fact and interpretation. The most trivial remark or gesture can be endowed in the minds of onlookers with symbolic significance because it is the last. And death is at once a great mystery and a plain mundane fact with practical consequences. Stanley is one of the most successful of all English biographers in making this paradox fruitful for his art.[28]

* * *

Arnold's moral and religious zeal comes across on almost every page as his dominant characteristic, and at least here Strachey's satire is fairly focused:

> All who knew him during these years were profoundly impressed by the earnestness of his religious convictions and feelings, which, as one observer said, 'were ever bursting forth'. It was impossible to disregard his 'deep consciousness of the invisible world' and 'the peculiar feeling of love and adoration which he entertained towards our Lord Jesus Christ'. 'His manner of awful reverence when speaking of God or of the Scriptures' was particularly striking. 'No one could know him even a little,' said another friend, 'and not be struck by his absolute wrestling with evil, so that like St Paul he seemed to be battling with the wicked one, and yet with a feeling of God's help on his side.'[29]

Such earnestness was highly attractive to a generation reacting to the Godless excesses of Regency England. This is one reason why Stanley's biography was so enthusiastically received. Other men, moved by Stanley's biography, modelled themselves on Arnold, and their biographers, encouraged by Stanley's success, made this trait their subjects' dominant characteristic, and an example for their readers to emulate. So it is understandable that to Nicolson earnestness came in 1844 with Stanley's biography, 'and with earnestness hagiography descended on us with its sullen cloud'.[30] But if the characteristic of moral earnestness is emphasised by Stanley it is because it is a characteristic supremely true of his particular subject. When other biographers stressed the same virtue, it was rarely, if ever, as appropriate as it was to Arnold. 'One can read dozens of volumes of *Life and Letters* ... and recognise that with greater or less skill, with greater or less truthfulness, the Stanley formula is being copied. And, almost always, as is fitting, the prevailing impression is that the imitators do not equal the pioneer.'[31] Nicolson reads later derivatives back into Stanley, and their distortions are wrongly assumed to be Stanley's too.

But despite 'the fixed earnestness and devotion which took possession of his whole heart and will',[32] Stanley's Arnold is not perfect. For all his high-mindedness Arnold remains deeply ambitious. 'It is evident', wrote Stanley, 'that he was not insensible to the attraction of visions of extensive influence, and almost to his latest hour he seems to have been conscious of the existence of the temptation within him, and of the necessity of contending against it.'[33] Stanley quotes a conversation Arnold had with a pupil in which he admitted to being 'one of the most ambitious men alive'.[34]

Stanley also mentions Arnold's inclination to treat people not as individuals but as types – of a sect or party (and certainly of sinful humanity). Arnold admitted in a letter to John Taylor Coleridge (which Stanley includes) that this led to 'the want of sympathy which I cannot but feel towards so many of those whom I meet with'.[35] 'With every wish to be impartial,' wrote Stanley, 'his natural temperament, as he used himself to acknowledge, made it difficult for him to place himself completely in another's point of view; and thus he had a tendency to judge individuals, with whom he had no personal acquaintance, from his conception of the party to which they belonged ...'[36]

In addition, Stanley refers more than once to Arnold's 'vehemence of language which he often used, in speaking of the subjects and events of the day'.[37] This, Stanley explains, was provoked by his 'deep, ineffable scorn and indignation at the sight of vice and sin'.[38] That was understandable, perhaps, but Stanley is clearly uncomfortable with what he describes as a defect which caused offence. He gives as an example Arnold's virulent and self-righteous article on 'The Oxford Malignants'. In 1836 the Prime Minister, Lord Melbourne, appointed Renn Dickson Hampden to the regius chair of divinity at Oxford. The Tory High Church party regarded the Whiggish Hampden as a heretic, and expressed their outrage in a malicious attack. Arnold counter-attacked, using language that more than matched the Tractarians', whom he accused of fanaticism, deceit and hypocrisy. In a letter to his mother, Stanley described the article as

> ... the most unfortunate thing which could possibly have happened – I am quite shocked, as I have no doubt you will be, at the uncharitable and unchristian way in which he speaks of Newman and Pusey. To anyone living at Oxford in the daily knowledge of the goodness of these men such phrases as 'moral wickedness'–'pretended holiness'–'deliberate dishonesty' must appear monstrous and shocking to the last degree.[39]

Stanley's disapproval was calmer when writing the biography seven years later, and he is now determined not to judge. Nonetheless, his dismay and disquiet are still evident:

> ... with his usual rapidity of composition, he gave vent to his indignation in an article in the Edinburgh Review ... Though only a temporary production, it forms a feature in his life too strongly marked to be passed over without notice. On the one hand it completely represents his own deep feelings at the time ... on the other hand it contains the most startling and vehement, because the most personal, language which he ever allowed himself deliberately to use. The offence caused by it, even amongst his friends, was very great ...[40]

It is significant that Stanley omitted this notorious article from his collection of Arnold's writings, published a year after the biography.[c]

*　　*　　*

Stanley concentrates on Arnold as headmaster rather than historian, or political or religious controversialist. He does this for three good reasons. First, his role as Headmaster of Rugby was the most central and important in Arnold's life, despite his interests and engagement in the world outside. Second, this focus allows Stanley to deflect attention away from Arnold's public persona as a trenchant critic of Church and society. Here, Stanley is saying, is the other, more important side of the man, previously hidden from view behind the walls of Rugby. And third, this is the Arnold Stanley knew and loved so well, and here he can speak from direct and recent personal experience.

The two lengthy chapters on Rugby are the most absorbing of the biography. Neither is supported by Arnold's letters, and this makes the *Life* unevenly balanced, and these chapters in danger of bias.

---

[c] *The Miscellaneous Works of Thomas Arnold, D.D.*, 1845.

Introduction

Furthermore, Stanley does not seem interested in Arnold's life before Rugby. His family background, his childhood, his schooling at Winchester – all this is disposed of in fewer than six pages. We learn on the first page that Arnold's father had 'died suddenly of spasm in the heart'[41] but no hint of a connection to Arnold's own identical death is given. Even when we get to Arnold's surprising appointment as Headmaster of Rugby at the early age of thirty-three there is no explanation as to why he was chosen.

Such imbalance is not unusual in biography. If the biographer knows his subject personally it is not likely to be until some moment in adulthood. 'The better he knew him in old age,' writes Cockshut, 'the harsher is the contrast between mere evidence about the early years and haunting memories of later years. The more vivid the memory, the more brilliant its recreation, the bleaker the contrast.'[42] This is exactly the problem Boswell faced with Johnson. Though they were acquainted for only the last 21 of Johnson's 75 years (and during this time Boswell was in Johnson's company for just 276 days) he devotes four-fifths of his biography to the time they were companions. The detail and vigour of this narrative is second to none. Though it is true that Boswell describes the rest of his subject's life better than Stanley does, the same imbalance is there.

There are several moments when Stanley is writing about Arnold at Rugby when Stanley's own fond memories and affections are suddenly engaged, and his usual objectivity is pierced by the subjective. Then the prose ignites, and the setting and the character of Arnold come vividly to life. It is as though we are present sharing the excitement Stanley felt as a boy. He is aware of this, and apologises for it at the start of his first chapter on Rugby: 'Something must, indeed, be forgiven to the natural inclination to dwell on those recollections of his life, which to his pupils are the most lively and the most recent.'[43] Here is Stanley's description of being taught by Arnold in the sixth form, the highlight of his and others' time at Rugby, and, one might well assume in Stanley's case, the highlight of his life:

> [Arnold's pupils] will remember the glance, with which he looked round in the few moments of silence before the lesson began, and which seemed to speak his sense of his own position and of theirs also, as the heads of a great school; the attitude in which he stood, turning over the pages of Facciolati's Lexicon, or Pole's synopsis, with his eye fixed upon the boy who was pausing to give an

answer; the well-known changes of his voice and manner, so faithfully representing the feeling within. They will recollect the pleased look and the cheerful 'Thank you', which followed upon a successful answer or translation; the fall of his countenance with its deepening severity, the stern elevation of the eyebrows, the sudden 'Sit down' which followed upon the reverse; the courtesy and almost deference to the boys, as to his equals in society, so long as there was nothing to disturb the friendliness of their relation; the startling earnestness with which he would check in a moment the slightest approach to levity or impertinence; the confidence with which he addressed them in his half-yearly exhortations; the expressions of delight with which, when they had been doing well, he would say that it was a constant pleasure to him to come into the library.[44]

A description like this is compelling because it provides an authentic snapshot. We are there, with Stanley, sitting before Arnold in the library tower in 1832. This is a boy's-eye view, not the view of a dispassionate biographer, focusing on his subject. What we miss is insight into what Arnold is thinking, what he really feels about teaching those boys: was he excited or was he bored by translating the same texts year after year? On the other hand, there is sympathy, wonder and enthusiasm here, and this communicates Arnold's gifts as a teacher in a way that no other biographer could. The reader feels that power for himself, as though he too were one of Arnold's pupils.

* * *

The best test of a biography's veracity is to compare it with other accounts. For Stanley's *Arnold* there are two classic texts to compare, Thomas Hughes's semi-autobiographical novel, *Tom Brown's Schooldays*, and the poem 'Rugby Chapel' by Arnold's son, Matthew.[d] They were both published in 1857, fifteen years after Arnold's death. Stanley recognised their importance in his preface to the twelfth edition of the *Life*. He describes them as the only two important additions 'to the better understanding of the subject of these volumes'. In *Tom Brown*, he says generously, 'a more vivid picture of Dr. Arnold's career is conveyed in the occasional allusions and general tone of that charming book than is given in the elaborate descriptions in this work.' 'The

---

[d] The poem was written in answer to Fitzjames Stephen's attack on Arnold in his reiew of *Ton Brown's Schooldays*.

other portraiture,' Stanley adds, 'which touches the more historical and universal key of his character, is in the pathetic poem entitled "Rugby Chapel".'[45]

Tom Brown's Schooldays proved even more popular than Stanley's *Life*,[e] and this is hardly surprising. *Tom Brown* is a readable novel, a fast-moving adventure story, interspersed with moments of melodrama. The fiction provides a different perspective but nonetheless a complementary one, and the two books are fascinating to compare.

Hughes arrived at Rugby five years after Stanley started and so they only just overlapped. Where Stanley was scholarly, responsible and virtuous, Hughes was a typical schoolboy, in trouble sometimes, and certainly keener on games than work. His novel describes an ordinary boy's ups and downs, and the lessons he learns in the rough and tumble of Rugby life. When Stanley first read it he was amazed to discover aspects of Rugby of which he said he had been entirely ignorant.[46] The characters are drawn from Hughes's own experience but only Dr Arnold is undisguised. Although Hughes's own view of the headmaster could not be that of a clever and sympathetic member of the sixth, the *impact* of Arnold that he describes is nonetheless much the same as Stanley's. 'What a testimony', Stanley told Mrs Arnold, 'to the character which could produce an impression so precisely alike in characters so wholly unlike!'[47] Seventeen years later, in an address in Rugby chapel, Stanley described *Tom Brown's Schooldays* as 'that admirable book (which) gives you the best idea of what Arnold was to Rugby'.[48]

Hughes's Arnold, like Stanley's, is a strict disciplinarian, and the boys are in awe of him. He is violent at times, as when he boxes a boy's ears for failing to construe a Latin passage. Stanley, on the other hand, plays down the beatings, which at the time were as prevalent at Rugby as at every public school. His Arnold is a flogger but a reluctant one. Stanley omits one notorious and much-publicised incident which happened when Stanley was in the sixth. The occasion was much the same as the one Hughes describes. Arnold was examining lower pupils when he asked a boy to construe a passage from Xenophon. The boy replied that the form had not read that far. Arnold called him a liar, and lying in Arnold's book was the gravest offence a boy could commit. He was beaten eighteen times. It soon transpired that the boy had been telling the truth. 'At once Arnold was filled with remorse,' wrote a later biographer. 'He told the lad how

---

[e] Five editions of *Tom Brown* were published in its first year, and 11,000 copies sold.

sorry he was, told the class so as well and even went so far as to apologise to him in front of the whole School.'⁴⁹

Stanley and Hughes are agreed that, as they grew older, boys came to recognise a tender heart beneath Arnold's stern appearance: what Stanley describes as 'a deep undercurrent of sympathy which extended to almost all, and which from time to time broke through the reserve of his outward manner'.⁵⁰ Both authors describe Arnold playing with his children, as here in *Tom Brown*:

> The Doctor looked up from his task; he was working away with a great chisel at the bottom of a boy's sailing boat ... Round him stood three or four children; the candles burnt brightly on a large table at the farther end, covered with books and papers, and a great fire threw a ruddy glow over the rest of the room. All looked so kindly, and homely, and comfortable ...⁵¹

Tom Brown gets himself into all kinds of scrapes, and eventually Arnold arranges for him to share a study with a new boy who is likely to find life at Rugby hard to take. This is George Arthur, a sensitive and pious orphan of a clergyman, and supposed to be Arthur Stanley.ᶠ Tom rises to the challenge, encourages Arthur, and protects him from the bullies. On his last day at school, a master explains to Tom what the Doctor had intended:

> '... we both agreed that you in particular wanted some object in the School beyond games and mischief, for it was quite clear that you never would make the regular school work your first object. And so the Doctor, at the beginning of the next half-year, looked out the best of the new boys, and separated you and East, and put the young boy into your study, in the hope that when you had somebody to lean on you, you would begin to stand a little steady yourself, and get manliness and thoughtfulness. And I can assure you, he has watched the experiment ever since with great satisfaction. Ah! not one of you boys will ever know the anxiety you have given him, or the care with which he has watched over every step in your school lives.'⁵²

Compare this to Stanley's '"If he should turn out ill," [Arnold] said of a young boy of promise to one of the assistant-masters, and his voice

---

ᶠ Hughes refuted any suggestion that his characters (apart from Arnold) were modelled on particular persons. He said that the portrait of Arthur was not drawn directly from Stanley, though in several respects he might have sat for it.

trembled with emotion as he spoke, "I think it would break my heart."'53

Stanley commended *Tom Brown's Schooldays* especially for its final chapter, which, he said, 'gives you the best notion of what [Arnold's] scholars thought and felt when they heard of his death'.54 The overwhelming effect that Arnold's unexpected death had on his children and pupils is represented in different genres but with the same intensity in Stanley's biography, *Tom Brown's Schooldays* and Matthew Arnold's elegiac poem:

> The lights come out in the street,
> In the school-room windows; – but cold,
> Solemn, unlighted, austere
> Through the gathering darkness, arise
> The chapel-walls, in whose bound
> Thou, my father! art laid.
>
> There thou dost lie, in the gloom
> Of the autumn evening. But ah!
> That word, *gloom* to my mind
> Brings thee back, in the light
> Of thy radiant vigour, again;
> In the gloom of November we pass'd
> Days not dark at thy side;
> Seasons impair'd not the ray
> Of thy buoyant cheerfulness clear.
> Such thou wast! and I stand
> In the autumn evening, and think
> Of bygone autumns with thee.

And here is the epilogue of *Tom Brown's Schooldays*, when Tom, a few years later, returns to Rugby. He is first on a fishing trip in Scotland when a companion brings him the dreadful news that 'your old master, Arnold of Rugby, is dead'.

> [Tom] felt completely carried off his moral and intellectual legs, as if he had lost his standing-point in the invisible world. Besides which, the deep, loving loyalty which he felt for his old leader made the shock intensely painful ...
>
> One thing only Tom had resolved, and that was, that he couldn't stay in Scotland any longer: he felt an irresistible longing to get to Rugby, and then home ...

> As he walked up to the town, he felt shy and afraid of being seen, and took the back streets – why, he didn't know, but he followed his instinct. At the School-gates he made a dead pause; there was not a soul in the quadrangle – all was lonely, and silent, and sad. So with another effort he strode through the quadrangle, and into the School-house offices.
>
> He found the little matron in her room in deep mourning; shook her hand, tried to talk, and moved nervously about. She was evidently thinking of the same subject as he, but he couldn't begin talking.
>
> 'Where shall I find Thomas?' said he at last, getting desperate.
> 'In the servants' hall, I think, sir' ...
> 'Where is he buried, Thomas?' said he at last.
> 'Under the altar in the chapel, sir,' answered Thomas. 'You'd like to have the key, I dare say.' ...
> Tom nodded, and the bunch of keys were handed to him ...
> All that was left on earth of him whom he had honoured was lying cold and still under the chapel floor. He would go in and see the place once more, and then leave it once for all. New men and new methods might do for other people; let those who would, worship the rising star; he, at least, would be faithful to the sun which had set ...
>
> If he could only have seen the Doctor again for one five minutes – have told him all that was in his heart, what he owed to him, how he loved and reverenced him, and would, by God's help, follow his steps in life and death – he could have borne it all without a murmur. But that he should have gone away for ever without knowing it all, was too much to bear.[55]

*   *   *

Stanley himself was not as well served by his first biographers as Arnold was by Stanley. A year after his death, George Granville Bradley delivered three lectures in Edinburgh, published in 1883 as *Recollections of Arthur Penrhyn Stanley*. He had also been a boy at Rugby under Arnold and returned there to teach. He was six years younger than Stanley, who had left Rugby three years before Bradley arrived. But he soon learnt of Stanley's reputation, and when he went up to University College, Oxford to sit the scholarship examination he was thrilled to be welcomed by Stanley, who had just become a fellow. Forty years on, when Bradley was beginning his last year as master of the college, he

Introduction

told a congregation in the college chapel: 'I was elected a Scholar here and greeted by him as a pupil of his own master, Arnold, with that indescribable grace and warmth which drew to him so many hearts. His face still shines out of the mist of years, I may surely say so now, as the face of an angel.'[56]

Bradley attended Stanley's lectures, and Stanley became Bradley's tutor for his final year. They remained friends, and Bradley followed him as a fellow of the college and later as Dean of Westminster. He had something of the same infatuation for Stanley that Stanley had for Arnold. Unlike Bradley, though, Stanley worried about his feelings, feared that they were idolatrous, and tried to restrain them. The detachment and objectivity of his *Life of Arnold* testifies to his success, but the same cannot be said of Bradley's *Recollections of Stanley*. He admits in his introduction that he has 'disclaimed from the very first any attempt to speak of Arthur Stanley otherwise than as a deeply attached and grateful friend'.[57] Here, for example, is Bradley's panegyric on Stanley as a tutor:

> The fascination, the charm, the spell, was simply irresistible; the face, the voice, the manner; the ready sympathy, the geniality, the freshness, the warmth, the poetry, the refinement, the humour, the mirthfulness and merriment, the fund of knowledge, the inexhaustible store of anecdotes and stories, told so vividly, so dramatically, – I shall not easily enumerate the gifts which drew us to him with a singular, some of us with quite a passionate devotion.[58]

Bradley's lectures are no more than what he called 'a short biographical sketch'.[59] The biography proper had to wait another ten years and its genesis was long and frustrating. Stanley entrusted his copious collection of letters and papers to three literary executors, Hugh Pearson, Theodore Walrond and Bradley's brother-in-law, George Grove.[g] Pearson and Stanley's sister Catherine invited Augustus J. C. Hare[h] to be the biographer but Grove would not allow it. Stanley had wanted Grove himself to write it but he was too busy establishing his new college of music. Walrond accepted the task but died four years later in 1887, leaving a vast mass of materials and only a fragmentary record.

---

[g] Hugh Pearson, vicar of Sonning near Windsor, was probably the closest of Stanley's friends. Theodore Walrond, another of Arnold's pupils, travelled with Stanley to Sinai and Palestine. (Sir) George Grove was the first Director of the Royal College of Music.

[h] Hare was Arthur's and Catherine's cousin. He was an accomplished artist and prolific writer of memoirs and travel books.

At this point Bradley took over, but by 1891 he had come to the reluctant conclusion that 'increasingly delightful as the work was, the duties of my position (Dean of Westminster) were such as to make it difficult, nay, almost impossible, to find the uninterrupted hours essential to work which demanded consecutive and unbroken attention.'[60] He had, however, written the first twenty-five years of Stanley's life, and this and Stanley's papers were handed to Roland Prothero to complete the work, which he did in just two years. Prothero's father had been a canon of Westminster and he had boyhood memories of Stanley. Otherwise it was a curious choice: he had written a book on English farming and became editor of the *Quarterly Review* in 1893, the same year the biography was published.[i] But Prothero did at least have the advantage of a dispassionate and professional approach. He put this to good use, not least by re-ordering Bradley's account and reducing it by more than a half.

Prothero's *Life and Correspondence* (1893) is a good example of those Victorian monumental obituary biographies which followed in the wake of Stanley's *Life of Arnold*. 1,100 pages in two volumes, plus a third volume of additional letters and verses, are typical. It is dedicated to Queen Victoria, and in scale and and sentimental reverence it stands comparison with the biography of Prince Albert she had authorised nearly thirty years before.[j] Prothero's *Life* is certainly lucid and readable and full of information, but it lacks any strong literary quality, and has never been read much except by scholars and those with a taste for ecclesiastical Victoriana. This is one reason why Stanley is not more widely remembered today. Cockshut is critical of Prothero's 'rosy view of human nature', and sees this as typical of many of the less distinguished ecclesiastical biographers of the time:

> A boy such as Stanley was in the year 1832 can only be prevented from rising in the world by disease or sudden death. He was well-born, well-connected, serious, sensible and highly intelligent. A prize pupil under Dr Arnold at Rugby, he is about to become a prize pupil at Balliol. His opinions, formed by Arnold, but modified by a cooler, more detached mental faculty than Arnold could command, are developing in the direction of a decorous Broad Church liberalism. In due course, he will attract the favourable

---

[i] Prothero went on to become Conservative MP for Oxford University and President of the Board of Agriculture. He was made Baron Ernle in 1919.
[j] Sir Theodore Martin, *Life of H.R.H. The Prince Consort*, i-v, 1875–80.

notice of Queen Victoria, and the admiring confidence of statesmen, who like churchmen to be men of the world rather than fanatics ... In the fulness of time, but not too soon, he will marry Lady Augusta Bruce, a close intimate of the Queen.

The preceding account, I dare say, will appear to have a satirical ring. If so, it is the biographer and not Stanley himself that has attracted the satire ... Prothero's unspoken assumption (and here he stands for many remembered and many forgotten biographers) is that since the world was kind to Stanley, and since Stanley deserved its kindness, the world must be a kind place. And we do not need the sour hindsight of our century to see that this was not so. We can appeal to the classic writers of Stanley's own time, to Newman, to Dickens, and to Ruskin.[61]

A problem for any subsequent biographer has been the disappearance of most of Stanley's correspondence, as well as Prothero's and his predecessors' working papers. There is no record of what Prothero did with these documents, and it is assumed that most were destroyed. Bundles of letters have been deposited at Pusey House, Oxford and among the Stanley family papers at the Cheshire Record Office, and individual letters can be found in various archives.[k] However, these comprise a small proportion of Stanley's papers. Prothero's *Life* and his collection of Stanley's letters provide therefore the only known evidence for much of Stanley's correspondence, and are a necessary and invaluable source. They are not without disadvantages, however: namely, undetectable inaccuracies, and the frequent omission of dates and names of correspondents.

---

[k] See primary sources, Select Bibliography, p. 380.

PART ONE
Alderley and Rugby
1815–1834

I
'In Possession of a Good Fortune'
1815–1828

IN JUNE 1815, six months before Arthur Stanley's birth, Britain had fought and won the Battle of Waterloo. This final end to twenty years of war with France marked a turning-point in English history. Peace, and the lingering impetus of the Revolution, produced fresh energy of thought and feeling, giving birth to new ideas and movements, political, religious and philosophical. The nineteenth century could begin at last.

Arthur Wellesley, the Iron Duke, was the hero of Waterloo. His characteristics of duty, discipline and determination were to become the virtues of Victorian England. Wellington's long post-military career in politics kept him and all he stood for firmly in the public eye. Stanley was not the only boy at the time to be christened Arthur.[a]

But though the nineteenth century had arrived with Waterloo, change took time. Jane Austen's *Emma* was published in 1815, dedicated to the Prince Regent, and it was into Austen's tranquil world of lords and baronets, patrons and parsons, country houses and Queen Anne rectories, that Arthur Stanley was born. That world survived for at least as long as Stanley was a boy.

*   *   *

Arthur's uncle was Sir John Stanley, the 7th baronet and 1st Baron Stanley of Alderley in the county of Cheshire. He had been an officer during the war with France, and when stationed in Sussex he met Lady Maria Josepha Holroyd, the eldest daughter of the 1st Earl of Sheffield. She was among the most intellectual women of her day, and had been a pupil of her father's friend, the historian Edward Gibbon. She and John Stanley married in 1796 and settled at Alderley Park. It had been the manor house since 1779 when the family's seventeenth-century Alderley Hall was burnt to the ground.[b]

---

[a] Queen Victoria's third son, Prince Arthur, was born 35 years later on Wellington's 81st birthday.
[b] Alderley Park had been the estate bailiff's house. It was altered and extended but was of little architectural merit and in 1931 it too was destroyed by fire.

Arthur's father, Edward Stanley, was Sir John's only brother and the youngest child of the family. He was born on 1 January 1779 and had been rector of the family church at Alderley since 1805. His brother, as patron, had insisted that this was the second son's responsibility, not the naval career Edward would have much preferred. He was remembered as 'a little man, active in figure and in movement, with dark, piercing eyes, rendered more remarkable by the snow-white hair which was characteristic of him even when very young. With the liveliest interest on all subjects – political, philosophical, scientific, theological; with inexhaustible plans for the good of the human race in general, but especially for the benefit of his parishioners and the amusement of his seven nieces at the Park, he was the most popular character in the country-side.'[1]

In 1810, five years before Arthur was born, Edward married Catherine, the eldest child of the Reverend Oswald Leycester. The Leycesters lived nearby at Toft Hall, and the two families had been friends and neighbours for centuries. 'Kitty', as she was called, was thirteen years younger than Edward, and had loved and admired him for as long as she could remember. They were engaged when she was just sixteen and married two years later.

In personality and appearance Kitty might have been one of Jane Austen's heroines. Her portrait,[c] drawn the year after her marriage, shows her dressed in a long, white, high-waisted dress, complete with shawl, bonnet and book in hand, and hair swept up in a chignon with ringlets flowing over her brow. While engaged to Edward, Kitty spent time in London where Maria, her future sister-in-law, acted as her chaperone. She and Sir John introduced her to the Whig circle of Holland House which she impressed with her sense and sensibility. There she met the wit Sydney Smith who praised what he called her 'porcelain understanding'. It is a curious but compelling phrase which Arthur translated in his memoir of his mother as 'delicacy of intelligence'.[2]

Arthur was the third of Kitty's and Edward's five children, all of whom were born and brought up in the rectory at Alderley. Their adoptive cousin, the author Augustus J. C. Hare, has left a charming description of the parsonage as 'a low house, with a veranda, forming a wide balcony for the upper storey, where bird-cages hung amongst the roses; its rooms and passages filled with pictures, books, and the old carved oak furniture, usually little sought after or valued in those days, but which the Rector delighted to pick up amongst his cottages'.[3] The

[c] Illustration 1b.

garden was of Dutch design, and the rhododendron that Edward planted to commemorate Waterloo is still to be seen.

At the end of the garden stands the church, built of red and grey sandstone, with a stout square tower, partly covered with ivy. It is a church rich in history. Grooves have been worn in the walls of the south porch where the villagers once sharpened their arrows. When Arthur was six, the fourteenth-century font was dug up in the churchyard where it had been hidden during the Commonwealth. An outside flight of steps led to the Jacobean gallery reserved for members of the Alderley Park family. The mansion was just a mile's walk across the park, and Arthur and his brothers and sisters were frequent visitors. Sir John and Lady Stanley had eleven children, the youngest of whom, Elfrida, was closest in age to Arthur, but she was drowned in a bathing accident when she was three and he was one. The next youngest was Emmeline who was five years older than Arthur. So their playing together was limited, though Owen and Mary, Arthur's elder brother and sister, were close in age to Emmy. In any case, strong familial ties, proximity, and much the same social standing threw the cousins together, and they spent idyllic holidays riding, boating and picnicking in the park. When they were older there were balls, supper parties and drawing-room concerts. 'There was constant intercourse between the Park and the Rectory, and the two families with a large circle of friends led most interesting and busy lives. The Rector took delight in helping his seven nieces with their Italian and Spanish studies, in fostering their love of poetry and natural history, and in developing the minds of his own young children. He wrote plays for them to act and birthday odes for them to recite.'[4]

The older nephews, Edward (who succeeded to the title) and William, were twins, born in 1802. Arthur looked up to them and remembered the week of celebrations to mark their twenty-first birthdays (Arthur was nearly eight). The tenants' hall was garlanded with evergreens, the villagers flew flags from their chimneys, and at noon a twenty-one gun salute was fired. This delighted William who had joined the Grenadier Guards and was there resplendent in scarlet and gold. There was a fancy dress ball, fireworks and ninety bonfires. Two bullocks and six barrels of ale were consumed by the village poor, and the children ate plum-cake and drank twenty-six gallons of tea. Arthur's brother, Owen, home from Charterhouse for the occasion, wrote a verse in honour of his cousins – 'On the Coming of Age at the Park':

> Ring the loud bells of the Alderley Steeple,
> And call up together the Alderley People –
> For the Twins of the Park are just turned twenty one,
> And their birthday let's keep with both feasting and fun.

*   *   *

To the north of the estate, close to the rectory, was Radnor Mere, one of those beautiful sheets of water common in Cheshire. Further north was Alderley Edge, a rocky ridge rising as sharp as a cliff. On its summit was an ancient beacon-tower to warn of insurrection or invasion. As a boy, Arthur was fascinated by it, as he was by all things legendary or historical, and not least his own ancestry. He took pride in discovering the Stanley family's entanglement in some of the most decisive moments in English history.

Arthur Stanley's first recorded ancestor was the aptly forenamed Adam de Audithlegh. He was supposed to be descended from the Emperor Charlemagne. Audithlegh was a village in Normandy, and Adam came over to England with William the Conqueror. He fought bravely on the field of Hastings and was rewarded with English land. His grandson, William, married Joan Stanley, heiress of the manor of Stoneley in Staffordshire. Her family was Saxon in origin and of great antiquity, and William made Stoneley his seat and changed his name to Stanley. Four generations later, in 1282, another William Stanley married another Joan, this one the daughter and heiress of Sir Philip Bamvile. Sir William had inherited the rangership of the forest of Wirral and the manor of Stourton near Birkenhead, and he migrated from Staffordshire to Cheshire. He adopted what became the Stanley shield with its three stags' heads.

Sir William's great-grandson, Sir John Stanley, also married well to Isabel, the daughter and heiress of Sir Thomas de Lathom, Lord of Knowsley and Lathom in Lancashire. Sir John became Lord Lieutenant of Ireland. In 1405 Henry IV made him a Knight of the Garter and granted him the Isle of Man, which he and his descendents ruled as sovereign lords until 1736. From the Lathoms the Stanleys acquired their curious crest of an eagle preying on a swaddled baby. Sir John's grandson, Sir Thomas Stanley, made an auspicious marriage to Jean Goushill, heiress of Elizabeth Plantagenet, daughter of Edward I. He too was a Knight of the Garter and comptroller of the royal household, and was raised to the peerage in 1456 as 1st Baron Stanley. By the end of the fifteenth century the house of Stanley was well established in

Cheshire and Lancashire as a landed family of knights and squires, growing rapidly in power and prosperity which were soon to reach dangerous heights.

Sir Thomas's eldest son (another Thomas) is the most famous and notorious of the Stanleys, 'a shrewd man and quick to see on which side his bread was likely to be buttered'.[5] He too wed extremely well, first to Eleanor Neville, Richard of Gloucester's cousin. In 1482 he married Lady Margaret Beaufort, widow of Edmund Tudor, 1st Earl of Richmond, whose son was to become King Henry VII. This Sir Thomas Stanley's career is an extraordinary story of machiavellian survival at the height of the Wars of the Roses, and lends the family motto, *Sans Changer,* a poignant irony. He held high office under three kings: Esquire of the Body to Henry VI (and knighted by him in 1460), and Steward of the Household to Richard III and before him to Edward IV, who made him a Privy Counsellor and Knight of the Garter. Thirty years among the changes and chances of court schooled him in the art of resilience, of which, under Richard III, he became an astute practitioner.

Richard recognised Stanley's unreliability but also his influence, and sought to buy his loyalty. When he came to the throne in 1483 he made him Constable of England and a member of his council. When Lord Hastings was arrested on a charge of treason, Stanley was wounded in the affray and confined to the Tower. But he survived, winning back Richard's favour, though never his trust. Stanley's wife, Lady Margaret, was already conspiring with her son. Two years later in 1485 Henry Tudor and his army landed at Milford Haven. Stanley was set to join his stepson, but at the Battle of Bosworth he was careful to place his forces in an ambiguous position between the two armies. Richard was wary, taking Stanley's own son hostage and sending the Duke of Northumberland to spy on his troops. Once the King moved close enough to attack Henry, Stanley brought his men in from the flanks and engaged the royal party. It was the decisive moment of the battle, and Richard and his bodyguard were killed. The rest is immortalised by Shakespeare, who in the final scene of *Richard III* has Stanley on the battlefield setting Richard's crown on Henry VII's head. Stanley had backed the winning side again and ingratiated himself with a fourth king. The earldom of Derby followed and another twenty years of royal favour.

The 2nd earl, Sir Thomas's son, fought at the Battle of Flodden in 1513 ('"Charge, Chester, charge! On, Stanley, on!" Were the last words of Marmion' in Sir Walter Scott's eponymous poem). The Stanleys of

Alderley descend from Sir Thomas's younger brother, John. He married Elizabeth, daughter and heiress of Thomas Weever of Alderley and Weever in Cheshire. His descendents lived at Weever until his great-grandson, another Thomas, who was High Sheriff of Cheshire in 1572, made Alderley manor his seat, and was the first Stanley to be buried there.

Thomas's grandson acquired through marriage manors in Derbyshire which were sold to purchase Nether Alderley in 1602. By now the Stanley estates were extensive, not least from lands granted through five centuries of prudent marriages. His son was made High Sheriff of Cheshire in 1634, and at the outbreak of the Civil War he took the side of Parliament, though avoided the fighting. A trimmer like the 1st Earl of Derby, he offered support to the exiled Charles II when the Commonwealth was about to end, and was created a baronet at the Restoration.

By the time of the 6th baronet, Sir John Thomas Stanley (1735–1807), Arthur Stanley's grandfather, the family was firmly Whiggish in its politics. That was unusual for the gentry, who – like the clergy – were usually Tory. But Sir John boasted of the 1st baronet's siding with the Parliamentarians (though in true Stanley fashion he also served George III as a gentleman of the privy chamber). He too made an advantageous match when in 1763 he married the beautiful Margaret Owen, daughter and heiress of Hugh Owen of Penrhos, Anglesey, adding more Welsh territory to his extensive holdings in Cheshire. They had five daughters (two of whom died in infancy) and two sons, John and Edward, Arthur's father.

* * *

As a child, Edward Stanley had moved between Alderley and his mother's home in Anglesey, and his education suffered frequent changes of private school and tutor. He did not have the advantage of the classical education that public school would have provided, and he acquired his only mathematics at one of his earliest schools. This put him at a considerable disadvantage when he arrived at St John's College, Cambridge, but hard work and determination produced a first in mathematics. Nonetheless, Edward's lack of a good school education and his indifference to study left him ignorant of the books and subjects which were to absorb his brilliant and studious son. Arthur was well aware of this, and he describes in his memoir of his father how 'the want of a regular classical education, as well as the peculiar turn of his own mind, indisposed him to purely literary studies, of which the nicer subtleties, whether in scholarship, metaphysics, or theology, were on every account distasteful to him'.[6]

On the other hand, natural history held much the same fascination it had for the curate of Selborne.[d] Ornithology was Edward's favourite study and he wrote a popular book entitled *A Familiar History of Birds* (1836). 'It was a constant source of amusement and interest to him in his parish walks and rides to notice the flight and habits of birds, to collect remarkable specimens of their organisation, and to gather from his parishioners stories of any peculiarities which they had themselves noticed.'[7] But Edward's greatest love was always the sea:

> In early years he had acquired a passion for the sea, which he cherished up to the time of his entrance at college, and which never left him through life. It first originated, as he believed, in the delight which he experienced, between three and four years of age, in a visit to the seaport of Weymouth; and long afterwards he retained a vivid recollection of the point where he caught the first sight of a ship and shed tears because he was not allowed to go on board. So strongly was he possessed by the feeling thus acquired, that as a child he used to leave his bed, and sleep on the shelf of a wardrobe, for the pleasure of imagining himself in a berth on board a man-of-war. Nor was this a mere boyish fantasy which a few years' experience of the hardships of sea-life might have dispelled. His whole character eminently qualified him for the naval profession. A cheerful and sanguine temper – readiness of decision – fertility of resource – activity and quickness of mind and body – and a spirit of enterprise that knew no danger, no impossibility, no difficulty – could hardly have failed to ensure success in the sphere to which his tastes had been thus early turned.[8]

It was the cause of considerable sadness to Edward that duty dictated a career in the Church,[e] but characteristic that he never complained. Instead he embraced his destiny and brought to bear in his ministry many of the traits that would otherwise have made him an outstanding officer.

---

[d] The Revd Gilbert White, author of *The Natural History of Selborne* (1789).
[e] The same can be said of Nelson who was expected to follow his grandfather, father and brother into the Church. He shared Edward's early enthusiasm for the sea and was able to persuade his father to allow him to join the navy.

Edward left Cambridge in June 1802 and set off immediately on a grand tour. He and a college friend travelled first to France and then on to Switzerland, Italy, Spain and Portugal. His long letters home were full of detailed accounts of the destruction left by the reign of terror, often accompanied by sketches. Like William Wordsworth (who had been at St John's seven years before), Edward had at first been enthused by the Revolution, but (again like Wordsworth) the devastation and carnage Edward saw in France (including five executions on the guillotine) made him abandon his earlier idealism.

Edward returned to France in 1814 after the collapse of the empire and Napoleon's banishment to Elba. He was present in Paris at the Tuileries when the King ('to me a very secondary person')[9] reviewed his troops. Two years later he was at Waterloo on the first anniversary of the battle. With him were Kitty; her brother, Edward Leycester Penrhyn[f] who had travelled with Edward in 1814; and their mutual friend Captain Donald Crawford, a veteran of the battle. Kitty's letters home make fascinating records of the impressions of this first wave of battlefield tourists. Here, for instance, is part of a long letter to her niece, Lucy Stanley, then aged seventeen:

> On the 18th of June, how can I begin with any other subject than Waterloo? ... At 8 this morning we mounted our Cabriolets for Waterloo. Donald put on his Waterloo medal for the first time, and a French shirt he got in the spoils, and a cravat of an officer who was killed, and I wrapped myself in his Waterloo cloak, and we all felt the additional sensation which the anniversary of the day produced on everybody ...
>
> At Mont St. Jean Donald began to know where he was. Here he found the well where he had got some water for his horse; here the green pond he had fixed upon as the last resource for his troop; here the cottage where he had slept on the 17th; here the breach he had made in the hedge for his horses to get into the field to bivouac; here the spot where he had fired the first gun; here the hole in which he sat for the surgeon to dress his wound. He had never been on the field since the day of the battle, and his interest in seeing it again and discovering every spot under its altered

---

[f] Edward Leycester had inherited the considerable fortune of his father's cousin, Lady Penrhyn, who had directed in her will that he should assume the name Penrhyn. She died in December 1815, the month Arthur Stanley was born. Edward Penrhyn was his godfather and Arthur was given Penrhyn as his middle name.

circumstances was fully as great as ours ... Henceforward I shall have a clearer idea, not only of Waterloo, but of what a military position and military plan is like.[10]

On his return from the grand tour Edward had assumed command of the Alderley Volunteers, a defence corps raised by his brother in expectation of a French invasion. He was ordained the following year and served his curacy in Surrey. Like all clergy at the time, Edward had no theological training: an Oxford or Cambridge degree (albeit in mathematics), and an obliging bishop and incumbent were all that were required. The curacy provided whatever training was necessary, and two years later Edward was presented to the long-promised family living of Alderley. And there he laboured for thirty-two years.

In her novel *North and South* (1855), Mrs Gaskell contrasts the dirt and disaffection of industrialised Manchester (Milton-Northern in Darkshire) with the idyllic charm and peace of rural Hampshire (the 'beautiful, beloved Helstone'). She might have been comparing Manchester to Alderley, though these places were only twelve miles apart. Manchester's cotton industry had been the catalyst for the industrial revolution, and by the time Arthur was born, 11,500 men, women and children were toiling in the factories. But the village of Alderley was untouched by this, and its 1,300 inhabitants still lived much the same lives as they had for centuries.

When Edward started as rector, the parish was in a poor state of neglect, not untypical of the Georgian Church. The previous incumbent had often been absent and would boast that he had never entered a sick person's cottage. Services were kept to a minimum and were poorly attended. Edward set to work at once to improve things, driven as much by a naval officer's demand for duty and order as by any religious zeal. 'His parish was his ship. The same sense of the importance of strict obedience to orders, the same strict requirement of obedience from others, that would have regulated his conduct as captain of a man-of-war, pervaded his view of the sacred trust committed to him in his parochial cure.'[11]

Edward was motivated too by the paternalism and *noblesse oblige* he shared with his brother, who was always a conscientious and benevolent squire. Edward made visiting the poor of the parish a priority, and he did so weekly and in systematic order. Arthur's description of these visits is admiring and sentimental but nonetheless conveys the vigour and dedication of his father's ministry:

> In his rides round the parish, the children used to run out of the houses to catch the wonted smile, or gesture, or call, of the Rector as he passed, or to claim the cakes and gingerbread that he brought with him for those whose hands and faces were clean; and the poor cottagers long afterwards described how their hearts beat with pleasure as they heard the short quick trampling of his horse's feet as he went galloping up their lanes, and the sound of his voice as he called out to them before he reached the house to come out and speak to him, or hold his pony as he went in. When he entered a sick chamber he never failed to express the joy which neatness and order gave him, or to reprove where he found it otherwise. Whatever was to be done in the parish for their good, they were sure to find in him an active supporter.[12]

Stanley's father regarded education as a vital part of his work. He extended and equipped the old parish school which had stood in the churchyard since 1628, and is referred to by Dickens in *The Old Curiosity Shop*. He introduced twice-yearly examinations which he modelled on the college examinations at Cambridge. The children were required to learn by heart a chapter of the Bible and to answer questions. Edward did the examining himself, and once a year he rewarded the children with pewter medals and books, followed by lunch at the rectory, and sometimes, as a special treat, a boat trip on the Mere.

* * *

Edward married Catherine Leycester five years after his induction as rector of Alderley. She was from the start a strong support to him in his work at Alderley, and later when he became Bishop of Norwich. Kitty was a remarkable woman. 'There was', wrote Arthur, 'a quiet wisdom, a rare unselfishness, a calm discrimination, a firm decision, which made her judgment and her influence felt through the whole circle in which she lived.'[13] Her own mother had suffered long periods of ill-health, and while still only a child herself, Kitty had brought up and educated her sister, Maria, who was six years younger. This experience led to her busy involvement in her own children's upbringing.

Kitty was highly intelligent and perceptive, and many people found her formidable; certainly fools were not suffered, gladly or otherwise:

> She was the best of listeners, fixing her eyes upon the speaker, but saying little herself, so that her old uncle, Hugh Leycester, used to assert of her, 'Kitty has much sterling gold, but gives no ready

change.' To the frivolity of an ordinary acquaintance, her mental superiority and absolute self-possession of manner must always have made her somewhat alarming; but those who had the opportunity of penetrating beneath the surface were no less astonished at her originality and freshness of ideas, and her keen, though quiet, enjoyment of life, its pursuits and friendships, than by the calm wisdom of her advice, and her power of penetration into the characters, and consequently the temptations and difficulties, of others.[14]

She was a prolific letter-writer and journal-keeper, and her writings (on people, politics and religion) reveal an extraordinary sensibility and moral discernment, as well as considerable learning. She also wrote delightful accounts of her children, of their differences of character and their development, and the pleasure they gave her. She recorded their faults and virtues, and her attempts to shape their personalities. Arthur was two when Kitty wrote to Maria:

How I have enjoyed these fine days, – and one's pleasure is doubled, or rather I should say trebled, in the enjoyment of the three little children basking in the sunshine on the lawns and picking up daisies and finding new flowers every day, – and in seeing Arthur expand like one of the flowers in the fine weather. Owen trots away to school at nine o'clock every morning, with his Latin grammar under his arm, leaving Mary with a strict charge to unfurl his flag as soon as the clock strikes twelve. So Mary unfurls the flag and then watches till Owen comes in sight, and as soon as he spies her signal he sets off full gallop towards it, and Mary creeps through the gate to meet him, and then comes with as much joy to announce Owen's being come back, as if he was returned from the North Pole. Meanwhile I am sitting with the doors open into the trellis, so that I can see and hear all that passes.[15]

Owen was born in 1811, a year after Edward and Kitty married. From his Welsh grandmother, Margaret Owen, he inherited his name and (like his father) the same dark eyes and black hair. Mary was born eighteen months later, and Arthur three years after Mary. Mary and Arthur were always the closest of the brothers and sisters. She never married and devoted her life to the poor and sick, and nursed in the Crimea. After Arthur came Charles who was with him at Rugby for his last two years and joined the army as an engineer. He died of fever, aged thirty, while serving in Van Diemen's Land.[g] The youngest child was Catherine. She married Arthur's schoolfriend, Charles Vaughan, who became Headmaster of Harrow. None of the five had children of their own, and when Catherine died in 1899 this line of the Stanley family was extinguished with the nineteenth century.

In 1821 Owen was sent away to school at Charterhouse in London. His two cousins at the Park had been to Eton but Edward and Kitty preferred Charterhouse, not least because of its rising reputation. A year before Owen started, the Duke of Wellington had heard that his friend Lady Shelley intended to send her son to Eton. He wrote to her to protest: 'I am astonished that you don't send your son to the Charterhouse, which I believe is the best school of them all.'[16] Owen's contemporaries included the novelist William Thackeray; George Paget, Regius Professor of Physic at Cambridge; and Henry Liddell, the Greek lexicographer and father of Alice in Wonderland.

Charterhouse's classical training was both rigorous and brutal, and it did not suit Owen. His parents had intended him for the bar but he was a physical, practical, adventurous boy, with a leaning to science and mathematics. He took after his father from whom he also inherited the same passion for the sea, and from earliest childhood Owen had busied himself with drawing, building and sailing model boats. Edward encouraged him and they would visit regattas and reviews and talk together of ships and the navy. In his third year at Charterhouse, Owen went with his family to a gala day on board HMS *Hecla* and *Fury*. The ships were at Deptford being fitted by the Arctic explorer Captain Edward Parry for a voyage in search of the North-West Passage. Parry was soon to marry Owen's cousin, Isabella, Sir John Stanley's fourth daughter. Over 300 guests were present to see the arrival of the admiralty barge bearing the First Sea Lord in his gold-laced uniform and plumed cocked hat. Owen absorbed every detail of the ships and the ceremony.

As soon as he returned to Charterhouse, Owen wrote to his parents to say that he wanted to leave immediately to join the Royal Naval College at Portsmouth. 'If you will let me chuse my profession, I chuse the Navy. Don't think it is an idle fancy. I have thought a great deal about it ...'[17] His father was more than sympathetic, and remembering how painful his own career sacrifice had been, he readily gave his

---

[g] The penal colony renamed Tasmania in 1853, four years after Charles's death.

consent. Kitty was not so sure but she had never understood Owen, and she seems to have found him exasperating. To be fair to her, Owen was by all accounts a disagreeable character – proud, self-centred, wilful and violent-tempered. 'He is selfish,' wrote Kitty when Owen was eight, 'concentrated on his own amusements and occupations: independent of other people – no sympathy with them, or with any kind of feeling – he cares for no one except in proportion, and for the time that they amuse him … It seems as if the powers and exercise of mind had usurped all other parts of his character.'[18] Thomas Huxley, who was surgeon-naturalist on Owen's last ship, HMS *Rattlesnake*, wrote much the same about him thirty years later.

Owen and his father had much in common and, despite his temper, Owen was Edward's favourite. Arthur was very different from Owen and his father, and he sensed that his own cerebral and introspective nature put him at a disadvantage with both. As always, Kitty's observations were acute:

> Owen, every bodily sense always on the alert, active in all outdoor exercises, with the entire command of his limbs, and no shyness, no forwardness. Arthur, sensitive and retiring, hesitating in manner (not leading one to suppose the clearness of his perceptions), and as helpless and void of common sense and exertion as ever. I was so amused the other day, taking up the memorandum books of the two brothers! Owen's full of calculations, altitudes, astronomical axioms, &c.: Arthur's of Greek idioms, Grecian history, parallels of different historical situations.[19]

The lack of sympathy between Arthur and his father was balanced by the closeness he felt towards his mother, and she towards him. Everything Kitty found distasteful in Owen she found the opposite in Arthur, and loved him the more for it. Owen, for instance, was disinclined to read: from the age of five Arthur would spend all day with a book. Owen was materialistic and matter-of-fact ('his imagination only wanders amongst realities, and in hearing Bible stories he is more interested to know exactly how Abraham built the altar, than about Isaac being put on').[20] Arthur was often lost in a world of his own imagining. As Owen was Edward's favourite child, so Arthur was Kitty's. After visiting Alderley with his parents, Thomas Arnold's son, Tom, described 'the entire union of heart and mind that existed between her and her son Arthur' as 'something very beautiful to witness'.[21] Arthur remained a devoted son until his mother died; he was by then approaching fifty and still unmarried.

* * *

Kitty's letters and journals give an unusually detailed picture of Arthur's childhood, and her affection for him. 'Arthur [aged three] is grown so interesting, and so entertaining too, – he talks incessantly, runs about and amuses himself, and is full of pretty speeches, repartees, and intelligence: the dear little creature would not leave me, or stir without holding my hand, and he knew all that had been going on quite as much as the others.'[22] Sixteen months later in January 1820 Kitty wrote to her sister: 'As for the children, my Arthur is sweeter than ever. His drawing fever goes on, and his passion for pictures and birds, and he will talk sentiment about *le printemps, les oiseaux,* and *les fleurs,* when he walks out.'[23]

Kitty played a very important part in her children's early education, and in Arthur she found an especially gifted and willing pupil. Instead of making her children learn lists of names and dates, as was usual, 'Mrs. Stanley's system was to take a particular era, and, upon the basis of its general history, to pick out for her children from different books, whether memoirs, chronicles, or poetry, all that bore upon it, making it at once an interesting study to herself and them, and talking it over with them in a way which encouraged them to form their own opinion upon it.'[24] It was a style of teaching which encouraged independent thought and imagination, as well as wide reading and a strong sense of history. Arthur benefited from all of these and foundations were laid for his future career.

Although Kitty welcomed Arthur's precocious intelligence and his studious, sensitive nature, she worried when he found it difficult to fit in with other boys. He was delicate, shy, timid, and often languid and disinclined to play. There was 'nothing of a boy about him except his love of horses and hatred of dolls, ... very liable to be spoiled, with simple pretty ways, and a kind of hanging on, dependent manner, that calls for tenderness ... with a strange sense of delicate beauty that runs through everything ... in ecstasies over every new flower ...'[25] His aunt Maria called him 'the little sylph', and his father 'Prince Pitiful'.

Understandably, Kitty was anxious at the prospect of Arthur's starting school, and 'she dreaded that the companionship of other boys at school, instead of drawing him out, would only make him shut himself up more within himself.'[26] On the other hand, it was felt that

Arthur's weak constitution needed the bracing benefits of sea air, and so he was sent away, aged eight, to board at a school for twelve boys at Seaforth where his cousins had been. Seaforth was five miles from Liverpool and just half a mile from the sea. It was where the father of William Gladstone had his house, and William had left the school just three years before Arthur started. Maria wrote with evident relief in August 1824:

> Arthur liked the idea of going to school, as making him approach nearer to Owen. We took him last Sunday evening from Crosby, and he kept up very well till we were to part, but when he was to separate from us to join his new companions, he clung to us in a piteous manner and burst into tears. Mr. Rawson[h] very good-naturedly offered to walk with us a little way, and walk back with Arthur, which he liked better, and he returned with Mr. R. very manfully. On Monday evening we went to have a look at him before leaving the neighbourhood, and found the little fellow as happy as possible, much amused with the novelty of the situation, and talking of the boys' proceedings with as much importance as if he had been there for months ... He is very proud of being called 'Stanley', and seems to like it altogether very much. The satisfaction to Mamma and Auntie is not to be told of having disposed of this little sylph in so excellent a manner.[27]

But school, as Kitty feared, was not an antidote to diffidence. Indeed, on his return home for Christmas, Kitty described how 'the shyness, reserve, colouring, susceptibility, seem to be rather increased, and he is less altered than I should have thought possible – as helpless, and void of common sense and common exertion as ever.'[28] At the end of his first year at Seaforth she wrote:

> School has not transformed him into a rough boy yet. He is a little less shy, but not much. He brought back from school a beautiful prize-book for history, of which he is not a little proud; and Mr. Rawson has told several people, unconnected with the Stanleys, that he never had a more amiable, attentive, or clever boy than Arthur Stanley, and that he never has had to find fault with him since he came.[29]

---

[h] William Rawson had been appointed vicar of Seaforth (and headmaster of the school) by Gladstone's father on the recommendation of the Cambridge Evangelical, Charles Simeon.

Kitty was still keen to encourage him to get outside and play more. In his last year he wrote to reassure her that 'I had much rather ride well than write Latin verses',[30] but he also admits 'I have not yet conquered my dislike to cricket so much as not to be glad that I was not at home on Owen's birthday to meet the terrible company of twenty-four boys.'[31]

Arthur always preferred to read. In the same year, 1828, Kitty wrote to the Reverend Augustus Hare, who was soon to marry her sister Maria:

> I have Arthur at home ... he suffers so much from a laudable desire to be with other boys, and yet, when with them, finds his incapacity to enter into their pleasures of shooting, hunting, horses, and to take theirs for his. He will be happier as a man, as literary men are more within reach than literary boys.[32]

Arthur's reading for pleasure included Homer, Plutarch, Herodotus, Cicero, Horace, Virgil, Sophocles, Shakespeare, Bunyan, and Scott, his favourite. From the time he was seven his first love had been poetry. At eleven he wrote: 'April has begun at last, and a most beautiful beginning it is here, the sun shining, and so warm and nice that to-day, when I had to write some Latin verses, I wrote five or six lines about Spring. And besides this I have written some more English verses on the Return of Coriolanus. I walk in the paths of poetry every Thursday, and of course I like it better than any other lesson.'[33] 'A constant process of verse-making seems to be going on his head,' recorded Kitty in her journal. 'He writes nothing down till it is all composed, and then it comes out as fast as he can write it.'[34]

In November 1827 Captain Parry's and Isabella's first child was born at Alderley. Immediately on hearing the news Arthur wrote to his sister Mary and included a long birthday ode which begins:

> Hail, thou lovely little stranger,
>   Thou, whose smile, so bright and sweet,
>   Shall thy noble father greet
> Now escap'd from ev'ry danger;
>   Him, whose brave undaunted soul
>   Dar'd explore the Northern pole,
> Storm and ice and snow defying;
>   Him who, with ecstatic joy,
>   Kisses now his lovely boy,
> In the lowly cradle lying ...[35]

Soon after, Parry paid Arthur a surprise visit at school: 'About 7 a.m., as I was coming downstairs ... I heard a voice that I thought I knew; I came quite down, and there I saw a great tall man and a little man. You may guess who they were. Papa talked to Mr. Rawson, Captain Parry to me; they had breakfast here, so all the boys saw the *celebrated man* ... They were much pleased; but were quite enchanted with him when he asked for a holiday for us.'[36]

Six months later Arthur was invited with another boy to the Gladstones' home. They were to have breakfast with William, who had recently left Eton and was soon to go up to Oxford:

> ... so we went, had breakfast in grand style, went into the garden and devoured strawberries, which were there in great abundance, unchained the great Newfoundland, and swam him in the pond; we walked about the garden; went into the house and saw beautiful pictures of Shakespeare's plays, and came away at twelve o'clock. It was very good fun, and I don't think I was very shy, for I talked to William Gladstone almost all the time about all sorts of things. He is so very good-natured, and I like him very much. He talked a great deal about Eton, and said that it was a very good place for those that liked boating and Latin verses. I think, from what he said, I might get to like it ... He was very good-natured to us all the time, and lent me books to read when we went away ...[37]

One of the books was an anthology of Thomas Gray's poetry. Stanley read it immediately and Gray became another favourite.

* * *

The letter home about Gladstone concludes: 'Oh! How soon – next Tuesday week, and then the sea, the Pyrenees!'[38] This was to be Arthur's first visit abroad, and the excitement of anticipation remained as strong throughout ten weeks of travels in the south of France. This was the journey that inspired in Arthur a lifelong love of travel and travel-writing.

The party consisted of Edward and Kitty, Mary and Arthur, their aunt Maria and cousin Lucy,[i] and Arthur's and Mary's beloved nurse, Sarah Burgess. They left Liverpool early on 17 July 1828, took a steam-packet to Dublin and from there a sailing-ship to Bordeaux. Arthur kept a detailed diary in two closely-written volumes and they make a

---

[i] Lucy Stanley was seventeen years older than Arthur and was his godmother.

fascinating record of those first experiences of a foreign country and its mountain scenery. Arthur's narrative and descriptive powers are already formidable. Here, aged twelve, is his account of what he regarded as the high point of the tour – the expedition to the Port de Venasque and the Maladetta:

> At last we came into a vast amphitheatre of stupendous rocks, out of which it seemed impossible to pass, and all their tops were glowing in the morning light. At the bottom of this magnificent place was a small lake, which was joined to some smaller ones. Its water was black as ink; but the rocks and rosy sky were reflected in it beautifully. We looked round, not knowing how we were to pass out, for the rocks towered above us and surrounded us as if with a wall; but we followed the guide, who led us winding on, till all of a sudden there appeared a pass – very narrow – looking just as if it had been cut into Spain, just what I could fancy the Brèche de Roland to be. There was scarcely room for more than two to pass at a time; but the moment we had got through the snowy range the mountains of Aragon burst upon us, and mighty and stupendous above them all, with its awful and magnificent height covered with eternal snows, the Maladetta rose before us! Never shall I forget what I felt on seeing it burst forth so suddenly in all its grandeur and desolation – so well deserving the name of Maladetta,[j] with its many dark granite peaks, rising out of the vast beds of snow with which it was crowned, its vast girdle of grey rocks, and the wild cliffs beneath only speckled with black pines.[39]

That first sight of the Maladetta made a strong impression on Arthur, and preoccupied his thoughts and poems for years to come.

The thrill of travel conquered Arthur's usual languor. He seems to have escaped the worst of the sea sickness he describes other passengers suffering. Instead, 'the Channel waves were magnificent, and Lucy, Mary, and I sat on deck screaming with rapture; for they came swelling and rolling and foaming, and the vessel heaved and rolled, and once when we were unprepared a great wave came, and we all three fell from our seats, and lay prostrate on the floor.'[40] Arthur was sure to be there on every excursion, often going an extra mile in search of something that had been overlooked. He enjoyed riding and was delighted with

---

[j] Maladetta means 'cursed'.

his little black pony. The expedition to the Maladetta lasted from midnight until three-thirty in the afternoon, and he returned home 'not in the least tired'.[41]

*   *   *

Arthur returned from the Pyrenees to start his final year at Seaforth. The question where he was to go next had been taxing Kitty. His peculiar strengths and weaknesses would, she feared, be difficult to accommodate in any of the schools she knew. Owen's unhappiness ruled out Charterhouse. Eton she felt was unruly, socially demanding and too expensive. But what of Shrewsbury or Rugby or Winchester?

Kitty sought advice from Augustus Hare. Hare was the same age as Kitty and an eccentric, and not to be confused with his nephew Augustus J. C. Hare. He had been at Winchester as a boy and then New College, Oxford where he stayed on as a fellow. After marrying Kitty's sister, Maria, he became vicar of Alton-Barnes in Wiltshire. 'Do you think,' Kitty wrote to him in February 1828, 'from what you know of Arthur's character and capabilities, that Winchester would suit him, and *vice versa*?' Hare replied first from Naples and then again three weeks later from Florence. Both these letters are remarkably prophetic and informative – about Arthur and Dr Arnold, as well as about public schools at the time:

> Are you aware that the person of all others fitted to get on with boys is just elected master of Rugby? His name is Arnold. He is a Wykehamist and Fellow of Oriel, and a particular friend of mine – a man calculated beyond all others to endgraft modern scholarship and modern improvements on the old-fashioned stem of a public education. Winchester under him would be the best school in Europe; what Rugby may turn out I cannot say, for I know not the materials he has there to work on.[42]

> I am so little satisfied with what I said about Arthur in my last letter, that I am determined to begin with him and do him more justice. What you describe him now to be, I once was; and I have myself suffered too much and too often from my inferiority in strength and activity to boys who were superior to me in nothing else, not to feel very deeply for any one in a similar state of school-forwardness and bodily weakness ... You may conceive what wretchedness this is likely to lead to, in a state of society like a school, where might almost necessarily makes right ...

About his school, were Rugby under any other master, I certainly should not advise your thinking of it for Arthur for an instant; as it is, the decision will be more difficult. When Arnold has been there ten years, he will have made it a good school, perhaps in some respects the very best in the island; but a transition state is always one of doubt and delicacy.[43]

Kitty wrote to Dr Arnold the following October. She described Arthur's peculiarities and asked whether he felt Rugby might suit him. After receiving his reply she wrote her sister a letter even more prescient than Hare's: 'Dr. Arnold's letter has decided us about Arthur. I should think there was not another schoolmaster in his Majesty's dominions who would write such a letter. It is so lively, agreeable and promising in all ways. He is just the man to take a fancy to Arthur, and for Arthur to take a fancy to.'[44]

2

'Under the Boughs of a Mighty Oak'

1829–1834

DESPITE HER FAITH in Dr Arnold, Kitty was as anxious about Rugby as she had been about Seaforth. Arthur was still frail and sensitive: what in Cheshire dialect was contemptuously called *nesh*. Public school, no matter how good the headmaster, was bound to be a trial. Arthur felt much the same. Four years later he wrote to a friend: 'I looked forward on my coming here to a long farewell to all goodness and happiness, and wondered how I should ever come out safe again.'[1] It was not just the physical rigours of boarding school that troubled Kitty and Arthur; Kitty worried too about the temptations and bad examples of other boys. Though she would have strongly disagreed with Squire Brown's indifference to learning ('I don't care a straw for Greek particles, or the digamma; no more does his mother') she would most certainly have sympathised with his desire for Tom to 'turn out a brave, helpful, truth-telling Englishman, and a gentleman, and a Christian'.[2]

Boarding schools in 1829 were brutal places. Kitty's friend and admirer, Sydney Smith, described them as 'evils of the greatest magnitude' whose 'system of premature debauchery ... prevented men from being corrupted by the world by corrupting them before their entry into the world'.[3] *Tom Brown's Schooldays* gives a graphic account of the fighting, flogging and fagging that were rife in schools before Arnold's reforms began to take effect. The novel's most contemptible character is the sadistic Flashman, the School House bully, who tyrannises the younger boys and 'left no slander unspoken, and no deed undone, which could in any way hurt his victims, or isolate them from the rest of the house'.[4] Hughes's descriptions of 'blanket-tossing' and 'roasting' can strike terror today in a boy or parent who fears such tortures still exist.

The chief fault of schools at the time was the inadequacy of the teachers, who were mostly poorly paid parsons supplementing their salaries with parish work (a practice Arnold was the first to abolish). So boys were left to their own devices, unsupervised for long stretches of time. Readers of William Golding's *Lord of the Flies* know how savagely boys can behave when deprived of adult direction. At Eton the collegers (scholars) of all ages were imprisoned in their dormitory at eight in the evening and not released until the following morning. Evidence given in the 1860s to the Public Schools Commission includes the following:

> The Long Chamber was then (1824) in its prime – that is to say, it had attained the maximum of age, dirt, squalor, neglect and desolation ... The condition of a junior Colleger's life at that period was very hard indeed. The practice of fagging had become an organised system of brutality and cruelty. I was frequently kept up until one or two o'clock in the morning, waiting on my masters at supper and undergoing every sort of bullying at their hands. I have been beaten on my palms with the back of a brush, or struck on both sides of my face, because I had not closed the shutter near my master's bed tight enough or because in making his bed I had left the seam of the lower sheet upper-most ... The rioting, masquerading and drinking that took place in College after the doors were closed at night can scarcely be credited. I do not think there was even an alarm-bell, although I have seen many a blaze that seemed to threaten destruction to the whole building.[5]

Frankly, there was not much to choose between Dickens's Dotheboys Hall and the dormitories of any public school at the time.

Woven into this culture of cruelty was a contempt for religion, and it is this which most provoked Arnold's fury and reforming zeal. Stanley appended a letter from George Moberly, Headmaster of Winchester, to the third chapter of his biography. The letter praises Arnold's good influence on recent undergraduates at Oxford. Before that, 'the tone of young men at the University, whether they came from Winchester, Eton, Rugby, Harrow, or wherever else, was universally irreligious. A religious under-graduate was very rare, very much laughed at when he appeared; and I think I may confidently say, hardly to be found among public school men.'[6] *Tom Brown's Schooldays* has a famous account of this disdain for religion. When George Arthur arrives at Rugby, Arnold arranges for Tom to look after him. On his first night in the dormitory, Arthur makes the fatal mistake of kneeling by his bed to say his prayers. 'Two or three boys laughed and sneered, and a big, brutal fellow who was standing in the middle of the room picked up a slipper, and shied it at the kneeling boy, calling him a snivelling young shaver ... It was no light act of courage in those days, my dear boys, for a little fellow to say his prayers publicly, even at Rugby.'[7]

* * *

Arthur Stanley and his father arrived at Rugby on 31 January 1829, after a long, cold and uncomfortable journey. They had travelled first by carriage from Alderley to Manchester, and then by a four-horse stagecoach to Birmingham, an eighty-mile journey which took twelve hours. After changing coaches at Birmingham they arrived six hours later at Dunchurch, a village to the south of Rugby. There they had breakfast and hired a post-chaise for the last three miles. One of Stanley's contemporaries remembered his first appearance in the school, and it was not a promising start:

> He was then thirteen years of age, short in stature, of slight frame, small and delicate features, with the gentle and amiable expression which marked him to the close of his life. His general appearance was feminine, and obtained for him the passing nickname of 'Nancy'... I recall him dressed in a round, blue, many-buttoned jacket, and grey trousers adorned by a pink watch-ribbon, being somewhat earlier than the general run of boys were trusted with watches. His manners were as gentle as his appearance indicated. He was shy and timid, but full of vivacity when accosted.[8]

Stanley was to board with the Reverend C. A. Anstey,[a] but his house was not finished and so for his first half-year[b] he lodged instead in Townsend's, a house of just fourteen boys in the middle of Rugby near the Eagle Inn. On 4 February Arthur wrote the first of many long letters home to his sister Mary (he usually called her Mäi) in which he described his school life in considerable detail:

> We drove through the town, which is just behind the school, and stopped at Mr. Townsend's. There we saw him and his wife. We went to look at the studies, some of which were ranged round a yard, and some upstairs ...
> Papa and I then walked to Dr. Arnold's, and presently Mrs.

---

[a] Charles Alleyne Anstey had been a boy at Rugby and returned to teach in 1819. He was appointed chaplain in 1825, and when he resigned six years later, Arnold combined the role of chaplain with that of headmaster.
[b] The school year was divided into two: the first half from August to December, and the second from February to July.

Arnold came in – she was very nice indeed. At last came the Doctor himself; but I certainly should not have taken him for a Doctor. He was very pleasant, and did not look old. When Papa asked him whether I could be examined, he said that if I would walk into the next room he would do it himself; so, of course, in I went with him, with a feeling like that when I am going to have a tooth drawn. So he took down a Homer, and I read about half a dozen lines, and the same with Virgil; he then asked a little about my Latin verses, and set me down without any more ado in the great book as placed in the fourth form ...

I went to Mr. Townsend's again to dine with the boys. The dining-room was a place with a large fire, and a table with benches, on the former of which was placed the dinner (which consisted of pudding and meat), and on the latter the boys – in number about seven – and two men-servants to wait upon us. Not a word was passed between me and them the whole of dinner-time ... The bell rang for us at a quarter-to-ten, and at ten we were all in bed. Now don't you expect some dreadful story of pulling toes, &c.? I am afraid Mamma and you will be very much disappointed, for I slept very quietly all night ...[9]

Given Arthur's character, and the rigours of schools like Rugby, he survived his first days surprisingly well, thanks in part to not having to sleep in a dormitory. He felt lonely and homesick, but in a letter to Owen written in July during his first holiday, Arthur reckoned that he had had a more agreeable start than Owen at Charterhouse. 'At my boarding house, there was very little fagging & no bullying except smoking & squirting thro' the study doors for each boy had a study to himself some of which are miserably small ... Upon the whole I am very happy – Garside [sic] Tipping[c] & some other big boys are very kind to me so that I have been remarkably fortunate.'[10]

That kindness was secured through the respect Stanley won for his cleverness, and the assistance he was willing to give other boys. Already in his 4 February letter he says that his form master had warned another boy that this new boy will soon be his equal. In those days pupils were promoted from one form to another according to ability not age. The fourth was the highest of seven forms that a new boy could join, so Stanley had evidently impressed Arnold when he tested him. He was

---

[c] Gartside Tipping came from Knutsford near Alderley and had started at Rugby in 1822 aged ten.

soon at the top, and after winning an essay prize, was promoted at Easter to the form called the shell, and then to the fifth form at the end of his first half-year. This was an extraordinarily rapid rise, and gained not only the admiration of his fellows but also some welcome privileges: the boys of the fifth were excused fagging and from being out of bounds. Stanley was delighted, and wrote to Mary to boast that 'at all events, I think I can say what no other at the school can, that at the beginning of one half-year I was in the fourth and had to sweep out another boy's study, and at the beginning of the next I had fags to sweep out my own.'[11]

Stanley was much in demand for help with other boys' work. 'As soon as I come into school in the morning about half a dozen boys run up to me, exclaiming, "Give me a construe, give me a construe"; and each one tries to get me, and one pulls one way and another another, till at last they all come and sit, stand or crouch round me whilst I give them one.'[12] A fortnight later, Stanley wrote to Mr Rawson: 'I thought of you, sir, the other night – as I was chosen to write out one of the praepostors' prize essays, on account of my writing such a *good hand*.'[13] 'I am never bogled[d] with smoke or squirts,' he told Mary, 'and so long as I do not fag[e] at my lessons very much I am not teased at all.'[14] Kitty wrote with relief: 'Arthur never gets plagued in any way like the others, his study is left untouched, his things unbroken, his books undisturbed.'[15]

Nonetheless, Stanley was still the same solitary and lonely boy who found it difficult to make friends. This was partly because he was such an atypical schoolboy, but also because he found it difficult to get close to anyone except his mother and sister. 'Do you want to know', he asked Mary, 'how – and I get on? Why, we are very amicable, &c., but I am afraid that he is a sphere above me. I think we shall always go on well and peacefully, but never be loving friends – like Waverley and Flora MacIvor!'[16] This is an odd analogy to describe his relationship with another boy.

Stanley did his best to get involved in the kind of school life that Tom Brown relished. He told Mary that he played football three days running. Rugby's peculiar version of the game allowed as many as a hundred players a side, with only throttling and strangling forbidden in the scrum! 'To be sure, I am a very poor player, but it is a great thing to have broken thro' the ice; for the last half-year, to say the truth, I don't

---

[d] Rugby slang for 'bothered'.
[e] The verb to 'fag' in Rugby parlance had two senses: to act as servant to a senior pupil and (in this context) to study hard.

think I ever played at any game in the playground. I do really like it ... though I sometimes catch myself looking at the sunset instead of the ball.'[17] 'I shall go on playing, I think, though it is a joke among the boys ... as I do very little more than run backwards and forwards after a crowd for the space of two hours.'[18] With two other boys he tried to stay up all night, 'partly to fag, partly to see what it is like'.[19] Another time he broke the rules by letting off squibs before being caught by Mr Anstey and given a hundred lines of Horace to translate.

Poetry remained Stanley's first love, followed by hard work at his books. At the end of his first year he was 'fagging away terribly, taking up Extras – in Divinity, Leslie on Deism; in Greek, half the Hippolytus; in History, some of the reigns of the kings of England; and under Mathematics, some Conversations on Natural Philosophy. Arithmetic is the only thing that I almost despair of.'[20] Promotion to the fifth form seems to have given Stanley the confidence he needed to 'rub up my poetry, for it has grown rusty'.[21] 'Old Moor', his eccentric form master, enthused him by devoting a lesson each day to writing English verses on a given subject, the best of which he read out with infectious delight. In October the subject was Brownsover, a small village on the River Avon a mile and a half from Rugby where Lawrence Sheriff, the founder of Rugby School, was born. Stanley's poem was judged the best in the form, despite the fact that he was modest enough not to overdo it since he was still new in the fifth. His next poem came top as well, and his first nickname, 'Nancy', was soon replaced by 'Poet'; his study was called 'Poet's Corner'.

* * *

To boys in the lower school Arnold was a remote and condescending figure. Stanley's only encounters with him were when he came every month to examine his form. 'We have been examined again by Dr. Arnold in Latin,' he told Mary, 'and he seemed very pleased with me, and said I had done extremely well. He is very particular; the least word you say or pronounce wrong he finds out in an instant, and he is very particular about chronology, history, and geography.'[22] Seven weeks later Arnold examined Stanley's new form, the shell: 'How particular he is; but at the same time so mild and pleasant ... He asks very much about history, and asks queer out-of-the-way questions ... He seems very pleased when I answer anything.'[23]

Stanley won another of many school prizes when in the fifth form he entered an English essay competition; the title set was 'Sicily and its

Revolutions'. He read everything he could find on the topic. 'So much for Sicily; my head is full of it – tyrants and princes and successions all rolling about in it, and making it like Mount Etna.'[24] And then, 'as I was running home from school, a cry of "Stanley to Dr. Arnold!" reached my ears. I turned, and bursting through the outstretched arms, and "You have got it," stood before Dr. Arnold. He said he congratulated me upon having gained the prize. Oh! what a moment! and when I came out such a shaking of hands, such congratulations.'[25]

Arnold wrote to Edward Stanley to invite him to hear his son read his essay on speech day. When the day came Stanley was terrified and largely inaudible, and looked pitifully small as he stood on the stage in the speakers' uniform of white trousers and silk stockings. 'There are many jokes on me: "Oh! Stanley must have a stool to stand on, and a wheelbarrow to wheel away the prize."'[26] But the prize-winner also won the admiring attention of one boy who was to become one of his closest friends. Charles Vaughan was eight months younger than Stanley, and had arrived at Rugby at the start of his second year. In the sermon he preached at Stanley's funeral, Vaughan described how he had first noticed Stanley when he won the prize: 'It is just more than half a century ago since I first looked upon that face, "as the face of an angel", which is now finally hidden from the sight of all the living. It was when I saw him enter the crowded School Chapel at Rugby, radiant – his look showed it – with the joy of his having just gained his first prize.'[27] The attraction Vaughan felt to Stanley is plain too in a reminiscence he wrote for Prothero's biography:

> The first time that I remember seeing our friend was on the Good Friday afternoon of that first half-year, when he came into chapel ... his face turned by blushes from rose-colour to scarlet in the joy and pride of his first triumph, the prize for the Fifth Form English Essay having been just adjudged to him. His face and look are as vividly before me as if it were a scene of yesterday – the black hair, cut close as always, the bright ingenuous child's face, the round jacket and twilled trousers, and the quick gliding movement, three steps to a man's one – all these I could draw, if I were an artist, into a far livelier picture of him than any of those that are left to us.[28]

* * *

Thomas Arnold was young and new to Rugby: he had started, aged thirty-three, just six months before Stanley. His reforms had hardly begun, though he had introduced an examination to be taken by the fifth form to decide who was to be allowed promotion to the sixth. Stanley sat these tests in the summer of 1831 and came top, despite being a year younger than most of the other candidates. The three years he spent in the sixth were his most enjoyable, and their effect was profound and far-reaching.

Stanley's joining the sixth coincided with Arnold's becoming chaplain as well as headmaster. He had preached occasionally in chapel but from now on he addressed the school almost every Sunday afternoon.[f] From the start Stanley had been enthralled by Arnold's sermons. and he continued to record and reflect on every word he could remember. 'Years have passed away,' he wrote in his *Life of Arnold,* 'and many of his pupils can look back to hardly any greater interest than that which, for those twenty minutes, Sunday after Sunday, they sat beneath that pulpit, with their eyes fixed upon him, and their attention strained to the utmost to catch every word that he uttered.'[29]

The intriguing question is how these sermons could have had such a bewitching effect on Stanley and other boys. One sermon he found particularly memorable was preached in February 1832 at the start of the half-year. When, ten years later, the sermon Stanley preached at Rugby after Arnold's death was published, he attached Arnold's sermon as an appendix. A virtuous boy called Henry Bland had died suddenly during the holiday. He was a year older than Stanley but had started at Rugby at the same time and was in the same house. All the essential ingredients of an Arnold sermon are here in this epitaph, with its earnest appeal to the boys to take stock of their sinful lives, join battle with temptation, and throw themselves on the mercy of Christ:

> He is safe – but we are yet in danger; – and here is the great consideration for us all. He is safe from those temptations against which we have still to struggle; and would that we all felt as we should do the blessedness of that safety. For though not yet ours, yet it may be so hereafter; we may attain to it as surely, as he has reached it actually. A blessed state indeed it is, when we feel what a conflict is now hourly besetting us; and how we can never dare to rest but for a moment without adding to our danger. Yet Christ

---

[f] Owen Chadwick (*The Victorian Church,* i) describes the sermons as the finest of the century. They were published in six volumes and Stanley would have heard most of those in i and ii.

will bring us to it in his own good time, if we bear our present struggle as becomes his soldiers, bravely yet humbly, striving earnestly ourselves, with our trust, not in what we can do, but in what He has done for us.[30]

What was undoubtedly compelling about Arnold's sermons was the seriousness and passion of his moralising. He sternly rebuked the wickedness he saw in his boys, and urgently pleaded with them to repent and amend their ways. In a sermon preached in 1831 on the text 'The law was our schoolmaster to bring us unto Christ', Arnold emphasised the central theme of his school sermons, and certainly of the early ones. He quotes the religious pamphleteer John Bowdler, who shared Sydney Smith's cynical view of schools: '"Public schools",' he says, "are the very seats and nurseries of vice. It may be unavoidable, or it may not; but the fact is indisputable. None can pass through a large school without being pretty intimately acquainted with vice; and few, alas! very few without tasting too largely of that poisoned bowl."'[31] Arnold explains exactly what this means, and the directness and frankness of his rhetoric would not have been lost:

That is properly a nursery of vice, where a boy unlearns the pure and honest principles which he may have received at home, and gets, in their stead, others which are utterly low, and base, and mischievous, – where he loses his modesty, his respect for truth, and his affectionateness, and becomes coarse, and false, and unfeeling. That too, is a nursery of vice, and most fearfully so, where vice is bold, and forward, and presuming; and goodness is timid and shy, and existing as if by sufferance, – where the good, instead of setting the tone of society, and branding with disgrace those who disregard it, are themselves exposed to reproach for their goodness, and shrink before the open avowal of evil principles, which the bad are striving to make the law of the community ...[32]

Arnold's sermons worked because they penetrated to the heart of the boys' lives at school. He showed a surprising knowledge of their closed and private world, holding up an uncomfortable mirror to those boys whose consciences were already afraid. And he gave them too the means to escape, not only by pointing them to Christ, but by standing there before them as a Christian hero and a man to emulate: a strong, brave and virtuous man, determined to root out evil and turn Rugby into a truly Christian school. Here is Stanley re-living what he had felt so strongly as a boy:

> But more than either matter or manner of his preaching, was the impression of himself ... It was the man himself, there more than in any other place, concentrating all his various faculties and feelings on one sole object, combating face to face the evil, with which directly or indirectly he was elsewhere perpetually struggling. He was not the preacher or clergyman who had left behind all his usual thoughts and occupations as soon as he had ascended the pulpit ... He was still the instructor and the schoolmaster, only teaching and educating with increased solemnity and energy. He was still the simple-hearted and earnest man, labouring to win others to share in his own personal feelings of disgust at sin, and love of goodness, and to trust to the same faith, in which he hoped to live and die himself.[33]

Arnold's combustible mixture of righteous indignation and strength of personality cast a spell over the boys, though none perhaps was ever as deeply affected as Stanley. 'How few of my thoughts are original, and how many of them come directly or indirectly from Dr. Arnold's sermons.'[34] These thoughts shaped Stanley's deepest Christian convictions, and especially his own sense of virtue and moral conviction.

When Stanley was in the sixth, Arnold's weekly sermon turned awe into something deeper. 'Idolatry' is what Stanley called it, and as time went on, and as Arnold impressed the perils of sin, it troubled him. Just before leaving Rugby, Stanley wrote to Vaughan: 'I fear I have passed the limits, and made him my idol ... You too love him and admire him as much as he deserves – but not more, and not dangerously, and you can help me – I would hardly say to love him less – but to love God more.'[35]

*   *   *

Dr Arnold taught classics, history and scripture to the sixth, and his teaching had almost as potent an effect on Stanley as his preaching. 'The chief source of [Arnold's] intellectual as of his moral influence over the school', he wrote, 'was through the Sixth Form. To the rest of the boys he appeared almost exclusively as a master, to them he appeared almost exclusively as an instructor. The library tower, which stands over the great gateway to the school-buildings, and in which he heard the lessons of his own form, is the place to which his pupils will revert as the scene of their first real acquaintance with his powers of teaching, and with himself.'[36]

What were those powers which Stanley experienced? Arnold was a clever and learned man and a gifted and enthusiastic teacher, but he never regarded the academic side of school as the most important. He had no respect for mere cleverness, and regarded it as 'more revolting than the most helpless imbecility, seeming to me almost like the spirit of Mephistopheles.'[37] 'What we must look for here', he told his prefects, 'is, 1st religious and moral principle; 2ndly, gentlemanly conduct; 3rdly, intellectual ability.'[38] To Arnold, teaching was essentially a religious activity which served a higher purpose, namely the pursuit of truth, and truth that was morally enlightening. This approach could be inspiring but it could also prejudice Arnold's pupils and impede dispassionate judgement. For instance, Stanley recalled that Arnold's strong moral disapprobation prevented his appreciation of the genius of Juvenal and Aristophanes. And when it came to history, 'no direct instruction could leave on their minds a livelier image of his disgust at moral evil, than the black cloud of indignation which passed over his face when speaking of the crimes of Napoleon, or of Caesar, and of the dead pause which followed, as if the acts had just been committed in his very presence.'[39] Stanley's other good friend in the sixth, William Lake,[g] recorded similar memories of Arnold's teaching:

> The lessons in the Sixth were to many of us a real enjoyment, and all the more because they were so evident an enjoyment to himself. He inoculated us with his likings for his favourite books and characters, for Thucydides and Tacitus, for Alexander, and for some of the earlier Romans like Scipio, and his strong dislikes for Caesar and Augustus; and when we came to his modern history lectures, there were no characters which he taught us more to admire than some of the religious characters of the Middle Ages, such as St. Louis of France and Pope Innocent III.[40]

Given the fact that Arnold's moral opinions were so forcefully expressed, his style of teaching was surprisingly socratic. 'His whole method', Stanley explains, 'was founded on the principle of awakening

---

[g] W. C. Lake was two years younger than Stanley and started as a day-boy when he was eight. His father had been severely wounded at Waterloo. He overlapped with Stanley at Balliol where he became a fellow and later Dean of Durham.

the intellect of every individual boy. Hence it was his practice to teach by questioning. As a general rule, he never gave information, except as a kind of reward for an answer, and often withheld it altogether ...'[41] Arnold seems to have intended that his boys should form their own opinions, and not take them on trust from him. 'It would be a great mistake', he once said, 'if I were to try to make myself here into a Pope.'[42] Nonetheless, the strength of his beliefs and convictions meant that Arnold expected his pupils to agree with him, and they often did.

Stanley rated Arnold's scripture lessons above his other subjects, as he explained in a letter to his uncle Augustus Hare:

> You may be very sure that if there was nothing else at Rugby I liked, [Dr Arnold's] being here would incline me to stay as long as ever I can ... I may safely say that there is not a word that goes out of his mouth in the way of teaching that I do not treasure up ... I have indeed cause to be thankful to you for sending me here to a man whom I hope I shall look up to with reverence all my life. What I consider as the most valuable of his instructions, as being the least attainable from any other quarter, are what he gives us in divinity whether from his sermons or in the regular lessons in that branch: I confess I am rather disappointed with his classical knowledge; tho' it seems I suppose very presumptuous of me to say so, & if one does lose something in the way of minute scholarship, it is fully overbalanced by the originality and goodness of his general remarks ...[43]

The Bible was as essential and fundamental to Arnold's divinity lessons as it was to his sermons. 'There was nothing of exaggeration or anything that could be called preaching about them,' wrote Lake; 'his comments, generally short and simple, were always "given in a tone and manner which left an impression that from the book which lay before him he was seeking to draw his rule of life," and the impression which he left upon us was that the one guide for this was Scripture.'[44] Arnold's reverence for the Bible was Evangelical in its intensity. He was convinced that its pages contained the supreme revelation of the will of God and the duty of man. But Arnold did not share the Evangelical's insistence that every word of the Scriptures was literally true. Indeed, Arnold held unusually advanced notions about how the Bible was to be interpreted and applied, and he was not afraid to share them with his pupils.

During Stanley's first months in the sixth, Arnold was writing a fifty-page pamphlet *On the Right Interpretation and Understanding of the Scriptures*. It brought Arnold's ideas to public attention, and was the first of a series of controversial books, articles and pamphlets. Arnold included it as an appendix to his second volume of sermons, and always regarded it as the most important of his writings, and also the most misunderstood. He sets out to answer a young man's difficulties when he finds obscurities, inaccuracies and immoralities in the Bible. Arnold gets round these by explaining that the Bible is not 'like the Koran, all composed at one time and addressed to persons similarly situated'.[45] Instead revelation is gradual and progressive like education. God accommodated himself to the time, and spoke to men differently in the Old Testament than he did in the New – just as a schoolmaster might speak differently to a new boy than to a sixth-former. What is important in Biblical exegesis, explains Arnold, is to read any passage in its historical context, and to understand that what God may have commanded in the Old Testament, during 'the childhood and youth of the human race',[46] does not necessarily apply to later generations. This may seem a sensible approach today but when Stanley was a boy it was radical and innovative. He and other pupils took his new methods to heart, and it is clear that learning to read the Bible like this helped later to preserve their confidence in the essential truths of Biblical revelation in the face of increasing criticism.

Stanley loved being taught by Arnold. 'What a wonderful influence that man has had on my mind!' Stanley wrote at the time. 'I certainly feel that I have hardly a free will of my own on any subject about which he has written or spoken.'[47] In turn Arnold treated Stanley almost with deference, looking increasingly to him as the pupil on whom he could rely for an accurate answer to his questions, and perhaps for an agreeable reflection of his own opinions. '"Stanley," he would ask, "what do you think about that?" ... – folding his gown and leaning upon the table, and looking towards him with such *respect*, shown in the very tones of his voice, and always getting a good answer.'[48]

Stanley probably exaggerated the extent to which Arnold dominated his understanding, but what is certain is that Arnold stimulated his passion for books. The range of Stanley's reading in the sixth is extraordinary, and gave him an enormous variety of ideas and opinions to set alongside what he had learnt from Arnold. His letters home reveal what Prothero calls 'his insatiable avidity for knowledge'.[49] We know, for instance, that he read in their entirety (and made notes on) the complete works of Milton (more than once), all eight volumes of

Mitford's *History of Greece*, Whately's *Historic Doubts relative to Napoleon Buonaparte*, Gibbons's *Decline and Fall*, Walton's *Lives* of the poets, Boswell's *Johnson*, and Keble's *Christian Year*. In describing Stanley, Lake borrowed Sydney Smith's description of the Whig historian, Lord Macaulay: 'he was a born "book in breeches".'[50]

* * *

All thirty members of Arnold's sixth form were prefects, or praepostors. Arnold had borrowed this system of boy leadership from his own school, Winchester, but he transformed it, and made it what Stanley calls 'the keystone of his whole government'.[51] This is the method Arnold employed to put the strong moral principles he taught and preached into practice in the school:

> The importance which he attached [to the system] arose from his regarding it not only as an efficient engine of discipline, but as the chief means of creating a respect for moral and intellectual excellence, and of diffusing his own influence through the mass of the school. Whilst he made the Praepostors rely upon his support in all just use of their authority ... he endeavoured also to make them feel that they were actually fellow-workers with him for the highest good of the school, upon the highest principles and motives – that they had, with him, a moral responsibility and a deep interest in the real welfare of the place.[52]

In the fifth form Stanley had found it difficult to exercise even limited authority: 'I am not one that could command anything,' he told Mary.[53] But now he relished being a praeposter, and this was because of the confidence Arnold placed in him. Arnold deliberately chose to entrust moral authority to the cleverest boys and not, as later in public schools, to the strongest athletes. Indeed Arnold was convinced that the sixth were best able to 'secure a regular government amongst the boys themselves, and avoid the evils of anarchy; in other words, of the lawless tyranny of physical strength'.[54]

Stanley's authority was tested by an incident in his second year in the sixth. This is loosely described in *Tom Brown's Schooldays*, though Hughes did not arrive at Rugby until the following year. Rugby boys had from the start been allowed to fish in the muddy waters of the Avon. However, by Arnold's time the landowners were beginning to object and the sport was forbidden. The boys continued regardless, and in May 1833 a keeper caught seven boys and tried to seize their nets. In the fracas that followed, the keeper fell into the river and the boys escaped. The squire was furious and stormed into Arnold's study. The culprits refused to own up, an identity parade was held, and the keeper picked out six boys whom Arnold expelled on the spot. The school felt that their ancestral fishing rights had been denied and were ready to rebel. Into the commotion stepped Stanley, supported by Vaughan and Lake, and he managed to persuade the school that resistance was hopeless, and that Arnold was right to punish as he had. Stanley confided later that he had 'rather enjoyed the excitement'.[55]

Stanley, Lake and Vaughan were the brightest pupils in the sixth and became close, helping Stanley to overcome his inherent difficulty in making friends. They shunned games and went instead for long walks together. Lake was always the most detached of the three, and the least admiring of Arnold, and regretted this in later life. 'Nothing could be closer than the friendship of Stanley, Vaughan, and myself; but to me it was the loss of what had been my earliest friends, the cricket-ground and football. These I gave up almost as a matter of course when I became an intimate friend of Stanley.'[56] When the three were not out walking they sat in Stanley's book-lined study. 'We discussed all things – ,' Vaughan reminisced, 'politics and politicians, theology and theologians ... (Stanley's) own prize compositions, which I used to write out for him, furnished a fruitful subject. School politics, at times somewhat revolutionary, were treated as moral matters, with a little too much (it may be) of grown-up sternness.'[57]

In his first year in the sixth, Stanley won two of Rugby's most glittering prizes, one for an English essay and the other for an English poem. The subject of the former was 'Novels and Novelists', and Stanley attacked the research with the same vigour and enthusiasm as for his essay on Brownsover. The poem was on the Frankish ruler, Charles Martel. Stanley stayed up late, night after night, reading 'Gibbon, Hallam, Percy's Reliques, Ellis's Metrical Romances, Mémoires de l'Académie, Bayle's Dictionary'.[58] He asked Mary to hunt for further sources as he tried to establish the precise topography of the decisive Battle of Tours in 732. In April Arthur wrote again to Mary: 'I have got the English Verse! I sent in 192 lines. On Thursday reports were disseminated of the extraordinary goodness of one copy – particularly one master, who told his pupils that it was the best school exercise ... ever shown up, or that he had ever seen, or the best ever done at Rugby.'[59] The poem, written in heroic couplets, was so exceptional that no second prize was awarded, and Arnold gave the school a half-day holiday. Again

Stanley's father came to Rugby to hear him read the poem and essay on speech day. His younger brother Charley had recently joined the school and was present too. Stanley was recovering from mumps but two glasses of wine eased his throat and his confidence. 'I was all this time not in a very great fright, not near so much as in my fifth-form essay, but still in a very great tremor.'[60] With prompting, Stanley managed to get through both readings, and when he went up to receive his final prize, 'there rose from all sides a tremendous peal of clapping. Those few moments certainly gave me as much pleasure as I have ever had.'[61]

*   *   *

Kitty was delighted with her son's glowing reports about Arnold: 'Arthur's veneration for him is beautiful ... what good it must do to grow up under such a tree.'[62] Everything she had hoped for was being realised, and soon Stanley's father was working hard to get Arnold a bishopric, though preferably not before Arthur had left Rugby. In July 1833 Kitty wrote in her journal: 'It was too damp to go out this evening, so I stayed at home, with Arthur's notes of Arnold's sermons. I have said it before often enough, I dare say, but I must say it again and again every time, what a peculiar feeling of gratitude it gives one to the man who makes such thoughts pass through one's child's mind.'[63] Kitty shared Arnold's distaste for Christian dogma and the divisive disputes that follow in its wake. She agreed with him that the Bible and the Christian religion are essentially practical not theoretical: their purpose is to provide a moral guide and inspiration for living a good and dutiful life. Kitty also admired Arnold's frank and robust approach. After reading his *Essay on the Interpretation of the Scriptures*, she noted that here 'is the very man as he appeared to me at that breakfast at Rugby – the bold, open avowal of truth as it stands on that very difficulty of the accommodation of Scripture ... my convictions all go with Dr. Arnold.'[64]

The Stanleys were anxious to repay Arnold's hospitality and to get to know him better, and in November 1832 Arthur was despatched to invite him, his wife and eight children to stay at Alderley. Arthur was not so enthusiastic: 'I don't think they will come, and, on the whole, for myself at least, I had rather they would come after I am gone from here; because, though I do like him very much, yet I stand in such exceeding awe of him, that I don't think that I could ever have a perfectly comfortable talk with him till our relations as schoolmaster and school-boy are snapped asunder.'[65] But the Arnolds accepted for the following summer, and Arthur travelled with them on the coach. 'We set off at seven o'clock; he and I outside ... I certainly could hardly credit my senses that I had him actually there; it certainly was a most total change from the exalted state in which he has appeared to my eyes for the week before – such childlike joy and simplicity ... He talked of his talk with Coleridge the other night, about chivalry, geology, and phrenology, and Queen Caroline and mobs, and Niebuhr[h] and Thucydides and triremes and genealogies and races, &c. &c.'[66] The Arnolds' son Tom (who was ten at the time) has left a perceptive description of the Stanleys:

> What charming manners, what delightful friendliness was conspicuous in every member of that dear family. The Rector, though a convinced Whig, (and hence in thorough political sympathy with my father) was an aristocrat to his very finger-tips; brave, chivalrous, but without a spark of hauteur.
>
> Mrs. Stanley had a powerful mind, and on the intellectual side was more in sympathy with my father, for whom she had a strong regard, than with the good Rector. The entire union of heart and mind that existed between her and her son Arthur was something very beautiful to witness.[67]

To Arthur's relief the visit proved an enjoyable success, and by the end he was hoping that Arnold would invite him to stay in Westmorland, as he had Vaughan and others. 'I was rather alarmed,' he wrote, 'for the carriages were at the door, and the children packed in, and all on the point of setting out, and not one word of my going to the Lakes when he at the last gave me the fullest invitation to come whenever I liked.'[68]

Arnold was passionately attached to the Lake District and went there every school holiday for rest and regeneration. When Stanley first stayed with the family they were renting a house at the head of Lake Grasmere while their own house, Fox How, in the Rydal valley, was being built. Arnold had chosen the spot not least because it was close to the home of his friends, William and Mary Wordsworth. Meeting the great poet was among the high points of Stanley's stay at the end of that summer holiday, 1833. 'In the afternoon with Dr. Arnold to Rydal Mount. Wordsworth had come back on Friday ... he is an old man with silver-grey hair, and rather untidily dressed. I don't think there is

---

[h] Barthold Niebuhr, the Danish scholar and diplomat. Arnold learnt German in order to read his *History of Rome* which he greatly admired.

anything peculiar in his face except perhaps a great mildness. He went with us to give his opinion on Fox How. He recommended for planting, oaks, birches and Spanish chestnuts ...'[69] Another day he and Mary came to dinner. 'Wordsworth, they said, was quite himself, for of late he has been in a very gloomy mood. Unfortunately the conversation did not turn on anything in which he could talk advantageously, but he was very merry and laughed heartily.'[70]

*   *   *

The clamour for political reform in the years before 1832 penetrated the walls of Rugby. Arnold's Whiggery, and his strong views on what a Christian society should be like, put him in favour of the Reform Bill. Stanley read the newspapers diligently and wrote home to ask his mother to fill a letter with political knowledge because he thought that perhaps his paper perverted the truth. Parliamentary reform was a regular topic for the new debating society which (to Stanley's surprise) elected him as its first president. Given his family's and Arnold's politics, it is not surprising that he joined what he called the 'small and growing Whig minority'.[71] As soon as the bill was passed on 4 June Arnold helped to arrange a public celebration in the town. Stanley wrote home to Mary: 'There is going to be a grand feast of a roasted ox given by the Reformers of Rugby to the people – on occasion of the Bill; the church bells have been ringing for 2 days – & a flag is at the top of the steeple.'[72]

Arnold's thoughts on social and political reform turned naturally to what he saw as a desperate need for reform of the Church. 'The Church, as it now stands,' he wrote on 10 June, 'no human power can save.'[73] Certainly the Church of England at the time was in the main lethargic, complacent and introspective, and dominated by a worldly, conservative and self-satisfied clergy. It was jealous of the privileges of being the established Church and dismissive of other denominations. Arnold sat down to write a pamphlet on the *Principles of Church Reform*. Again he discussed his ideas with the sixth, and this debate, and the pamphlet itself, had an important and enduring effect on Stanley's understanding. 'Arthur', wrote Kitty, 'was a running commentary upon Arnold's Church Reform – knowing so well what he meant by this, what led him to that, and recognising his illustrations and references.'[74] The uproar the pamphlet provoked made Stanley defensive of Arnold, and he collected in a scrap-book every reference to the controversy he could find.

Arnold was a deeply convinced Christian who saw all life and experience as subject to Christian truth and morality. He was annoyed therefore by any hard and fast division of secular and sacred. A secular society meant Godlessness and moral evil, just as a separate Church bred priestcraft and sectarianism. A national Church like the Church of England existed for no better purpose than to Christianise the nation, and transform society in accordance with Christian principles. In their ideal form, Church and State were not two societies but one. 'In other words, religious society is only civil society truly enlightened; the State in its highest perfection becomes the Church.'[75] This was the theory, but the reality was very different. 'The more I think of the matter,' wrote Arnold, 'and the more I read of the Scriptures themselves, and of the history of the Church, the more intense is my wonder at the language of admiration with which men speak of the Church of England ...'[76]

In the pamphlet, published early in 1833, Arnold produced an astonishing manifesto of reforms. He argued that, as a national Church, the Church of England should be more comprehensive, and should therefore be reconciled at least to Nonconformists. Such a Church must therefore allow a variety of doctrines, and no doctrine must be too precisely defined. Parish churches should permit Methodists, Baptists, Presbyterians and others to hold their own services there. The Church should be more democratic, and instead of being led by a caste of priests, lay people should be more involved and should share responsibility. Arnold argued too for the creation of suffragan bishops, the revival of the order of deacons, the use of churches on weekdays, and for variety in forms of worship. These ideas were remarkably prescient and took at least a hundred years to find favour. At the time they were roundly condemned, and Arnold was attacked in newspapers and denounced from pulpits.

*　　　*　　　*

So precocious were Stanley's talents that it was not unreasonable for him to think of applying to Oxford when he was only sixteen. His uncle Augustus Hare had been a fellow and tutor at New College and Stanley wrote to him for advice, 'as being my great authority in all my present business, as my father knows so little about it'.[77] Hare persuaded Arthur to wait another year because he thought he still had much to learn from Arnold, and from being at the top of the school. He should, however, certainly apply to Oxford, and for a scholarship, but to which college? Oriel is not as popular as it was, he said, and Balliol scholarships are not valuable (he must have meant financially, though their worth had recently doubled). 'The best, meaning by best the most distinguished, scholarships in Oxford are the Trinity: & I shall hope one of these days ... to hear of your standing for one & getting in.' But Hare's soundest advice was to 'make a friend of Dr Arnold and consult him'.[78] Arnold was firm that, financially valuable or not, Stanley must apply to Balliol, and be the first boy from Rugby to win this blue ribbon of university success.

In 1806 Balliol had followed Oriel in opening its fellowships to competition;[i] previously a scholar of the college had an almost automatic right to be elected. Twenty years later Balliol had done the same for scholarships, which at Oxford colleges were usually restricted to the founders' descendants, or to boys from a particular county or school (Blundell's in Balliol's case). By the time Stanley sat the examination, Balliol had stolen the march on other colleges, and its open scholarships were the most highly valued of Oxford's prizes, and attracted some of the most brilliant young men in the country. Though in *Tom Brown's Schooldays* the boys' sporting hero, 'Pater Brooke', boasts, 'I know I'd sooner win two School-house matches running than get the Balliol scholarship any day',[79] the distinction of a Balliol scholarship is implied.

Stanley burnt pints of midnight oil toiling over his books before going to Oxford to sit the examinations, and he pushed himself to the point of exhaustion. He was all too aware that the papers would be difficult and the competition severe, but a strong measure of personal ambition, and the chance to bring glory to Arnold and Rugby, spurred him on. When at last Stanley arrived at Oxford in the last week of November 1833 he was full of excitement, and wrote one of his detailed letters home to Mary:

> My heart did jump within me certainly when we got to Oxford – and turned out in the High Street where some of our friends showed us our lodgings and took us to dinner. – I then went at about 9 to Greenhill[j] at Trinity – and there was something so

[i] Oriel's open fellowships produced an intellectually vigorous common room unusual at the time. Its members included Thomas Arnold, who was one of a group of sceptical, liberal fellows known as the 'Noetics'. Other fellows included the leading Tractarians, Keble, Newman, Pusey and Froude.
[j] William Greenhill had left Rugby the year before and gone up to Trinity with an exhibition.

Part One: Alderley and Rugby 1815–1834   65

impressive in the dark colleges with their gateways and towers and quadrangles. The next day was fine so that I had a good walk all about with Greenhill – chiefly calling on men in different colleges; which very much surpassed all my expectations. Do you recollect the part of High Street where Queen's and All Souls are – and a place where you look at the Radcliffe Library, St. Mary's, and All Souls at once? – and Christ Church Hall too ... We Rugby men never see one another except in the morning and at night when we meet to tell our adventures; all the day I am with Greenhill, or dining, breakfasting &c with other men – and in short I am so happy and comfortable as possible: every body seems so kind – and all to go on so delightfully – tho' at the same time I have some doubts as to how I shall like residing here for good.[80]

There were two scholarships on offer and thirty candidates, including a remarkable seven from Rugby, and a formidable colleger from Eton, who was viewed as the favourite. This was James Lonsdale, who became a fellow of Balliol and later Professor of Classical Literature at King's College, London. The examination lasted a week and included two consecutive days of eight hours' writing. The papers consisted of translations and compositions in Latin, Greek and English, as well as examinations in mathematics and divinity. Stanley provides a unique description of how the result of the examination was announced, and again Stanley's own pride and enthusiam are unmistakable:

We all assembled in the Hall and had to wait an hour – the room getting fuller and fuller with Rugby Oxonians crowding in from various parts to hear the result. – at last the door opened – the Master's servant appeared – and called for Mr Stanley – I clapped my hands – rushed forward amidst congratulations – every body ran to the door – where you may conceive how angry I was to find it was only a note from some one to breakfast ... Well – another ¼ of an hour passed – every time the door opened my heart jumped – but many times it was nothing. At last the Dean appeared in his white robes – and moved up to the head of the table. – He first began a long preamble – that they were well-satisfied with all – that those who were disappointed were many in proportion to those who were successful, &c. &c. – all this time every one was listening in the most intense eagerness – and I almost bit my lips off – till 'the successful candidates are – Mr Stanley' – I gave a great jump – and there was a half shout among the Rugby men –

(the next was Lonsdale from Eton). The Dean then took me into the Chapel, where was the Master and all the fellows in white robes. And there I swore that I wd not dissipate the property, reveal the secrets, or disobey the Statutes of the College – I was then made to kneel on the steps and admitted to the rank of Scholar and Exhibitioner of Balliol College, nomine Patris, Filii et Spiritus. – I then wrote my name in a book and so was finished – I am to be matriculated to day – and so shall get back to Rugby in good time ... You may only think of my joy. The honour of Rugby is saved – and I am a Scholar of Balliol.[81]

Stanley arrived back at Rugby in the small hours of Sunday morning and was greeted as a hero. Arnold's admiration was complete, and to mark his star pupil's triumph, he awarded the school another half-holiday. 'It was the greatest delight to see Dr. Arnold after it,' Stanley wrote to his parents, 'and all the masters are very much pleased.'[82]

* * *

Success at Balliol overcame any doubts or misgivings Stanley had about Oxford. 'My visit', he told his parents, 'has certainly most wonderfully reconciled me to what I had before such a dread of – going up to reside there, as now, instead of being associated with gross bigotry and gross profligacy as before, it is associated with the recollections of one of the happiest weeks I ever have had'.[83] Stanley refers to the hostility Arnold's writings had received from the High Churchmen in Oxford. Keble had ended their friendship, and Newman had even raised the question whether or not Arnold was a Christian. Nothing had changed but Stanley felt now that he had a mission to champion Arnold's cause.

Stanley had six more months at Rugby. Although he feared that school would be dull after his week in Oxford, he actually relished his high standing in the school and the challenge of further achievements. His reputation for brilliance, modesty and kindness made him a figure of wonder and admiration. 'It seemed almost impossible', wrote a younger boy, 'that such a clever fellow should be so humble, and entirely unspoilt by such success.'[84] Thomas Hughes recalled an invitation to breakfast with Stanley when he started at Rugby in February 1834. He found Arnold's study packed with other new boys:

> His welcome filled us with joy, and induced us at first to haunt the walk under Arnold's garden-wall to get a nod from him as he scuffled, to or from Anstey's, with his hat on the back of his head

and mighty books under his arm ... I don't think I ever *spoke* to Stanley again at Rugby, but I was one of the heartiest shouters on the topmost bench in the big school ... when he got all the prizes which it took two fags to carry ...'[85]

Stanley busied himself winning every prize he could. He even competed precociously for the Newdigate Prize for poetry at Oxford. Before the end of March he was able to announce that 'my circle of prizes is complete. I have got the Greek Iambics and the Latin Prose, i.e. all that can be got ... I have done enough for myself at Rugby; what remains is to establish the fame of Rugby elsewhere'[86] – and by Rugby he meant Arnold.

Stanley's last speech day was the Wednesday before Easter 1834. It was an altogether more confident occasion than any before:

> The Latin Prose I read, and then came the last of the sixth-form prizes with the Greek Verse ... I had always been told before that I could not be heard; so this time – the last speech I shall ever make in Rugby School – I shouted at the top of my voice. When I went up for the last of my six prizes, Dr. A. stood up and said: 'Stanley, I have now given you from this place every prize that can be given, and I cannot let it pass without thanking you thus publicly for the honour you have reflected upon the school, not only within these walls, but even already at the University.'[87]

Still to come was the final school examination, on the results of which depended the award of exhibitions. The outside examiners were the poet's nephew, Christopher Wordsworth, fellow of Trinity College, Cambridge, and George Moberly, fellow of Balliol and later Headmaster of Winchester. The result was announced on 6 July, the last day of the half-year, and Stanley tied for first place with Vaughan. Vaughan had won a scholarship at Wordworth's college, and would succeed him ten years later as Headmaster of Harrow.

At last, that evening, came the dreaded farewell. 'I went to take leave of the Arnolds, with as heavy a heart as was compatible with the relief of all being over ... He was going out, so I saw him only for a few minutes, but those few minutes were worth much. After saying how sorry he was to lose me: "God bless you, Stanley," he said, "here and hereafter, and let me see you and hear from you as often as you can." And then he called me in again after I had gone out, and again blessed me ... And so we parted.'[88]

PART TWO
Oxford
1834–1851

3
'Trailing Clouds of Glory'
1834–1837

BEFORE STARTING AT Oxford in October 1834 Stanley spent six weeks staying with Julius Hare, his uncle Augustus's younger brother. Julius had recently resigned his fellowship at Trinity College, Cambridge to take up the lucrative family living of Herstmonceux in Sussex. Augustus had died of consumption earlier in 1834 and Stanley had written to Vaughan to say that his uncle had been like a father to him. Augustus's young widow, Maria (Kitty Stanley's sister), had gone to live with Julius at the rectory.

Julius was a learned, cultivated man and a friend and disciple of Samuel Taylor Coleridge. Every room, staircase and corridor of his rectory was packed from floor to ceiling with books and paintings, including a Raphael which Julius had brought back from Florence. Stanley wrote home:

> The house was just as I expected ... and, dinner over, Julius showed me over the pictures. Looking at them by day, I don't know that I should have observed the Raphael Madonna particularly, but I should have noted the Vision of Ezekiel ... I have been looking about at all the books, of course ... The German part is quite astounding; if they are so good, and so much better than English books as to take up so much more room, what a gap there must be in all Englishmen's minds. I was looking at them in the drawing-room when Auntie came in. I was startled, at first, for I had not imagined her to myself in her widow's weeds. She sat down before me and cried very much for some time, but she soon recovered herself, and now she talks as calmly and as cheerfully as usual.[1]

Coleridge and Hare were among the first in England to read the modern German philosophers and theologians, and Hare encouraged others to do the same, Augustus's friend, Thomas Arnold, included. In 1835 Maria adopted the youngest of the five children of Augustus's and Julius's feckless elder brother, Francis. This was the author Augustus

J. C. Hare, who was frightened of Julius but remained devoted to his adoptive mother, writing her eulogy in two rambling volumes of *Memorials of a Quiet Life*. Interestingly, Maria's husband had been similarly adopted as a child by his widowed aunt. Such family adoptions were not then uncommon: there is a fictional example in Jane Austen's *Mansfield Park*, in which Sir Thomas and Lady Bertram adopt her impoverished niece, Fanny Price.

The purpose of Stanley's stay at the rectory was to be tutored by Hare, who as well as being well-versed in German literature, was a classical scholar and a fastidious philologist. 'Now you shall have my week,' Stanley wrote to Mary –

> I get up between 7 and 8. Julius comes down at 9, having always sat up till 2 a.m. Then prayers in the dining-room and breakfast ... Auntie comes down about 10.30, and I learn my work in the drawing-room, where she sits or lies down. On Monday Julius and I began with the Antigone (of Sophocles) which I had not read. – and this we shall do until we finish it which will be Monday next week. I learn it before with a German-Greek Lexicon: which teaches me both languages at once. – and then about 11.30 do it with him which takes till (luncheon intervening) 2.00 p.m... . He does it very thoroughly and with all his books about it. You will be amused to see how we begin by having four books (i.e. four editions) and end by having twenty on the table ... it is quite delightful, much in the style of Arnold; only that taking more time and having more books for it, he does it of course more thoroughly.[2]

In the evenings Julius would read aloud – Milton's speeches, Shakespeare's sonnets or Wordsworth's prose. Even when Stanley allowed himself some exercise it seemed that he could not escape from books: on a ride home from Ashburnham he saw 'a little ragged cottage girl, perched up on the hedge-bank, with a dirty doll stuck in a hollow tree, herself busy with a book, – a sight I never saw before'.[3]

Julius Hare's curate was John Sterling. He had been his pupil at Trinity and was an early member of the Cambridge Apostles, a discussion group dedicated to the pursuit of truth, however unorthodox.[a] Stanley

---

[a] The Cambridge Conversazione Society, better known as the Apostles. Sterling's friend F. D. Maurice, the theologian and Christian socialist, was also a member: he too was Hare's pupil and an ardent disciple of Coleridge. Later members include the philosophers A. N. Whitehead, Bertrand Russell and Ludwig Wittgenstein; Lytton Strachey, Leonard Woolf and J. M. Keynes of the Bloomsbury group; and the spies, Anthony Blunt and Guy Burgess.

was impressed by Sterling and excited by his conversation, and the breadth and vigour of his ideas. His sermons often moved Stanley to tears, and he thought they were 'the next best after Arnold I have ever heard, and like him in several things. He has the same evident and positive conviction of perception of truth, the same undercurrent of a great system, and to-day he had nearly (except in one flowery sentence) the same beautiful language that Arnold's later sermons have.'[4] Sterling and Stanley went out for long walks on most afternoons. 'He talked about the various systems of mythology, and we went to the poorhouse, where he reads the Bible once a week ... Then he took me to his house, and showed me his books, chiefly of odd theology and philosophy, among them twelve volumes of Puritan divines, St. Augustine, Spinoza (which he said was the profoundest book there was). He lent me a German-Latin book on the Revelation, and a paper with Coleridge's view of the Atonement.'[5]

Sterling was also devoted to Coleridge and visited him regularly at Highgate until his death just a month before Stanley's arrival at Herstmonceux. 'Sterling', wrote Stanley, 'idolises Coleridge as I do Arnold, having known him intimately.'[6] Arnold's own thinking had been strongly influenced by Coleridge, whom he described as 'a very great man indeed, whose equal I know not where to find in England'.[7] Much of the attraction that Stanley found in Coleridge was in identifying this influence and understanding Arnold better. He would certainly have recognised similarities between Coleridge's views on the Bible and Arnold's in his pamphlet *On the Right Interpretation of the Scriptures*:

> Mr. S. brought me the 'Letters on Inspiration'[b] to read before they are sent to Dr. Arnold. On the whole, I like them very much. The spirit is beautiful, and some of the passages ... and some of the outbursts of indignation, are quite magnificent. I think, however, as I thought I should, that in some Dr. A. will not agree. Indeed I don't think the argument throughout is clear. As far as I can judge, he, Dr. A., will not like the placing of the whole Bible ... on a footing with all good books. However, he will delight in the comprehensive spirit of not making it an article of the Christian faith to believe every word, or receive every book.[8]

To Stanley's mind, Arnold was superior even to the colossal Coleridge:

---

[b] Coleridge's [7] *Letters on the Inspiration of the Scriptures* were published posthumously as *Confessions of an Inquiring Spirit* (1840).

'If he had but been able to write like Arnold, what a man he would have been!'[9] Nonetheless, Stanley was aware that, in reading Coleridge, 'I had got a new element into my mind.'[10]

Like many of his generation, Sterling discovered in the philosopher-poet the ideas and inspiration to escape the arid rationalism of the previous century, as well as what Coleridge called the 'bibliolatry' of the present, by which he meant the fundamentalism which resisted any attempt to question or criticise the Scriptures. Nonetheless, faith never came easily to Sterling, and he resigned his curacy at Herstmonceux not long after Stanley had started at Balliol. His life then became almost as chaotic as Coleridge's, and he spent his next and final ten years scraping a living as a writer, and battling with ill-health and domestic tragedies. He died in 1844 aged thirty-eight. Four years later, Hare published Sterling's *Essays and Tales* with a biographical preface which claimed that Sterling had in fact always been an orthodox believer. Thomas Carlyle was incensed by this and wrote his own *Life of John Sterling* (1851), a book 'remarkable for its inversion of the usual proportion between biographer and hero. Johnson for once writes upon Boswell.'[11]

Stanley found those heady weeks in Herstmonceux thrilling and exhausting. 'I had never been in a place so intellectual before;' he wrote to Mary, 'everything seems to breathe with learning and deep thought; and, having no conversation of an ordinary sort, I feel quite as if it was a dream when I go to bed at night. Julius so poetical, and Mr. Sterling so philosophical, and Auntie so heavenly.'[12] Kitty wrote to her sister to thank her and Julius for having him to stay: 'I cannot speak of the blessing it has been to have Arthur so long with you. He says he feels his mind's horizons so enlarged.'[13] Looking back thirty years later, Stanley recalled that 'to pass from common clerical society, however able and instructive, to Herstmonceux Rectory was passing into a house where every window was fearlessly opened to receive air and light and sound from the outer world'.[14]

*   *   *

Stanley left Sussex in the second week of October and crossed the border into Kent to stay with the Hussey family at Scotney Castle. He seems to have had no intention of going home to Alderley before starting at Oxford, though he was determined to visit Arnold and Rugby. He had already written to his mother to explain that it would enable him to meet Vaughan and Lake, and 'to see Dr. A. and have some talk with him before I go to Oxford, and hear him preach once more. It would do me good too, I think, to have a little ordinary conversation with my equals, and loose the strings of my tongue for Oxford.'[15] Stanley seems to have expected his mother to disapprove of so premature a return to school, and to win her approval he proposed to call on her brother, Edward Penrhyn, and his family,[c] who lived next to Richmond Park. The strategy worked and Kitty was delighted. Stanley's later fondness for children is anticipated in his looking forward to reading Coleridge's poems to his nieces, and in his account of ringing their door-bell and hearing them 'jumping and screaming within, and then their bright faces and kisses! The little girls looked more beautiful than ever.'[16]

The next morning Stanley boarded a packed coach from London to Dunchurch, and after stopping at St Albans and seeing the abbey church, he arrived at Rugby at five. His excitement was as intense as ever:

> Such a joy to be with my face towards Rugby! I ran over as fast as I could, found at Lake's house that Mrs. A. was expecting me at the Praetorium so ran on and came in just as Dr. and Mrs. A, and Vaughan and Lake, were going in to dinner. They welcomed me most cordially. Dr. A took me up to my room where I washed my hands and face, and then dined. Talked about Coleridge and the 'Letters on Inspiration', the publication of which he approves ... talked about Wordsworth also; very excellent he was about them; then about old times at Rugby.[17]

Stanley extols 'this seventh heaven, where I now am' and 'the time of the most luxurious happiness I have ever had – so unbrokenly delightful'.[18] On Sunday he heard Arnold preach very well, he thought, though after Julius Hare's variety of tones, he found his voice too low and rather monotonous. This was the first of regular returns to Rugby.

Although Stanley's journey to Oxford was eased by the company of two Rugbeians, a long letter to Mary gives a graphic account of the discomfort of travelling on the outside of a coach so full that it was in constant danger of tipping over. There was also driving rain and a sharp wind to contend with before they arrived at last at seven on what turned out to be a fine moonlit Friday evening. While Stanley was waiting for his luggage to be unloaded, John Penrose, Arnold's nephew,

---

[c] Penrhyn had married Lady Charlotte Stanley, daughter of the 13th Earl of Derby.

who was already up at Balliol, came to meet him. He took him first to the Mitre Inn (where Stanley booked a room for the night) and then on to Balliol for tea in his rooms. The next morning Stanley went to find his own rooms which were on the west side of the college, overlooking the church of St Mary Magdalen. A sketch plan in the same letter shows a large, square sitting-room with two tables, a sofa, an armchair, bookcases and cupboards, and with an adjoining bedroom and lumber-room.

> I found my cap & gown which I put on and sallied out to Chapel. I had been instructed by the Porter as to which place I was to go to and a fine Chapel it is – with venerable painted windows[d] – the Chapel too where I was made a Scholar and swore not to squander their property, reveal their secrets or break their statutes. I found that it being a Saint's day I ought, as a Scholar, to have worn a surplice.[19]

*   *   *

The Oxford of 1834 was a very different place from the Oxford of today. Suburbs had not stretched far, and the city's distant spires and steeples could still be seen across meadows and cornfields from miles around. 'The great thing of beauty in every walk is Oxford itself,' wrote Stanley, 'rising with all its towers out of its solemn grove of trees.'[20] The colleges though were not as beautiful as they are today. Their golden stone was blackened and flaking, their quadrangles and courtyards dimly lit by gas, and their lawns were not striped and manicured but rough-hewn with scythes.

Oxford University, like the Church of England that dominated it, did not emerge from the eighteenth century until well into the nineteenth. When Stanley arrived it was still 'that magnificent and venerable seat of Learning, Orthodoxy, and Toryism'[21] that Dr Johnson had known a hundred years before. Undergraduates were set apart from one another according to social rank. Gladstone, who had gone up to Christ Church in 1828, thought it only right and proper that 'the distinctions of the outer world should have their echo in Oxford'.[22] Noblemen (most of whom were at Gladstone's college) were splendidly attired in gowns of purple silk and black velvet caps ('mortar-boards') with a golden

---

[d] This was Balliol's second chapel built c.1525. It was demolished in 1854 to make way for the present chapel designed by William Butterfield, and in which the venerable painted windows (1635) survive.

tassel.[e] Gentlemen commoners, who were sons of the gentry, had black silk trimmings on their gowns; scholars, like Stanley, wore plain black gowns with full sleeves, and commoners wore gowns with no sleeves. These different classes of undergraduate sat at separate tables in hall, and in some colleges the noblemen, and even gentlemen commoners, sat with the fellows at high table. The noblemen were said to lead idle and dissolute lives, and often left Oxford early without taking a degree. The gentlemen commoners were often much the same and 'kept up a style of living as is usual in large country houses'.[23] The 'reckless, loose young spendthrift'[24] Drysdale, the Etonian in Thomas Hughes's sequel, *Tom Brown at Oxford*, is a gentleman commoner.

Though many of the college fellows remained Georgian caricatures (bewigged, obese and pompous), others were diligent and conscientious, at least so far as the system allowed. Tutorials then were not occasions for one-to-one discussion; instead they were more like school lessons with a mixed ability class of undergraduates. 'I think sometimes I'm back in the lower fifth;' complains Tom Brown, 'for we don't get through more than we used to do there; and if you were to hear the men construe it would make your hair stand on end.'[25] Ambitious undergraduates often had to employ a private tutor or 'coach' from outside the college to help them through schools.[f]

Oxford was dominated by parsons and privilege. Almost all fellows had to be in holy orders and unmarried, just as they had to have been scholars of their college or descendants of the founder, or attended a particular school, or been born in a certain county or diocese. Except at Oriel and Balliol there was, as Lord Melbourne famously said of the Garter, no damned merit in it. The fellows usually held office for a decade or so until they were offered a college living and could afford to marry. Jane Austen's father was a fellow of St John's College for ten years before he was appointed rector of Steventon in Hampshire, which he held in plurality until he married three years later and had to resign his fellowship. Pluralism, absenteeism and nepotism were common abuses in Church and university. Richard Jenkyns, the Master of Balliol in Stanley's time (and Jane Austen's great-uncle), persuaded a well-connected cousin to suggest his name to Robert Peel when the deanery of Wells became vacant. He was appointed but continued as Master of Balliol until his death nine years later.

[e] The tassel explains the nobleman's nickname 'tuft'; those who cultivated him were known as 'tuft-hunters'.
[f] Oxford's name for courses of study and final examinations.

Oxford was almost an Anglican seminary with a responsibility to uphold Christian doctrine as taught by the Church of England. Every undergraduate had to subscribe to the Thirty-Nine Articles in order to be allowed to study for a degree that for many was simply a step on the road to ordination. Chapel was compulsory and in most colleges undergraduates had to attend a service at least once on weekdays and twice on Sundays, as well as holy communion once a term. In 1830 almost a third of the undergraduates were parsons' sons, and of those who graduated that year, two-thirds took holy orders. Of more than 25,000 men who matriculated at Oxford in the first half of the century, over 10,000 were ordained.

* * *

In the 1830s the colleges *were* Oxford and the university as a separate entity scarcely existed. Apart from the Bodleian Library, the university church, the press and the old Ashmolean Museum, there were no university institutions, and most teaching took place in the colleges. The heads of the twenty-four colleges, together with the vice-chancellor and the two proctors (fellows appointed to oversee discipline), made up the university's governing body, the hebdomadal board.

Stanley's college was founded in 1263 by John de Balliol, the rich and powerful lord of Barnard Castle, and his wife, Dervorguilla, and is almost certainly the second oldest Oxford college. A century later John Wycliffe, credited as the first to translate the Bible into English, was master. By the end of the fifteenth century, Balliol was prosperous and had by then ten fellows and a full complement of buildings. The college had remained faithful to Rome even in Wycliffe's time. Nonetheless it just survived the Reformation, and on Mary's accession the master was rewarded with the bishopric of Gloucester. He was one of the judges who condemned the Protestant bishops, Latimer, Ridley and Cranmer, to be burned at the stake near the master's lodgings in Broad Street.[g] Balliol's Catholic sympathies persisted until the end of the sixteenth century. During the Civil War, Balliol (like other colleges) was obliged to support the King's army garrisoned at Oxford, and sent all its plate to be melted down and coined. By the Restoration in 1660, Balliol's finances were in a parlous state, but fund-raising in the 1670s helped to fill the coffers again, and crumbling buildings were repaired.

The master of Georgian Balliol was Theophilus Leigh, who was

---

[g] The 1843 martyrs' memorial to the west of the college is misleadingly positioned.

elected in 1726: his principal qualification was that he was the Visitor's nephew. The college declined during the sixty years of his mastership. Finances at least were improved under John Davey, Leigh's successor, though numbers remained low. The election of John Parsons in 1798 marked the beginning of Balliol's emergence from eighteenth century torpor and its ascent to academic pre-eminence. Unusually, Parsons had been elected to a fellowship from outside the college (he was an undergraduate at Wadham) and he made this precedent a key ingredient in his reforms. In 1806 he insisted on the election of another outsider in preference to three scholars, persuading the Visitor to overrule the protestors and settle the policy once and for all. So Balliol joined Oriel in making fellowships competitive, and Parsons was able to recruit talented fellows who made effective tutors. The college became attractive to aspiring undergraduates, and a greater demand for places allowed for selection. Parsons's aim to raise academic standards gathered momentum.

When Parsons died in 1819, his vicegerent, Richard Jenkyns, succeeded and remained master for thirty-five years. Jenkyns was a pompous, snobbish, even ridiculous figure, nicknamed the 'Little Master'. 'He was short of stature and very neat in his appearance; the deficiency of height was more than compensated for by a superfluity of magisterial and ecclesiastical dignity.'[26] But Jenkyns was also strong-willed, an efficient administrator and a shrewd judge of character, and he shared Parsons's academic ambitions. In 1827, in a move that, to John Jones, Balliol's historian, was 'the making of Victorian Balliol',[27] Jenkyns encouraged the fellows to award scholarships solely on the basis of an open examination and to double their value. This reform proved even more successful for the college than its open fellowships. 'By the mid-thirties, Balliol was generally recognised as the leading college: its Open Scholarships and Fellowships were the greatest distinctions in the University a young man could aspire to, and it was dominant in the Honour Schools, having risen as Oriel and Christ Church declined.'[28] The twenty Balliol scholars in the ten years from 1832 to 1841 (fourteen of whom had come from Rugby or Eton) included an Archbishop of Canterbury, two Lords Chief Justice, two Cabinet ministers, three cathedral deans, three university professors, two eminent poets, and a Master of Balliol.

*   *   *

After chapel and breakfast on his first morning, Stanley paid a courtesy call on the master and on his tutor, George Moberly, who had been one of the two external examiners at the end of his time at Rugby. Neither was especially welcoming and Stanley returned to his rooms 'feeling very desolate, and more so by contrast with the past week, the happiest week that ever I remember'.[29] He went to Christ Church to find a Cheshire friend and on the way met a Rugby acquaintance with whom he 'lunched homelily on bread and butter'[30] (always Stanley's favourite food). After leaving letters from Rugby at various colleges (the penny post was still six years away), and making some calls, he returned to Balliol, arranged a few of his books, 'threw into the fire, one after the other, about fifty programmes of tradesmen',[31] and dined with the other scholars at their table in hall.

Once Stanley had adopted the routine of college life, or at least of the studious undergraduate, he began to feel more at home, and better able than at first to 'believe that the shadow of the cap on the wall belongs to my head'.[32] After chapel at eight, mornings and early afternoons were spent at lectures or in reading, until dinner at four. The time between five and six was often spent at a wine-party in friends' rooms, and the hours from six to nine were set aside for exercise. In Stanley's case that meant walking with one or two acquaintances out beyond Oxford into the countryside. There was, however, chapel again at seven for those who chose to attend or who had missed the morning service. Supper was at nine, followed by more reading until bed at half-past ten.

Edward Gibbon said of himself that he had 'arrived at Oxford with a stock of erudition that might have puzzled a doctor, and a degree of ignorance of which a schoolboy would have been ashamed'.[33] Much the same might be said of Stanley. Certainly the range of reading and thorough grounding in the classics that Arnold had provided stood him in good stead for the broad Oxford curriculum. The schools then for all undergraduates consisted of Literae Humaniores (the Greek and Latin languages, ancient history, and the poetry and philosophy of classical writers); the rudiments of the Christian religion (the gospels in Greek, Old and New Testament history, the Thirty-Nine Articles and William Paley's *Evidences of Christianity*); plus the basic elements of mathematics and physics.

John Parsons, with the heads of Christ Church and Oriel, had been the driving force behind the reforming examination statute of 1800. What had been little more than an informal and even frivolous conversation was replaced with a public viva voce on prescribed texts. Furthermore, in what was the beginning of the honours system, the

Part Two: Oxford 1834–1851

statute introduced a voluntary examination which could be taken instead by those who wanted to prove their superior abilities. By the time Stanley arrived at Oxford, thirty per cent of undergraduates read for a class and not a pass; at Balliol the percentage was higher. By then most of the examinations were written not oral, and this was not only a more rigorous and accurate way of testing, but it saved the examiners' time: in 1822 it had taken 12 weeks to hear 200 candidates.

Balliol had more scholarly and conscientious tutors than other colleges. The best was George Moberly, Stanley's tutor until he left a year later to become Headmaster of Winchester. Nonetheless, Stanley found their lectures generally disappointing. At his first on Livy 'we construed in the old way, word for word, in turn, with one or two unimportant remarks'.[34] Stanley reported home that his first lecture on Mark's gospel comprised a few commonplace observations from the tutor and remarkable ignorance from his fellow students. He found two out of three classical lectures 'absolutely useless'. Moberly on Herodotus though was 'from time to time really excellent', and Stanley adds that he is reputed to be one of the three best tutors in Oxford. But the fact that Moberly is also criticised ('he makes no observations whatever except occasionally a joke on some of the men, or even on Herodotus himself')[35] implies that fault may have lain as much with Stanley's own intellectual haughtiness as with the weaknesses of the tutors. Stanley was clever and extraordinarily well-read, and it was all too easy for him to feel superior. As a schoolboy he had found even Arnold's classical knowledge limited, and had not been slow to say so.

As at Rugby, Stanley's reserve and shyness made it difficult to form friendships. Ten days into his first term he wrote priggishly to Vaughan at Cambridge to describe the five college sets he had observed: 'the most disreputable', 'the idle, though respectable', 'those who read much but are not over-gentlemanly', 'literary, but rather dull men, who profess not to know classics, second-rate speakers at the Union, &c., but very respectable and gentlemanly', and 'men who are both clever and gentlemen'.[36] Stanley looked to the latter for companions, but even here 'when I go out walking with them I am disappointed. They all dogmatise very much. When they are together, this is softened down, so as to be amusing and lively, but when I am alone with them, I find it tedious and unsatisfactory, and when to this is added constant exaggeration ... the matter is worse still.'[37] Part of the problem was political: Stanley was a rare Whig among Tory High Churchmen. In a letter to Lake he describes one such undergraduate:

a good type of his class apparently, who quotes the Articles as Scripture, the Church as infallible. I went out for a walk with him other day – suddenly a look of horror appeared on his face. 'I did not know that such a thing was tolerated in Oxford,' pointing to a notice on the wall. I imagined it to be 'something dreadful'; it was an innocent *To the chapel*. 'Oh!' said I, 'you mean the Dissenting chapel?' 'Yes, how could it have been built here? I wonder they did not pull it down long ago.'[38]

Early in his first term Stanley went to hear a lecture on the *Odyssey* given by the Professor of Poetry, John Keble. He described him to Mary as 'a middle-sized, rather sharp-faced man, and with very twinkling eyes ... I am ashamed to say that I so tired myself with trying to see his face that I only heard a long argument, in part certainly most curious, to show that Homer was a Tory – not a poetical Tory, but a thoroughly downright political Tory – in words as plain as Latin can express it.'[39] Stanley refers here to his own chronic myopia (he wrote similarly when he described Newman preaching: 'You forget that I cannot see his face with my poor eyes.').[40] Soon after, he was invited to dine with Philip Shuttleworth, the Whiggish Warden of New College. There he met his future tutor, Archibald Campbell Tait, who eight years later was to succeed Arnold at Rugby. Stanley's record of the evening includes: 'Tait told me that Moberly came back convinced that Rugby was the first school in England.'[41]

Stanley wrote regularly to Vaughan in letters that were invariably warm, even garrulous, though never affectionate. Vaughan asked Stanley to visit him at Cambridge, and he went in December at the end of his first term. He was not impressed. 'The change from the sweep of High Street and Broad Street to the wretched narrow, winding, college-less streets of Cambridge, was at first quite overwhelming ... I could hardly conceive it possible for a university to exist with any degree of grandeur in a place so vile!'[42] The colleges, on the other hand, he did admire. Vaughan's college, Trinity, he found 'somewhat finer than Christ Church, as being larger and more diversified ... The view of the colleges from the gardens, through which flows the Cam, is finer than Ch. Ch. meadows, and King's Chapel is not to be spoken of in the same breath as any of the Oxford chapels ... being superior inside and outside beyond comparison.'[43]

Stanley stayed overnight at Trinity and had breakfast with Julius Hare, who had returned for a meeting. He introduced Stanley to his friend Connop Thirlwall, the classical historian who was about to leave for a parish in Yorkshire. He had been forced to resign as a tutor at Trinity after publishing a letter[h] that questioned the inclusion of religious teaching in the Cambridge curriculum. Hare also introduced him to another friend and fellow, William Whewell, the mathematician and future Master of Trinity. At a party at Downing College, Stanley met Christopher Wordsworth, who had shared the Rugby examining with Moberly. He too was a Trinity fellow and a brilliant classicist. Stanley found the senior men less polished than those at Oxford but kinder and more welcoming. 'They seem very happy all of them together, and with much less restraint among them than I should think there was among men of the same standing at Oxford.'[44] Before Stanley left Cambridge, Vaughan took him to see the portrait of Oliver Cromwell in the hall at Sidney Sussex College, and the mulberry tree supposed to have been planted by Milton in the fellows' garden at Christ's.

*   *   *

Stanley's arrival at Oxford coincided with the start of a decade of fierce religious strife and revival. Stanley followed it all closely and involved himself as much as he was able. It was the crucible in which he tested what he had learnt from Arnold and started the process of forging his own core beliefs and convictions.

The first controversy was over subscription. Like all Oxford undergraduates Stanley was obliged to subscribe, or sign up to, the Thirty-Nine Articles of Religion, the doctrines of the Church of England. It was the university's method of ensuring that its members were also members of the established Church, and that Roman Catholics, Nonconformists, Jews and freethinkers were therefore excluded. This rankled with Stanley and others of a liberal persuasion. Arnold's teaching and his pamphlet on the *Principles of Church Reform* had taught Stanley that the Church of England, if it was to be a truly national church, had to be more comprehensive. Arnold had argued for the inclusion of Protestant sects though not Roman Catholics or Quakers, whose doctrines he believed to be too incompatible. But Stanley was already going further than Arnold. In Stanley's Church of England all English men and women who called themselves Christians were to be included. He had been encouraged in this by Hare and Sterling. Hare was of the view that there should be not thirty-nine but only one article,

---

[h] *Letter on the Admission of Dissenters to Academical Degrees* (1834).

the divinity of Christ. Stanley agreed, but because he wanted to make love for God the supreme qualification, the exclusion even of Unitarians troubled him. In a letter to Vaughan from Herstmonceux Stanley had written:

> ... their individual members are not so far from the Communion of Saints ... which I take to be the communion of all good men, in all ages and countries, of all who have loved God and served man; including, therefore, chiefly real Christians, but also the Jewish saints, who lived before Christ, and all those, such as Socrates, &c., whom we value among the pagans, or those whom we might have to value among Unitarians or Deists.[45]

In March 1834, when Stanley was still at school, a petition signed by members of the university senate at Cambridge in favour of abolishing religious tests and admitting Dissenters was presented by the Prime Minister to the House of Lords. The second reading of a bill founded on this petition was carried in the Commons in June, causing excitement and alarm in both universities, but especially in the more conservative Oxford. Reams of pamphlets and letters were published and circulated. The Regius Professor of Divinity wrote to the new chancellor, the Duke of Wellington: 'I never remember any occasion on which so strong or unanimous a feeling has been shown in Oxford.'[46] On 1 August, after much lobbying, the bill was rejected in the upper house by a large majority. 'Alas for the Dissenters Bill!' lamented Stanley in a letter from Toft Hall, his grandparents' house.[47]

Nonetheless, there remained in Parliament a view that compulsory subscription was too demanding on the religious scruples of boys fresh from school. Urged by the chancellor to modify the arrangement, Oxford's hebdomadal board framed a statute which proposed instead a declaration of general assent to the worship and teaching of the Church of England. The statute still excluded Dissenters but at least it eased the subscriber's conscience. But this too provoked a storm of opposition from traditionalists. Stanley's account of the issues, and what happened next is as clear and complete as any:

> The old form was that at matriculation everyone signed his name in a book to the Articles. Of this everyone gives a different interpretation. The natural one, of course, is that the subscriber agrees with every word of what he signs; but this being too absurd to be upheld, when the subscribers are boys, of whom not one-third

have read, and not one out of fifty have thought about, the Articles, other explanations are given: that it expresses your submission to the Church's authority; that it means that you are a member of the Church of England; that it means a denial of heresy ... (or) a profession of your parents' belief ... that they are conditions of thought to be borne in mind while engaged in the University studies, &c., &c. All these interpretations make it impossible for anyone to know what the subscription means. Accordingly, it was proposed to substitute a Declaration quite as exclusive, but with the great advantage of being intelligible.[48]

Stanley goes on to describe the meeting of convocation[i] in May 1835. Stanley waited outside the Sheldonian Theatre, hoping to catch a glimpse of Arnold, and as soon as undergraduates were allowed into the gallery he watched the door for his appearance:

The place below was filled with M.A.'s. The doctors of divinity sat clothed in scarlet, and among them a bishop ... Then came the twenty-four heads – Hawkins and Hampden[j] were hissed by the undergraduates. The Declaration was read, received with a scornful laugh, and proposed, 'Placetne vobis, domini doctores?' 'Non placet' ejaculated the bishop and various others. 'Placetne vobis, magistri?' 'Non placet' roared the Masters, and thereupon they waved their hats and caps, and gesticulated and yelled, the undergraduates responding from above.

They, the majority, behaved themselves more like schoolboys in rebellion than clergymen employed in defending what they call the last barrier of orthodoxy.[49]

Stanley adds that, though some voted against for good reason, many others did so through 'horror of innovation, which would equally induce them to vote against any improvement in our system'.[50]

The Duke of Wellington's lobbying behind the declaration was not the first time he had been seen to meddle in affairs of Church and university. In 1828, when Prime Minister, he had changed his mind over Catholic emancipation[k] because he feared that Irish unrest might lead

---

[i] The assembly of Oxford M.A.s with power to approve or reject measures proposed by the hebdomadal board.
[j] Edward Hawkins (Provost of Oriel) and Renn Hampden (Principal of St Mary Hall) were both known to favour the proposal.
[k] The attempt to repeal the Test Act (1673), which had excluded Roman Catholics from Parliament.

to civil war. To force this through Parliament he secured the support of the leader of the Commons, Sir Robert Peel, who sat for Oxford University. But Oxford had elected Peel twelve years before as its anti-Catholic champion[l] and was incensed at this sudden betrayal. He was obliged to resign his seat in 1829 but he offered himself for re-election. In rowdy scenes in convocation, similar to those which were to accompany the vote over subscription, Peel's proposer and seconder were shouted down and windows broken. The election was bitterly fought and Peel was defeated.[m] Oxford's High Churchmen were satisfied with the vote and glad to see the back of Peel, but the Government's readiness to put the interests of the Church second alarmed them. It was time for the Church to place its confidence elsewhere, and it was with Peel's defeat that the Oxford Movement began.

Four years later, on 14 July 1833, John Keble preached before the judges of assize in the university church on the subject of 'National Apostasy'.[n] The Whig Government had proposed the suppression of ten out of twenty-two Irish Protestant bishoprics and the confiscation of their revenues. 'Twenty-two Protestant bishops', wrote G. M. Trevelyan, 'drew £150,000 a year, and the rest of the Church £600,000 more, very largely from the Catholic peasants.'[51] Again the Government needed to ease tensions in Ireland, and again this initiative roused a storm of protest in England. Keble was incensed: to him this was nothing less than flagrant erastianism, a profane intrusion by the State in the affairs of the Church. 'Is APOSTASY', he asked, 'too hard a word to describe the temper of the nation?'[52]

By the time Stanley arrived at Balliol in 1834 the Oxford Movement's aims and ideas had become more clearly defined, its leaders identifiable, and its followers greater in number and enthusiasm. Drawing on the High Church tradition, the movement looked elsewhere for identity and authority than to the established Church's links with Crown and Parliament, links which now seemed threatened. It found inspiration instead in the Church of England's roots in the catholic and apostolic Church. 'We are Catholics without the Popery,' declared Hurrell Froude, 'and Church of England men without the Protestantism. The

---

[l] Convocation opposed emancipation for the same reason it opposed the abolition of subscription: it did not want any threat to the Church of England's monopoly.

[m] The words 'No Peel' can still be seen hammered into a door at the foot of the hall staircase in Peel's college, Christ Church.

[n] Newman regarded this sermon as the start of the Oxford Movement but it was in fact more the spark that inflamed the fire that had been smouldering since Peel's defeat.

Reformation was a limb badly set – it must be broken again in order to be righted ... Let us give up a *national* Church and have a *real* one.'⁵³ The movement's teaching, expressed in sermons and a series of published *Tracts for the Times*, emphasised the continuity of apostolic succession, the sacredness of priesthood and sacraments, and the importance of devotion and penitence.

On his first Sunday in Oxford, Stanley heard Edward Pusey preach a university sermon at St Mary's. He remembered that its text was from the Song of Solomon, and that it was 'very long and disproportioned, most of it learned and clever'.⁵⁴ The next week he caught his first glimpse of John Henry Newman and was fascinated. Newman was famous in Oxford, and the man and his sermons were much discussed. Stanley was especially intrigued because he knew how much Arnold distrusted him. Newman had succeeded him as a fellow of Oriel in 1822, and when, six years later, another fellow, Edward Hawkins, became provost of the college, Newman succeeded him as vicar of the university church. He combined his incumbency with a popular and energetic tutorship at Oriel until 1831 when Hawkins dismissed him and two other tutors,° largely because he was jealous of their possessive and unilateral actions, and fearful of their proselytising.

Like Arnold, Newman preached every Sunday afternoon and undergraduates flocked to hear him. The effect he had on them was much the same as Arnold's at Rugby. 'We came to regard Newman with the affection of pupils for an idolised master,' wrote J. A. Froude.ᴾ 'The simplest word which dropped from him was treasured as if it had been an intellectual diamond. For hundreds of young men *Credo in Newmannum* was the genuine symbol of faith.'⁵⁵

> Men recalled in after years every detail of those great occasions; the listeners all breathless with expectation, the gas light at the left of the pulpit, lowered that the preacher might not be dazzled, while they stood perhaps in the half-darkness of the gallery, the preacher's manner of presenting truth, simple and direct, his attitude quiet and unostentatious. There was no movement of the body, scarcely a movement of the hands. But the eye was full of life and the voice powerful, yet melodious. He stood in the pulpit a frail thin form as one who had stepped forth from another world.⁵⁶

° Hurrell Froude and Robert Wilberforce (second son of William Wilberforce).
ᴾ James Anthony Froude was a younger brother of Hurrell. His later disillusionment with Christianity is described in his autobiographical novel, *The Nemesis of Faith* (1849).

It is instructive to compare the two men's preaching, as Oxford Rugbeians did. 'There were things', Stanley told Lake, 'that reminded me that he was the High Churchman, but the general tone, the manner, the simple language, reminded me of no other than Arnold himself. There was the same overpowering conviction conveyed that he was a thorough Christian – I had almost said, a man of the purest charity.'[57] It is a fact that the sermons share much the same directness and lucidity. The same moral urgency is there too: like Arnold, Newman was passionate in his warnings of the consequences of evil and wickedness. But their solutions were different. For Newman, salvation was to be received through membership of the Church, whereas for Arnold it was to be found in moral rectitude. And Newman's sermons have a poetic, literary quality lacking in Arnold's (Newman used to say that he re-read *Mansfield Park* every year in order to perfect his style). There was also in Newman's preaching an imaginative and spiritual depth, and a sense of mystery.

Stanley could not help being fascinated by Newman, and he found himself surrounded by friends and acquaintances who were devoted to the man and his cause. Stanley acknowledged his many gifts and virtues, and told Lake that 'he does appear to be a man of the most self-denying goodness that can well be conceived, and to do good to a very great extent'.[58] Stanley dreaded a collision between Arnold and Newman, and believed that 'they are really of the same essence'.[59] Nonetheless, Stanley remained loyal to Arnold, and the liberal Churchmanship and Whiggish politics he espoused. He agreed, for instance, with Arnold's rejection of the idea that apostolic succession was fundamental to a true understanding of the episcopate, and therefore to all priestly authority. Arnold had attacked the doctrine in an appendix to his third volume of sermons. He regarded the idea of a divine right of the clergy, grounded in an unbroken line from the apostles to the present bishops, as 'a mischievous superstition'.[60] Similarly, Stanley was 'more and more convinced of the unChristian, un-Anglican tendency of the Apostolical Succession',[61] and in a letter to Mary he explained that the doctrine amounted to 'saying that every Christian society which has not Bishops is no more likely to be saved than Jews, Heathens, or Mohametans'.[62]

* * *

It was Napoleon who said that to understand a man fully you need to know what was happening in the world when he was twenty. What was happening at that age in Stanley's world was the appointment in 1836 of Dr Renn Dickson Hampden to the regius chair of divinity. The bitter crisis that followed brought to light the true colours of the Newmanites, as well as the vehemence of Arnold's antagonism. And even more than before, it showed Stanley's even-handedness, and his scrupulous determination to see good in all sides of an argument.

The professorship fell vacant in January on the death of Edward Burton. The regius chair is, as the title implies, a Crown appointment, and responsibility fell to the Prime Minister, Lord Melbourne. He consulted the Archbishop of Canterbury, William Howley, who had occupied the same chair twenty-five years before. Howley produced a list of names which included Pusey, Newman and Keble. But Melbourne wanted a Whig, not a High Church Tory, and though only a second year undergraduate, Stanley was asked his views. His cousin, Edward Stanley, was then Secretary to the Treasury and he wrote to Arthur from Downing Street to enquire what the opinion was in Oxford of those in the running and, in particular, how Hampden stood as a scholar and divine. 'You may imagine my astonishment on opening the letter,' Stanley wrote home, 'which was marked *private* ... I never felt in so important a situation before, and my answer was one of the most nervous jobs I have ever had.'[63] Stanley's reply has not survived but in any case it did not arrive until after Melbourne had made his decision. What is clear is that Melbourne favoured either Thomas Arnold or Renn Hampden, and after taking soundings at Oriel where both had been fellows, he chose Hampden, whose appointment was announced on 17 February. Perhaps Arnold would have been appointed if Stanley's letter had been read in time.

Once again a violent storm erupted. Hampden was not only a Whig but his theological opinions were regarded as heterodox. He was known to favour the ending of subscription, and his 1832 Bampton lectures[q] had caused concerns because they seemed to drive a wedge between the Church's dogma and the revelation of the Bible by arguing that the former was both misleading and divisive. The lectures were now revisited, the criticisms clarified, and Hampden was publicly accused of denying the Trinity. The King was petitioned, pamphlets and counter-pamphlets were circulated, and the row hit the national press. But Melbourne refused to change his mind. Agitation grew, and a

---

[q] John Bampton left a legacy in 1751 for the foundation of an annual series of eight divinity lectures to be delivered in the university church.

month after the appointment had been announced, the hebdomadal board submitted a statute to convocation which deprived the regius professor of two of the duties of his office: the nomination of certain preachers and the doctrinal scrutiny of Oxford sermons.

To his regret, Stanley had to miss the meeting of convocation on 22 March but he was there at Hampden's inaugural lecture five days before. 'It was one of the most pathetic and impressive sights I ever saw – the Regius Professor defending himself before the whole University against the charge of heresy in the old magnificent school of divinity – especially when he appealed to God that he had never for a moment swerved from the true faith of Trinity in Unity and Unity in Trinity.'[64]

At convocation the two proctors exercised their right of veto, and according to a report in *The Globe*, 'amidst shouts, groans and shrieks from galleries',[65] the proceedings came to an abrupt close. The statute was brought back to Convocation in May. This time the doors were barred to undergraduates, causing more broken windows, and the statute was carried by 380 votes.

Stanley's own views on Hampden are critical but typically conscientious and restrained. When he was appointed, Stanley described him as 'a man of excellent private character and learning, but with the most extraordinary faculty of writing obscurely that any man ever had'.[66] He could understand therefore why he gave the wrong impression of what he believed, but he took the view that writing so unintelligibly ought itself to have disqualified him. In short, 'it is a most complicated and difficult subject. I think it was a bad appointment on account of his great obscurity, but I think all the petitions and proceedings against him ... have been worse. He is, I believe, really orthodox, though from this said obscurity, apparently heterodox.'[67]

The Tractarians' attacks on Hampden were vindictive and libellous, and fuelled in some cases as much by jealousy and disappointed ambition as by zeal for orthodoxy. All this 'provoked [in Arnold] in equal measure his anger and his scorn, his sense of truth and justice, and his natural impetuosity in behalf of what he deemed to be right'.[68] At least that is how Stanley came to see it eight years later; at the time he was shocked and offended by the ferocity of Arnold's counter-attack in an article entitled 'The Oxford Malignants and Dr. Hampden'[r] in which Arnold castigated Hampden's opponents as lying fanatics and hypocrites. Stanley was even more troubled by this than he had been by

---

[r] Published in the *Edinburgh Review*, April 1836; the provocative title was the editor's.

the language and tactics of Hampden's opponents. He feared for his hero's reputation, but he also recoiled again from lack of charity to those with whom one disagrees. Stanley described Arnold's article as 'a most sad thing, and will, I fear, make the breach irreparable. The most objectionable thing is "pretended holiness," and the general contempt with which he spoke of them as well as the imputation of deliberate dishonesty.'[69] Stanley sent a letter to Arnold to tell him so: 'I have written to him much more openly than I had yet done, telling him how much his article was regretted at Oxford, and saying that I did not see why the general principles of the Newmanists, or the particular act of persecution of which they had lately been guilty, should necessarily involve their whole moral character, or shake my belief in the very strong evidence I had for their being good men.'[70]

The row over Hampden left a lasting impression on Stanley and shook his admiration for Arnold. He had been dismayed and scandalised by the vindictiveness and cruelty on both sides in this religious dispute. He had come to know Newman, Keble and Pusey, and though he disagreed with their views and disapproved of their vilification of Hampden, he could see that they were essentially devout and virtuous men. Arnold's personal attack was therefore intemperate and unfair, and suddenly Arnold was no longer the mighty oak he had been. Stanley told Vaughan in May:

> I was looking over my old M.S. notes of Arnold's sermons the other day, and they call back old times most painfully – at least I believe I must say painfully, though there is no great reason why it should be so. The change is great from the time when I used to go on from day to day in a state of such undoubting trust and confidence, and conscious of gaining day by day improvement in all my powers, and looking forward to furthering the interest of the great man to whom I owed so much by my own exertions at Oxford, and passing once a week twenty minutes in the evening chapel on Sundays. Now there is doubt and controversy, and rival men and principles to demand my attention, and perpetual fear lest I'm going backward instead of advancing, and want of anyone on whom I may repose with confidence, or from whom I may gain any moral or intellectual food such as I can be sure will endure.[71]

* * *

Two outstanding new tutors, W. G. Ward and A. C. Tait, joined Balliol at the start of Stanley's second year, and both became his close friends. Stanley had met the eccentric William Ward during his first term:

> There bounced in on Sunday a huge moon-faced man, Ward, once of Christ Church, now of Lincoln. The first words almost that he spoke, having just come up from town, were that Arnold's Sermons (vol. iii.) were on the point of coming out. It seems that he idolises Whately,[s] and Arnold almost, though not quite, as much, purely from their books, without any knowledge of them.[72]

Ward was only three years older than Stanley. After Winchester he had gone up to Christ Church and thrown himself into the Union. He won a scholarship to Lincoln College and from there sat the fellowship examination at Balliol with a view to teaching mathematics. He was said to have startled the examiners by stretching out on the floor and sleeping for an hour before putting pen to paper. Stanley described him in a letter to Vaughan:

> Ward I see more than any one else, and I like him exceedingly ... He is very uncouth in appearance as you know, and also uncouth in his tastes, at least he has no taste for beauty of scenery and not very much for beauty in poetry, though on the other hand he is passionately fond of music ... On these points therefore ... we have not much in common. But what I do like very much in him is his great honesty and fearless and entire love of truth, and deep interest about all that concerns the happiness of the human race. These I never saw so strongly developed in anybody ... He is the best arguer and the most clear-headed man that I ever saw, I think – though in one way his logical faculty is one of his defects, for it has attained such gigantic height as rather to overshadow some of the other parts of his mind.[73]

Stanley and Ward would go on long afternoon walks together when Ward would hold forth with passion on whatever topic happened to excite him at the time. He was envious of Stanley's intimacy with Arnold, and wanted to learn everything he could about his opinions. In 1838 he went to stay at Rugby and questioned and argued with him so fiercely that Arnold had to retire to bed exhausted. Ward soon lost confidence in Arnold's liberalism and was drawn deep into the Tractarian camp.

---

[s] Richard Whately, Archbishop of Dublin, had been a fellow of Oriel with Arnold.

Tait's was a very different character – wise, calm, and sensible. He had been brought up in Scotland as a Presbyterian, and after studying at Glasgow University he came to Balliol as a Snell Exhibitioner.ᵗ He succeeded Moberly as Stanley's tutor, and soon gained a reputation as a kind and conscientious mentor and the ablest lecturer in Oxford. Tait was Lake's tutor too when they arrived together in October 1835: 'He gave me at once the impression of strength of spirit which I always associated with him through life.'[74]

Although they remained on friendly terms, Tait and Ward fell out over Newman and his followers. Tait had, of course, subscribed to the Church of England's formularies but he retained respect for his Presbyterian background. 'He found himself all at once in the midst of a system of teaching which unchurched himself and all whom he had hitherto known. In his simplicity he had believed ... that neither Episcopacy nor Presbytery availeth anything. But here were men – able, learned, devout-minded men – maintaining that outward rites and ceremonies were of the very essence, and that where these were not, there is no true Christianity.'[75] As Ward's Tractarianism deepened, Tait became increasingly troubled by his opinions, and told him that they were not 'the right ones for a fellow of this college to hold'.[76] In the end, in 1841 (and much to Stanley's disappointment), Tait persuaded the master to ask him to resign as a tutor.

In November 1835 Benjamin Jowett won the top scholarship to Balliol and entered into residence the following October. He and Stanley became friends and began to exert a considerable influence on one another. Jowett later recalled that Stanley had 'an almost extravagant regard for me when he was young and said that he learned more from me than from any one except Dr Arnold'.[77] They shared many of the same characteristics and physical features, and must have looked an odd pair on their daily walks or as they sat together at the scholars' table. Like Stanley, Jowett had been 'a pale delicate child with little physical strength but remarkable intelligence'.[78] He was small and effeminate with a high-pitched voice, and his nickname at school was 'Miss Jowett'. His smooth, chubby face was often described as 'cherubic'.

Jowett's childhood had been very different from Stanley's but it left him with the same shyness and reserve. He was born in London in 1817, the third of nine children of a furrier turned printer who had fallen on hard times. He went at twelve as a day-boy scholar to St Paul's

---

ᵗ In 1679 John Snell had founded exhibitions at Balliol for graduates of Glasgow University.

School, then under the shadow of Wren's cathedral. Incredible though it may seem, Jowett lived alone for seven years in lodgings on the City Road, including most of his school holidays. He missed out on the company and pursuits of other boys, and spent his time reading voraciously and committing classical texts to memory. By the time he left school he could repeat most of Virgil and Sophocles. Jowett shared Stanley's high intelligence but had a more original and philosophical mind. Stanley's first impression was that he was almost as disputatious as Ward, and Tait's view (as his tutor) was that Jowett was much more worthy to have taught him.

* * *

Stanley spent part of his first summer vacation in Dublin, where he joined his father at the fifth annual meeting of the British Association for the Advancement of Science. By his own admission he was 'unable to enter into the scientific business from my ignorance of the subject'[79] but he was interested in hearing the debates on social questions.

The angry reaction in England to the drive in Parliament for Catholic emancipation, and the suppression of Protestant bishoprics in Ireland, encouraged father and son to see all they could of the Roman Catholic Church, and to understand it better. Edward Stanley (with Arthur's help) wrote a pamphlet entitled *A Few Observations on Religion and Education in Ireland*. Its main purpose was to protest against the contemptuous attitude to Catholic dogma by those who wished to advance the cause of Protestantism in Ireland. Arthur wrote to Vaughan at the time to say that 'I have been reading many Roman Catholic books lately, and learned their doctrines better than I knew them before. I am convinced that Protestants in general treat them with shameful ignorance and unfairness.'[80] In another letter to Vaughan he explained:

> The important points which form our differences, viz. the priesthood, the infallibility of the Church, the indispensable nature of ceremonies, the Apostolical Succession, and the Real Presence in the Eucharist, are all virtually held by Newman and his followers ... I do not see any more reason for saying that Roman Catholics are of a different religion from ourselves, than for saying that the High Churchmen are.[81]

In the same letter Stanley expressed his thanks that 'God has given us youth to form our opinions in before we have publicly to act upon and express them'.[82] It is clear that Stanley's later convictions about

Christian unity, the inclusiveness of the national Church, and the importance of doctrinal tolerance are already present. When Mary wrote to him to say that she was anxious that, in wanting to do justice to the Church of Rome, their father was doing less than justice to the Evangelicals, he replied:

> Ask him to consider whether it is not as possible to abstain from balls and plays with sincerity as to fast with sincerity ... whether an over-reverence for the Bible, shown by interpreting it absurdly, and supposing its inspiration to extend to every word of it, is not much more harmless than an over-reverence for the Councils of the Church, shown by supposing their decrees to be infallible, and to have a claim on every Christian's obedience ... You must remember that the great point in the general question about Catholics is, that they are Christians, and therefore may be, and sometimes are, fellow-workers with Protestants against their common enemies, the world, the flesh, and the devil ... I suppose you have to thank Arnold that I am not illiberal towards the Evangelicals from being liberal towards the Catholics.[83]

Soon after Stanley's return to Oxford in October 1835 Queen Adelaide[u] paid a visit to the city and university, riding through the streets in an open carriage accompanied by the Duke of Wellington. She attended the chapels of New College and Magdalen, lunched at Queen's, and was received by the university at a grand reception in the Sheldonian. Later in the day she held court at the Angel Inn, where she received invited guests. Stanley was not enthusiastic: 'There was', he wrote, 'the usual display of rank Toryism.'[84]

A month of the next long vacation was spent with his mother and both sisters in the German town of Baden-Baden. He was fascinated and amused by the people there. 'The needy Scotch baronets, the newly married couples, the vulgar people trying to scrape themselves into good society, the gossips, the princes, the wicked ex-Elector of Hesse, and the noble ex-Duchess of Baden, are all very curious.'[85] Stanley seems to have taken to the Grand Duchess Stephanie, describing her conversation as 'superior to anyone's that I ever heard, except Arnold in his best moments'.[86] Kitty wrote a long letter home to Maria in which she gave a graphic account of a remarkable woman:

---

[u] Princess Adelaide of Saxe-Meiningen married the Duke of Clarence, George III's second son and future William IV.

She found out I lived near the Château, so asked me to come there to a much smaller and pleasanter party, and then she asked me to show her my drawings ... She looked them over with great interest, said that if I could finish as well as I began I should have *un grand talent* ... She spoke of the comfort her taste for beauty and for the picturesque had been to her; of the rare pleasure of finding anybody who could understand her; and of how she often longed to be a poet to express what she felt ...

Perhaps you know more of the story than I did – that she was a Beauharnais, married by Bonaparte to the Grand Duke of Baden against his will, bringing with her as dowry the southern part of the Duchy ... Her two sons, it is suspected, were poisoned by the uncle who succeeded to the Duchy.[87]

*   *   *

Nine months later in May 1836 Stanley's father received an unexpected letter from the Prime Minister inviting him to become Bishop of Norwich. The previous bishop, Henry Bathurst, was a character out of the Barsetshire novels, and it is easy to believe that Trollope had him in mind when he created Bishop Grantly. They were both bishops of the old school – amiable, worldly and indulgent. Bathurst, aged eighty-three, had been suffering a long and lingering illness, just like Grantly at the beginning of *Barchester Towers*. They both had sons who were their archdeacons, and who harboured ambitions to succeed them.

Bathurst was a Whig and had been the only bishop to vote for the Reform Act of 1832. Melbourne was determined that another Whig should succeed him. Furthermore, 'the Dead See', as Norwich was known, was in desperate need of reform. Bathurst had started there as bishop in 1805, the same year that Edward started as rector of Alderley. Bathurst had never been an energetic pastor or administrator, and old age and infirmity only increased his inertia and neglect. All the abuses of the Georgian Church were rife, making 'the Diocese of Norwich a byword for laxity amongst the sees of the Church of England'.[88] Edward Stanley's reputation for energy, efficiency and naval discipline recommended him to Melbourne. 'He was still the commanding officer of the ship: the difference was only that he had a mightier vessel to direct, and more stormy seas to encounter.'[89]

Edward and Kitty and their daughters were plunged into what the family called 'a terrible taking'[90] when Edward received the invitation. They certainly did not want to leave Alderley, Norfolk was an unattractive prospect, and Edward felt unworthy of episcopal office which he also regarded an uncongenial. By contrast, Arthur's reaction was sanguine:

> I came up to town to-day for two days to have a tooth out, and here I found my father just in the agonies of deciding on the Bishopric of Norwich. It is all over, and he is appointed. I had not the least expected it; no more, I imagine, has the world at large. I have hardly figured yet to myself the change that it will be. To me the parting from Alderley will be far less painful than to the rest. Indeed, I shall not care much about it ... Of course he is a fit man in many respects, but my heart groans at the exclusion of Arnold.[91]

It is extraordinary that even at a moment like this Stanley was thinking of the Doctor. The pride and pleasure that he might have been expected to feel on his father's elevation are qualified by feelings of disappointment that it was not Arnold who had been chosen. Such feelings were not shared by many outside a tight Whiggish circle of Arnold's admirers which included Edward and Kitty. It is true that Melbourne had considered Arnold for the bench before, and he had been recommended for Norwich by Lord John Russell. But his pamphlets on Biblical interpretation and Church reform had made him unpopular with the clergy, and his recent attack on the Oxford Malignants had damaged his reputation still further. Furthermore, Melbourne was so wounded by the uproar provoked by his appointment of Hampden that he was sure he could not afford to be liberal again.[92]

Edward tried to restore some respectability to Arnold by giving him the honour of preaching at his consecration in the chapel at Lambeth Palace. However, the cautious Archbishop Howley would not allow it on the grounds 'that such a step would be so "very ill received by the clergy in general"'.[93] Howley asked Edward to appoint another preacher but he stood his ground and refused to do so. In the end the sermon was delivered by one of the archbishop's chaplains.

Stanley relished the family's new life in the cathedral close and wrote an excited letter to Owen, who was serving on HMS *Terror* in the Arctic:

> I was the first who saw the Palace stript of the remnants of the old Bishop's furniture, and, to a certain degree, made comfortable, so that my first impressions are the most favourable; and as I entered

the gate for the first time, I was more struck with the size than the ugliness of the Palace, and with the surpassing beauty of the Cathedral, which overshadows it ... I never saw any house like it; it is among houses, I should think, what Moscow is among towns – rooms which we may really call very fine side by side with the meanest of passages and staircases ...

Then, as to the living attractions of the place, it is more in my way than Alderley was. I find it exceedingly interesting to see so many clergy passing constantly before one's eyes and ears; such letters at breakfast – complimentary, abusive, sermons in verse; such faces at dinner – all overcast, as soon as they come into the dining-room, by the remembrance that it was the scene of their examination for Ordination in past times ... Then, I think the Bishop of Norwich seems to be an unusually important Bishop in his diocese, whether from the old one having been so much out of the way for so long, or from the county being so much at the world's end ...

I am afraid that this letter will have given you the idea (which they say at home is the case) that I am the only one puffed up by the accession of dignity.[94]

The visit to Dublin had brought father and son together, and Stanley enjoyed helping his father write his pamphlet on religion in Ireland. He wrote frankly to Vaughan to tell him how much he had enjoyed the vacation, 'having become much more at ease with my father and talked more with him than I ever did before. From his having had so different an education, and having such totally different pursuits and feelings we have very little in common with each other, so that I am very glad of anything which we can have in common, as this pamphlet.'[95] Stanley was now determined to build on this and help his father with his installation sermon.

Stanley's contributions to the sermon were considerable. He encouraged his father to make two central and, as it turned out, controversial points: that tolerance of dissent was neither sinful nor schismatic, and that combining secular with religious instruction was a desirable way of elevating and enlarging the mind. Though many of the Norwich clergy were Cambridge men and therefore less affected by the Oxford Movement, Tractarian thinking was still influential, and opposed to both these points. The second point was especially offensive to the Tories because there was a rumour abroad that the Whig ministry was about to introduce a national system of education entirely divorced from all religious teaching.

The installation took place on 17 August 1837 and was the first enthronement of a Bishop of Norwich for over thirty years. The cathedral was packed, and the congregation included 1,200 charity children who were there to represent the National Society for Church education. The service was impressive, with numerous processions and much pomp and circumstance. According to Stanley, 'The Bishop was deeply affected by this cordial and solemn entrance into this new office, and expressed publicly, at the close of the day that "till then he had never felt anything like consolation for the sacrifice he had made in parting from his former charge".'[96] But what Edward did not know until the evening was the offence his sermon had caused. At a public dinner in his honour, an aristocratic Tory clergyman proposed the Bishop's health but broke with custom by not requesting publication of the sermon. This omission was rebuked by the archdeacon but then defended by another speaker. A general uproar ensued and the row reached the Tory press with stories of a liberal bishop's heretical sermon. In the end the sermon was printed and sold out immediately, and the row rumbled on for several months. 'It was', regretted Stanley, 'an ill-omened accompaniment to what might otherwise have been an auspicious inauguration, and the scene left on his mind an unfavourable impression of the temper of his clergy which was not easily effaced.'[97]

*   *   *

Stanley had been able to afford these ecclesiastical distractions at home and at Oxford because studying for his degree was relatively easy. Arnold's teaching in the sixth form far surpassed the lectures at Oxford, and Stanley's reading was so wide and thorough that he had studied most of the prescribed texts already. 'Alas!' he exclaimed to Lake, 'most truly was it said that the last year at school surpassed a hundredfold the first year of college.'[98] Stanley's attitude to responsions (the first year examination) was identical to Mark Pattison's: 'I was examined in two plays of Sophocles, Juvenal, Euclid I. and II., and Latin writing. The examination was one I could as well have passed the first day I set foot in Oxford. The College had thus spent a year and two months upon me in preparing me to do what I was ready to do before I entered it.'[99]

Stanley was in danger of losing interest in his work, and there is certainly in his letters a dampening of the enthusiasm he had shown at school. Prizes, however, still provided incentive, and he was determined to win two of the most prestigious and demanding, the Ireland Scholarship for Greek and Latin composition, and the Newdigate Prize for English verse.[v] For Stanley's first attempt at the Ireland in 1835 he read from nine to two and from seven to eleven every day, and 'I practise composition much, alas!!'[100] Surprisingly, Stanley was never very good at writing Latin verse: indeed he found the work 'odious' and 'utterly useless'.[101] For his second attempt he engaged a private tutor, Thomas Claughton, a Rugbeian and fellow of Trinity College, and forty years later the first Bishop of St Albans. His task was 'to polish up, or rather to create some Latin verse spirit within me'.[102] In January Stanley was 'reading on an average eleven hours a day, devoting my mornings to "De Oratore" first, and then to Aristophanes ... My evenings are given to composition. I have improved much in lyrics and tolerably, I think, in hexameters. Greek iambics I find I can get up fast.'[103] Stanley's exertions were endangering his health, and in March 1836 he failed again but wrote a gracious letter to Vaughan, who had just won an equivalent prize at Cambridge:

> You will be sorry to hear that your triumph has not been followed up. The examination was as much against me as possible ... [But] I am even in better spirits than last year. However great would have been my joy if we had both succeeded, it is a most exceeding happiness that we have not both failed. In short, I owe to you the good spirits I at present enjoy ...
>
> Arnold sent me a most kind and thoughtful message by Lake, begging me not to worry myself about having the responsibility of the school on my shoulders, as I had quite enough from my own anxiety without their unreasonable expectations.[104]

Stanley had one more chance of winning the Ireland, but whether or not to put himself through the ordeal was a difficult decision. 'If I had only to read poets and criticism, I would do it most willingly, but it is in Latin verses and Greek iambics that I fail, and these will entirely divert me from my degree work, inflict upon me the greatest misery, and will all perish in the using.'[105] In the end Stanley took Claughton's advice and entered the lists. This time he was victorious and wrote again to Vaughan:

---

[v] The first was founded in 1825 by John Ireland, Dean of Westminster, 'for the promotion of classical learning and taste'. The second in 1805 by Sir Roger Newdigate, M.P. for Oxford University.

It has been a great pleasure to me – far more than I ever could have anticipated – for it was so long since I had gained any honour, or received any congratulations, that I had almost forgotten what it was.

And it has been doubly (or rather, I should say, tenfold) delightful to be reminded in almost every letter that I have had on the subject that it is not my own fame only or chiefly which is advanced by my success, but the fame of Arnold, to whom I do most sincerely feel that I am indebted for my present happiness, and for whose sake it was always my chief aim, and is now my chief joy, to gain the Ireland.[106]

Stanley's compositions had been so excellent that at first the examiners suspected that he had cheated by gaining prior access to the papers. The master and fellows of Balliol were mortified at such a slur on the college's good name, and for his part Stanley appealed to the vice-chancellor, who soon concluded that the insinuation of dishonesty was entirely groundless. On 4 March the examiners published a signed apology and 'there was shouting from one end of Balliol to the other'.[107]

Two months later, Stanley won the Newdigate Prize with a 270-line poem on the set subject of 'The Gypsies'. It uses the same poetic form and descriptive power as his prize-winning poem at Rugby, but it shows a surer, more confident touch:

> Drear was the scene – a dark and troublous time –
> The Heaven all gloom, the wearied Earth all crime;
> Men deemed they saw the unshackled Powers of ill
> Rage in that storm, and work their perfect will:
> Then, like a traveller, when the wild wind blows,
> And black night flickers with the driving snows,
> A stranger people 'mid that murky gloom
> Knocked at the gates of awe-struck Christendom!
> No clang of arms, no din of battle roared,
> Round the still march of that mysterious horde;
> Weary and sad, arrayed in pilgrim guise,
> They stood and prayed, nor raised their suppliant eyes;
> At once to Europe's hundred shores they came,
> In voice, in feature, and in garb the same ...[108]

Stanley was asked to call on the Professor of Poetry, and thirty years later he recalled Keble's 'quiet kindness of manner, the bright twinkling eye, illuminating that otherwise impressive countenance, which greeted the bashful student into the Professor's presence'.[109] Keble suggested some improvements and spoke warmly of one of Arnold's sermons. Stanley admired Keble's saintly character, and every Sunday for the rest of his life he read the appropriate poem in *The Christian Year*, Keble's devotional anthology.

Stanley's parents were invited to hear Arthur read his prize poem in the Sheldonian at the end of the summer term. They brought Mary and Catherine with them and stayed at Balliol with the master. Vaughan came too and acted as Stanley's prompter. 'I heard Stanley recite his "Gypsies" in the Theatre in 1837;' wrote W. Tuckwell in his *Reminiscences of Oxford*, 'the scene comes back to me as of yesterday – the crowded area; the ladies in their enormous bonnets; handsome, stately Dr. Gilbert[w] in the Vice-Chancellor's chair; the pale, slight, weak-voiced, boyish figure in the rostrum; the roar of cheers that greeted him.'[110] Stanley's father was so touched by the applause that he was unable to conceal his feelings and hid his face in his hands.

When Stanley returned to Oxford after his father's enthronement he had less than three months to revise for finals. He wrote at the time to Owen: 'Here I am at Oxford, in the last agonies before my final examination in November, when I shall be at once and for ever freed from the great burden that has been hanging over me for the last three years.'[111] Stanley set to work as hard as he had for the Ireland, and after taking a short break at Rugby, he wrote to Vaughan: 'I am quite surprised at my health and success. Logic, Aristotle, history questions, English prose into Greek and Latin, Greek and Latin poetry into English, are now past, all quite to my satisfaction. The examination acted upon me like magic, dispelled all my headaches, and I only broke down in the intervals.'[112] Stanley was so confident of success that he was critical of his examiners, accusing them of making 'prodigious mistakes' in the questions to which he said he had made 'several impudent answers'.[113] Fortunately this did not count against him: the examiners were impressed and Stanley was awarded the predicted first class. He wrote defiantly to Mary: 'All is over ... nothing could be better – in Divinity especially I have proved I hope quite sufficiently that the son of a Whig Bishop and a pupil of Arnold's knew as much as other people.'[114]

---

[w] Ashurst Gilbert was Principal of Brasenose and later Bishop of Chichester.

4
'From the Dust of Creeds Outworn'
1838–1842

THE FACT THAT Arthur Stanley was Arnold's disciple and a Whig bishop's son caused the fellows of Balliol to have their doubts about his joining them. Jowett said later of an Oxford fellowship that it was 'as good a start to life as a young man can have',[1] and Stanley had set his heart on one at Balliol almost from the moment he arrived. But the Balliol common room had become an uneasy and divided place, and the Tractarian element was already anxious about the growing number of Arnoldian liberals in the college.[a] Jenkyns, the master, was not supportive. He was a High Churchman of the old school who felt uncomfortable with any form of enthusiasm, putting peace and quiet in the college before the pursuit of religious truth.

Stanley had heard rumours that his hopes of obtaining a fellowship were likely to be disappointed. 'Listen,' he wrote to Vaughan in December 1837, 'listen to what will make your Cambridge hair stand on end with astonishment.' He explained that he had reason to believe that one after another of the fellows had 'given in to the overwhelming terror of the outcry against Balliol as a heretical and Arnoldian college, and declared that they had rather not elect me in November'.[2] In a letter to Mary, Stanley described an interview with Jenkyns:

> The Master affected some surprise at there being any objection raised to me – said it was quite new to him – that he had not meant anything by his urging me to stand at Oriel – that he had been surprised and grieved at my proposing to do so – that he himself had no objection whatever to me, but on the contrary had the highest opinion &c, &c ... This of course rather throws things back again, but as I knew that he *had* known of this before, though I could not tell him so, it rather throws a doubt over all that he said. – And though he also spoke with great dislike of Newmanism, yet I found

---

[a] Stanley and Lake had been joined by another of Arnold's star pupils, the poet Arthur Clough. Tait and Jowett also shared their liberal opinions.

it rather hard to bring him to the point on my theological opinions. He said that he should certainly make it a point to put down any party arising in the college: the fear of which is in fact his real reason for having any doubts at all about me ...[3]

The prospect of not being elected to a Balliol fellowship was bitterly disappointing and provoked a crisis in Stanley's thinking. Was he right to reject Tractarianism and hold fast to Arnold's teaching, and in so doing forfeit the opportunity to stay at Balliol? Or should he revisit the tracts and, if convinced, join forces with Newman and renounce Arnold? Certainly Newman and Arnold were poles apart, and no convenient compromise was possible. In a letter to Vaughan at the end of February, Stanley described Newmanism as 'a magnificent and consistent system shooting up on every side, whilst all that I see against it is weak and grovelling'. On the other hand, he still believed that Paul's epistles were strongly against it. But what paralysed his thinking and made decision impossible was the fear of parting company with Arnold:

> I feel that to become a Newmanist would be a shock to my whole existence, that it would subvert every relation of life in which I have stood or hope to stand hereafter. I dread to think of it even as a possibility, and I dread also a long and dreary halting between two opinions, which will mar the pleasure of every opinion I hold for an indefinite period. With this feeling you may be sure I shall not join it without a desperate fight, within and without, that I will leave no stone unturned which may enable me to keep in that line of life to which I had thought God had called me, and from which a conversion to Newmanism would lead me away into a path utterly unknown to me.
>
> I know of no system to which I can hold except Arnold's; and if that breaks down under me, I know not where I can look.[4]

A few days later Stanley felt, he said, 'more at peace about Newmanism'. He felt more confident now about the Biblical objections, and was content 'to lay the question on the shelf for a time, and not read the Fathers[b] till I have possessed myself as much as possible with the spirit of the New Testament'.[5] When Stanley returned to the struggle the

---

[b] The theologians of the Church's patristic period from the end of the 1st to the close of the 8th century. The Tractarians regarded their writings as especially authoritative sources of orthodox doctrine.

following term he saw the dividing issue as essentially that of doctrine and belief versus morality and virtue. For example, to Newman's mind the main point to be embraced was the Trinity, the intricate belief that God is both three and one. For Arnold, what mattered was that God had sent his Son to deliver us and his Spirit to sanctify us, and the precise nature of the relations between Father, Son and Holy Spirit were unintelligible and mysterious. 'The fault of Newman's view seems to me to consist, not in requiring us to believe that such secrets and mysteries exist, but in requiring us to make them (not their practical side) the food of our religious belief and feelings.'[6]

Stanley's Rugby and Balliol friends, William Lake and Arthur Clough, went through much the same heart-searching. Lake had never fallen for Arnold in the way Stanley had, and from the start he maintained an emotional independence, regarding Arnold as admirable but not perfect. Like so many of that Oxford generation, Lake was attracted to Newman; indeed at the end of his life he confided that for fifty years he had felt a higher admiration for Newman than for anyone.[7] But Lake's was not a passionate nature and he experienced no Damascene conversion. Instead he came to combine the liberal, tolerant instincts of Stanley with a staunch if moderate Tractarianism.

The poet Clough was a different case. At Rugby he had perhaps been even closer to Arnold than Stanley; he was head of School House and often stayed with the Arnolds in the holidays (his own family was living at the time in America). He certainly shared Stanley's hero-worship and became another model pupil, winning every prize, and a Balliol scholarship the year after Stanley. Arnold wrote to Clough's uncle to say that he had passed eight years at Rugby without a fault, and was 'regarded by myself, I may truly say, with an affection and interest hardly less than I should feel for my own son'.[8]

Clough arrived at Balliol in 1837 and found that Ward was his tutor. Ward was by now disillusioned with Arnold, and was becoming instead a passionately convinced, even fanatical Tractarian. It is clear that he took an immediate fancy to Clough, admiring his intense conscientiousness and high-mindedness, not to mention what he later called 'his singular sweetness of disposition'.[9] Clough replaced Stanley as Ward's companion on his afternoon walks, and he used them to bombard Clough with criticisms of Arnold's liberalism. Looking back thirty years later, Ward confessed the damage he had done:

I fear that, from my point of view, I must account it the calamity of his life that he was brought into contact with myself. My whole interest at that time (as now) was concentrated on questions which to me seem the most important and interesting that can occupy the mind ... It was a very different matter to force them prematurely upon the attention of a young man just coming up to college, and to drive him, as it were, peremptorily into a decision upon them: to aim at making him as hot a partisan as I was myself.[10]

For his part, Clough felt, when being talked to by Ward, 'like a bit of paper blown up the chimney by a draught, and one doesn't always like being a bit of paper'.[11] Ward provoked a severe crisis in Clough by undermining the convictions he had brought from Rugby without being able to provide him with acceptable alternatives. When Stanley saw them on one of their walks he remarked, 'There goes Ward mystifying poor Clough, and persuading him that he must either believe *nothing* or accept the whole of Church doctrine.'[12] Clough certainly admired Newman and found at least the devotional aspects of Tractarianism attractive, but these were not enough to convert him to the cause. Like Stanley he was sure that to have done so would have been a shameful betrayal of Arnold. But where Stanley was able in the end to stay loyal to Arnold's teaching, Clough remained torn and confused, and with the additional pressure of overwork, his health began to suffer. He had to postpone his final examinations, and when he sat them he missed the first he deserved. He walked from Oxford to Rugby in despair to confess his failure to Arnold.

Clough was also disappointed when it came to a Balliol fellowship. His rejection was entirely on academic grounds, though it was a close contest and he was one of three front-runners. Balliol's earlier rejection of Stanley, on the other hand, had been partisan, and knowing the outcome, he did not sit the examinations. That year there were four vacancies at Balliol, two of which were filled by Lake and Jowett (who was still an undergraduate).

*   *   *

Being the son of a bishop afforded Stanley some rare privileges. His father had rented a large house in Lower Brook Street in Mayfair, and Stanley escaped from Oxford in May to stay there with his family. He wrote again to Vaughan to say that he had been twice to the House of Lords where (since Owen was at sea) he had the eldest son's right to stand on the steps of the throne. He heard the Prime Minister, Lord Melbourne, and found him 'a most pleasant speaker, and a most agreeable-looking man'.[13] In the bishops' robing-room he met the High Church Tory Henry Phillpotts, then in the eighth of nearly forty years as Bishop of Exeter. Stanley spent time wandering around Lincoln's Inn and the Temple, and felt reconciled to the life of a lawyer if, when it came to ordination, he found it impossible to subscribe to the articles.

On Thursday 28 June 1838 Stanley was present at the Coronation of Queen Victoria, sitting high up at the west end but in full view of the throne. In another long letter to Vaughan, he gave the fullest and most vivid of all eyewitness accounts.[c] With his mother, sisters and brother Charles, Arthur left home at five-thirty in the morning, and found London all awake and the streets crowded. They reached Westminster Abbey at seven and had to wait three and a half hours for the Queen to arrive. The service lasted five hours. Stanley's account shows how excited and awe-struck he was ('I never saw anything like it; tears would have been a relief'), but he was also aware of the service's dramatic shortcomings, and the rude behaviour of sections of the congregation of 10,000. There had been no rehearsal and the officiating clergy were confused. They began the litany too soon, and towards the end of the service the Bishop of Bath and Wells turned over two pages at once, whispered to the Queen that the service was over, and then had to fetch her back from St Edward's Chapel to which she had retired with her ladies and train-bearers. The Queen was shocked to see the chapel altar covered with sandwiches and bottles of wine. Nonetheless, Melbourne, who had already dosed himself with brandy and laudanum, helped himself to a glass, feeling exhausted by the weight of the sword of State which, according to Disraeli, he held like a butcher. The Archbishop of Canterbury managed to force the ruby ring on to the Queen's fourth finger, not realising that it had been made to fit the fifth, and during the homage one nonagenarian peer caught his foot in his robes on the steps of the throne and rolled to the bottom, causing frantic cheering.

Stanley walked home while the family waited for their carriage to make its way through the crowds. He was wise to have done so because it took the coachman four hours to reach the Abbey. 'It was all more like a dream than a reality – ', he wrote, 'more beautiful than I could

[c] Appendix I.

have conceived possible ... I shall wish almost never to see [the Queen] again, that as this is the first image I ever had of her, so it should be the last!'[14]

*   *   *

Stanley returned to Oxford immediately. He had already been approached about a fellowship at University College. In tune with the founder's will, preference was to be given to candidates who had been born near Durham, but in order to recruit Stanley, the master and fellows had decided to set aside this restriction. This was a controversial step though not the first time the college had waived such conditions.[d] Stanley was undecided. On the one hand he was confident of being elected; on the other hand, he thought University 'not a very agreeable college'.[15] It was certainly a backwater in Oxford, unfashionable and undistinguished. In the end he swallowed his pride and sat papers that were no more than a formality. On the evening of the election he wrote to his father: 'I am a Fellow of University – I hope it will be for the best, though it is impossible not to feel that it is a change which nothing but the certainty of this election contrasted with the uncertainty of the other, could justify.'[16]

The same evening Stanley wrote to Tait: 'I cannot help writing to say how much obliged I am to you for your endeavours to keep me at Balliol – if all my friends had done the same, I should probably not be where I am now.'[17] To Stanley a fellowship at University College not Balliol was 'the Bishopric of Man, instead of the Archbishopric of Canterbury'.[18] He felt that he was in exile and for the next few weeks was very miserable. He quibbled about the depressing silence of the senior common room and 'the utter impossibility even of procuring toast for breakfast'.[19] With encouragement from Tait he even considered resigning and submitting an application to Balliol.

Part of this was temperament: Stanley never liked change and he had suffered similar feelings when he arrived at Rugby and Balliol. According to Prothero, the first consolation came to him in the college chapel on the festival of St Simon and St Jude (28 October), when he heard the thanksgiving for Alfred the Great, 'first Founder of this House'. Stanley was an historian and it is unlikely that he regarded a ninth-century foundation by Alfred as any more than fanciful legend. Nonetheless, he

---

[d] Mark Pattison assumed that his own northern roots would guarantee success and was horrified to find Stanley also sitting the examination.

seems to have relished the idea, as indeed did the fellows in 1872 when they celebrated the college's first millennium. Stanley was by then Dean of Westminster but he returned to give one of thirteen speeches at the commemorative feast.

The true founder of University College was William of Durham, who died in 1249. The original college consisted of just four fellows who studied theology. Early in the sixteenth century undergraduates were admitted, and in the seventeenth the buildings on the High Street began to take on something of today's appearance. The college was unusually vigorous in the 1760s and 1770s during the first half of the mastership of Nathan Wetherell. Two years into his forty-three year reign the brilliant polymath William Jones had been elected a fellow. Jones transformed the college's reputation for scholarship while Wetherell transformed its teaching. Regrettably, the second half of Wetherell's mastership was marred by loss of interest and subsequent decline.

The master when Stanley joined the college was Frederic Plumptre, who had been elected in 1836. He was unusually tall and thin, and was prone to hide his natural shyness 'under a carapace of dignified imperturbability, if not pomposity'.[20] But he was an energetic and enterprising master, and by the time Stanley arrived he had already improved conditions for the scholars and endowed two more. Plumptre supported the steps taken to recruit Stanley, and in the month of his fellowship examination he was able to record that 'there has been much competition for our Scholarships and the nature of the examinations for them requires that a young man should possess decided ability in order to obtain one'.[21]

But it was still early days, and Stanley found himself in a very different college from Balliol, as George Bradley describes. Bradley was six years younger than Stanley but very much in the same Arnoldian mould as Stanley, Lake and Clough. At Rugby he had excelled in Greek and Latin composition and he is said to have been the model for Tom Brown's friend 'little Hall, commonly called Tadpole, from his great black head and thin legs'.[22] Bradley sat the Balliol scholarship examination in November 1839 but was unsuccessful. Arnold encouraged him to try for University where he could at least expect to be taught by Stanley. This time he succeeded and came up in the autumn of 1840. Stanley was his tutor and the two became close, with Bradley looking up to Stanley almost as much as Stanley had done to Arnold. After returning to Rugby to teach, Bradley followed another Rugby house master, George Cotton,[e] as Master of Marlborough. He returned to University as master in 1870 and was less successful than he had been as headmaster. Eleven years later, Bradley succeeded Stanley as Dean of Westminster. In an address in the chapel after Stanley's death, he gave a detailed description of University College as he found it when he arrived forty years before, and when Stanley was starting his third year as a fellow:

> The College, it was said (at Rugby), was not a leading college. Quite the reverse, but for all that had much to recommend it, and now that they had elected Arthur Stanley there was everything to be hoped for it. His name from the immense impression that he had made at school and at Oxford ... was quite familiar to me; I had read and could repeat with enthusiasm his youthful compositions, and I can hardly recall a happier day than that in which I was elected a Scholar here and greeted by him as a pupil of his own master, Arnold ...
>
> We were a smaller, far smaller society than we are now: not more I think than about half our present number ... For that and perhaps for other reasons, the social feeling in the College was strong ... The number of Scholars was also smaller and there was no Scholars' table; the proportion of men in easy or even affluent circumstances was large ... There was much idleness in the usual sense of the word ... men were regular at lectures, but *read little*. There was much vigorous athletic life ... great recent successes on the river were filling us all with unbounded delight; some few of us, a very few, read hard and discussed our favourite authors in private; but as a rule such [pastimes] found little favour ... loose conversation was to be heard, if you wished to hear it, in the rooms of certain men; but those who *hated* it need never do so ... In regard to religion there was much tension and interest among thinking men; fierce discussions, sharp and even bitter dispute; for the air above us and around us was full of controversy ... There was of course much indifference to religion ... We came to Chapel as part of our regular daily duty, some of course coming as little as they could ...
>
> Our relations to our elders – to the fellows of the College – were

---

[e] Cotton was perhaps the kind young master in *Tom Brown's Schooldays*. He was engaged to Arnold's eldest and favourite child, Jane, and distress caused by his breaking off the engagement may have contributed to Arnold's sudden death.

not close but pleasant and friendly – we attended lectures regularly in our tutor's rooms; but there was so far no private work of any kind that I can recall.[23]

There were aspects of the college which were bound to be uncongenial to someone as serious-minded as Stanley: indeed Stanley summarised 'the curse of our College' as 'that atmosphere of childishness and frivolity',[24] and told Vaughan that it was 'chiefly composed of all the most bigoted men in Oxford'.[25] Nonetheless, there were good sides and the new master was already introducing the kinds of reform of which Stanley approved. Some of Stanley's complaining was prompted by anxiety about change but much of it was petulant, the product of lingering disappointment over Balliol. Fortunately for both Stanley and the college, his feelings of disdain were soon to mellow.

*   *   *

The life of a probationary fellow, and indeed of any fellow who was not also a tutor or the holder of a university or college office, was one of ease and comparative luxury. The college expected very little in return for the status and comforts it bestowed, and in most cases even residence was not required. Conscientious fellows filled their hours with private study, coaching or competing for Oxford's prizes. Stanley spent much of the early months of 1839 learning Hebrew and researching and writing three prize essays: the Chancellor's English Essay, the Ellerton Theological Essay (in both of which he was unsuccessful until the following year), and the Chancellor's Latin Essay (which he won). The latter's subject was *Quaenam sint Academiae erga Rempublicam officia*, 'The Duties the University Owes the State', and marked the start of Stanley's thinking about university reform. He was invited to read his essay at commemoration in July 1840. Arnold came to hear him and to see his friends Wordsworth and Chevalier Bunsen (the Prussian diplomat and scholar) receive honorary degrees. 'Arnold's coming up,' Stanley told Mary, 'being unable to resist the triple temptation of the honours to be conferred on Wordsworth, Bunsen, and – me!'[26] But the ceremony in the Sheldonian turned out to be a disappointment. The proceedings (which included Keble's tribute to Wordsworth) were lengthy and exhausting, and by the time it was Stanley's turn to take centre-stage the audience was already leaving.

Stanley was making friends with some at least of his new colleagues at University. He spoke of the kindness of Travers Twiss, who had been the driving force behind his election. Twiss had been a fellow since 1830 and was another polymath, examining in both mathematics and classics before becoming professor first of political economy and then of civil law. Like Arnold and Julius Hare, he was one of the few Englishmen at the time who could read German. In 1836 he had published a concise version of Barthold Niebuhr's *History of Rome*, a book which had a powerful influence on Arnold's approach to ancient history. Twiss married in 1863 and resigned his fellowship; nine years later he severed all links with old friends after allegations were made about his wife's sexual past.

Stanley had fortnightly walks with another fellow, William Donkin, whom he described as 'shy and silent, but very gentlemanlike, and I believe very clever'.[27] Donkin had been a scholar at University and was the first undergraduate of the college to win firsts in both literae humaniores and mathematics. He devoted himself to science and in 1842 became Savilian Professor of Astronomy. He was a keen amateur instrumentalist and, with the Oxford philologist Friedrich Max Müller, the host of popular musical evenings. A third fellow, Frederick William Faber, was the college's only prominent Tractarian. As an undergraduate he had been a devout Calvinist but was converted to Newmanism by Pusey's preaching. He and Stanley had occasional discussions, but unlike the mercurial Ward at Balliol, Faber had little influence on either undergraduates or fellows, and was indeed non-resident for most of the time. In 1845 he followed Newman and converted to Rome.

While staying at Herstmonceux during the summer vacation Stanley received a letter inviting him to join Tait in Bonn, where he was studying the German university system. It happened that Faber was on the Ostend steamer with Richard Church, then a fellow of Oriel and friend of Newman, and later the historian of the Oxford Movement and Dean of St Paul's. Stanley travelled with them by canal as far as Bruges. His frequent letters home were full of his descriptive eloquence and enthusiasm for travel and historic places. The Palais de Justice, with its historic associations; the procession of the host, with the Bishop of Bruges under a gilded canopy; the Hospital of St Jean, with its ark of relics and 'black-dressed sisters moving about from bed to bed'[28] – every detail was carefully recorded. From Bruges the three took a carriage to Ghent which Stanley found 'not so striking as Bruges – an unequal town, streets of convenience, not of majesty'.[29] From Ghent he travelled alone to Bonn via Liège, Aix and Cologne.

Stanley worked hard as Tait's research assistant. Tait was already full of ideas for reforming Oxford and he wanted to understand the workings of a very different university. The pair attended lectures and sermons, questioned professors and students, and joined and observed their social life. They discovered that there had been 300 duels that term and this struck Stanley (like much at University College) as 'more childish than anything else'.[30] When having his hair cut short, the barber supposed that it was 'to prevent my antagonist catching me by it when I fought'.[31] Stanley was not impressed by the general effect the university had on the students: 'They seem to have all the vices of schoolboys, with all the liberty of men, and no one, I should think, could doubt that it was a bad system.'[32] When they returned home, Tait wrote an anonymous pamphlet, with Stanley's help, entitled 'Hints on the Formation of a Plan for the Safe and Effectual Revival of the Professorial System at Oxford', published in November 1839.[33] The main recommendation was that after studying for their degree, undergraduates should remain at Oxford for a fourth year in order to attend professorial lectures. This would in turn free tutors from at least some of their college lecturing, enabling them to devote more time 'to the moral superintendence of their pupils'.[34]

* * *

After a twelve-month probationary period Stanley was obliged to be ordained if his fellowship was to become permanent. This worried him. He had felt for as long as he could remember that ordination would be the right step, but it was to him a sacred and solemn matter, and not to be undertaken lightly or hurriedly, and certainly not as a qualification for a secular profession. His conscience was troubled too about having to subscribe again to the Thirty-Nine Articles. He even thought for a time of exchanging his fellowship for the lay fellowship held by Faber, leaving him free to choose his own time for taking holy orders. But he abandoned the idea when the college allowed him to defer for six months until December 1839.

Arnold had imparted to Stanley his own conscientious understanding of ordination, in an age when for many young men orders were merely a matter of duty or worldly advantage. One of Arnold's sermons that Stanley had taken especially to heart was on the subject of vocation:

Some of you are old enough to inquire what is God's call to you, as to the choice of a profession; that is to say, what course of duty is pointed out to you by the particular dispositions and faculties of your minds ...

Family convenience, prospects of preferment, must not outweigh higher considerations; and this applies especially to that most solemn of all callings, and in which, above all others, worldly well-doing in it may be quite independent of the fitness of our hearts and minds for the discharge of its duties ... But how many do we see every day, who are wished, and who consent readily, to enter into Christ's spiritual warfare, to become ministers of Christ's Gospel, while their minds are wholly disinclined to heavenly knowledge, and their hearts without any relish for heavenly love ...

But you are young yet, and you may hope, that before the time comes when you will actually enter on the ministry, you may have gained that desire to know and to do God's will, and to save the souls of others, which as yet you cannot pretend to feel. Then if you have this hope, do your best to realise it; if you think that God does call you into his service, live as worthy of that call: at school and at university, if your friends' wishes and your own prepare you to enter hereafter into the ministry, see that you regard yourselves as vessels fashioned to honour, and to be preserved especially pure and bright for our heavenly Master's use.[35]

In a letter written ten years later, in which Stanley explained his own sense of a calling both to ordination and to academic life, it is clear that he had kept these ideals alive and tried to live up to them: 'The real thing which long ago moved me to wish to go into orders ... was the fact that God seemed to have given me gifts more fitting me for orders, and for that particular line of clerical duty which I have chosen, than for any other ... I hope I shall always feel ... that, in whatever work I am engaged now or hereafter, my great end ought always to be the good of the souls of others, and my great support, the good which God will give to my own soul.'[36]

Stanley's chief obstacle during the autumn months before ordination was subscription, and it caused him much anxiety and heart-searching. His wish not to exclude men from university on religious grounds had made him uneasy about subscribing as an undergraduate, but these feelings were now intensified by his sense of the greater demand for truth and a clear conscience imposed by ordination. Stanley's scruples focused on Article VIII, which declares that the Athanasian creed, with its assertion that those who do not assent to certain doctrinal definitions are damned, 'ought thoroughly to be received and believed'. Anathemas like these were contrary to Stanley's understanding of the all-embracing love of God, as was a creed that condemned every man, woman and child who was not an orthodox, catholic Christian. 'The Athanasian creed', wrote Prothero, 'was diametrically opposed to his own spirit of toleration and breadth of theological thought.'[37]

Stanley's agonising about whether or not he could subscribe became an obsession, aggravating his tendency to what he called his 'fatal irresolution',[38] and 'darkening with the shadow of exceeding gloom the most momentous period of his life'.[39] Stanley's friends urged him to put his scruples aside. Arnold had written from Fox How in June: 'My own answer must be clear to you from my own practice ... I read the Athanasian Creed, and have and would again subscribe the Article about it, because I do not conceive the clauses in question to be essential parts of it', and furthermore, 'Church subscriptions *must* be taken in their widest rather than in their strictest sense.'[40] Though Stanley was still troubled, he decided in November to present himself to the Archdeacon of Oxford as a candidate for ordination at Christmas. He was required to sit an examination and used it to raise his concerns. In answering the question, 'What are the tenets of the Church on the sufficiency of Scripture?', he contrived to tackle the question whether Article VIII refers only to the doctrines of the Athanasian creed, or also to the damnatory clauses. Writing to Mary, Stanley gave a verbatim account of his subsequent interview with the archdeacon:

> I am just returned from the Archdeacon. He sent for me this morning, and I went with a palpitating heart. I record the conversation as a standing memorial of the verdict of the authorities in the Diocese of Oxford on the censures of the Athanasian Creed.
>
> *Archdeacon.* Pray sit down, Mr Stanley; do you leave Oxford immediately after the ordination?
> *A.P.S.* Yes, sir.
> *Archdeacon.* I thought you might wish to see me on the point to which you adverted in your answers. *You need be under no apprehension about it; when several bishops have expressed their opinion, there can be no doubt that you may be at ease on the point.* You seem to have paid a good deal of attention to it.
> *A.P.S.* Yes, it gave me a great deal of anxiety and trouble, and I thought the fairest way was to state it at once fully in my answers.

Archdeacon. Oh! I am very glad that these points should be entered into. My own view on the three clauses is pretty much the same as yours. I don't think they ought to be considered as part of the Creed, but merely as anathemas which were then always affixed to any statement of doctrine.[41]

Stanley signed the following day, and on Sunday 22 December 1839 he was ordained deacon by the Bishop of Oxford, Dr Bagot, in Christ Church Cathedral. He told Mary that it turned out to be an altogether happier occasion than he had expected:

The ordination lasted from 10 till 2; the great number of the candidates of both orders (30 I think of each) made it very imposing, and nothing could be better arranged. It all floats before me like a dream. There was very little in the service with which I could not heartily sympathise; and the sermon[f] was happily such as hardly jarred with my own feelings on the subject even once. One of the most pleasing recollections I have throughout was hearing the voice of the Archdeacon breaking in from time to time in the service – the same voice which had in the conversation on Friday sanctioned my protest against the clauses. I feel as if I was gradually awaking into a new life; the old one really seems, and I hope I shall feel it to be, lying far behind, and separated from me by an impassable barrier. If anything could have added to the solemnity of the thing, or taken the sting out of the troubles of making the irrevocable step, it would have been the beautiful letter which I enclose to you from Arnold.[42]

Arnold reassured Stanley that when he was ordained in the same cathedral almost exactly twenty-one years before, he had experienced similar scruples and difficulties but had overcome them. He concluded, 'God bless you ever in this and in all your undertakings, through Jesus Christ.'[43]

Stanley went to Norwich for Christmas and stayed for six weeks. He spent most mornings in his room at the palace reading and writing at his standing-desk by the fireplace. At other times he began to put his deacon's orders into practice in the cathedral and in various churches in the diocese. He read prayers, administered communion and buried the

---

[f] Preached by Henry Liddell, then a tutor at Christ Church and later dean. He advised the ordinands to 'Avoid controversy, if possible. Few have ever entered into controversy without repenting of it.'

dead. His preaching does not appear to have been a success. After his first sermon in the village church at Bergh Apton two old women were overheard: 'Well I do feel empty-like!', said the first. 'And so do I,' replied the second, 'that young man doesn't give us much to feed on.'[44] Stanley admitted to Vaughan that he found preaching 'very unnatural and strange, a sort of being oneself and not oneself'.[45] It is clear in the same letter that he was still struggling with Tractarianism: 'The question is ... whether I shall be nothing whatever, except an obedient, quiet and so far happy, follower in the train of Newmanism or whether I shall be a great agitator in the cause of (some sort of) Reformation. I am in somewhat better spirits, but still in a horrid confused state.'[46]

Though Stanley's own worries about subscription had been eased, he wanted to do what he could to relieve others who experienced similar reservations. His father's chaplain, Canon Wodehouse, happened to be preparing a petition to the House of Lords to call attention to the discrepancy between the terms of subscription and the beliefs of the majority of clergymen. Wodehouse wanted Parliament to alter the words of the offending article and creed. Stanley argued against this, fearing that any revision might make subscription even more stringent. He hoped instead to provoke a discussion which would elicit from the bishops a declaration that they did not regard subscription as binding the conscience to a literal agreement with every clause. With some reluctance, Stanley added his signature to the petition which was presented to the Upper House in May 1840 by Arnold's Oriel friend Richard Whately, now Archbishop of Dublin. Stanley's father spoke in the debate, and with Arthur's help, emphasised the burden imposed by subscription on scrupulous consciences, and admitted: 'I never yet met with one single clergyman ... who allowed that he agreed in every point, in every iota, to the subscription which he took at ordination.'[47] But he was opposed by the Bishop of London, Charles Blomfield, who spoke with 'withering ferocity',[48] scuppering any chance of relaxing the terms of subscription. The petition was rejected.

* * *

Stanley was suffering again from nervous exhaustion, worn down by worries and scruples over ordination. With the freedom his fellowship allowed, he decided to spend the next ten months travelling on the Continent, the first of many long tours abroad. He left England with Tait on 10 July 1840, and with his pockets filled with books, he retraced his route to Bonn. From there, he travelled alone via Mayence,

Freiburg and Basle to Berne, teaching himself Italian on the way. When Stanley arrived at Freiburg he discovered that the Grand Duchess Stephanie was staying at her schloss a few miles away and he travelled by carriage to visit her. In Berne he found the theologian F. D. Maurice and his wife staying at the same hotel. Stanley had already been introduced to Maurice by Julius Hare, who had been his tutor at Trinity. Maurice had married John Sterling's sister-in-law, and after her death in 1845, he married Hare's sister (Hare was already married to Maurice's sister). Maurice had left Cambridge without a degree because he was not prepared to submit to the articles, though by the time Stanley met him in Switzerland, he was ordained and had just been appointed Professor of English Literature and History at King's College, London.

Stanley went the next day to stay at Chevalier Bunsen's house. Christian von Bunsen was a Lutheran friend of Arnold, Hare and Niebuhr, who had secured for him the post of secretary to the Prussian embassy in Rome, where he stayed for twenty-two years and became an expert in oriental languages. He was transferred then to Switzerland as minister. Stanley had met him a year ago in Oxford and then in London where they had discussed various theological questions. 'I never had so satisfactory a talk with any man,' he told Mary, ' – a most fortunate encounter.'[49] Again in Berne, Bunsen's conversation 'flowed like a fountain',[50] and topics included Swiss life, the condition of Italy and Rome, the renovation of Prussia, Church and State, and English national education. In private, Bunsen was passionately anti-Rome and showed Stanley his candle-snuffer. 'It was a hollow figure of a Jesuit with his arms folded and Bunsen's delight is to put him on the candlestick, and imagine him to say, as the smoke rises round him, "Thank Heaven, I have extinguished a light."'[51] Bunsen told him that on his last night in Rome he had taken his sons onto the balcony of their house and, like Hannibal, had made them look towards St Peter's and swear eternal enmity.

After a week with Bunsen, Stanley set off with Maurice to the Bernese Oberland where he was unimpressed by the mountain scenery. He went on to Geneva to meet Edward Goulburn, who had won a Balliol scholarship the year after Stanley and was about to take up a fellowship at Merton. He had been a boy at Eton and was to succeed Tait as Headmaster of Rugby. On 3 September they departed for Milan and spent five weeks among the lakes and towns of northern Italy. Stanley was enthralled by Venice, and his descriptions of the floating city are as vivid and captivating as any:

The Piazza is quite unrivalled. I shall never forget the first view, when we issued into it from a dark lane on a glorious day of Italian sunshine. It seemed as if, at one glance, the whole of Venetian history was unrolled before us. It was not beauty, nor magnificence alone, nor grotesqueness. We have been vainly searching after words to describe the peculiar effect. It is a sort of sublime quaintness – the work of a mighty child, with all the strange and lively fancies, and yet with none of the weakness or innocence of a child. The clock-tower with its two gigantic figures, the sea opposite with the ventures of Antonio, and the two granite columns from Tyre, surmounted by the winged lion, his wings and tail standing out in the clear blue sky, and by St. Theodore, the earliest patron-saint, with his right-handed shield and left-handed sword, standing on the amphibious crocodile; the long array of the ancient library, procuratory, and Ducal Palace, carved as if with a fantastic network, fretted with innumerable pinnacles, and shining through innumerable windows; the three red flagstaffs of the three subject kingdoms of Candia, Cyprus, and Morea; the red porphyry stone on which a banished man stood for two days in the presence of the people; the two marble columns from St. Jean d'Acre; the supposed statues of Harmodius and Aristogeiton; the pigeons, which are to Venice what the bears are to Berne, feeding by hundreds on the chequered pavement; the tall tower of the Campanile, and, above all, the gorgeous Church of St. Mark, with its six domes, its bright painted front, its four horses of Lysippus, its porphyry columns and brazen gates and winged lions ...[52]

This extract from a letter home illustrates Stanley's fascination with the historic and legendary significance of places. Architecture and natural scenery, on the other hand, were of little interest to him. The Alps, for instance, struck him as 'unformed, unmeaning lumps'.[53] But places connected with famous people, important events, colourful legends, or scenes in literature delighted and absorbed him. 'Where man had set his mark upon a place, there his interest was keen and his memory unerring.'[54] 'As a general rule,' wrote Bradley, 'he looks on nature not as a poetical interpreter of nature ... but as one who seems never to feel that he has thoroughly mastered any event, or chain of events, in human or sacred history, till he has seen the spot and breathed the air which give to such occurrence its peculiar and local colouring.'[55] Stanley was able to visualise the people and incidents of the past, and to see them in the place where they belonged; and, having done so, he had no wish to return. 'On the first sight of scenes of this sort', he explained, 'a whole new world opens before me; floods of thought come in which are indelible, and there is nothing new in a second visit.'[56] Stanley's longing to see notable places engendered an extraordinary enthusiasm for travel which mastered his physical frailties. Foreign travel in the nineteenth century was still a very uncomfortable and exhausting business but Stanley was rarely discouraged or wearied. Bradley refers to the 'insatiable avidity'[57] with which he would fatigue the most indefatigable of his fellow-travellers.

From Venice, Stanley and Goulburn travelled overland by carriage to Ancona where they took a steamer to Corfu. Stanley's brother Charles was stationed there as a lieutenant in the Royal Engineers and he took leave in order to accompany them to Greece. Here Stanley was thrilled to see the places he had absorbed from his long study of Greek history and literature, and indeed to find them very much as he had imagined them. 'Not only did almost every mile recall an ancient hero or poet, but it called up with me the more substantial form of a modern friend from England. The visions of the library at Rugby, and of the lecture-room at Balliol, were constantly blending themselves with the visions of battles, and temples, and oracles.'[58] Stanley and his companions visited Mycenae, Delphi, Corinth, Marathon, Olympia and Athens, which he found more familiar to him than any place in the world except Alderley. 'Scene after scene passed by as in a magic-lantern, and it was not till I went to bed, and lay awake for two hours in a fever of excitement, that I could believe I had seen the realities.'[59]

Stanley sailed on alone to Malta where he was put in quarantine for five days with a crowd of other young men whose language and drinking disgusted him. He travelled next to Naples where he met another friend, Hugh Pearson. Pearson had started at Balliol with Goulburn and was said to have combined an exceedingly ugly face with a heart of gold. He spent most of his life as a devoted parson in Sonning, a village on the Thames near Reading, and was often Stanley's travelling companion and confidant. After visiting Herculaneum and Pompeii the two journeyed to Sicily and Rome, which they reached in March 1841. Though for Stanley nothing in Italy compared with the glories of Greece, he did catch a glimpse of unrivalled papal splendour:

My first sight of the Pope[g] was at S. Maria, on the Feast of the

---

[g] Gregory XVI (1831–46).

Annunciation, when he goes there in state to give dowries to poor girls. There was nothing much in the prelude to his appearance, except the strangeness of seeing the whole church lined with the Papal guards, with their caps and plumes, and their lines only broken by the priests and monks running about to make preparations. At last, through this file, the procession began: cardinals, &c., &c., and, last of all, high in the air I saw the waving of enormous fans of white peacock feathers, which announced the coming of the great sight. Under these fans, raised on a chair on the shoulders of men, high above the heads of the people, wearing the triple crown, motionless as a corpse, except when his two fingers moved in blessing, his whole figure visible from head to foot, sat the Pope. The moment he appeared the whole congregation, guards, and people, fell on their knees, calling out, 'Benedice, Santo Padre.' It was a most impressive, almost an awful, sight to see the old man so very near, in such a tremendous position – the prostration of the people making his own exaltation more striking.[60]

Stanley stayed a month in Rome and then headed for France via Florence, Pisa, Genoa and Turin. He spent a week in Paris and arrived home in London on 26 May 1841, after nearly a year abroad.

* * *

Significantly it was while in Rome that Stanley heard about Tract XC, and what Newman called 'the immense commotion'[61] that had followed in its wake. 'O, my dear Belvedere,'[h] he wrote playfully to Tait, 'what have you been doing? Rome is only in a less state of excitement than Oxford ... What has happened? First comes a letter from London to Pearson, intimating that a Tract has appeared and that you are in a state of frenzy ... Pearson and I are in a state of ferment beyond bounds.'[62]

The ninetieth *Tract for the Times* had been published anonymously at the end of February 1841. The Oxford Movement's attempt to revive Catholic dogma and ritual, and regenerate the Church of England's understanding of itself as descended from the early apostolic Church, was encouraging an increasing number of its followers (Ward especially) to feel drawn towards Rome. This pull to the more obvious representative of the primitive church was intensified by the Protestant character of the Thirty-Nine Articles which outlawed such Romish

---

[h] Tait's sobriquet, derived from the resemblance of his curly hair to that of the Apollo Belvedere, an ancient marble sculpture in the Vatican museum.

doctrines as purgatory, transubstantiation, and the sacrifice of masses. For those Tractarians who were beginning to believe that there may after all be truth in these dogmas, Rome looked a more viable and welcoming prospect than Canterbury.

Newman's intention in writing Tract XC was to keep these followers in the Anglican fold by demonstrating that the articles were not in fact incompatible with Roman Catholic teaching. 'In the first place,' he wrote, 'it is a *duty* which we owe both to the Catholic Church and to our own, to take our reformed confessions in the most Catholic sense they will admit.'[63] He argued that while certain doctrines were condemned, the articles' intention was only to condemn the aberrations associated with them, and not the doctrines themselves. 'The Articles are not written against the creed of the Roman Church, but against actual existing errors in it.'[64]

Tait had never felt any sympathy towards Newman and his followers. In John Shairp's[i] opinion, 'his Scotch nature and education, his Whig principles and, I may add, the evangelical views which he had imbibed, were wholly antipathetic to this movement ... To his downright common sense the whole movement seemed nonsense, or at least the madness of incipient Popery.'[65] Now the Popery had become far more than incipient and, with three other Oxford tutors,[j] Tait wrote a protest to the editor of the tracts which was published in the *The Times*: 'The Tract has, in our apprehension, a highly dangerous tendency, from its suggesting that certain very important errors of the Church of Rome are not condemned by the Articles of the Church of England[k] ... but only certain absurd practices and opinions which intelligent Romanists repudiate as much as we do.'[66] The four tutors were especially concerned that if the tract's principles were generally recognised, 'the most plainly erroneous doctrines and practices of the Church of Rome' would be 'inculcated in the lecture-rooms of the University'.[67] A few days later the hebdomadal board censured the tract, and the Bishop of Oxford asked for the series to be discontinued. Newman agreed to the request immediately.

Stanley got to hear of all this through Tait's letters, and he expressed his own views in his replies. With perhaps his ordination sermon in mind, he was glad that goodwill had been preserved during the storm.

---

[i] Shairp came to Balliol in 1840 as a Snell Exhibitioner and after teaching at Rugby was Principal of St Andrews and Professor of Poetry at Oxford.

[j] T. T. Churton of Brasenose, H. B. Wilson of St John's, and J. Griffiths of Wadham.

[k] The protest mentions purgatory, pardons, the worship of images and relics, the invocation of saints, and the mass.

He was concerned (as he had been in Norwich) that in reacting to the tract, the articles themselves might be too tightly defined, and that that in turn might exclude not just Roman Catholics. Writing from Genoa at the beginning of May, Stanley admitted that he saw no reason against Roman Catholics becoming Anglicans, though he admitted that this would be impracticable. Here again Stanley expressed his own inclusive, comprehensive ideal of the Church of England, an ideal he had derived first from Arnold but had extended. The day after arriving in London, Stanley wrote similarly to Pearson: 'I have read No. 90 and almost all its consequences. The result clearly is, that Roman Catholics may become members of the Church and universities of England, which I for one cannot deplore.'[68]

Ward thought that Newman had been too cautious and compromising. To clarify matters he wrote two pamphlets, *A Few Words –* and *A Few Words More – in Defence of Tract 90*, in which, rather than supporting the tract, he insisted that the framers of the articles were not in truth Roman in sympathy but Protestant. That meant, he said, that some at least of Newman's interpretations in the tract were forced. Furthermore, while Newman denied that the articles were a difficulty for Catholics, Ward emphasised that indeed they were, though the difficulty was not insurmountable.

Ward's sympathy with the Roman Church was unmistakable in both pamphlets. Tait withdrew his invitation to join him as a tutor at Balliol, and tried to persuade the master that his Roman bias made him unfit for his lectureships in logic and mathematics. Jenkyns liked Ward as much as he disliked theological controversy, and was reluctant to concede to Tait's demands. 'Tait was the great mover against Ward,' wrote Stanley, 'and they are still on perfectly good terms with each other. The master shed tears in the final interview, and is very much disturbed about it; it is said that he is overheard grumbling to himself, "I wish Mrs. Jenkyns would take care of the flowers instead of the cabbages," ... and then in the next breath, "I wish Mr. Ward would not write such pamphlets."'[69] Ward eased the master's plight by resigning: 'Really, Ward,' he responded, 'this is just like your generosity.'[70] Stanley despaired of Oxford's animosity, regretting Ward's loss of £250 a year, and fearing more 'turning out of tutorships' and 'keeping out of fellowships'[71] on religious grounds. He dreaded what seemed to be Ward's next, inevitable step, and even thought of leaving Oxford behind and moving to Durham.

* * *

On the day Stanley arrived back in London after his travels, the leader of the opposition, Sir Robert Peel, defeated Melbourne's ministry after a fierce debate on the budget. Nine days later Peel obtained a majority of one on a vote of no-confidence. The Government tottered on for a while, and in a scene reminiscent of the opening pages of *Barchester Towers*, Dr Nares, the Regius Professor of Modern History at Oxford, collapsed and died. He was seventy-nine and had occupied the chair for nearly thirty years. Would Melbourne's ministry last long enough for him to appoint a Whig as Nares's successor, or would Peel be given the chance to appoint a Tory?

Stanley's father had been working hard since his enthronement to persuade the Whigs to offer Arnold a plum piece of preferment. He suggested to Melbourne that he give him a canonry at Christ Church or Durham, or any deanery worth £1,000 or more. But after the fracas over Hampden, Melbourne was nervous about appointing Arnold: 'I have, as you know,' he wrote, 'a high opinion of Dr Arnold ... but [he] has published some indiscreet opinions.'[72] Nonetheless, in his last week in office when he had nothing more to lose, Melbourne offered Arnold the regius chair.

Stanley had wondered for a moment whether he himself might have been a candidate, but this was unrealistic, and he realised that it would have meant 'a burden of labour and responsibility greater than I could have borne'.[73] He was surprised, but of course delighted, that Arnold's abilities had at last been recognised, and that he had been given an opportunity to return to Oxford where his name was subject to abuse and misapprehension. Stanley was also glad for himself that he would be able to sit at Arnold's feet again, and he looked forward to his lectures as 'the advent of a fresh invigorating breeze across a parched and sultry plain'.[74] He hoped that Arnold's energy and convictions would not only revive the professorial system, but also provide a compelling counterpoise to the doctrines of the Oxford Movement.

Arnold wrote to Stanley for advice on 'the best line to choose for my lectures',[75] and to reassure him that, though he would not humour his audience or decline to speak the truth, he would not strike a hostile note or 'seek occasions of shocking men's favourite opinions'.[76] One of the advantages of this chair for Arnold was that it was not residential, so he was able to combine it with Rugby. The inaugural lecture was to be given on 2 December 1841, and Arnold and his wife travelled by train to Oxford and returned the same day. They were accompanied by their two older children, Jane and Matthew (who had just finished his first term at Balliol), as well as by Stanley and Clough. Stanley did not have the conversation he was hoping for because Arnold spent the entire journey correcting examination papers.

In his first lecture Arnold challenged any hard and fast line between the civilisations of Greece and Rome, and the progress of what was called modern history. Stanley's various accounts of it in letters and in the biography are full of his own excitements. Here is part of a letter he wrote two days later to a Rugby friend, John Simpkinson:

> Every one who loves Arnold ought to have been present at the august scene of his Inaugural Lecture last Thursday, and if you were not there in the body, I feel bound, so far as in me lies, to make you so in mind.
>
> The usual place is a small room in the Clarendon Buildings; but fortunately we had so far anticipated the amount of the audience as to secure the Sheldonian Theatre. But the numbers were far more than any one could have expected, far more than any professor has addressed in Oxford since the Middle Ages.
>
> Imagine that beautiful building with the whole of the area and the whole of the lower gallery completely filled; the Vice-Chancellor in state; the Professor himself distinguished from the rest by his full red Doctorial robes. It was certainly one of the most glorious days of my life; to listen once more to that clear, manly voice in the relation of a pupil to a teacher, to feel that one of the most important Professorships was filled by a man with genius and energy capable of discharging its duties, to see him standing in his proper place at last and receiving the homage of the assembled University, was most striking and most touching. The lecture lasted just an hour. It was listened to with the deepest attention, and began and closed with a burst of general applause.[77]

Arnold was required to deliver an annual series of eight lectures during the first three weeks of the Lent Term, and a further three lectures on biography. He returned to Oxford therefore in January and rented a house on Beaumont Street to accommodate his family. On 2 February he met his arch-rival, Newman. They found themselves sitting next to each other at a gaudy in Oriel where Newman still held the fellowship he had inherited from Arnold. According to Stanley, 'they talked on different matters, and got on very well together.'[78] Newman reminded Arnold that there had in fact been a previous encounter fourteen years before when Arnold was examined for the degree of bachelor of divinity. He realised that on that occasion he had mistaken Newman for Pusey. Nearly fifty years later, Arnold's son Tom recalled his father's account of the meeting: 'I recollect as well as if it were yesterday how pleased and radiant dear Papa looked when he came back to the Beaumont Street lodgings, and how he described Newman's cordiality (which was evidently more than he quite expected).'[79]

The lectures made frequent use of phrases like 'if I am allowed to resume these Lectures next year', 'if life and health be spared me', 'if God shall permit' and, looking back, it was evident to Stanley that Arnold had a 'sense of his coming fate'.[80] On Sunday 12 June 1842, four months after the final lecture, Arnold died suddenly of a heart attack aged forty-six. He had awoken early that morning with a sharp pain across his chest. The pain grew more severe and the doctor was summoned. He arrived at a quarter to seven, applied remedies and explained that Arnold was suffering a spasm of the heart. When asked whether any of his family had ever had disease of the chest, Arnold replied that his father had died of it at fifty-three. Tom Arnold was called to the bedside. The pain returned and Arnold asked whether his condition was fatal. 'Generally,' replied the doctor. He prepared laudanum but before he could administer it Arnold suffered a final and violent attack. The other children in the house were sent for but their father was no longer conscious. After a heaving of the chest and deep gasps Arnold breathed his last.

Stanley was in London when later that day he heard the news of what he described as 'this dreadful calamity'.[81] He was completely overwhelmed and took to his bed for the rest of the day. He set off for Rugby the next morning and arrived at eight-thirty in the evening. He wrote to Mary the following day to describe 'the bitterness of waking this morning to the sight of this place with the thought that he who was its light and life is gone!'[82] Stanley wrote to her again on Wednesday, and the letter shows that he was already trying to make sense of the tragedy, and to see signs of good in it. Nonetheless, though 'the exclusiveness and vehemence of my veneration had naturally been abated by years, I feel that I never saw, or shall see, his like again. Others, abler and better and wiser I may meet of course, but none who can stand in the same relation to me – none whose position and qualities so combined to attract respect and love.'[83] In a letter to Pearson three days later, he described the calamity as 'the greatest that ever has – almost the greatest that ever can befall me.'[84]

As soon as Stanley arrived at Rugby he collected every detail, not only of Arnold's last hours but his last days and weeks as well. Lake was staying with the family when Arnold died, and had spent the previous evening walking with him in the garden, discussing interpretations of the eucharist. Lake had much to tell Stanley, as did Mrs Arnold who later wrote down everything she could remember. Stanley also spoke to the doctor, who gave a full account of Arnold's last hour and of the family's grief. Stanley conveyed all this immediately to Mary, albeit in a form that he admitted was 'broken and indistinct'.[85] By the time he came to tell the story of Arnold's last days in his biography, he had become convinced that Arnold had had intimations of his own mortality, and that there was divine purpose and meaning in this untimely death of an unusually virtuous and faithful man. This interpretation was, of course, a profound personal comfort to him. Furthermore, the combination in his narrative of detailed description and unfolding drama helps to make the death scene one of the finest in any biography. Arnold's last weeks take eleven pages to reach the promised end:

> The physician then quitted the house for medicine, leaving Mrs. Arnold now fully aware from him of her husband's state. At this moment she was joined by her son, who entered the room with no serious apprehension, and, on his coming up to the bed, his father, with his usual gladness of expression towards him, asked, 'How is your deafness, my boy?' (he had been suffering from it the night before) – and then, playfully alluding to an old accusation against him, 'You must not stay here; you know you do not like a sick-room.' He then sat down with his mother at the foot of the bed, and presently his father said in a low voice: 'My son, thank God for me;' and as his son did not at once catch his meaning, he went on, saying – 'Thank God, Tom, for giving me this pain; I have suffered so little pain in my life, that I feel it is very good for me: now God has given it to me, and I do so thank Him for it.'... Meanwhile his wife, who still had sounding in her ears the tone in which he had repeated the passage from the Epistle to the Hebrews, again turned to the Prayer Book, and began to read the Exhortation, in which it occurs in the 'Visitation of the Sick'. He listened with deep attention, saying emphatically – 'Yes,' at the end of many of the sentences. 'There should be no greater comfort to Christian persons than to be made like unto Christ.' – 'Yes.' 'By suffering patiently troubles, adversities, and sickness.' – 'Yes.' 'He entered not into His glory before He was crucified.' – 'Yes.' At the

words 'everlasting life,' she stopped, and his son said, – 'I wish, dear Papa, we had you at Fox How.' He made no answer, but the last conscious look, which remained fixed in his wife's memory, was the look of intense tenderness and love with which he smiled upon them both at that moment.[86]

Arnold died on the morning of the last day of the school year. The news spread quickly, and was met by the masters and boys with bewilderment and agitated enquiries. Arnold's nine children, aged seven to twenty-one, had been left fatherless. Matthew and two of his sisters had already started their holiday at Fox How, and Lake was despatched to break the news and bring them back to Rugby: he did so on what would have been their father's birthday. Matthew, Stanley and William Hall, an Oxford friend of Arnold, went to Rugby's chapel to decide exactly where Arnold should be buried. They chose a place in the vault under the chancel and facing the altar. The funeral took place at noon on Friday, led from Arnold's stall by the rector of Rugby, with the chapel draped in black. This was the first funeral Stanley had attended. The night before, he had gone with Matthew to Arnold's room:

> The coffin was on the floor – otherwise, all as it was when he died, as it was the last time but one that I saw him ... The window opens to the school-field, commanding a glimpse of the Shuckburgh Hills over the trees – the only distant view about Rugby, and one, therefore, in which he especially delighted ... Matt and I knelt down by the coffin, and I said a short prayer for us both.[87]

The following Sunday Stanley took the services in the chapel, attended by the family. In the afternoon he read the last of Arnold's sermons that he had heard as a boy: the subject was faith triumphant in death.[1] 'I knew it was very applicable, but when I came to read it aloud in the Chapel it was quite startling ... I hear that at the end of it Mrs. Arnold looked up with a gleam on her face, not of comfort, but of happiness – the first they have seen.'[88] The next Wednesday, just ten days after Arnold's death, the family left their Rugby home for the last time. Stanley went with them to the station. 'I felt when the bell rang for their departure, and the train whizzed off, that the last act of this sad week was over.'[89]

---

[1] Preached at Rugby on 5 December 1841; Stanley had returned from Oxford with Arnold after his inaugural lecture.

5
'O for ... the Sound of a Voice that is Still!'
1842–1851

ARNOLD'S DEATH LEFT two important positions unfilled – the headmastership of Rugby and Oxford's regius chair of modern history. Though only twenty-six, Stanley was a potential candidate for both. He put his name forward for the professorship because Arnold had once expressed a hope that he would follow him. 'I shall stand', he wrote to Pearson, 'rather from a duty to our departed father than from any love of the office itself. My tangible claims are my Honours and my English Essay, and I suppose having been a pupil of Arnold's will now be a recommendation rather than otherwise, even with Peel.'[1] But he admitted to Mary that the post was probably out of his reach: he was not appointed.[2]

Filling Arnold's shoes at Rugby was much more difficult because, in the minds of so many masters and former pupils, Arnold and Rugby had become confused. 'Whether in the school itself,' wrote Stanley in the biography, 'or in its after effects, the one image we have before us is not Rugby, but ARNOLD.'[3] When it came to finding a successor, Bradley thought there was 'a sort of inflated idea that Rugby was the centre of the world, and that no one but a man of genius could preside over it'.[4] Not surprisingly, Stanley's closeness to Arnold and his academic reputation made him a popular choice with many of the most prominent masters and Rugbeians. But Stanley was aware of what he called his 'tremendous deficiencies'[5] and did not apply.

Only a brave or foolish man would have dared to put on what Lake called 'that giant's armour'.[6] Nonetheless, there were eighteen candidates, among them Stanley's schoolfriend, Charles Vaughan, who was now an incumbent in Leicester; his tutor, Archibald Tait; and Bonamy Price, who had been a pupil of Arnold at Laleham and then for a decade on his Rugby staff. Arnold's family wanted Julius Hare to apply but he too declined. Stanley took a keen and active interest in the contest, but a combination of intensity and irresolution indicates that he was still deep in the throes of bereavement. He found it hard at first to choose between Tait and Vaughan. On balance he supported Tait (and had indeed encouraged him to apply) but he began to think him an inferior scholar to Vaughan. He tried then to get Tait to withdraw. When Tait's appointment was announced at the end of July, Stanley was filled with guilt and sorrow for his own 'mess of misunderstanding'.[7] The extraordinary letter he wrote to Tait reveals both his continuing pain at Arnold's passing, and his deep regret that there could be no one worthy to take his place:

> The awful intelligence of your election has just reached me ... I have not heart to say more than that I conjure you by your friendship for me, your reverence for your great predecessor, your sense of the sacredness of your office, your devotion to Him whose work you are now more than ever called upon to do, to lay aside every thought for the present except that of repairing your deficiencies ... Read Arnold's sermons. At whatever expense of orthodoxy (so called) for the time, throw yourself thoroughly into his spirit. Alter nothing at first. See all that is good and nothing that is bad in the masters and the Rugby character.[8]

Stanley wrote again a few days later: 'Forgive me, if in the first agony of distress, when your election brought before me what I had lost – not only in him at Rugby, but in you at Oxford – I may have spoken too sadly. You must not expect that I could go scatheless through so terrible a convulsion as this has been.'[9]

Tait's appointment was announced when Stanley was staying with Hare, helping him to prepare for publication the last volume of Arnold's *History of Rome*. From Herstmonceux he travelled to Leicester to commiserate with Vaughan, and then on to Rugby where the school was reassembling. Seeing Tait for the first time in Arnold's study was 'overpowering'. 'It was true that the rightful master was gone; but I rejoiced to think that his labours were over, that the School would now meet, and he would feel no more vexation or anxiety about it from this time forward for ever. And then when I turned to look at his successor, I really felt that there was a moral dignity about him, and a consciousness of the shadow of the past which in itself fitted him for his great position, and held out the happiest prospect for the future.'[10]

The main service on the first Sunday of the term, 14 August 1842, was dedicated to the memory of Arnold, and since Tait had not known him well, Stanley was asked to preach. He was reluctant and found it a difficult assignment. 'The whole service of the Chapel', he wrote, 'was most awful. Tait sitting in the old place, all the boys assembled, and the pulpit and desks hung with black, made a confusion of past and present that one could not understand.'[11] Stanley was not pleased with the sermon though the sixth form expressed their approval. This is surprising because, even by Victorian standards, the eulogy was long as well as repetitive and rambling, revealing a disturbed, grief-stricken state of mind. It was hastily published and Stanley was not able to revise the proof-sheets. 'I hate the sight of it;' he told Pearson, 'it has been a horrible mess altogether, bred out of the confusion of the last two dreadful months.'[12]

* * *

Three months before Arnold's death Stanley had been appointed college lecturer (praelector) in Latin. In July he moved from the poet Shelley's[a] old rooms into a set on the top floor of University College's New Building, with views from the front onto the High Street, and from the back onto the fellows' garden. On the ground floor beneath him was Stanley's lecture-room, which he found damp and sparsely furnished. However, 'the only unpleasant part I find in my lectures', he wrote, 'is the total absence of any expression of feeling in the faces of my twelve auditors. Not a shadow of joy or sorrow ever passes over their immovable features.'[13]

Although lecturers had a lower status than tutors, and tended to teach only one part of the curriculum,[b] the two positions were much the same in that lecturers and tutors were only required to lecture. This was how undergraduates were taught, with two or more college lectures a day. Richard Whately described a college lecture in 1831:

> Let the stranger to Oxford imagine a long table, spread with books, maps, or mathematical diagrams, as the occasion may require, and thronged with students, generally from the age of sixteen to twenty-one; and at the head of this class (usually from five to fifteen in number), a master of arts presiding, and conducting the business ... If the subject of a lecture be a classical author, the several members of the class are called on in turn, to translate a portion; questions are put by the tutor, as occasion offers, and

---

[a] Shelley arrived as a scholar in autumn 1810 and was expelled the following March after writing a pamphlet on *The Necessity of Atheism*.
[b] Latin, Greek or mathematics. Tutors often taught the whole range of classical subjects, as well as divinity.

remarks are made by him, on points of grammar, philology, and criticism, as well as on the subject-matter of the book, whether it be history, philosophy or poetry. At the same time, directions are given, as often as may be needful, respecting the method of preparing for these lectures, the books to be consulted, method of analysing and illustrating, and the like ...[14]

Whately gives an idealised depiction which was rarely achieved. It is true that lectures were more like old-fashioned, text-centred school lessons, but the poor quality of many tutors and their pupils meant that they were often rowdy and fruitless affairs. Mr Verdant Green, the eponymous and gullible hero of Cuthbert Bede's comic varsity novel, was lectured at Brazenface College by Mr Slowcoach and the eccentric and short-sighted Rev. Richard Harmony. 'His infirmities, instead of being regarded with sympathy ... were, to Mr. Verdant Green's surprise, much imposed upon; for it was a favourite pastime with the gentlemen who attended Mr. Harmony's lectures to gradually raise up the lecture table by a concerted action, and when Mr. Harmony's book had nearly reached the level of his nose, to then suddenly drop the table to its original level'.[15] Mark Pattison had found his tutor at Oriel incapable of explaining any difficulty in Aristotle's *Rhetoric* and barely capable of translating the Greek.[16]

Some of the texts Stanley used for teaching have been preserved,[17] and it is clear from their detailed and ingenious annotations that he approached the task with unusual energy and care. His copy of the *History* of Herodotus includes notes which are often colour-coded, and the text of Aristotle's *Politics* is similarly underlined with coloured crayons. 'How well two or three of us remember that well-marked Herodotus which he freely lent us,' wrote Bradley. 'It had its special marks in coloured lines to indicate, first, passages noteworthy for the Greek; secondly, passages bearing on Greek history, or on the time of Herodotus; thirdly, passages containing truths for all time.'[18] In lecturing on the *Politics*, Stanley advised his pupils to do the same, and to use red for enduring truths, blue for the truths of Aristotle's time, and ('with a humorous twinkle of his eye')[19] black for truths for the schools.

In December 1843 Stanley was ordained priest and appointed a tutor. Like his friend Jowett at Balliol, Stanley was determined to do more for his pupils than lecture. Both men had been influenced as undergraduates by the example of Tait (whom Jowett had succeeded). Though Tait had had no time for Newman's theological views, he had shared his vision of the tutor's role as pastoral, moral and spiritual, and not just formal and academic. Furthermore, Stanley's conscientious approach to the duties of ordination reinforced this novel approach to tutoring. 'We walked with Stanley, sometimes took our meals with him,' wrote Bradley,

> – frugal meals, for he was at the mercy of an unappreciative college servant, who was not above taking advantage of … his indifference to any article of diet other than brown bread and butter; we talked with him over that brown bread and butter with entire freedom, opened our hearts to him; while his perfect simplicity, no less than his high-bred refinement, made it impossible to dream that any one in his sober senses could presume upon his kindness… We always knew that he treated us and felt to us as a friend; cared for us, sympathised with us, gave us his heart, and not his heart only, but his best gifts; that we did not sit below the salt, but partook with him of all that he had to give; and what he gave us was just that which was most calculated to win and attract, as well as to inspire and stimulate.[20]

Stanley used his afternoon rambles to get to know the undergraduates, as well as to excite their intellects, and help prepare them for their examinations. His conversations ranged widely, and he often spoke with such enthusiasm that it was wise to walk on the side of the road. 'His sympathy with his pupils and absorption in his subject was so great that, otherwise, he would keep drawing nearer and nearer to his companion, until he drove the inside member of the party into the ditch.'[21] Stanley showed considerable kindness and generosity to pupils who were struggling or in trouble. He was quick to write them letters of sympathy or advice, and he even administered medicines when they were ill. He was also ready to give money to those who could not, perhaps, afford a holiday, and he would do so with sensitivity: 'One line to say that, supposing a prolonged expedition would not interfere with your reading, but is impeded by want of supplies, you must not let that be an obstacle, but, on the same conditions of silence, &c. as before, regard me as "the Ural Mountains", and see Prague or whatever it may be. I should lament your losing the sight of it when it had been in my power to help you to it.'[22]

Stanley set a new standard as a tutor, and by the end of the 1840s University had become a very different college from the idle, athletic and mildly dissolute place that Bradley found when he arrived at the start of the decade. In a letter to Pearson in 1843, Stanley had expressed his hope to elevate his pupils' minds 'above that atmosphere of childishness and frivolity which is the curse of our College'.[23] Better quality applicants (many from Rugby) were attracted by the college's growing reputation, a trend started in October 1842 when Arnold's son Tom arrived as a scholar (Matthew had gone up to Balliol the year before). Better tutoring and clever undergraduates meant improved results. In 1844, for instance, two of the four firsts in literae humaniores were awarded to University men, and three others achieved seconds. The firsts went to George Bradley and Edward Plumptre, nephew of the master, who also won the only double-first[c] that year.

* * *

Alongside his work as a tutor Stanley was writing his *Life of Arnold*. It was, he told Julius Hare, hard and anxious labour,[24] and apart from a week's visit to Paris with Vaughan in July 1843, it absorbed every moment he could spare from his college duties.

Mrs Arnold invited Stanley to write a memoir almost as soon as her husband had been buried. As a schoolboy he had imagined himself doing just this and he accepted immediately. He followed her to Ambleside, and he and William Lake took lodgings close to Fox How. There he began the task of reading through Arnold's journals and letters, and sometimes Mrs Arnold read them aloud to him. He discovered new aspects of Arnold's character and thinking, and found the experience exhilarating. 'If', he wrote, 'I am not able to make out of (Arnold's papers) one of the most remarkable biographies that has appeared for a long time, it will be my fault, not theirs.'[25]

Dr Johnson complained that biography had often been allotted to writers who seemed scarcely acquainted with the nature of their task, or were negligent about its performance.[26] That could certainly not be said of Stanley. He may not have written a biography or any book before, but his reading had included a range of biographical literature. At Rugby he had studied parts of Xenophon's *Memorabilia* of Socrates and Plutarch's *Parallel Lives* of Greeks and Romans, as well as Walton's *Lives* of Donne and Herbert. He had also read Boswell's exemplary *Life of Samuel Johnson*, Southey's *Life of Nelson* and, at Balliol, he had tackled Lockhart's seven volume *Life of Sir Walter Scott* ('second only to Boswell in the art of biography').[27] It is instructive to compare these

---

[c] both classics and mathematics, taken in the same term.

last three *Lives* with Stanley's own biography, and trace any influences they might have had.

First, Southey's graphic description of the wounded hero's last, dark hours below the decks of *Victory* would have impressed any schoolboy reader, and would have shown Stanley the importance of a moving and well-written death scene. Secondly, Lockhart followed Boswell's semi-autobiographical method by weaving into his narrative letters, diaries, writings and (supremely) conversations, in order to allow his subject to speak for himself. Stanley adopts something of the same method, though rather than incorporating Arnold's correspondence into his text, he reproduces the letters at the end of chapters. This is less satisfactory but nonetheless the same intention is there as it is in Boswell and Lockhart. Thirdly, both these biographers were determined not to be panegyrists but to include vices as well as virtues. Stanley's biography has been accused of hero-worship but this is not the case. His admiration for his subject is unavoidable, but he makes a determined effort to remain impersonal and unbiased, and he too is prepared to include words and incidents that illustrate Arnold's less attractive characteristics. And last, Stanley's clear and direct style also seems indebted to the examples of Boswell and Lockhart, both of whom are masters of simple, translucent prose.

Stanley told Pearson that there were times when the biography hung like a millstone round his neck,[28] and he used to say later that it was the hardest thing he had done in his life. He was relieved when *The Life and Correspondence of Thomas Arnold, D.D.* was published in two volumes on 31 May 1844. It was an instant success. The first edition of a thousand copies sold out in three weeks, and before the end of June, Stanley was at work on the second. A third edition was called for in November, and the sixth edition was published in 1846.

Since Newman was often mentioned, Stanley sent him a copy, and in reply he 'expressed most kindly interest in it all through'.[29] Like other opponents who disliked and mistrusted Arnold, Newman discovered a more pious and humble man than he had perceived. Stanley confessed 'to having an almost restless desire to hear what is said about the book, not I really believe from vanity, but because it does give me such intense pleasure, as it always did, to find that dear Arnold is known and loved, and that the great labour, I might almost say agony, of the last two years has not been thrown away.'[30]

Arnold's lesser known work as Headmaster of Rugby was now publicised, and that account, told intimately and sympathetically by

Stanley, helped to create a more balanced understanding of his character and achievement. This aspect of the biography also had a considerable impact on the teaching profession, as Arnold's example inspired subsequent generations of schoolmasters. In a sermon in Balliol chapel after Stanley's death, Benjamin Jowett explained that 'through the influence of this book Arnold may be said to have lived after his death more truly than in his life, for there is no public school in the kingdom which has not been profoundly affected by the picture which the disciple drew of his beloved teacher and friend.'[31] It was Stanley's *Life* that established Arnold's unrivalled reputation as a headmaster, not *Tom Brown's Schooldays* published thirteen years later.

The effort required for the *Life of Arnold* exhausted Stanley, and there is a view that, though at twenty-eight he had established an enviable literary reputation, he never again achieved anything of such quality.[d] The process certainly had a cathartic effect and allowed him to close a very important chapter in his life. Reading everything that Arnold had written, assembling facts and the opinions of others, spending weeks every holiday at Fox How with the family and talking to Mrs Arnold, selecting and interpreting his material, and then straining in his writing to remain detached so as 'to describe a man to those who did not know him that they shall really understand him'[32] – all this biographer's work required Stanley to stand back from the man he had once adored. Writing the *Life* did not disillusion him (his feelings of gratitude and reverence remained strong for the rest of his life), but he was no longer in thrall, the spell had been broken, and he was free to develop his own ideas and convictions. From Stanley's point of view it was perhaps a blessing that Arnold had died so young.

* * *

Immediately after the *Life* was published, Stanley found himself embroiled in another round of *odium theologicum*. Ward's *The Ideal of a Christian Church Considered* was published in June 1844. Its 600 turgid pages comprised an outspoken and uncompromising attack on the Church of England, and a passionate and unqualified defence of the Roman Catholic Church. The hostility of bishops and university to Tract XC three years before had hardened the hearts of the more extreme Tractarians against the English Church, and driven them

---

[d] This was Jowett's opinion: 'The Life of Arnold written before he was [29] was his greatest real success.'

further into the arms of Rome. 'The restoration of active communion with that Church', wrote Ward, 'is the most enchanting earthly prospect on which my imagination can dwell.'³³ Ward had been harrying Newman to admit that the Thirty-Nine Articles were in truth Protestant in spirit and intention, and that the Roman Church was the only true descendant of primitive Christianity. Newman objected to being driven by Ward's logic faster and further than he and his followers were ready to go, and this in turn increased Ward's frustration. *The Ideal of a Church* threw down the gauntlet, and challenged the authorities to declare finally whether or not assent to Roman dogma was compatible with subscription to the articles. Ward still hoped that it might be, provided the articles could be interpreted in a non-literal sense, but he doubted that Oxford would agree.

Ward was summoned to appear before the hebdomadal board in November, and asked to withdraw six of the most extreme passages in his book. He refused, and ten days later the vice-chancellor published a notice giving details of the intended proceedings. The extracts were given in full, and included 'I know no single movement in the Church, except Arianism in the fourth century,ᵉ which seems to be so wholly destitute of all claims on our sympathy and regard as the English Reformation', and 'We find, oh most joyful, most wonderful, most unexpected sight, we find the whole cycle of Roman doctrine gradually possessing numbers of English Churchmen.'³⁴ It was proposed that convocation be summoned on Thursday 13 February 1845 to pass a resolution to the effect that the passages were inconsistent with the Thirty-Nine Articles and with Ward's subscription to them. If passed, a second resolution was to follow to degrade Ward – in other words, to deprive him of the degrees which had been conferred on the strength of his subscription. A third measure consisted of a test by which, as Stanley explained nearly forty years later, 'it was asserted that the articles for the future must be accepted, not according to the subtle explanations of the nineteenth century, but according to the rigid definitions of the sixteenth.'³⁵ Stanley was contemptuous of convocation and disgusted by this whole affair: had it been the sixteenth century, he observed, 'just the same men, with just the same arguments, would have been voting, not for degradation, but for burning.'³⁶

The third resolution was resisted by both Tractarians and Broad

---

ᵉ Arius's teaching that God the Son was subordinate to God the Father was condemned by the Council of Nicaea in 325.

Churchmen, who opposed any erosion of the Church of England's latitude in matters of belief. Were the resolution to be passed, it would exclude liberals like Hampden and Whately, as well as Ward and the more extreme Tractarians. Tait wrote and published a letter to the vice-chancellor to approve of the proceedings against Ward (whose liberty he said had degenerated into licence), but to condemn the test. 'There is no need of our narrowing the limits of the Church of England because some amongst us wish to make it too wide.'[37] The test was withdrawn, though a resolution was substituted to censure Tract XC, in which Newman had argued that the articles were actually consistent with Roman dogma: an opinion Ward thought disingenuous.

The meeting of convocation was as bitter and intense as it had been when Hampden had been 'tried' ten years before. This time Stanley was present, and has left a dramatic account of events which he obviously enjoyed:

> At last came the memorable day, which must be regarded as the closing scene of the conflict of the first Oxford movement. It was February 13, St. Valentine's Eve. It was a day in itself sufficiently marked by the violent passions seething within Oxford itself, and aggravated to the highest pitch by the clergy and laity of all shades and classes who crowded the colleges and inns of Oxford for the great battle of Armageddon, which was to take place in the Convocation of Oxford that day assembled in the Sheldonian theatre ... The excitement of the day was yet more fiercely accentuated by one of the most tremendous snow storms which had down to that time taken place within the memory of man. Fast and thick fell the flakes amidst the whirlwinds which snatched them up and hurried them to and fro ... The undergraduates, who ardently participated in the excitement of their seniors, watched the procession, as it passed under their windows, with mingled howls and cheers; and one of them, of more impetuosity than the rest, climbed to the top of the Radcliffe Library, and from that secure position pelted the Vice-Chancellor with a shower of snowballs to testify his detestation of the obnoxious measure.[38]

The proceedings were all in Latin, though Ward was permitted to defend himself in English. He spoke for over an hour, and began by questioning the legality of the proposals, and then reminded the audience that they were there not to decide on the merits of his beliefs, but on their consistency or not with his subscription to the articles. 'Your belief that certain doctrines are ever so pernicious can have nothing to do with the question whether they are allowed by the symbolical documents of the English Church; and yet I cannot but fear that vast numbers of you[f] mix up in your minds these absolutely distinct matters.'[39] Ward restated his full assent to all the doctrines of the Roman Church, and at the same time his readiness to repeat his subscription in what he called a 'non-natural', or metaphorical, sense. The speech over, the vice-chancellor proposed the resolution. The first (the censure of the passages) was carried by 770 to 380, and the second (the degradation which Stanley expected to be lost) by 570 to 510. When it came to the proposal to condemn Tract XC, the proctors[g] bravely exercised their right of veto, as they had when Hampden was charged, and the proceedings were over. 'It is very remarkable to observe', wrote Stanley, 'how peculiar a feeling is excited the moment that the slightest attempt is made to eject Newman, as if men had an instinctive fear of touching even a hair of his head. Men who had prepared to sacrifice Ward without a struggle recoiled in horror when they found that they were called upon to sacrifice Newman too.'[40]

As soon as Ward left the Sheldonian he slipped and fell flat on his face in the snow, his papers flying in all directions. He picked himself up and walked back to Balliol with Tait, followed by a large crowd of cheering undergraduates, most of whom regarded Ward's condemnation as narrow-minded and backward-looking. Though Tait had voted against Ward, he praised the peroration of his speech, which consisted of an eloquent appeal to all those who loved the liberty of the English Church to make common cause with him. 'I am glad you liked it,' replied Ward. 'These rhetorical efforts are out of my line, but Stanley said there should be something of the kind. He wrote it for me.'[41]

Ward had already resigned his lectureship at Balliol, and since he had been reduced to an undergraduate *in statu pupillari*, he now surrendered his fellowship. Then much to his friends' amazement he announced that he was secretly engaged. The marriage a year later of a man who had advocated clerical celibacy scandalised many of his followers, who lost confidence in his Catholic credentials. Jowett likened it to the end of *The Beggar's Opera* when an execution is turned into a wedding.[42] His conversion to Rome followed in September 1845,

---

[f] About 1,500 M.A.s were present, mostly country parsons.
[g] The junior proctor was Richard Church, a friend of Newman and Ward and later Dean of St Paul's. He wrote the classic history of the Oxford Movement.

preparing the way for Newman's secession the following month, and the end of the Oxford Movement. The Tractarians' valiant attempt to recover the Church of England's Catholic heritage lay in ruins.

*   *   *

Stanley had been in need of a change of scene after the hard labour of the biography. He and Jowett spent six weeks in the summer of 1844 touring Germany and the cities of Prague and Vienna. They travelled across France as far as Rheims, and from there they crossed the border at Trier. There they found the 'holy coat' on show for the first time since Napoleon had given permission in 1810. Stanley describes a medieval scene of processions, sacred banners and hordes of pilgrims crowding into the cathedral to venerate the seamless robe, supposed to have been worn by Christ at his crucifixion.[h] Guarding the shrine stood two knights of Malta in scarlet uniforms, drawn swords in their hands. A hundred priests in richly coloured vestments assisted at the pontifical high mass.

After visiting Bingen, they reached Nuremberg which Stanley found enchanting, 'a Pompeii of the Middle Ages, for its national spirit still hangs about it and gives it the appearance, not of death, but of sleep. It is exactly a German Venice, a very German Venice indeed.'[43] They took a steamboat down the Danube to Vienna, which Stanley thought uninteresting, and from there they travelled to Prague, which excited Stanley so much that he could hardly sleep. He saw the magnificent bridge over the River Moldau, the oldest German university, the Jesuit seminary, the cathedral, palaces and churches, and, as before, it was the historical associations of the city that fascinated him.

Heading home, the pair arrived at Dresden where they discovered that many of Germany's leading scholars were attending a congress of philologists. They made their way to the assembly and found Professor Böcking, who had been Stanley's host in Bonn. He introduced them to Professor Hermann of Leipzig, the president of the assembly. Stanley described him to Mary as 'the father of German philologers, a very old man, but still strong and vigorous'.[44]

> It was very curious to have such a constant succession of persons, whom we had only known from the backs of books, passing before you – such a sudden transformation of names into men of

---

[h] Tradition has it that Helena, mother of Constantine the Great, discovered the relic in the Holy Land, and had it sent to Trier where Constantine lived before becoming emperor.

flesh and blood. There was Lachmann, with long, streaming yellow hair, the editor of the Greek Testament which you have often seen in my rooms.ⁱ There was Immanuel Bekker, and others whose names would not interest you, whom I was very glad to see.⁴⁵

The scholar Jowett most wanted to meet was Professor Erdmann of Halle, the disciple and interpreter of Hegel, whose *History of Philosophy* was about to be published. Jowett had insisted that he and Stanley spend two or three hours a day on their travels studying the German text of Kant's *Critique of Pure Reason*.ʲ On this, wrote Stanley with irony, they 'supported their weary minds by alternate reading, analyzing and catechizing'.⁴⁶ Jowett's study of Kant had awakened an interest in Hegel, and he wanted to consult Erdmann on how best to approach his master's works. This important conversation marked the start of Jowett's pioneering study of German idealism, and its introduction first to Balliol, and then into mainstream British philosophy.

After watching a performance in Greek of Euripedes' *Medea*, the friends travelled to Berlin, stopping on the way at Wittenberg where Luther had been professor, and where he launched his great protest against the corruptions of Rome. In Berlin Stanley met the Protestant Church historians, von Ranke and Neander, both of whom he found disappointing. The city though was 'teeming with intellectual energy – with purely intellectual energy, beyond any place I ever saw'.⁴⁷

The friends returned to Berlin the following summer, and Stanley's sisters joined them at Ischl. Catherine recorded fifty years later that her brother and Jowett 'were deep in those days in the study of Hebrew, and could hardly be persuaded to look up from their books and contemplate the beauties of the scenery through which we passed. We used to exclaim, "Oh, do look! How beautiful!" And they would hastily raise their eyes, cry out, "Yes, very fine," and as hastily return to the contemplation of their Grammar.'⁴⁸

* * *

In October 1845 Stanley was appointed a select preacher to the University of Oxford. The honour of preaching four sermons in St Mary's

---

ⁱ Professor Karl Lachmann was the founder of modern textual criticism. Stanley and Jowett used his Greek text for their commentaries on the Pauline epistles.
ʲ Jowett and Stanley were unusual in Oxford in knowing German: Tait had started what became something of a fad at Balliol.

before a congregation which included the vice-chancellor, heads of colleges, fellows and undergraduates, signified his growing reputation. Though Stanley always lacked the wit, passion or single-minded conviction of the greatest preachers, he thought sermons important, and occasionally preached at services in University College chapel which had previously lacked a homily. How successful these sermons were is difficult to tell, though a letter written to his mother in 1847 is not encouraging: 'I preached again in chapel last night, but with the unfortunate drawback of – having a glove on my head! Entirely unknown to me till I was told by an undergraduate this morning.'[49]

Stanley took his preparation of the four sermons extremely seriously, asking friends for advice, showing drafts to Jowett,[50] and reading them aloud to the family when at home in Norwich. Stanley was a candidate for a new chair of Biblical exegesis, and he knew that his chances of being appointed depended not least on the impression the sermons made. He had already established a reputation as a theological liberal, and though this was welcome in some Oxford circles, he was regarded by many as heterodox. He was renowned as Arnold's champion, and Arnold's opinions, particularly on Biblical interpretation, were viewed with suspicion. Furthermore, Stanley was known to have met and read some of the German theologians, notorious in England for their rationalism and free-thinking.

Stanley chose the Church's earliest, apostolic age for his subject, and focused on three apostles, Peter, Paul and John, 'the three great Fathers of the whole Christian world'.[51] He posed the question, 'What were the human media through which the Divine life, and those Divine truths, were in the first instance communicated to man?'[52] Stanley answered as an historian, setting 'the Galilean fisherman, and the Pharisee of Tarsus, and the aged Apostle of Ephesus'[53] in the context of their time and place, and viewing them 'in their purely human, historical, individual characters'.[54] He tried in the sermons to hold up the apostles as exemplars and witnesses to all ages, and not least to the undergraduates living in the immediate aftermath of the collapse of the Oxford Movement. 'If amidst the controversies, the thoughtless selfishness, the positive sins or temptations of this place,' he concluded his first sermon, 'our excitement is sobered, our carelessness checked, our principles strengthened, by the thought of what He was and is – of what He has done and will do for us – then to others and to ourselves His name receives a witness from us, more humble, but not less real, than it once received from Peter, Paul, and John.'[55]

Today the sermons seem orthodox and reverent in content, and it is difficult to see why Stanley should have been so anxious about their reception. But Arnold's and the German influences are apparent, and furthermore, it has to be remembered that the Bible, and certainly its most saintly dramatis personae, were regarded at the time with an awe and piety that prevented their being approached in the same objective, critical way that an historian might approach any other book or historical person. And this was exactly what Stanley was doing in his sermons.

The first, introductory sermon was preached in February 1846. Stanley was nervous about it, and told Mary that the day before he had been 'alarmed by an access of sick headache, cold, and all the usual accompaniments'. He dreamt that night that it was already seven on Sunday morning, he was stranded at a village eight hours from Oxford, and was due to give his sermon at half past ten.

> However, I was all right in time, and duly drest up in cassock, bands, hood, &c. It lasted not quite an hour, and is reported to have been more audible than the last ... I have not heard very many judgments, but on the whole I should think it was successful. The undergraduates took it very well... and our Master[k] declares his opinion that there was no reasonable ground of offence to anyone.[56]

Stanley feared that the second sermon in May was not so well received, though Jowett thought otherwise. But the third, and especially the final sermon, went better, and Stanley wrote in triumph to his mother: 'the sermon seems to have been highly successful ... The Master has just been congratulating me, and says, or rather implies, that the impression produced on the Heads was so favourable that it may affect the election materially.'[57] Unfortunately the encouragement given to Stanley was partial. To many, the sermons were profane and fanciful, and the critics won the day: Edward Hawkins, Provost of Oriel, was elected the first Ireland Professor of Exegesis.

Stanley was never a man to dwell on personal disappointment, or compromise his convictions to win favour or preferment. Despite the fact that the sermons may have hindered his appointment, he was determined to publish them in order to bring their method and ideas to wider notice. He delayed, however, because 'the Heads and my senior

---

[k] Frederic Plumptre, Master of University College.

friends, are dreadfully alarmed at the notion of precipitate publication'.[58] Then, in November 1847, much to Oxford's dismay, Renn Dickson Hampden was offered and accepted the bishopric of Hereford, leaving the regius chair of divinity vacant. Stanley was a candidate, and when he heard a rumour that he was postponing publication in order not to jeopardise his chances again, he rushed them into print.[l] 'I believe', he wrote, 'that they will turn out a failure as signal as the success of Arnold's Life'.[59]

*   *   *

The supposedly heretical Hampden had met fierce opposition when he was appointed professor, and convocation had deprived him of two of his duties.[60] Since then he had fulfilled his responsibilities, though without distinction. When in 1842 convocation was summoned again to debate the repeal of its earlier statute, the repeal was rejected on the grounds that Hampden had done nothing either to recant or clarify his theological views. So Russell's choice of Hampden for Hereford is difficult to account for, apart from the fact that he was a Whig, and was supported by the Queen, who favoured bishops of liberal views.

Opposition to Hampden was as impassioned as it had been in 1836 and 1842, though this time it spread beyond Oxford. An urgent protest signed by the clergy was despatched to the Prime Miniser. The octogenarian Archbishop of Canterbury, William Howley, remonstrated against the appointment, and the Dean of Hereford wrote a laborious 3,000 word letter to Russell to say that no earthly consideration would induce him to approve the Crown's nomination to the see of Hereford. In return, he received from Woburn Abbey a curt, twenty-four word reply, penned on Christmas Day: 'Sir, I have had the honour to receive your letter of the 22nd instant in which you intimate to me your intention of violating the law.'[61]

Stanley was never impressed by Hampden, whom he thought dull and worldly. He had also come to share Tait's view that his theology was shallow and uninspiring.[62] 'Oh that it had been an Arnold! ... how I would have moved heaven and earth in his cause!'[63] Nonetheless he condemned the outcry, as he had in 1836. And as with Ward, he thought it unjust because it was directed at a book which nine-tenths of the critics had not read.[m] Furthermore, the lectures it contained had

---

[l] *Sermons and Essays on the Apostolical Age* was published in November 1847
[m] *The Scholastic Philosophy considered in its relation to Christian Theology* (Hampden's Bampton lectures, 1832).

been delivered fifteen years before, and though they might have been largely unintelligible, they were not unorthodox.

As the agitation against Hampden increased, Stanley felt duty-bound to defend him. He decided to write for advice and support to his father and to Julius Hare's friend, Connop Thirlwall, now Bishop of St David's. But the result was not as Stanley had intended, as he explained in a letter to Mary:

> To these two letters I received no answer till yesterday morning, when I found two letters on my table, one – the enclosed – from Edward, the other from Cuddesdon.[n] I opened it, and I could hardly believe my eyes, till the truth flashed upon me that the letter designed for St. David's had gone to S. Oxon.[o] How I cannot conceive; I suppose that by a slip of the pen the word 'Oxford' had got into the direction instead of into the date, and this was the result. The immediate effect upon me was to fall into successive convulsions of laughter, from which I have hardly yet recovered; the absurdity of a letter designed for one Bishop going exactly to the antipodes and that other Bishop so innocently assuming it all as addressed to himself.[64]

Bishop Samuel Wilberforce had voted against Hampden in convocation eleven years before, and was known for his orthodox beliefs. He was Mrs Tait's cousin and the third son of the Evangelical philanthropist William Wilberforce. After only six months as Dean of Westminster he had been appointed Bishop of Oxford in 1845, and Stanley succeeded him as a university select preacher. He established a reputation, both as a champion of orthodoxy and a time-serving vicar of Bray[p] – hence his sobriquet, 'Soapy Sam'. Trollope's Archdeacon Grantly named his own third son Samuel, or '"dear little Soapy"' as he was familiarly called ... To speak the truth, Samuel was a cunning boy, and those even who loved him best could not but own that for one so young he was too adroit in choosing his words and too skilled in modulating his voice.'[65]

Stanley went straight to Cuddesdon with Jowett to explain the mistake, and found, as he had expected, that Wilberforce was firmly against Hampden's appointment, and that he and twelve other bishops

---

[n] The village near Oxford where the bishop had his palace.
[o] Samuel Wilberforce, Bishop of Oxford.
[p] The subject of an 18th-century anonymous poem who boasts the he has accommodated himself to the religious views of the reigns of Charles, James, William, Anne and George.

had just protested to the Prime Minister. Wilberforce was about to take upon himself the task of preventing both Hampden's consecration and the public scandal of a suit being brought against him in the court of arches.q But his handling of the negotiations proved clumsy and inept, causing offence to both sides. 'Sly Sam of Oxford', wrote Charles Greville[r] in his diary, 'has covered himself with ridicule and disgrace.'[66] Wilberforce thought his handling of the affair, and the royal disappointment it caused, cost him the archbishopric of Canterbury when Howley died.[s]

Russell stuck to his guns, and Hampden was consecrated in Lambeth Palace chapel on 26 March 1848. The new Archbishop of Canterbury, John Bird Sumner, was assisted by three Whig bishops, one of whom was Edward Stanley. 'So Hampden is over at last,' wrote Stanley. 'He called very civilly on me before he went; and I met Mrs. Hampden in the street, and told her that, in the words of George IV. to Louis XVIII., I hoped never to see her in Oxford again.'[67] Stanley was disappointed not to be appointed Hampden's successor as regius professor, but his recently published sermons confirmed his reputation as unorthodox, and Russell was not going to risk another controversy. The vice-principal of Magdalen Hall, William Jacobson, was chosen instead. Writing to Mary, Stanley was magnanimous, though not without a touch of cynicism at the end:

> I regard the appointment of Jacobson with almost universal satisfaction, partly as setting the question at rest, and partly from the great pleasure which it gives me to see him there, both on his own account and because, though not brilliant, he is such a thoroughly honest, straightforward, sensible man ... And he is so safe a man that the Government will almost cover their appointment of Hampden by it.[68]

Six months later the regius chair of modern history fell vacant and Stanley's friends urged him to apply, knowing that for this secular post his theological opinions would not be such an impediment. Stanley was attracted by the prospect but he was nervous about a second rejection. In the end he allowed his name to go forward but half-heartedly.

---

q The ecclesiastical court of the Canterbury province.
r Clerk to the Council, 1821–59.
s This was highly presumptuous: Wilberforce had been Bishop of Oxford for only two years when Howley died in February 1848.

Charles Vaughan's cousin, Henry Halford Vaughan,ᵗ was elected: 'a capital appointment in every respect,' wrote Stanley, 'except as regards the immediate interests and pleasures of A.P.S.'⁶⁹ 'My paradise is lost,' he told Pearson, 'but I hope to regain it elsewhere.'⁷⁰

*   *   *

News of revolution in France reached Oxford on 26 February 1848. The spectre of another 1789 filled many English hearts with fear and dread, and certainly of the ruling class. Stanley, on the other hand, was thrilled at the thought of history unfolding:

> I had come back late from a dinner at Cuddesdon the night before, and overslept myself, so I did not hear it till just before my lecture at ten. 'The Abdication of Louis Philippe'; 'The Palais Royal Stormed'; 'The Tuileries Sacked'; 'The King on his Way to England'. I could hardly get through my lectures ... Then came the excitement of the evening papers, and we were met as we came up from chapel by undergraduates shouting that the Republic was proclaimed.⁷¹

Jowett shared his excitement, and was determined to visit Paris and the scenes of turmoil as soon as the Easter vacation began – despite the fact that his parents (who had been living in the Rue Madeleine) had fled to Bonn. Stanley was keen to join him. He envied his father's visits to France after the first revolution, and he wanted to experience and not just read about another turning-point in history. Stanley's family was anxious about the dangers but Bunsen assured them that Paris was no more perilous than Kennington Common. In case of danger the travellers were given letters of introduction to the British and American embassies, and to various friends of friends. On Saturday 8 April, Stanley and Jowett left Folkestone for Boulogne. They were accompanied by two of Jowett's pupils at Balliol, Francis Palgrave,ᵘ who had recently been elected a fellow of Exeter College, and the undergraduate, Robert Morier,ᵛ who had been born in Paris and spoke better French than English. Jowett was especially fond of Morier and they became lifelong friends.

ᵗ In the sixth form at Rugby when Arnold arrived in 1828; a contemporary of Gladstone and Liddell at Christ Church, and a fellow of Oriel.
ᵘ Professor of Poetry at Oxford, 1885–95, and editor of the famous *Golden Treasury* (1864).
ᵛ Ambassador at St Petersburg, 1884–93.

On reaching France the four were greeted by a huge placard announcing the planting of a tree of liberty. There were tricolours flying everywhere and constant cries of '*Vive la République!*' The spirit of 1789 was alive again. After travelling overnight by rail they arrived in Paris early on Sunday morning. The streets were empty, and when they reached the Tuileries 'not one of us spoke; but it was truly awful to see the vast grey mass standing as before, with the consciousness of all within gone, or dead for ever.'[72] More evidence of the revolution followed: broken barricades, posters proclaiming the provisional Government, the words *Liberté*, *Egalité* and *Fraternité* scrawled on the walls, and the *garde mobile* 'everywhere – at the entrance of public buildings, walking round the Trees of Liberty, parading in half-formed regiments through the streets ... all in blouses or in common ragged coats or cloaks, mostly boys, almost reeling under the weight of their muskets and bayonets.'[73]

The visitors went to the Comédie Française (renamed the Théâtre de la République) to see a new, topical play about the flight of Tarquin.[w] At the end, 'Rachel', the famous actress playing Lucretia,[x] came forward to sing the Marseillaise, wrapping herself in a tricolour 'as if with a determination that nothing should ever part her from it – a love, an adoration as if it were an animated creature ... Had Nero fallen instead of Louis Philippe, the impression conveyed could not have been more ferocious.'[74] They visited two of the clubs, or political associations. The Club de la Sorbonne was held in the amphitheatre of the university's theology faculty, and reminded Stanley of the Sheldonian in Oxford. 1,500 were present, 'chiefly of the common people, in blouses, beards, long flowing hair, women &c.'[75] They were there to debate the law regulating the elections. Stanley was surprised by the perfect order of the proceedings. 'Speeches, if not liked, were heard in silence; the ringing of the president's bell was instantly attended to; in short, the House of Commons could not have been under better control.'[76] The next day they went to the Club des Intérêts du Peuple and found a very different atmosphere. In a letter home, Stanley described the uproar caused by a dispute between the president and the secretary:

---

[w] The legendary king of Rome who was expelled after his son raped the virtuous Lucretia who then stabbed herself.

[x] Elisa-Rachel Félix started life singing on the streets of Paris to help support her impoverished family. She was discovered and became renowned for her passionate portrayal of tragic heroines.

Part Two: Oxford 1834–1851   149

What would you have given if you could have been mesmerically transported there, and seen the hall, dimly lighted with tallow candles, a French mob of 1,000 persons, shouting and yelling at the tops of their voices ... and the Poppet's[y] head enclosed within the embrace of two huge arms of a rough-bearded and bloused man, who was leaning over me, and every now and then pouring his complaints into my fraternising ears? Yet with all this the most perfect good-humour prevailed.[77]

On Palm Sunday, Stanley and his companions attended a packed mass in the cathedral of Notre Dame. They saw the Archbishop of Paris and heard the Dominican liberal, Henri Lacordaire, preach an intensely political sermon on labour. On his way back to the hotel, Stanley witnessed an immense parade on the other side of the Seine. It consisted of two lines, one of workmen, the other of soldiers of the national guard. Four days later, on 20 April, Stanley watched the return of the regular army which had not been in Paris since the revolution of 1789. He waited at the Arc de Triomphe from seven-thirty in the morning. At nine, members of the provisional Government arrived in carriages. Among them Stanley glimpsed the poet Alphonse de Lamartine, now foreign minister and idol of Paris. He was impressed by 'his very aristocratic appearance – a perfect gentleman, the one gentleman of the set'.[78] And then, at ten, 400,000 troops began to appear:

The spectacle itself was of its kind as grand as can well be conceived. From the platform raised half-way up the height of the Arc de l'Etoile, immediately under the colossal statues of Napoleon and France, whose huge limbs supported and sheltered the pigmy forms of living men, you looked down the Champs Elysées to the Tuileries; and the whole avenue ... was one continuous stream of bayonets, first grey in the dull morning, then, as the sun came out, glittering like silver waves, wave upon wave flowing steadily onwards between the dark banks of the crowd which lined it on either side. It began at ten, and I believe is still going on now (9 P.M.).[79]

Stanley was struck, not just by what he called 'the greatest military spectacle that I ever saw', but by the crowd's lack of enthusiasm, and by the democracy of the scene. 'On that splendid platform round the Ministers of State, with the judges and generals on each side, there were

[y] The family's pet-name for Stanley.

ranged, instead of the brilliant aristocracy which might have been expected, the commonest working-people, in mud-bespattered clothes, blouses, and even rags.'[80]

Stanley returned to Paris in October, this time with his Balliol friend Hugh Pearson. They were detained for a few hours in Boulogne, where they spent the time visiting Napoleon's column, the cathedral and the abattoir, a word neither men had heard before: they were surprised to discover that it was the slaughter-house. Stanley found Paris much changed since April. The second insurrection in June had been brutally suppressed, and revolution had given way to reaction. Soldiers were everywhere, with their white tents pitched along the Champs Elysées. The clubs had been broken up, the trees of liberty were dying, and the tricolours faded. They saw houses in ruins or pock-marked by shot and cannon-balls. They were there to hear Lamartine's celebrated speech to the assembly in a debate on the mode of electing a president. He described the presidents of old, including the Pope; the abyss into which the country would fall if the only hold the Government had on the people was through the assembly; the fall of Louis Philippe and the Orléanists; the prospects of the Bonaparte family; the president as the embodiment of every elector. Lamartine's eloquence was formidable, and his concentration of thought in single images reminded Stanley of Pericles.

*   *   *

Most of the first months of 1849 were spent preparing for a long excursion with Jowett to Palestine, planned to start in November. Goldwin Smith (another brilliant classicist of liberal views who had been elected to a fellowship at University College) was to take on Stanley's work as tutor, allowing him to be absent from college during term. In July Stanley started 'to read through all the geographical parts of the Bible in Hebrew, and have got as far as the Kings, with the increasing conviction that there is no other ancient geography, except Greece, which opens its arms so widely to receive, and to render up, the secrets of the past, as that of Palestine and Arabia.'[81]

But the journey was not to happen. A spate of family deaths and bereavements intervened, and changed the course of Stanley's life.

Stanley's father had been Bishop of Norwich for eleven years and had celebrated his seventieth birthday in January. He was in need of a rest and change of scene, and the family persuaded him to spend August in Scotland. Stanley travelled with his parents and sisters as far as

Derby, and from there he paid a visit first to Alderley and then to the Lakes, where he spent time with Mrs Arnold and Jowett. He then made his way north to rejoin the family in Perth. But on reaching Edinburgh he found a letter from Mary asking him to hurry to Brahan Castle in the Highlands, where they were staying with the head of the Mackenzie family. Stanley arrived during the evening of 5 September 1849 to find his father dying of 'congestion of the brain'.[82] He was already unconscious and breathing heavily, and died at half-past eleven the following night, with the family at his bedside. 'That moment', wrote Mary, 'it seemed as though the very life was drawn from one, no one moved for some time – then Arthur knelt down & prayed.'[83]

Two days later Stanley wrote to Mrs Arnold. He described his father's last hours and the impression made by the first dead body he had seen: 'the stone-like repose of the beloved countenance, with none of its energy and fire, but with nothing of the suffering and of that long-protracted struggle of expiring nature, nor yet of the restlessness of his often overworked and over-excited life.'[84] Stanley goes on to compare his father with Arnold, and to rejoice in the respect they had had for one another. As a boy, Stanley had held Arnold in greater esteem, and felt that he had more in common with his well-stocked and scholarly mind than with his father's practical and extrovert nature. Now the preference was less pronounced:

> How thankfully I recur at this moment to the recollection of how truly he honoured and was honoured by him whose death is the only event within my personal experience that I can compare to this! They were very different in many ways; the differences of taste and of education were so great that one almost wondered how they could understand each other; yet, in spite of this, there was the same manly, generous love of truth and justice united with purity and devotion in that rare union which outweighs hundreds of books of evidences, and each felt it in the other, and it was reserved for him to be the one Bishop in England who delighted to receive and honour him whom all England has since delighted to honour; and he, I trust, will in like manner receive *his* praise when he has been removed from the scene where he earned it.[85]

Edward Stanley had devoted himself to the care and reform of his diocese, just as he had for thirty-two years in his parish at Alderley. As parson and bishop he belonged to the best of the Church of England before the Evangelical and Tractarian revivals. He was driven not by their intense religious zeal, but by the combination of a practical and paternal sense of responsibility for people, the discipline and duty that would have made him a respected naval officer, a sincere and uncritical Biblical faith, a strong and confident morality, and a reverence for the Book of Common Prayer. He distrusted any sign of partisanship in the Church, and deplored the distrust and division they caused. Edward's concentration on Christian essentials produced an unusually broad and liberal outlook. He had striven for Christian unity, and for an established Church that was welcoming and inclusive. His influence on Stanley's beliefs and convictions is not to be underestimated.[z]

In Alderley, Edward had increased the number of communicants, provided a Bible and prayer book in every home, extended the school building, and started a Sunday school and parish library. When he moved to Norwich in 1837 he exchanged a parish church and a thousand parishioners for a thousand churches, a cathedral and nearly nine hundred clergy. After the long reign of his Georgian predecessor, the diocese was marred by what the new bishop called 'the laxity of bygone days'.[86] But Edward set to work to make improvements, and endured exhaustion and unpopularity as a result. The entry in his journal for 31 December 1848, seven months before he died, is gloomy and self-pitying, as he surveyed what he often called his bed of thorns:

> Seventy years of my life have passed and gone their way: forty-four of them in a profession dedicated to the service of God, of which the last eleven are the most especially important from the position in which circumstance so unlooked for and so unsought for have placed me. And though these latter years have been accomplished with much labour and pain and sorrow, more and more alive as I am, to the difficulties presenting themselves, still I feel satisfaction in what I have been fortunately instrumental in doing. How many parishes have I supplied with resident clergy, in which no pastoral care had been for years and years manifested. How many churches have had the full measure of services prescribed, in which for time immemorial the most scanty administration had been administered. And how many schools have

---

[z] Edward Stanley bears comparison with Trollope's Bishop of Elmham in *The Way We Live Now* (1875). Elmham was an ancient see which later formed part of the diocese of Norwich. Though Trollope intimated that the bishop was modelled on Charles Longley, Archbishop of Canterbury (1862–8), there are more similarities between him and Edward Stanley.

been established, for the benefit of the thousands who had been with most culpable negligence permitted to remain brutalized and uncivilized and perishing for lack of knowledge. To my impartiality in awarding preferment, I cannot but think my most bitter opponents will bear testimony. To the majority of vacancies I have appointed individuals differing from me politically and religiously, and for some of whom instead of gratitude I have been treated with a want of common courtesy and respect; too surely proving how little trust can be placed in men professing to be exclusively the supporters of their Church.[87]

The bishop's body was brought by sea from Invergordon to Yarmouth; on the way the steamer hit a fierce storm and Edward was almost buried at sea. He had expressed a wish to be interred in the churchyard at Alderley but had been given permission for burial in the cathedral at Norwich. The funeral took place on 21 September 1849, and the hordes of people who attended, and the feelings of sadness expressed, revealed a respect and affection for their bishop which Edward had never realised. Adam Sedgwick, Professor of Geology at Cambridge and a prebendary of Norwich Cathedral, left this account:

> It was the most touching and stirring ceremonial I have ever witnessed. The mayor and corporation in their civic dresses, covered with crepe, led the way. Then followed the coffin and pall-bearers – then the family and mourners ... About four hundred clergymen, in full robes, followed. There were also present most of the Nonconformist ministers of the city. And lastly, a great multitude of the respectable inhabitants in the city and neighbourhood. The procession was so very long that I could only see a very small part of it. When the doors of the cathedral were thrown open, on each side of the central aisle of the nave were seen eleven hundred children from the different schools of the city, arranged in triple rows ... There were thousands in the cathedral. All parts of the triforium were filled. The organ gallery was covered with spectators; all were in mourning; many were deeply affected. Almost every eye was dim with tears, and you could hear the modest and half-concealed sobs of the little children as you passed down the nave ... The day was beautiful, and between the palace gate and the Erpingham gate we marched, through, I should think, not less than 20,000 spectators, who were all respectful and silent, and many of them were sorrowful.[88]

The body was laid to rest in the centre of the nave, marked later by a black marble slab with an inscription which paid tribute to 'Edward Stanley, buried amidst the mourning of the diocese which he had animated, the city which he had served, the poor whom he had visited, the schools which he had fostered, the family which he had loved.' At Edward's request, the west window of the cathedral was restored as his memorial.

Stanley set to work to write a memoir of his father.[A] Much as he had done for his biography of Arnold, he wrote first to the clergy of the diocese asking for information and opinions. Stanley was as amazed as his father would have been by the warmth and admiration expressed in the replies. 'He had found (the diocese) a wilderness,' wrote one parson, 'and he left it in comparison a cultivated field ... Both clergy and laity, both rich and poor, felt that they had in him a father and a friend.'[89]

* * *

Stanley's bereavement led to a painful and puzzling exchange of letters. Jowett wrote a warm letter to his friend when he read of his father's death in the newspaper, and for the first time addressed him as 'My dear Arthur', instead of the customary use of surname. 'It would be a happiness to me to be with you if I could be of the least use in alleviating this overwhelming affliction ... Would you like to me to come to you? If so, I should like to stay in lodgings nearby'. The letter closed with the same intimacy: 'Believe me, my dear Arthur, Your affectionate friend, B. JOWETT.'[90] Stanley's reply was distinctly cool: 'Very many thanks for your kind thoughtfulness in proposing to come. No, my dear friend, it was not needed then, and is not now. We are enough in ourselves for ourselves, and hereafter I will not fail to let you know whether you can be of the slightest service to us.'[91] Behind this hauteur lies Stanley's shy, independent and private nature, and perhaps also a consciousness of the social superiority of his family. Subsequent correspondence reveals further tensions between the two friends over a collaborative effort to produce a critical edition of St Paul's epistles. On 1 October Stanley wrote to Jowett on the subject: 'You know that I believe myself to have learned more from you than from anyone else since Arnold's removal; and therefore I hope you will not misunderstand me when I say that I

[A] The brief memoir formed the preface to Stanley's collection of his father's addresses, published in 1851. An expanded memoir was published in 1879 and included extracts from his mother's letters and journals.

sometimes feel so much oppressed and depressed in talking to you about these things that I seem to have lost all will of my own. Some means must be taken for avoiding this. Perhaps the long interval and separation from all such topics will themselves produce all the independence which is requisite.'[92]

Arnold had been planning a Rugby edition of the Pauline epistles, and in 1847 Stanley and Jowett had agreed to take on the task, and work together to produce a modern, scholarly edition of their own. Each volume was to include a Greek text plus an introduction, translation, commentary and essays. Stanley was to tackle Corinthians, and Jowett, Romans, Galatians and Thessalonians.[B] While Stanley pressed on alone with his share of the work, Jowett became increasingly enthusiastic, and demanding of Stanley's time and attention. Stanley's letter suggests that he was finding Jowett's excitement smothering and invasive. At the start, in August 1847, Jowett had advised: 'I think we ought to do more towards it than we have done in the last two years, if we are to live to see it finished. I wish we could read through the New Testament together, to begin with: otherwise there will be no sort of unity in what we write ... My own wish would be, if it is to your taste, to work at it together, something in the same fashion that Liddell and Scott did at their Lexicon ... Next Term I could read the Epistles with you three or four evenings in the week, if you are not alarmed by such a proposal.'[93] Stanley *was* alarmed, and he deliberately distanced himself from Jowett. Two years later, Jowett had been made to understand that Stanley needed privacy and independence, and that their relationship would have to change. 'I know well', confessed Jowett, 'how much better and wiser I ought to be to be at all worthy of the high opinion you express. It will always be a motive with me to try and make myself very different from what I am ... I earnestly hope that the friendship that commenced between us many years ago may be a blessing to last us through life ... I have often felt the inability to converse with you, but never for an instant the least alienation. There is no one who would not think me happy having such a friend. We will have no more of this semi-egotistical talk: only I want you to know that I will do all that I can to remedy the evil, which is chiefly my fault.'[94]

*   *   *

[B] The commentaries were published in 1855. Though Jowett's included some radical theological views, Stanley's was relatively conservative and uncontroversial, and concentrated on describing the historic setting of Pauline Christianity.

Stanley's mother and sisters stayed on in Norwich until the end of 1849 when they moved to London and a new house in Grosvenor Crescent, where Stanley was a frequent visitor. With both his elder and younger brothers away in the Antipodes, Stanley had to assume the role of head of the family. He did so willingly, and the responsibility made him more practical and businesslike, more sociable and confident, and less preoccupied with his own affairs. He devoted himself to caring for his mother for the rest of her life. His nephew believed that 'he made her feel that she had still as much to interest her and give a zest to life as in the happiest days at Alderley and Norwich'.[95]

The Dean of Carlisle, Dr Samuel Hinds, was appointed to the see of Norwich. He was another Whig and had been chaplain to Archbishop Whately, as well as to the Earls of Bessborough and Clarendon. Russell offered the vacant deanery to Stanley, 'as due to your own merits, but also hoping that it would be considered as a tribute of respect to the memory of the late Bishop of Norwich'.[96] Stanley declined immediately and with unusual decisiveness. In a courtly reply to the Prime Minister, he expressed his family's gratitude to the honour paid to his father, 'but I trust that I shall not be misinterpreted if I add that I shall feel myself under still further obligation if Her Majesty would permit me respectfully to decline a post for which, however honourable in itself, I feel no peculiar qualification.'[97] Stanley went on to explain that his real interests remained in Oxford. Once the letter had been despatched, however, he began to have second thoughts. His mother and sisters had not wanted to live in Carlisle, but their sadness at the thought of leaving Norwich made him wonder whether they might not have been happier if he had accepted the post. 'If the refusal of the Deanery was a mistake,' he told Jowett, 'it is not so irreparable a one as the acceptance of it would have been, supposing it to be a mistake. I shall be very glad if you can say that you approve of the step. I am sorry to find that all my friends, from whom I have heard, think it was wrong.'[98] Jowett, always in favour of worldly advancement, replied to say that, though he must not expect too much from the cathedral, he ought to change his mind: 'It will give you a position & a right to speak, & money & unbounded leisure and raise you greatly in the opinion of all dignified persons, such as the Dean of Wells.'[99]

The only other position in the Church that Stanley had been offered was one his uncle's family had been keen for him to accept. This was four years before, when Charles Girdlestone, Edward Stanley's successor as rector of Alderley, was being urged to resign. Edward had approved the choice of 'one long and well known to me for his practical piety, his active zeal, and his Christian character'.[100] But Girdlestone soon fell out with Edward's curmudgeonly brother,[C] the patron of the living, and his family seem to have taken a spiteful delight in reviling 'Girdy', as they called him. In the end they refused to attend the church where they would have to listen to what Lady Stanley called 'his odious hypocritical voice'.[101] To Stanley, the prospect of moving back to Alderley to do what his father had done for over thirty years was absurd. 'To me personally', he wrote, 'the occupation would be almost so uncongenial as a mission to Labrador.'[102]

It is uncertain whether or not Stanley recommended him to Russell but in October 1849 Tait was offered Carlisle and gladly accepted. Rugby had prospered under his eight years as headmaster, but the work was not congenial. Furthermore, the pressures on Arnold's successor had been stifling, with masters, parents, and past and present pupils refusing to support any deviation from Arnold's principles and methods.[D] Certainly, Stanley had not helped him. In the sermon about Arnold preached on Tait's first Sunday at Rugby, he not only extolled the virtues of 'the greatest man who ever filled the office of Head Master, here or elsewhere', but compared him to Tait: 'there is not one whom I address, from him who now occupies his vacant seat, down to the humblest and youngest boy, who is not able, if he be willing, to bear his part in continuing the work of one who will rank amongst the greatest men who have adorned this Church and nation.'[103] The biography had enhanced Arnold's standing and pushed his successor further into the shade. The year before Carlisle was offered, Tait's health broke down, and on Ash Wednesday he dictated a farewell letter to the sixth. He recovered, and despite a phase of popularity, he welcomed the opportunity of less demanding work. Stanley was pleased, and wrote to Jowett to say that his own misgivings about

---

[C] The quarrel was over tithes, the tenth of the annual produce of land owned by a rectory and paid to the rector. The Tithe Commutation Act (1836) was passed the year before Girdlestone became rector. It turned payment in produce into payment in money of the estimated value of the produce. Where Edward Stanley had declined payment under the old system, Girdlestone insisted that he was paid fairly under the new.

[D] A Rugby master, G. F. Bradby, wrote a satirical school novel, *The Lanchester Tradition* (1913), about the trials that beset the headmaster who succeeds Dr Lanchester (obviously based on Arnold): 'The Lanchester tradition permeates the place like an atmosphere, invisible but stimulating ... Any change in the hour of a lesson or the colour of a ribbon is regarded as an outrage on the Lanchester tradition, and is popularly supposed to make the dead hero turn in his grave.'

Carlisle had passed away, not least because of 'this delightful appointment of Tait – I am sorry that Rugby is to be again at sea – but for his sake & with the great risk of his continuance there, I cannot imagine a place which would suit him better – I reflect upon it with conscious joy every hour of the day.'[104]

During the next nine months, Stanley and his family had to face the deaths of both his brothers. First, in December 1849, news arrived that Charles had died suddenly, aged thirty, in Van Diemen's Land. Charley was practical and adventurous like Owen. On leaving Rugby he had joined the Royal Engineers and achieved the rank of captain. He caused a stir at Alderley and Norwich when he became entangled briefly with what his scornful aunt called 'a half-foreigner' from Jamaica.[105] He then married Eliza Clayton, a banker's daughter from Preston. She was disapproved of at Alderley Park almost as vehemently as the girl from the Caribbean: 'No money *at all* I believe, no connexion or rather a very inferior one ... Kitty does not seem to like it, says the Bishop had such a horror at the possible alternative of the West Indies that it acted upon him like Emmy's fits.'[106] Charley was offered a position as private secretary to Sir William Denison on his appointment as Lieutenant Governor of Van Diemen's Land. He and Eliza set sail with him and Lady Denison (who was a friend of the Stanleys) in October 1846. Three years later, and three weeks before his father, Charley died of fever caused by gastro-enteritis.

Then in July 1850 news reached home that Owen too was dead, worn out by the hardships of over twenty years at sea. He had become an expert nautical surveyor, and had helped to map the waters and shores of the Mediterranean, South America, the Arctic, New Zealand and, finally, Australia and the island of New Guinea.[E] In April 1846 he had been given his first command of a twenty-eight-gun frigate, HMS *Rattlesnake*. After months of preparation, the ship set sail from Portsmouth for Australia, docking first at Plymouth. Edward Stanley was there with the family to say farewell, and was asked to preach on the quarter-deck to a thousand sailors from the *Rattlesnake* and other ships. He spoke of the value and importance of discipline at sea and in the Christian life.[107] The ship left Plymouth on 11 December, taking Owen's sisters, Mary and Catherine, as far as Madeira. Owen reached Van Diemen's Land in June 1847, and spent three weeks with Charley and Eliza. He took them with him to Sydney, and from there he set off

---

[E] The central mountain range in New Guinea is named after him.

north to chart the inner passage of the barrier reef on the edge of the Coral Sea. News of Charley's death reached him in October 1849, and his father's in February 1850. His irritability became worse, causing fits of anxiety and violent temper. A month later, in Sydney harbour, he was found lying in an epileptic seizure on the deck of his cabin. He had fallen on his head and remained unconscious until he died. He was thirty-eight. Stanley was distraught, and spent long periods alone, walking or closeted in his room. Kitty was heartbroken. 'I could think of nothing that could be worse than what poor Kitty was suffering,' wrote Lady Stanley. 'Such repeated bereavements, this so unexpected & at a time when all thoughts were busied in his return. How she will cling to Arthur, & when I look at him I do feel such dread of farther & deeper trials.'[108]

Stanley's responsibility for his mother and Mary was now complete. Catherine had married his schoolfriend, Charles Vaughan, Headmaster of Harrow, in the spring of 1850. The wedding provided a welcome respite from mourning, though news of Owen's death was soon to follow. Catherine herself had always been frail, and nearly died of a painful intestinal condition nine years before when she was twenty. It was, Stanley wrote at the time, 'the first time that I ever was in a house with serious illness, the first domestic sorrow we have ever had in our family'.[109]

With the deaths of his father and elder brother, Stanley inherited a small estate in Cheshire that provided a significant income for life, and certainly sufficient to disqualify him from his fellowship in Oxford. He was given a year's grace before he would have to resign.

*   *   *

Another theological controversy was raging in the background. Stanley followed it closely and entered the lists in July 1850 with an impassioned and learned article in the *Edinburgh Review*.[110] The crisis concerned a lengthy and litigious dispute between Henry Phillpotts,[F] Bishop of Exeter, and the Reverend George Cornelius Gorham, whom Phillpotts had refused to induct into a living in his diocese.

Gorham was a staunch Evangelical with Calvinist leanings. He had first aroused the High Church Phillpotts's suspicions in 1846 when, as a vicar in Penwith in Cornwall, he had advertised in the *Ecclesiastical*

[F] Phillpotts is caricatured in *The Warden* as Archdeacon Grantly's pugnacious son, Henry. His eldest son, the compromising Charles James, is a caricature of Blomfield, Bishop of London.

Gazette for a curate 'free from Tractarian error'. The following year Gorham accepted the Lord Chancellor's offer of the Crown living of Brampford Speke near Exeter. But before agreeing to induct, Phillpotts subjected Gorham to no fewer than 52 hours of theological examination in which he was asked 149 questions. These were principally on the efficacy of infant baptism, which the bishop regarded as an essential test of orthodoxy. Phillpotts believed firmly that in baptism the child was unconditionally regenerated: Gorham believed firmly that regeneration depended on the child's subsequent profession of faith. To Phillpotts this was a sure sign of unsound doctrine.

Gorham published an open letter protesting at this 'cruel exercise of episcopal power',[111] and claiming that, if the precedent were established, a bishop would be able to exclude from his diocese all clergy whose views differed from his own. A major principle was at stake, and Gorham resorted to the courts in what became one of the most famous legal actions of the century. After various stages the case came before the court of arches, and in August 1849 Phillpotts was upheld and Gorham was judged heretical. But Gorham was not to be deterred and he appealed to the judicial committee of the Privy Council. On 8 March 1850 the 'Gorham Judgment' reversed the ruling, with the decision that his views were 'not contrary or repugnant to the doctrine of the Church of England as by law established'.[112]

Stanley's article states that the most important aspect of the controversy was not in fact the theological issue of baptism, but the nature of the English Church, and especially the authority of the State to determine doctrinal boundaries. The influence of Arnold's ecclesiology is unmistakable. Stanley defends the supremacy of the Crown, and therefore the law, over the national, established Church. The decision of the Privy Council was not only wise and just but appropriate, and Stanley refutes the High Church charge of State tyranny: 'that is no tyranny which protects the minority, or it may be the majority, of the clergy from the inquisition of arbitrary prelates, and of tumultuous synods.'[113] The Church of England is by nature and history a comprehensive, latitudinarian Church which includes 'opposite and contradictory opinions'.[114] 'It is, by the very conditions of its being, not High, not Low, but *Broad*.'[115] Stanley explains in a footnote to the 1870 republication of the article that this was the first occasion when the expression 'Broad' was used, and that Clough had suggested it.[116]

When Stanley turns to the matter of baptism he reveals a strong doctrinal scepticism characteristic of Broad Churchmen. The nature of baptism, he says, is not susceptible to 'precise dogmatic statements',[117] and in any case, upholding the right doctrine is not essential to Christian faith. Disagreements over doctrinal definitions are misplaced and inappropriate, and as the Gorham controversy had shown again, divisive and destructive. 'It is not this or that tenet of any particular school, but the moral and spiritual character of religion itself which suffers in struggles like these.'[118]

> Let anyone look at a rustic congregation, and ask what it is which is expected from the Church of England by the rude farmer, the simple labourer, the hard shopkeeper, the timid woman, the ignorant child, that come to worship under that sacred roof. Do they wish to know whether their pastor has authority to teach them dogmatically the doctrines of Absolution and the Real Presence? Do they wish to be told whether Regeneration takes place in, before, or after Baptism? – whether their children have been regenerated by prevenient grace or by the sprinkling of water? ... Everyone knows that they want no such thing. Everyone knows that a clergyman who was constantly insisting on such matters in his pulpit would be regarded as hardly in his right mind. Everyone knows that what they desire, and what from any good pastor they will receive, is the permission and the help to worship God as their fathers worshipped Him – to serve Him truly in those various stations in which He has placed them – to be strengthened and built up in that holy faith which is indeed, in every sense, beyond and 'without controversy'.[119]

The article was welcomed by liberals who had been dismayed at what they saw as a benighted clash of ignorant armies. Nonetheless, Stanley had misgivings: he feared that he had only added to the controversy and its damage to the Church. He felt 'weary of all this wordy strife',[120] and recalled Liddell's advice (in his sermon at Stanley's ordination) to avoid controversy. No doubt bereavement played a part in these feelings of disenchantment. To raise his spirits Stanley set off in August with his mother and Mary on a six-week expedition to Como. They visited Strasbourg and Constance on the way, and returned to Paris via Milan, the Grande Chartreuse and Bourges.

* * *

While abroad Stanley received a letter from Downing Street inviting him to become secretary of a royal commission to inquire into the 'state, discipline, studies, and revenues' of the university and colleges of Oxford. The question of university reform had been agitated for fifty years. At Oxford, the Tractarian movement had proved both a distraction and a conservative force. After Newman's secession in 1845, attention turned again to improving the university. Stanley's responsibility was to give him a new prominence in Government circles. He was delighted, partly by the honour, but more because he had wanted to see reform in Oxford since his visit to Bonn with Tait in 1839. He had come too to share Jowett's ambitions for a more inclusive university, open to poor students as well as to those who could not subscribe to the Church of England's formularies, and he had been working with him and other liberal dons on a volume of essays on university reform. Stanley wanted to see a broader curriculum and the end of restricted scholarships and fellowships. His aim, in short, was to turn what in many respects was still a medieval institution into a modern one.

The urge for reform was also to be found at Westminster. In April 1850, James Heywood, the radical member for North Lancashire, moved for an address to Her Majesty for a royal commission of inquiry into the universities of Oxford, Cambridge and Dublin. Stanley had no confidence that Oxford would reform itself. After a meeting in his rooms[G] with other liberal dons (including Jowett, Goldwin Smith and Mark Pattison), Stanley wrote a letter to the Prime Minister, John Russell, 'to express a hope that, whatever course the Government may adopt with regard to the motion, your Lordship will not allow the discussion to pass without holding out a prospect of such friendly assistance as would, I conceive, be ultimately necessary for carrying out those changes which are essential to the real interests of the University'.[121]

Stanley was present in the Speaker's gallery for the debate on 18 July. He described the scene in a letter to Jowett:

> The Ministerial speeches were very feeble, perhaps purposely so, with a view of closing the debate. Gladstone's was very powerful, and said, in the most efficient manner, anything which could be said against the Commission.[H] His allusion to Peel[I] was very

---

[G] Stanley had moved into the main quadrangle in 1846; today his rooms are occupied by the master.

[H] Gladstone had been shocked by the Gorham Judgment and was afraid that the State would again challenge the Church of England's autonomy by abolishing its monopoly of the universities.

[I] Peel had died two weeks before and, like Gladstone, had been a member for Oxford University.

touching, and the House responded to it by a profound and sympathetic silence, with the exception of two M.P.'s who, having been for some time lying head to head in the Members' Gallery, were roused from repose by the pause and, on hearing what it was, exclaimed one to another: 'Balderdash!' 'd – d balderdash!' and so to sleep again.[122]

The motion was carried, clearing the path for the appointment of commissioners. They were carefully chosen by the Prime Minister rather than the university, and were decidedly liberal in outlook. Among them were Tait, Liddell and Hinds, the Bishop of Norwich. Goldwin Smith was appointed later as Stanley's assistant secretary and treasurer. The commissioners were charged to inquire into the current state of the university, to make recommendations as to how the university might be reformed, and to collect material necessary for legislation.

The commission met first at 10 Downing Street on 19 October 1850, but the start was not propitious. Stanley was suspected of being responsible for another epistolary mishap. Letters were sent to the university's chancellor, the Duke of Wellington, and the vice-chancellor. But they were placed in the wrong envelopes. Stanley, however, was adamant 'that it was the Bishop who had written, covered, and sealed the letters and that I had only franked them'.[123]

Between October 1850 and April 1852, eighty-seven meetings were held, mostly in London, and the volume of work on the secretary's shoulders was considerable, monopolising Stanley's time and energy. The commissioners remained painstakingly thorough in their approach, despite determined resistance from the university and colleges, many of which boycotted the inquiry, University College included. In the face of obstruction Stanley was, according to one of the commissioners, invariably patient, good-tempered and conciliatory.[124] Enough witnesses were found to make the report and its evidence what John Sparrow described as 'the fullest and most interesting account there is of Oxford in the nineteenth century'.[125] Much of the 'blue book' was written by Stanley, and its 260 foolscap pages covered statutes and governance; scholarships, fellowships and professorships; revenues and expenditure; curricula and examinations. The Duke of Wellington took it to bed to read, telling his son, 'I shall never get through it Charles, but I must work on.'[126] He died the same night.

The commission made stringent recommendations for reform. The university's governing body, the hebdomadal board, would be replaced by a council composed of the board, together with professors and public lecturers, and the senior tutor of every college. The student body would be extended to include 'a much larger and poorer class',[127] who should be spared the expense of being members of a college. Undergraduates would no longer be graded as noblemen, gentlemen commoners and commoners. Literae humaniores would cease to be the compulsory school, and the role of professors would be expanded. Scholarships and fellowships would be open to competition, and fellows would not have to be ordained. The commission was not empowered to discuss religious tests but they noted that subscription was a barrier to university extension.

Outside Oxford the report was well received, in Whig circles especially. The *Edinburgh Review* described it as 'a truly remarkable document, and one which is destined to form an era in the constitutional history of the country'.[128] But many in the university, and the heads of colleges especially, remained conservative, and resentful of Government interference. There were squabbles in colleges between diehard and reforming fellows, and it soon became clear, as Stanley had known from the start, that the university would not reform itself without legislation. Gladstone (now Chancellor of the Exchequer) realised that reform was unavoidable, and started to draft a bill that would protect the university's connection with the established Church. He asked Jowett for help, which he gave, though not without disagreement on a number of important points. The Oxford University Bill was a compromise, and was introduced by Russell in March 1854. After a stormy passage, it passed into law in August, and included many but by no means all the commission's main recommendations. Stanley was present in the Commons at one in the morning, and described

> a superb speech from Gladstone, in which, for the first time, all the arguments from our Report (without acknowledgement, of course) were worked up in the most effective manner. He vainly endeavoured to reconcile his present with his former position. But with this exception, I listened to his speech with the greatest delight. To see our labours of 1851-2 brought at last to bear on the point, to hear proclaimed on the housetop what we had announced in sheepskins and goatskins, to behold one's old enemies slaughtered before one's face with the most irresistible weapons, was quite intoxicating. One great charm of his speaking

is its exceeding good-humour. There is great vehemence, but no bitterness.[129]

* * *

Another royal commission was hard at work at the same time as Stanley's: to plan for the Great Exhibition of the Work of all Nations. This had been Prince Albert's big idea, and he was president of the commission: members included the Prime Minister and Gladstone, nine fellows of the Royal Society, and Charles Barry, the architect of the new Palace of Westminster. The exhibition was a massive undertaking with enormous problems to overcome, and required a building the size and structure of which had never been seen before. Joseph Paxton's Crystal Palace in Hyde Park, 'a blazing arch of lucid glass',[130] covered 16 acres and used over 4,500 tons of iron and nearly 300,000 panes of glass. Its length was more than three times that of St Paul's Cathedral. Over 100,000 exhibits were on show from all over the empire. 'Whatever human industry has created you find there,' wrote Charlotte Brontë after her second visit, 'from the great compartments filled with railway engines and boilers, with mill machinery in full work, with splendid carriages of all kinds, with harness of every description, to the glass-covered and velvet spread stands loaded with the most gorgeous work of the goldsmith and silversmith, and the carefully guarded caskets full of real diamonds and pearls worth hundreds of thousands of pounds.'[131]

Stanley was one of Prince Albert's honorary chaplains[j] and this, together with his new connections in Downing Street, ensured an invitation to the opening ceremony on 1 May 1851. Queen Victoria described it in her journal as 'one of the greatest and most glorious days of our lives'.[132] In a letter to Charley's widow, Stanley has left another detailed account of a celebrated historic occasion:

> It was not till we were fairly seated that we ventured to look round. The transept, as the nearest part, was the chief object. In the centre was the platform, covered with red cloth, and a dais for the Chair of State, immediately in front of which was the glass fountain, not yet playing. On each side were statues; in the north transept were the great green trees, and underneath them palm-trees and the like from the East India House, with another fountain, playing; and amongst these trees stood, statue-like, the

[j] In 1847 Baron Bunsen had recommended Stanley as tutor to the six-year-old Prince of Wales. He was not appointed but was added to the Prince Consort's chaplains.

Beefeaters ... At last 11.30 A.M. came, when the doors were finally closed, and no more invasion of our seats was possible. Then the clock reached 5 minutes to 12, the platform cleared, and the flourish of trumpets announced the arrival of the Queen. I have a very indistinct recollection of that moment: a dim vision of a procession amidst the palm-trees, and then the whole group gradually forming itself on the platform, and 'God save the Queen' bursting forth from the north organ. I never had so good a view of the Queen before, and never before saw her look so thoroughly regal. She stood in front of the chair, turning round first to one side and then to the other, with a look of power and pride, flushed with a kind of excitement which I never witnessed in any other human countenance ...

I cannot say, with the 'Times,' that the pageant of yesterday was the most magnificent I ever saw. In many essential points the Coronation was finer, in some the entrance of the Pope into St. Peter's on Easter Sunday. Of all occasional festivals that I have ever seen, not forgetting the Fête of Fraternisation at Paris in 1848, it was, however, the grandest; and whatever flaws there may be in the moral interest, it has at least that of being unparalleled. No one knew beforehand what it would be like, or knows now what will grow out of it.[K] The Master of Pembroke said at the Commission, what I suppose is true, 'There were never before gathered so many human beings under one roof since the world began.'[133]

[K] The proceeds were used to buy land in south Kensington where the Royal Albert Hall and the Victoria & Albert, Natural History and Science Museums were built.

PART THREE
Canterbury and Oxford
1851–1863

6
'Treading the Pilgrim's Ground'
1851–1858

STANLEY'S WORK FOR the university commission on top of his college responsibilities was wearying, and he complained to Pearson that Oxford was 'beginning "to come out at the nostrils".'[1] The Prime Minister, Lord John Russell, was sympathetic, and knowing that Stanley's fellowship had to end, he offered him the respite of a canonry at Canterbury. Stanley's Oxford friends were sad to see him go, but recognised that removal from the pressures of the university would do him good, if only for a while. One Balliol friend wrote prophetically: 'I am sure no man is better for living his whole life here, and if you come back (as I hope and believe you will), you will then feel the full benefit of the break.'[2]

Stanley's students wrote warmly 'to express their deep sense of your great kindness to them all during your residence among them, and their regret at losing the advantages they have so long enjoyed'.[3] They offered to pay for a portrait to be hung in hall. Stanley agreed to sit, and Eden Eddis was commissioned: the portrait hangs today above that of Plumptre, Stanley's master.[a] Stanley is shown with the report of the commission in his hand, but what is remarkable about the portrait is that he is made to look similar to Arnold in the famous portrait by Thomas Phillips.[4] Though Arnold seems active and Stanley contemplative, they are both holding a book, and their heads, turned a touch to the right, have identical black, curly hair and long sideboards. It is difficult not to conclude that Eddis modelled his portrait on Phillips's: indeed the undergraduates may have asked him to do so.

Stanley was installed in the cathedral in person and not by proxy (as was still often the case) on Saturday 16 August 1851. His stall[b] was in the gift of the Crown and he was 'presented by the Queen's

---
[a] For some unknown reason the portrait remained in Vaughan's possession until he gave it to the college in 1894.
[b] Stall v had been occupied 1803–38 by Canon William Nelson, who succeeded his famous brother as Baron Nelson of the Nile.

most generous majesty'. Stanley had to subscribe again to the Thirty-Nine Articles, which he did now with an easier conscience than at ordination. The following day he preached and read the offices. He then returned to Oxford until November when his house at 17 The Precincts became vacant. Stanley's final departure from Oxford was difficult, as such changes always were. 'I found him', wrote one of his pupils, 'in his rooms, literally cowering over the fire. "Think of me," he said, "lost in that huge Cathedral."'[5] After an unhappy start, Stanley had become firmly attached to University College. 'I feel deeply', he told Pearson, 'that my calling was *here*: and I feel as if I were passing from a land of reality into a land of shadows. How gladly would I lie down to rest under the threshold of this beloved chapel!'[6]

Born and brought up in the Georgian world of Jane Austen, Stanley found himself now at the heart of Anthony Trollope's Victorian Barchester.[c] Reform was in the air (as it was in the universities) but cathedrals were still served by old-fashioned High Churchmen like Septimus Harding and the Grantlys. The Dean of Canterbury was the worldly and learned William Rowe Lyall. Educated at Eton and Trinity, Cambridge, he was a protégé of Archbishop Howley, who had appointed him Archdeacon of Maidstone and a canon of Canterbury, before persuading Robert Peel to offer him the deanery. Lyall had been present at the famous conference at Hadleigh in Suffolk held ten days after Keble's assize sermon. That meeting is generally regarded as the start of the Oxford Movement, but Lyall's ambition and conservatism combined to distance him from a cause which soon became too radical for him. As dean, he enjoyed considerable patronage, much of which he bestowed on his family, securing lucrative livings for a brother, four nephews and three nephews-in-law.[d] Soon after Stanley arrived, Lyall suffered a stroke from which he never recovered, and died in the deanery five years later.

There were six residentiary canons in Stanley's time, and these included the two archdeacons. When Stanley started, three had been canons for over twenty years. Canon Lord Charles Thynne had become a fervent Tractarian. He was a son of the 2nd Marquess of Bath and was married to the daughter of Lyall's predecessor as Dean of

[c] *The Warden* (1855) and *Barchester Towers* (1857) were published during Stanley's time at Canterbury.
[d] See Clive Dewey, *The Passing of Barchester* (1991), for a study of Lyall and the relatives he appointed.

Canterbury, now Bishop of Bath and Wells.[e] A year after Stanley moved into the precincts, Thynne caused a scandal by converting to Rome. Stanley's aunt, Lady Stanley, was appalled: 'I think Arthur will return when he hears how the chapter at Canterbury is falling to pieces, but the news of Ld. Charles' perversion can have hardly reached him yet ... He gives up everything in the Church & has no private fortune – in a *better cause* one should honour the sacrifice to conscience – in *this* I can only see gross folly & blindness to Truth *as it is in Jesus*.'[7] Another canon, Benjamin Harrison, was Stanley's neighbour and became his closest friend in Canterbury. He was seven years older and had been a contemporary of Gladstone at Christ Church. He was another of Howley's favourites,[f] and had succeeded Lyall as Archdeacon of Maidstone, a position he held conscientiously until his death forty-two years later. Also like the dean, he had been an early but short-lived member of the Oxford Movement.

The chief concern of the dean and chapter appears to have been the administration of their considerable property and endowments. Renewal of leases, appointment of tenants, inspection of estates, repair of farm buildings, and the overriding desire to maximise profits dominated the weekly chapter meetings. None of this made any sense to Stanley, for whom arithmetic was a mystery and business a foreign language. An amusing letter from him headed 'The Audit Room Canterbury', and dated 26 November 1851, two days after his arrival, describes: 'A conversation in Chinese (as far as relates to me) going on between the Dean, Dr. Spry, and the sexmillenarian C – on leases and tithes at one end of a long table. The aged M – wrapped in the "Times", the infirm D – wrapped in vacancy; the auditor warming himself by the fire; Archdeacon Harrison really doing business; Lord Charles Thynne and A. P. S. writing letters as fast as the pen can carry us – which possibility is the redeeming feature of the whole affair, and really prevents it from being so intolerable as it would otherwise be.'[8]

Though Stanley was disinterested, he benefited personally from this lucrative endeavour. Canterbury Cathedral's revenues were very considerable, and they had in the past been shared between the dean and canons. Since 1840 the income from cathedrals' land and property could be commuted in return for a comparative grant from the ecclesiastical commissioners. In Canterbury's case the grant was sufficient to

---

[e] Richard Bagot, who had ordained Stanley when he was Bishop of Oxford.
[f] Harrison inherited Howley's books which are now part of the cathedral's Howley-Harrison library.

provide quarterly stipends of £500 for the dean and £250 for the canons – the equivalent of annual salaries of £150,000 and £75,000 today. For comparison, the average benefice was worth £13,500 in today's money. Furthermore, commuting was in its infancy, and additional miscellaneous income still found its legitimate way into the canons' coffers. And they could also hold benefices and their revenues, especially those in the gift of the dean and chapter.

The chapter set aside a portion of the grant to maintain and restore the cathedral. Here Lyall was unusually ambitious, devising a programme to overhaul the entire fabric, though not much more was achieved in his time than the repair of the cloisters. There had been considerable neglect in the previous century, and in the year Lyall was appointed an article in the *Ecclesiologist* noted with disapproval that 'a beautiful staircase turret to the south-east transept is entirely out of repair; and generally in this part windows are broken or their sills are vegetating with weeds ... The northern side of the cathedral ... is even deficient in rainwater pipes and the walls are streaked with green. The most valuable sculptures are here unheeded, the Chapter House is in disorder, damp and littered.' The article goes on to describe the cloisters as being used as a dumping ground for stone and ladders, and the crypt as unfit to be 'the resting place of some of the most illustrious Primates of the English Church'.[9]

Despite the notorious worldliness and lethargy of the eighteenth-century English Church, the daily offices said or sung in the choir had remained every cathedral's prime *raison d'être*. The quality was still often poor, as Charles Kingsley observed: 'The scanty service rattled in the vast building like a dried kernel too small for its shell. The place breathed imbecility and unreality, and sleepy life in death, while the whole nineteenth century went roaring on its way outside.'[10] The standard of worship at Canterbury was better than at most cathedrals. Daily sung services were resumed immediately after the Restoration in 1660, with matins at ten and evensong at three in winter, and four in summer. On Sunday mornings there was a long service consisting of matins, litany and ante-communion. Full communion was celebrated once a week, and in 1853 Canterbury was one of only twelve cathedrals where communion services were held more than twelve times a year. Sermons were preached in the cathedral twice on Sundays, and Stanley took this responsibility especially seriously. From an unpromising start as a preacher he had, through determination and practice, become proficient in the pulpit. His homilies, like Arnold's, were practical, not doctrinal.

They were now often lively and graphic, and – unusually at the time – used plain, familiar language. It is no surprise that Stanley's sermons in the cathedral, and in parish churches in the city, were popular and well attended. 'I am glad to say', he wrote to Pearson in January 1852, 'that I have at last succeeded in making myself audible, and I am also told that the sermons are beloved by the people.'[11]

Stanley's house in the cathedral precincts was a substantial Georgian dwelling of red brick.[g] It was at the north-east corner of the cathedral and was built on the site of the twelfth century prior's chambers. The dormers and sash windows on the front gave fine views of the top of the cathedral's Bell Harry Tower, finished in 1504, and of the beautiful corona at the east end, so-called because a slice of Thomas Becket's skull had been preserved there in a silver reliquary. Stanley had inherited a parrot on a perch in his garden, and he trained it to call out 'Thomas à Becket!' whenever a visitor called. Immediately in front of the garden were the ruined arches of a chapel which had once served the priory's infirmary; in Stanley's time, small houses (soon to be demolished) had been built into the arches.

Here Stanley made a home for his mother and Mary, as well as for the family nurse, Sarah Burgess, who died in 1856. She was an Alderley girl who had come to live at the rectory when Arthur was two, and he was always fond of her. To his cousin, Augustus J. C. Hare, 'the chief charm to Arthur Stanley in having a home of his own was that he could welcome his mother to it, and greatly did she enjoy her long visits to Canterbury, where she shook off at once all the influences of her London life, and threw herself with all her heart into the interests of the place and its associations. Never were the mother and son more wholly united than in these happy years, when every evening the literary work of the day was read to her, and received her deepest attention, often her severest criticism.'[12]

Stanley took considerable pride in being, as he put it, 'the servant and minister, not of some obscure fugitive establishment, for which no one cares beyond his narrow circle, but of a cathedral whose name demands respect and interest even in the remotest parts of Europe'.[13] As always, it was the narrative of history enshrined in the place, rather than its beauty, grandeur or ecclesiastical pre-eminence that most excited him. The story of Becket, his quarrel with the King and his

---

[g] Today the building is a boarding house (Linacre) for the King's School.

martyrdom in the cathedral, began to fascinate and engage his imagination. Two months after his arrival in Canterbury he wrote to Pearson: 'I am so entirely absorbed in Commission work that I have not read anything else whatever, except in the evenings accounts of Becket and Canterbury. I now know the story thoroughly, with many incidents quite new ... On December 29, the day of the murder, I went to the spot at 5 P.M. – the fatal hour – with what results you shall hear. The place absolutely teems with history and ghosts, ancient and modern.'[14] In future years Stanley would assemble his family and friends on the anniversary, and lead them in the dark on a graphic guided tour of Becket's last moments. He wrote a masterly essay on 'The Murder of Becket' which appeared in the *Quarterly Review* in September 1853. Minutely researched and detailed, it is also a gripping and at times melodramatic telling of the tale.[h] Stanley included it in his *Historical Memorials of Canterbury*, published in 1855, and dedicated ('with sincere respect') to Archdeacon Harrison. The three other essays are based on lectures given in Canterbury – on the landing of Augustine and the conversion of Ethelbert, Becket's shrine, and the Black Prince, whose splendid tomb and effigy are in the south choir ambulatory. The book was widely read, and helped to revive interest in the cathedral and draw attention to its dilapidated state.

The cathedral statutes determined that the dean and each canon should be resident in the precincts for ninety days each year. With twelve canons, it was intended that three would be resident at any one time. The Cathedrals Act had reduced the number of canons to six, and with similar reductions in every cathedral, the royal commission appointed in 1852 'to inquire into the State and Conditions of the Cathedrals' recommended that every member of the chapter should reside for nine months each year. However, it is clear from the Canterbury chapter minutes that the dean and canons continued to draw up a rota allowing each to reside for only two consecutive months a year. To critics of the Church, arrangements like this were a scandalous abuse and waste of manpower, and certainly there were plenty of cathedral clergy for whom absenteeism was a chance for indolence or the profits of pluralism. For others they provided a justifiable opportunity for contemplation, prayer or study. Stanley's Balliol contemporary Edward Goulburn (Tait's successor at Rugby before becoming Dean of Norwich) was convinced that what mattered above all in a cathedral

---

[h] See Appendix II, pp. 335ff.

were 'sacred learning, study, devotion, retirement from the world, and the maintenance of the perpetual worship of God'.[15] Stanley added travel to the list, and months of leisure, supported by a private income, enabled him to indulge his passion for visiting and describing the distant places of sacred history.

*   *   *

The report of the Oxford University Commission was published in May 1852, and Stanley was free at last to make his pilgrimage to the Holy Land which he had postponed when his father died. He left England in August with his mother, Mary and a niece, the daughter of Kitty's brother, Edward Penrhyn. Stanley's plan was to travel with them through Italy until November, when he would leave them in Rome and set off to Cairo en route to Palestine. In a long letter to Pearson, Stanley described first their visit to the papal states of northern Italy. They stayed at Ferrara which Stanley found 'a deeply uninteresting place', and Bologna 'which charmed us ... a great city ruled by a cardinal, Pontiffs in bronze or marble towering over every square, and the keys blazing on every gate, custom-house, and shield!' When they were there they heard that the Duke of Wellington had died two weeks before. Stanley asked Pearson to send details of the death and funeral arrangements of 'the greatest man in England, Europe, the world'. He had last seen him at the Great Exhibition, bent with arthritis. From Bologna they travelled to the ancient city of Ravenna on the Adriatic coast. Stanley was disappointed, finding nothing impressive or beautiful in either the town's situation or its buildings. Typically the whole interest of Ravenna centred on its history, 'as displayed in its tombs and mosaics within the churches'. He was fascinated by the vivid mosaic representations of the Emperor and Empress, Justinian and Theodora, in San Vitale: 'They seem', he explained in the same letter, 'to be the only existing pictures of the Byzantine court, and, though stiff like all mosaics, it is something to look on the very figures of those departed potentates.'[16]

From Ravenna the party travelled south, crossing the Rubicon to Rimini, popular at the time as a bathing resort. Then on to the little pilgrimage town of Loreto, famous for the sanctuary built on the site to which it is believed that angels transported the Virgin Mary's house (the Santa Casa) from Nazareth. Stanley saw the house inside, encased in marble and sculptured with statues. He was shown the window through which the angel Gabriel was said to have flown to make the annunciation. Stanley explained to Jowett that he found it 'a mournful spot to see ... especially mournful from the irreconcilably opposite aspects which it presents to us and to them. The Protestant's associations of Loreto are merely of a gross and monstrous fiction. In the mind of the Catholics it is not merely that they do not reject the fiction but that it seems hardly to enter into their consideration of the place.'[17] In a letter to Shairp, Stanley regretted that neither side considered the feelings of the other, and asked, 'Is it impossible that some new change might take place, equal to the Reformation in extent, but ending in understanding and harmony, instead of in rents and convulsions?'[18]

They reached Rome on 20 October, though Stanley never liked to return to places he had already visited. 'Were I to see Rome a thousand times at the interval of thousands of years, the first dawn of the Campagna and St. Peter's from the hills of Albano, the first waving of the peacock fans in Santa Maria, the first rise of the Capitoline steps under the thrilling feet, would still live unrivalled, and all subsequent impressions seem poor and tame in comparison.'[19] Nevertheless, he had not seen the Sistine Chapel before and was fortunate to find a place on the front row of the strangers' seats for a papal mass on All Souls' Day. He watched the cardinals arrive, one by one, kneeling and rising, and bowing to the altar, all dressed in funereal crimson and purple instead of scarlet.

> At last the great catastrophe arrived. The door on the left of the altar, after having poured in a host of magnificently arrayed canons round the Cardinal Archbishop who was to perform the service, and of scarlet prelates, opened finally. 'Il Pontefice,' whispered the spectators; the cardinals rose *en masse*.
>
> In walked Pius IX.,[i] with a high white mitre, white, but with a richly embroidered coat, a long train borne by two scarlet Monsignori, one of whom was our old acquaintance Talbot of Balliol.[j] What with the turning inwards of the whole body towards him, the robes, the train, and mitre, and also a portly person and large-featured face, there was something almost colossal about him – something very different from the dead corpse-like figure of Gregory XVI.[k] ...

[i] Pope, 1846–78.
[j] The Hon. George Talbot joined Balliol the year after Stanley. He converted to Rome in 1843 and was ordained priest. In 1849 he was appointed a canon of St Peter's and a chamberlain to Pope Pius IX. He was an *éminence grise* in Rome for twenty years.
[k] Stanley had seen him on his first visit to Rome in 1841.

1a Stanley's father as Bishop of Norwich

1b Stanley's mother, Kitty, the year after her marriage

1c Kitty Stanley, when she was living at Canterbury

1d Mary Stanley, after the Crimean War

2a The church and rectory at Alderley

2b Stanley as a pupil at Rugby

2c Thomas Arnold, aged 43, by Thomas Phillips, RA

3 Ackermann print of Rugby School

4a Sixth form schoolroom at Rugby

4b Charles Vaughan by George Richmond

4c Balliol College, the front quadrangle, 1810

5a Queen Victoria's Coronation, 28 June 1838

5b University College, Oxford, from the High Street

6a John Henry Newman, 1847, two years after his conversion to Rome

6b Stanley as fellow and tutor of University College, by Eden Eddis, 1851

6c Canterbury Cathedral in Stanley's time

7a The opening of the Great Exhibition, 1 May 1851

7b Archibald Campbell Tait as Headmaster of Rugby

7c Benjamin Jowett by George Richmond, 1850

8a The Duke of Wellington's funeral procession, 18 November 1852

8b R. D. Hampden by H. W. Pickersgill

8c Dean Liddell by George Richmond, 1858

Thrice at least he descended from the throne to be clothed and unclothed, mitred and unmitred, spread and unspread, and the whole service seemed to move in equal relations round him and round the altar. Never for a moment were you allowed to forget that the highest potentate of this earth was present in the chapel; never could you forget that you looked on an aged human being, living in this passing generation of the nineteenth century, but laden with the traditions and courtesies, and, must I add? superstitions and falsehoods of 1,500 years.[20]

Stanley received word that Wellington's funeral, the last of the great heraldic State funerals, was to take place on 18 November and he was determined to be there. So instead of journeying to Cairo to begin his eastern tour as planned, he left Rome on 14 November and reached London the night before the funeral. He was up at six the next morning on a bright, cold day and made his way on foot to St Paul's. He noticed that the crowds along the route of the procession were even denser than for the Coronation, with people on rooftops, and others leaning out of windows or hanging high up in trees. The clubs of St James's were hung with black, and Temple Bar was covered with black velvet, with silver vases at the top, burning with gas to look like incense. The crowds were jammed at Charing Cross, and Stanley was unable to move until eight. He took half an hour to reach the Strand, and St Paul's was to be closed at nine. Then suddenly the line moved on, Fleet Street was clear, and he reached St Paul's with fifteen minutes to spare. He had been invited to breakfast at the deanery where he first met Lord John Russell and the dean's wife, Mrs Milman. At ten he crossed the street with the dean's party, climbed the cathedral's spiral staircase, and sat with them on the balcony, overlooking Ludgate Hill. Once again, as with the coronation and the opening of the Great Exhibition, Stanley has left a graphic, first-hand description of a defining Victorian event:

If ever St. Paul's could bear comparison with St. Peter's, it was on that day. The space, from being entirely cleared, seemed far larger than usual; the crowds sat in numbers numberless on the roofs of the houses, but the Churchyard, and Ludgate Hill, and Fleet Street, between the avenues of troops on the pavement, was as vacant as the nave of St. Peter's.

It was, I think, about eleven A.M. that the procession first began to show itself. I must confess that it was not impressive. There were, it is true, many soldiers moving on in succession, but they were in such broken detachments, and the line was so often interrupted by coaches, and those often private coaches of the meanest appearance, that all sense of continuity was lost, and the pageant was neither military nor stately ... Two or three striking points, however, there were – the successive banners of the Duke, the standard, the banner of Wellesley, carried with all heraldic pomp; the eighty-three old Chelsea pensioners, toiling up with all the stiffness and slowness of age; and, above all, what came very nearly at the close of the procession, the funeral car – not, indeed, the car itself, for that was ungainly and extravagant[1] but the vast black mass which preceded it in the shape, or rather shapelessness, of the twelve black horses, so loaded with plumes and trappings that they might have been elephants. You knew not what. You saw only the vast pagoda towering high above, and before it all this mass advancing like a cloud of Death, a living Grave. Alone, of all the parts of the procession, this mighty monster passed through the gates of the Churchyard and stopped at the Cathedral doors.[21]

Stanley descended from the balcony and entered the cathedral to be seated in the gallery, looking down the nave, just as he had been for the coronation in Westminster Abbey. He was disappointed though because he had expected the interior to be dimly lit – instead the sun was streaming in the windows and reflecting on the white stone. However, he found the long procession of clergy robed in black and white as splendid as the cardinals. The psalms struck him as magnificent, every word of the lesson read by the dean was audible, and the rustling of paper as the vast congregation turned over the pages of their service-books sounded like a giant sigh. The dead march thundered as the coffin was lowered into the vault to take its place next to Lord Nelson's. The dean read the words of burial, and the Garter King of Arms proclaimed the duke's titles. The words were hardly audible to Stanley, except 'field marshal' and 'knight', repeated a hundred times. The blessing by the Bishop of London was followed by a boom of cannon at the Tower of London. 'To me', wrote Stanley, 'there was something awfully impressive in the mere Protestantism of the service: grand hopes of immortality, deep sense of irreparable loss, exhortations

---

[1] Inspired by Prince Albert, this massive car was 21 feet long by 12 feet wide and weighed 18 tons. It was decorated with trophies, heraldic achievements, and the names of Wellington's victories emblazoned in gold.

to duty, but not a word of prayer or thought, or wish for the dead himself.'[22]

As Stanley made his way out of St Paul's he met some of the college heads, there to represent Oxford where the Duke had been chancellor. They told him how they had been saying to each other, 'Oh! How Stanley would enjoy this sight!'[23] He travelled back with them to their hotel where he met the master of University College. Relations between the two men had been strained by the commission which Plumptre had resented. Nonetheless, he received Stanley warmly, as if he had 'descended from the stars in a flaming comet'.[24]

* * *

A fortnight later, Stanley set off again on his long-awaited tour of the East. He reached the centre of Paris on 2 December 1852, just in time for another dose of pomp and circumstance as the Second Empire was proclaimed. Since Stanley's last visit in October 1848, Napoleon's nephew, Louis Napoleon Bonaparte, had been elected President of the Republic. Three years later he had extended his term of office by a *coup d'état*, and a year after that, was voted hereditary emperor: as Napoleon III, he inaugurated the Second Empire.

> I was waked at 10 by the cannons from the Hôtel de Ville. This was the actual Proclamation. The *sight* was the entrance of the Emperor (oh marvellous, fateful, and heart-stirring word!). At 1 P.M. I stood near enough to see him distinctly. The roar of artillery and crash of martial music were wonderfully impressive, and gave it all the appearance of a great event. He bowed graciously to right and left, and looked pleased and well. I then flew up to the highest room in this house ... and thence saw the *cortège* enter the Tuileries, thus adding another chapter, another dynasty, another splendour, another fall to the history of that most awful palace.[25]

Kitty and Mary were on their way home from Italy, and Stanley met them at Avignon. From there he went on to Marseilles and boarded a ship bound for Egypt. Jowett was to have accompanied him in 1849 but now he was too busy at Balliol. Instead, Stanley took with him three younger men whom Jowett had recommended: Theodore Walrond, William Fremantle and William Findlay. Stanley wanted men he could teach, and who in return would be able to provide practical support on what was going to be a long and gruelling journey. Walrond was nine years younger than Stanley. He had been Arnold's last head of school and a pupil of Jowett. He had returned to Rugby to teach for two years before being elected to a fellowship at Balliol in 1850.ᵐ Findlay was curate of Hindley in Lancashire; he and Walrond had become friends as undergraduates. Fremantle was still a Balliol undergraduate and Walrond's pupil.ⁿ In a letter sent from their boat on the Nile, Stanley drew a plan to show the arrangement of their cabins. The crew called him 'The Sheykh', the holy man; Walrond they called 'The Pacha' because of his leadership of the party; Fremantle, 'The Fez' because of his cap; and Findlay, 'The Father of Guns' because he was fond of hunting.

Stanley chose to start the pilgrimage in Egypt because, after the patriarchs of Genesis, it was the place where the Hebrew history began. It was out of Egypt that Moses had led the Hebrew slaves on their exodus through the deserts of Sinai. There they received the Ten Commandments, before reaching the promised land of Palestine. Egypt was to provide the background and introduction to his visit to the Holy Land. The party landed at Alexandria, and from there they travelled on horseback to Cairo, where they witnessed elaborate celebrations for the birthday of Mohammed. Two days later, on Christmas Day 1852, they set sail on their 460-mile voyage up the Nile to Luxor. The long journey was not spent simply sightseeing like other passengers, but in reading the Bible and Koran, and books on Biblical history. Stanley lectured his companions on the Coptic Church, and after dinner they took it in turns to read aloud from *The Arabian Nights*.

Stanley was overwhelmed by the ruins of the ancient capital city of Thebes where Luxor now stands, and which they reached on 10 January. The temples, palaces, gateways, tombs and colossi made it 'the most interesting place in the world – after Rome and Athens – that I have seen'.²⁶ Stanley was struck especially by the statue of Rameses II, supposed to be the pharaoh at the time of the exodus, and the subject of 'Ozymandias', Shelley's famous sonnet:

> What spires are to a modern city – what the towers of a cathedral are to its nave and choir – that the statues of the Pharaohs were to the streets and temples of Thebes. The ground is strewn with their fragments. There were avenues of them, towering high above

---

ᵐ Walrond was a candidate for the headmastership of Rugby in 1869 and was to become one of Stanley's literary executors.
ⁿ Thirty years later Jowett invited Fremantle back to Balliol as chaplain. He edited Jowett's sermons for posthumous publication.

plain or houses. Three of gigantic size still remain. One was the
granite statue of Rameses II himself, who sat with his hands on his
knees, on the right side of the entrance to his palace. By some
extraordinary catastrophe, the statue has been thrown down, and
the Arabs have scooped their millstones out of his face. But you
can still see what he was – the largest statue in the world. He must
have been, even sitting, a hundred feet high.[27]

In this letter to Mary, Stanley reflects on the purpose of such an enormous monolith. It was the uninhibited representation of the conqueror of the then known world, of a king of kings who shared the same stature as the gods. 'It carries one back to the days "when there were giants in the earth". It shows how the king was, in that first monarchy, the visible god on earth ... No pure monotheism could for a moment have been compatible with such an intense exaltation of the reigning king.'[28]

After a second visit to Thebes, the party made ready to cross the Sinaitic wilderness on camels, which Stanley likened to 'passing through the desert on a mountain. You feel at once raised above all ordinary cares: no fear of fleas, if there are any; no glare or heat from the sand; a wide prospect, like what one used to enjoy from the highest summit of coach or diligence,° and the full enjoyment of every breeze which blows through the desert. The strangeness of the animal is inexhaustible.'[29] They arrived at Mount Sinai in the south early in March. Stanley held a service on the Sunday, attended by other travellers staying at the ancient monastery of St Catherine. 'I confess', he wrote, 'that it was with difficulty, that, in that place, I could read through the Ten Commandments.'[30] Despite the heat and discomfort of the journey, Stanley remained remarkably fit and resilient, and more so than his younger companions. He told Kitty and Mary that, to his surprise, he had found the desert a delight: 'not for a single day have I felt otherwise than richly repaid. Every day brought with it something new, something which made that day a period in itself. Every day also brought a new stock of health and refreshment, such as I have not known since Greece.'[31]

Nonetheless, Palestine was a relief, and for two reasons: first, it marked the high point of the journey; and second, it was a land of certainties and familiarities after the vagueness and ambiguities of

---

° A public stagecoach.

desert topography. 'It was quite startling', he wrote, 'to find the localities so absolutely authentic, and to hear the names of Carmel, Maon, Ziph, shouted out, in answer to my questions, from the Bedouin guides, or from the ploughmen in the fields, who knew no more of David's wanderings than those of Ulysses.'[32] Travelling in a train of horses and mules, Stanley and his companions reached Hebron, and set off north until 'a shout rang down the long file of horsemen, followed by a deep silence – BETHLEHEM!'[33] They were as overwhelmed by the associations of the place as any Christian pilgrim:

> Of the one great event of Bethlehem you are, of course, reminded by the enormous convent or convents, Latin, Greek and Armenian, clustering around the church ... The manger is in a *cave*. I do not think this is probable. Yet there is the deep interest of knowing that this is the oldest special locality fixed by the Christian Church ...
>
> I have said that you are reminded of the Nativity by the convent. But, in truth, I almost think it detracts from it. From the first moment that those towers and hills and valleys burst upon you, you have before you the thought that now at last you are in the Holy Land: it pervades the atmosphere ... no feeling that I have experienced in seeing famous places has been at all like it.[34]

Jerusalem was only five miles away, and 'the sight that for years I had most longed to see'[35] was soon in view. They entered the holy city through the Jaffa gate at half past four in the afternoon on Easter Saturday 1853.

> *Easter Sunday.* – I rose at 5.30 A.M., partly to have the pleasure, for once, of seeing the sun of Easter Day rise, 'very early in the morning,' over the shoulder of the Mount of Olives, partly to see if any ceremonies welcomed it in the great church. But there was nought. Strangely enough, here, as at Seville, Easter Day is nothing ... Our own service was at ten. I called on the bishop to offer my help, and had the great delight of reading the whole service. In the afternoon we walked down the Via Dolorosa by Gethsemane, up the Mount of Olives, round the valley of Jehoshaphat and Hinnom.[36]

They left Jerusalem on 31 March and headed up into the northern mountains of Judaea ('like the Lowlands of Wales or Scotland')[37] and on to Samaria, stopping at Bethel, Shiloh, Shechem and Jezreel with their Old Testament associations. They then descended from the hills towards the plains of Galilee, and the scenes of Jesus's life and work – Nazareth, Cana, Capernaum, Bethsaida. Stanley's party stayed in the Franciscan convent at Nazareth, the church said to have been built on the site of the Virgin Mary's house. Stanley wrote to Mary to say that he was intrigued to discover whether there was any evidence that might support the incredible claims of Loreto. He found, however, that here was another window through which it was said that the angel had flown, and, furthermore, that the outline of the house implied a large door where no door could have existed in the house at Loreto. 'I had thought before I came that possibly a likeness of situation might have suggested the story. There is, as you will have seen, none such.'[38]

Stanley travelled north-east to Damascus on the road where the apostle Paul was converted. Damascus reminded Stanley of Cairo but was more impressive. Fifty miles on in Lebanon were the ruined temples of Baalbek, the city of the Semitic sun-god, called by the Greeks Heliopolis. From there the party planned to travel 800 miles across Turkey on horseback to Smyrna (Izmir), traditionally the birthplace of Homer; and Ephesus where St Paul had challenged the cult of Artemis (Diana), and where it was believed St John the evangelist was buried. Stanley and his friends had been warned that robbers made the journey between the two cities especially dangerous. The British consul tried to dissuade them but they decided to go ahead, though not to carry money.

Constantinople (Istanbul) was to be the culmination of the Eastern tour, and Stanley had planned to be there on 29 May 1853, the 400th anniversary of the fall of the city to the Ottoman Turks and the end of the Byzantine empire. Stanley and his companions travelled for part of the journey by steamer along the Aegean coast, then through the Dardanelles (not far from Troy), and into the Sea of Marmara. 'What a journey! what a voyage! when Troy is but a speck, a cloud, in the rapid succession of interest.'[39] Stanley had the good fortune of the seaward approach to Constantinople, arriving at dawn and seeing the city's long line of domes and minarets silhouetted on the horizon. It reminded him of Venice, but on a much grander scale. 'I had imagined a background of mountains, as at Genoa. There is none such; it rises at once from the waters against the sky ... the nearer we approached the more stately and majestic the whole scene became ... No! there is no doubt that for situation Constantinople is absolutely unrivalled. No view of any city that I have ever seen can compare with it for beauty and grandeur combined – not Venice, not Genoa, not Edinburgh, not Prague, not Florence.'⁴⁰

Their first day in Constantinople was a Friday, and Stanley hurried to the Sultan's new palace to watch him pass on his way to the mosque. His pale and haggard appearance made him look weak and ordinary, 'yet still there was something dignified in the absolute immovability with which, statue-like, he rode through the silent crowd, the heir of all the great recollections of East and West, the successor of the last of the Caesars, and the last of the Caliphs, the supreme head of the Mahometan Church'.⁴¹ Stanley found Hagia Sophia by far the most impressive of all the mosques. He was fascinated by features that showed that it had previously been a Christian cathedral, with one peculiarity being an enormous gallery for women, now deserted. There were three windows placed over the altar at the command, it was said, of an angel to commemorate the Trinity. Stanley noticed that in order to face Mecca, the prayer-mats were 'turned aslant in total defiance of the architecture, so the whole building seems to have received a twist'.⁴²

There was just time before starting the journey home to travel seventy miles south-east to Nicaea (Iznik). Here in 325 the first general council of bishops had met at the command of the Emperor Constantine to determine whether the teachings of an Alexandrian priest named Arius were orthodox or heterodox.ᵖ A Greek priest gave them breakfast and showed them a painting of the council. The outcome was clear: the bishops were shown sitting in a semi-circle with Constantine wearing his imperial robes and crown on the right side of the altar, and the champions of orthodoxy, Alexander and Athanasius,ᑫ on the left. 'In the centre, ominously dressed in black, and looking thoroughly disgusted, were Arius and his followers.'⁴³

Stanley and his party returned to Constantinople on 28 May, just in time for the anniversary of the capture of the city. 'The Turks did not know the day of the month – their lunar calendar conceals it – but they knew that this was the 400th year, and had awful forebodings …'⁴⁴

*   *   *

Indeed dark clouds were already forming over the Black Sea. Before he departed for England in June, Stanley visited Lord Stratford, the British ambassador at Constantinople. Stanley asked him about Russia's

---

ᵖ See p. 137, fn. e.
ᑫ Athanasius succeeded Alexander as Bishop of Alexandria in 328.

demands for a Christian protectorate in the Balkans and about Turkey's refusal. The ambassador thought Russia's claims unjust, and that 'we are really on the verge of that most important event to which all the world has been looking for so many years, and that, after so many false cries, the wolf has come at last.'[45]

Ten months later, in March 1854, Britain and France joined forces with Turkey and declared war on Russia. All three countries had long been suspicious of Russian ambitions, until disputes over the safety of holy places in Palestine and Christians in the Turkish Empire, supplied the *casus belli*. In September allied troops landed at Balaclava on the Crimean peninsula and laid siege to Sebastopol.

The war was to bring notoriety to Stanley's sister, Mary. She and Arthur had always been close, and never more so than now she was living with him in Canterbury. Hers was a complex character – intense, self-absorbed, earnest, and like many young women of her class, frustrated by lack of opportunities in education and the professions. She envied her brothers' schooling and careers, and her sister's marriage to the Headmaster of Harrow. Mary had become fascinated by the Oxford Movement, and like many after Newman's secession, felt drawn to Roman Catholicism. These feelings were encouraged by Julius Hare's friend, Henry Manning,[r] the future Cardinal Archbishop of Westminster, who had become her spiritual mentor. Manning had been wrestling with his own attraction to Rome, until in 1847 the strain made him seriously ill. He took Mary with him to the eternal city to recuperate, and the visit changed her life. First, she was impressed by what she saw of the Church, and second, she was introduced to Florence Nightingale, who was also convalescing.[s] (Nightingale had in turn met Sidney Herbert, the future Secretary-at-War, who was to play a key part in her mission to the Crimea.) Florence had had a very similar Jane Austen upbringing to Mary, and she too was frustrated by its limited ambitions. But in Rome she had settled on nursing as her way to fulfilment, and Mary was captivated.

Seven years later, Herbert wrote to Nightingale inviting her to lead a detachment of nurses to the dilapidated barrack hospital at Scutari,

---

[r] Hare and Manning had been rectors of neighbouring parishes in the 1830s and were archdeacons in the diocese of Chichester in the 1840s.
[s] Nightingale and Manning are two more of Strachey's *Eminent Victorians*. Strachey's purpose was satire, and Manning is lampooned as a man divided between Anglican ambitions and Roman convictions. Nightingale, however, is almost admired as a woman of courage, vigilance and determination.

across the Bosphorus from Constantinople. Nightingale's party arrived on 4 November 1854 and comprised thirty-eight nurses, fourteen of whom were professionals and the rest Anglican and Catholic nuns. The appalling conditions they found are well-known: impossible numbers of sick and badly wounded soldiers on the one hand, and filthy wards, lack of equipment and supplies, and administrative incompetence on the other. To assist Nightingale with her overwhelming task, Herbert asked Mary Stanley to take out a second party as reinforcements. Mary was delighted, and turned for help to Frances Bridgeman, the domineering mother superior of the Catholic Sisters of Mercy in Dublin. Manning had directed Mary to the convent soon after their return from Rome, and she had remained under Bridgeman's influence. Mary's group was made up of nine ladies, fifteen nuns from Dublin with their chaplain, William Ronan, and twenty-two nurses. Stanley travelled with Mary on the train from London to Folkestone where she met her party and boarded a steamer for France. 'I waved my hat as long as they were in sight,' he told their mother, 'and felt that, if I were never to see her again, it would be as peaceful a last impression to bear away as it would ever be possible to have. I cannot but think that it may be the beginning of a new life to her, being the first complete opportunity of developing all her best powers that has occurred since she left Norwich.'[46]

Alas, the venture was doomed from the start. Though Florence and Mary were friends, Florence was furious that she had not been consulted: she had impressed on Herbert that she should be in sole charge. Furthermore, Florence did not approve of untrained, well-meaning ladies patronising her nurses and patients, and cluttering her wards. She was alarmed too at the high proportion of Catholics in Mary's party, and felt this also threatened her authority, and added an unwelcome controversy. Indeed, the Evangelical newspaper, *The Record*, was quick to attack Mary for this. Stanley was incensed, not least because he feared that this would drive Mary closer to Rome. 'In this nurse business', he wrote, 'there is no question that the rabid Protestant party have shown by far the greatest incapacity of tolerating anything beyond their own "infinitely little minds".'[47]

When Mary saw Florence in December 1854, soon after her arrival, she described her as 'dear Flo writing on a small unpainted deal table. I never saw her looking better.'[48] Two months later, Mary was complaining that 'few English-women of education would submit to the kind of subjugation she requires'.[49] Nightingale insisted on dividing Mary's detachment, sending Mary and half the group to the hospital at

Koulali, and with dire consequences. Gillian Gill writes in her Nightingale biography:

> Miss Stanley ran the nursing at the hospital according to her own system, and it was disaster for all concerned. Miss Stanley did not manage to set up extra diet kitchens or laundries, and she exercised no discipline over the other women. The army kept shipping men in from Balaclava who kept dying, and conditions on the wards were so horrid that after two days Miss Stanley could not bear to go near them ... The nurses spent their time drinking and flirting with the orderlies or else acting as ladies' maids. The ladies wafted around aimlessly, 'pottering and messing about with little cookeries of individual beef teas,' as Nightingale cuttingly put it in a letter to Sidney Herbert.[50]

Within four months Mary's health was broken, and she returned home in April 1855. She had been taking secret instruction from Father Ronan and he received her into the Catholic Church while they were still in the Crimea. Three years before, Stanley had written to Nightingale (on the grounds that she was his friend Arthur Clough's cousin) to ask her to discourage his sister from taking what he, and more so the family, regarded as a gravely reprehensible step. But Nightingale had refused on the grounds that the Church of England gave no responsibility to women. In February 1856 Mary finally found the courage to announce her conversion, and the Stanleys were devastated. Her cousin by marriage, Lady Henrietta Stanley, wrote to her mother-in-law:

> You will wish to hear how Aunt Kitty is – I went to see her by her desire this morning & she told me the sad story. It is what one had expected but when it does come it is most painful. Aunt is looking shockingly ill, & the mixture of grief & irritation is most trying. Poor Arthur suffers so much & it will be such a deep injury to him ... It is difficult not to think that there is great presumption in leaving the church God placed one in ... Mary will feel cut to the heart I should think when she is re baptised & the baptism of her Father set at nought.[51]

Mary tried hard to be reconciled to Nightingale but she was exhausted and would have none of it. 'Dearest Florence,' she wrote, 'if I have given you pain by any words or deeds of mine, I heartily ask your forgiveness.'[52] On the envelope Nightingale scribbled, 'Is she mad, bad, or silly?', and wrote in reply: 'I have no Mary Stanley and to her whom

I once thought my Mary Stanley I have nothing to write. She has injured my work. She has dampened my courage to pursue it by the grievous blow of finding want of faith in her whom I so loved and trusted.'[53] When there was talk of Queen Victoria presenting Florence and Mary with diamond brooches, specially designed by Prince Albert, Florence's brother let it be known that such an association would pain his sister. Only Nightingale received the honour.

Another member of the Stanley family was directly involved in the Crimean War, and that was Johnny, the son of Lord Edward and Lady Henrietta. Unlike his father and brothers who went to Eton, Johnny attended Harrow where Arthur's brother-in-law, Charles Vaughan, was headmaster. Johnny had been a delicate and rebellious child and was soon in trouble at Harrow. His offences (for which he was flogged) included foul language and 'secreting light & being up all night & also for jumping over the dinner table when Dr. Vaughan was there, which was considered a great breach of discipline'.[54] Johnny had to leave early, much to his father's annoyance with Vaughan ('these followers of Dr. Arnold', he wrote, 'who clothe themselves in his lion skin look more like other animals than lions').[55] Like his uncle William, Johnny was sent to Sandhurst and into the Grenadier Guards. He arrived in Constantinople in June 1855, aged eighteen, and reported for duty at Scutari. From there he was shipped across the Black Sea to the front at Balaclava and Sebastopol. In letters home he describes his fatigue, the stifling heat, and roads covered with shot and corpses. After only five days, Johnny collapsed with dysentery and was invalided home. He recovered, but to his family's relief, not in time to return to the war.

Stanley and his mother wanted to be away from England when Mary announced her secession. He chose Paris because the leaders of the nations were there to negotiate a peace settlement with Russia. Again Stanley wanted to be present where history was being made, and he made every effort to catch a glimpse of the delegates. While they were there, Napoleon III's son and heir, the Prince Imperial, was born, and Stanley noted that 'the burst of cannonade on Palm Sunday morning was in the highest degree effective'.[56] Back in London more cannon fire announced on 30 March 1856 that peace was concluded and the Treaty of Paris signed. Stanley was having dinner with friends, and 'had hardly sat down when everyone started to their feet at the same moment, with the same exclamation, "The Peace! the Peace!" ... The cannon sounded magnificently in the still night. I entreated them to wake the children, that the historical continuity of the event might be carried on to the next generation. But they slept too soundly in spite of all the exertions of their parents.'[57]

* * *

Sinai and Palestine was published in the same month, three years after Stanley's eastern tour. It had been a pleasure to write ('Nothing I have ever written has so much interested and instructed me'),[58] and, with a fourth edition in the first year, it proved almost as popular a Sunday school prize or confirmation present as his *Life of Arnold*. Stanley's letters, notes and journals provided the immediacy and accuracy of a first-hand account, as well as much of the text. 'You have nothing to do,' advised Goldwin Smith, 'but to piece together your letters, cut off their heads and tails, and the book is done.'[59]

Stanley had learnt from Arnold that history and geography are intimately connected. He had taught the sixth form that political events and national characteristics, cultures and customs are shaped as much by topography as they are by distinguished lives and decisive battles. Stanley wrote to Mrs Arnold a month before the book was published:

> It *is* a great pleasure to feel that anything which I write must come home to you and yours with usury, if it has anything worth reading, knowing, as you do, how large a portion of it is owing to the same source from which I have received so much. Not only does almost every page contain some term of expression which else I should not have had; but the framework of the book is a result of that sense of a connection of history and geography which I have never ceased to enjoy since it was first imparted at Rugby.[60]

With reference to a wide range of sources from Josephus to Niebuhr, Stanley weaves together detailed descriptions of places and scenery with people and incidents from the Biblical narrative. Take, for instance, his account of Jerusalem:

> In every approach to the modern Jerusalem, the first and most striking feature ... is the long line of walls and towers ... The same terror which has collected the entire population of Palestine from isolated houses into villages, has confined the population of its capital within the city walls ... the town is entirely enclosed, the gates locked at night, and the present walls ... thus become an essential feature in every view of the place from within or from without.

> ... Jerusalem must at all times have been in a state of insecurity too great to allow any neglect of fortification. From first to last, History and Poetry are always recurring to the mention of her walls and gates and towers. 'Walk about Zion, go round about her, tell the towers thereof; mark well her bulwarks.' David, Solomon, Hezekiah are all concerned in the fortifications of the city of the Monarchy. To have raised the walls of the city of the Restoration was the chief glory of Nehemiah. Herod's walls and towers, called after the favourites of his court and family, were amongst his most celebrated works.[61]

The deeper effect of illustrating the coincidence between historical narrative and geographical setting was to confirm the truth and authority of the Bible. Stanley was aware of this, and it was one of his intentions in writing the book:

> It is impossible not to be struck by the constant agreement between the recorded history and the natural geography both of the Old and New Testaments. To find a marked correspondence between the scenes of the Sinaitic mountains and the events of the Israelite wanderings is not much perhaps, but it is certainly something towards a proof of the truth of the whole narrative ... The detailed harmony between the life of Joshua and the various scenes of his battles, is a slight but true indication that we are dealing not with shadows, but with realities of flesh and blood. Such coincidences are not usually found in fables, least of all in fables of Eastern origin.[62]

F. D. Maurice thought that, with *Sinai and Palestine*, 'Stanley has done more to make the Bible a reality in the homes of the people than any living man.'[63] The Bishop of Argyll wrote to say that 'I have read no work of any description which has so raised and invigorated my faith and sight of the facts in the Old Testament history as your work on Palestine ... I have to thank you for putting the Old Testament into my hands as a new and more powerful weapon.'[64]

The book had its critics. The Christian Knowledge Society even agonised over whether or not to include it in its approved reading list. John Keble raised two objections. First, that Jesus is spoken of not as divine but as no more than a perfect man; and second (and Pusey raised this too), that miracles are explained away as natural phenomena.[65] Both criticisms illustrate the differences between Stanley's more modern, historical, critical attitude to the Bible, and Keble's and Pusey's traditional, devotional, literalist approach. Stanley's purpose was to describe the Jesus of history in his geographical setting, and not to preach the Christ of faith. As far as miracles were concerned, Stanley was open to natural explanations, and regarded them as just as useful as signs and wonders in confirming the historicity of Biblical events: 'If, for example, the aspect of the ground should, in any case, indicate that some of the great wonders in the history of the Chosen People were wrought through means which, in modern language, would be called natural, we must remember that such a discovery is, in fact, an indirect proof of the general truth of the narrative.'[66]

* * *

Though Stanley and his mother were distressed by Mary's conversion there was never a rift, and Stanley was soon writing to her as before as 'My dear Mäi' or 'My dearest Child'. In August 1856 he took her and Kitty on a tour through Scotland, visiting Dumfries, Glasgow, Fife, Skye and Glencoe. 'If I were a Scotsman,' he told Kitty, 'what a beautiful subject the history of Scotland would be!'[67] While travelling, Stanley heard an unlikely rumour that he was to succeed the dynamic Blomfield as Bishop of London. A friend wrote to him from Dundee to urge him to accept: 'Honesty, simplicity, general ability, and knowledge of the world, a good fortune and position, seem to me the best materials for a Bishop. All these you have; therefore do not hesitate, whether London or any other is offered.'[68] Jowett wrote from Balliol to say much the same. This is more surprising because Jowett knew Stanley well, and must have recognised that, for all his intellectual gifts and virtuous character, he was too independent-minded and lacking in worldly knowledge and confidence for such a public position.

In fact a number of bishops were being mentioned for what was then the largest Anglican diocese in the world. In the end, Palmerston wrote to Tait in September to offer him the see. This was almost as surprising as Stanley's appointment would have been. Just once during the last two hundred years had a man who was not already on the bench been appointed to London. Tait was only forty-four, and his experience as a tutor at Balliol, Headmaster of Rugby and, for the past six years, Dean of Carlisle, had not prepared him to lead such an extensive and senior diocese, with its wider Church and national responsibilities. The reason why Tait was so elevated was that Queen Victoria had taken pity on him, and wanted to console him after his terrible family tragedy. Six months before, between 6 March and 8 April, five of the Taits' seven children had died of scarlet fever, all girls aged one to ten.ᵗ The parents had borne their grief with superhuman faith and fortitude.

Tait accepted Palmerston's invitation immediately, and Stanley wrote to congratulate him: 'God grant you health to fulfil all your highest wishes, and may the mournful past bear its true fruits in a happy and useful future.'[69] Tait appointed Stanley as one of his six examining chaplains, responsible for assessing the orthodoxy of candidates for ordination. Stanley's reputation for liberalism caused the Evangelical Earl of Shaftesbury to write to Tait's sister, Lady Wake: 'I myself could have appointed Stanley a dean. I like much that he has written, but as for examining chaplain, avert it for heaven's sake!'[70] When Tait got to hear of this he wrote to his sister to defend his choice: 'I have known Stanley now for twenty years and more, and that very intimately. He is a man against whom efforts have at times been made to excite prejudice, but you know as well as I do how admirable is the Christian simplicity of his character.'[71] Tait considered inviting Stanley to preach at his consecration in the chapel royal at Whitehall in November 1856 but was cautious, and chose George Cotton, another of his examining chaplains. Cotton, who had taught at Rugby under Arnold and Tait, was now Master of Marlborough. Stanley was characteristically generous in his judgement of the sermon. 'Even had I preached the same,' he wrote, 'it was much better that it should have come from him than from me, and I am perfectly convinced that I should not have preached anything nearly so good. The one thorn, if there be one, was that I was not there to hear it.'[72]

*   *   *

A fortnight later, and three days before his 41st birthday, Stanley received a letter from Palmerston offering him the regius professorship of ecclesiastical history at Oxford, a position for which he was eminently suited. 'There is one and one only possible candidate,' wrote the Church historian Dean Milman of St Paul's, 'and that is Arthur Stanley.'[73] This was a new chair, founded in 1841, and the first professor, Robert Hussey, 'a monument of erudition',[74] had died suddenly of heart disease after fourteen years in office. The chair was attached to a canonry at Christ Church. This was not available when Hussey was

---

ᵗ Mrs Tait wrote a heart-rending account of their deaths: William Benham (ed.), *Catherine and Crauford Tait* (1879), pp. 279–393.

appointed, and he continued to live in the rooms that were already his as a student[u] of Christ Church. Stanley had to wait until February 1858 for the stall (and the house that went with it) to become available. He remained in Canterbury and combined his cathedral duties with those of the professorship. Stanley welcomed this arrangement because, as before, he was anxious about moving. He had also come to love Canterbury, and the freedom, leisure and family home his canonry provided. Indeed, Stanley came to the view that these were the happiest seven years of his life. He was also reluctant to return to the theological maelstrom of Oxford. 'Oh! this Professorship! I do not well see how I could have declined it,' he told Hugh Pearson. 'But at times my heart quite sinks at the prospect both of the work and of the place. I keep Canterbury till Christ Church becomes vacant.'[75]

Stanley's appointment had a mixed reception. His friend and fellow commissioner, Henry Liddell, the new Dean of Christ Church, was as enthusiastic as Milman, and had strongly recommended Stanley to Palmerston. 'Of all offices,' he wrote, 'this is the office for him; and of all men, he is the man for the office.'[76] The older, conservative generation at Oxford took a different view. The university commission and its reforms were still resented, and the Tractarian party would always regard Stanley as a dangerous enemy. Pusey wrote to Stanley to say that he viewed his appointment 'with sorrow and fear'.[77] 'How many letters of congratulation do you suppose I have received from residents in Oxford?' Stanley asked Pearson. 'One from Jowett, and – *not one besides*.'[78] Jowett was certainly delighted: 'As children go about saying to themselves, "This is Christmas Day", or "This is Easter Sunday", so I go about saying to myself that one of my oldest and best friends is Professor of Ecclesiastical History.'[79]

Stanley's lectures were open to all members of the university, though most of those who attended were undergraduates reading for holy orders. He welcomed this overlap with his duties as Tait's examining chaplain. Stanley found the work 'exceedingly interesting and instructive',[80] and was convinced 'that in point of influence and power the Chaplaincy is a more valuable post than my Professorship'.[81] Stanley's experience as chaplain, and the insights it gave him into the theological needs of ordinands, helped to inform the approach and subjects of his professorial lectures. He was required to give three inaugural lectures during the Lent Term of 1857, followed by a course of twelve lectures.

---

[u] Fellows of Christ Church are called students: see chapter 7.

He decided in the first year to focus on the Eastern Church, with six lectures on various aspects of the Council of Nicaea, and four on the history of the Church in Russia.ᵛ

The introductory lectures were delivered in the Sheldonian, twenty years after Stanley had recited his prize poem on the same platform. Though Liddell offered him accommodation in the deanery, he preferred to lodge in the same rooms at 115 High Street that Arnold had occupied when he was a fellow of Oriel. Stanley could not fail to recall the excitement of Arnold's lectures as Regius Professor of Modern History, delivered in the same theatre shortly before he died. He followed Arnold's example by using the inaugural lectures to give a general introduction to his subject, and to try to make it exciting and attractive. His first lecture on 'The Province of Ecclesiastical History' was strikingly innovative in starting the Biblical narrative with Abraham. It had been assumed in Oxford (though not in European universities) that Church history began with the apostles, and so a course of lectures like these might open with the apostolic age, or the fathers of the early Church, or even perhaps the Reformation. But it was characteristic of Stanley's all-encompassing theology to regard Abraham as 'the first figure in the long succession which has never been broken ... the first Father of the universal Church'.[82] The same Arnoldian comprehensiveness is there too in what Stanley says about the relation of civil and ecclesiastical history. He argues that the range of the history of the Church is as wide as that of the history of the world, which it was destined to permeate. 'Never let us think that we can understand the history of the Church apart from the history of the world, any more than we can separate the interests of the clergy from the interests of the laity, which are the interests of the Church at large.'[83]

The second and third lectures, on the methods and practical advantages of Church history, argue that a thorough understanding of history and biography can foster sympathy towards dogmas and parties that might otherwise seem arid or alien. 'How immensely do [doctrines and opinions] gain in liveliness, in power, in the capacity of being understood and appreciated, if we view them through the medium of the lives, characters, and circumstances of those who received and taught them!'[84] Here is the strongest protection against

---

ᵛ Published as *Lectures on the History of the Eastern Church* (1861). The book remained on the reading lists at Oxford until the 1930s. When he is sent down, Evelyn Waugh's hapless hero in *Decline and Fall* (1928) is reminded by the college chaplain to return his copy of Dean Stanley's *Eastern Church*.

partiality or exclusiveness. 'The wrath which is kindled by an anathema, by an opinion, by an argument, is often turned away by a homely fact. It is like suddenly meeting an enemy face to face, of whom we have known only by report; he is different from what we expected ... he has ceased to be an abstraction, he has become a person.'[85]

The lecture series itself began in May and was well attended. After a general lecture, Stanley turned to Nicaea, describing in graphic detail the council's causes, characters and conclusions, and with the same dramatic vitality as in his essay on the murder of Becket. Here is his description of the arrival of the Emperor Constantine:

> The whole assembly rose and stood on their feet; and then for the first time set their admiring gaze on Constantine, the Conqueror, the August, the Great. He entered. His towering stature, his strong-built frame, his broad shoulders, his handsome features, were worthy of his grand position. There was a brightness in his look and a mingled expression of fierceness and gentleness in his lion-like eye, which well became one who, as Augustus before him, had fancied, and perhaps still fancied, himself to be the favourite of the Sun-god Apollo. The Bishops were further struck by the dazzling, perhaps barbaric, magnificence of his dress. Always careful of his appearance, he was so on this occasion in an eminent degree. His long hair, false or real, was crowned with the imperial diadem of pearls. His purple or scarlet robe blazed with precious stones and gold embroidery. He was shod no doubt in the scarlet shoes then confined to he Emperors, now perpetuated in the Pope and Cardinals. Many of the Bishops had probably never seen any greater functionary than a remote provincial magistrate, and gazing at his splendid figure as he passed up the hall between their ranks, remembering too what he had done for their faith and for their Church, – we may well believe that the simple and the worldly both looked upon him, as though he were an angel of God, descended straight from Heaven.[86]

Stanley spent the summer vacation 1857 in Russia, researching his autumn lectures on the Russian Orthodox Church. He travelled first to Sweden, before departing from Stockholm on 1 August, bound by Baltic steamer for the imperial city of St Petersburg. This time his companion was Arthur Butler, a Rugbeian whom Stanley had taught at University College, and who was now a fellow of Oriel. From St Petersburg Stanley travelled 350 miles south-east to Moscow. It was a difficult journey because, as Englishmen in Russia after the Crimean War, they were treated with suspicion, at times with hostility. Furthermore, they did not have an interpreter until they reached Moscow, and neither men knew a word of Russian. They found it almost impossible to interpret the meaning and significance of the Church's rich symbols, pictures and rituals. 'One moves about,' Stanley told Jowett, 'like a Homeric hero in thick darkness, protected sometimes by a god or goddess, sometimes by a very inadequate Hermes, and has to guess at the world as it passes before one.'[87]

As soon as they arrived in Moscow they hired a carriage and drove to the Kremlin: 'How strange is the sensation ... to rush forward to a site long imagined, but beheld for the first time! How delightful, I must confess, to feel that even after Athens, Rome, Thebes, Jerusalem, there is a flood of enthusiasm to be let forth at one more glorious view!'[88] To Stanley, the Kremlin was 'the Tower, Westminster Abbey, Canterbury Cathedral, Windsor Castle, Lambeth, all crammed together within the space of a quarter of an hour's circuit'.[89] 'Such a collection of historical and architectural marvels as I have not seen in one place out of the great Piazza of S. Mark's.'[90]

Of the three cathedrals, Stanley found the patriarchal cathedral, dedicated to the repose of the blessed Virgin, the most impressive. Here tsars were crowned and patriarchs and metropolitans buried. Stanley was there on the festival of the Assumption and saw the Metropolitan of Moscow, the aged and saintly Philaret Drozdov:

> ... at the head of the gorgeous procession – copes, and dalmatics, and crowns, and mitres, that might have roused envy, not only in the minds of poor craving Puseyites, but of any Pope or cardinal in the West – came tottering between his two enormous archdeacons, wan as a shadow, his lips moving, but his gentle whisper itself inaudible, our good old friend Philaret ...
>
> Some parts of the Sacramental Service were, I thought, exceedingly curious and instructive ... One striking circumstance was, that whenever the Metropolitan advanced from the altar to give his blessing, which he did many times over, there was always thrown under his feet a carpet embroidered with the eagle of old Pagan Rome, to indicate that the Christian Church and Empire of Constantinople had succeeded and triumphed over it.[91]

Stanley had been granted a private interview with Philaret at his country residence, and was impressed by 'the almost supernatural sweetness of his voice' and his 'deep-sunk expressive eyes'.[92] Through an interpreter they discussed sacred pictures and statues, the eccentricities of German Protestantism, and the apparent cruelty and vindictiveness of the Old Testament. Stanley also attended a service in the same cathedral to commemorate the coronation the year before of Tsar Alexander II. Stanley mentioned 'the silver, trickling rill'[93] of Philaret's voice as he read the gospel: 'Render unto Caesar the things that be Caesar's, and unto God the things that be God's.'[w]

*   *   *

Stanley poured everything he had learnt in Russia, and much of what he had written in letters, into the lectures he delivered during the Michaelmas term, 1857. He then returned to Canterbury to keep his final residence. Dean Lyall had died in February and been succeeded by the Biblical scholar, Henry Alford.[x] He was a liberal Churchman who wanted to increase the preaching in the cathedral and open its doors to Nonconformists. Stanley shared his aims, but the other canons proved so obstructive that Alford even recommended to the archbishop that they be abolished. Stanley threw himself into his work with renewed vigour, preaching every Sunday in the cathedral and in parish churches, representing the chapter at the mayor's banquet, entertaining visitors, examining the boys of the King's School, and lecturing in the city on its history or on Russia. He still found chapter business mystifying. After a long audit meeting to discuss the substitution of rents for leases, an archdeacon remarked: '"I wonder, Stanley, whether you quite understand the meaning of fines." "I have not the remotest idea", was the prompt reply.'[94]

At last, the third stall in Christ Church Cathedral became vacant on the death of the notorious pluralist, Dr John Bull, and Stanley was obliged to leave Canterbury. He did so at Easter, and with a heavy heart. 'It will be a satisfaction', he wrote, 'that Canterbury will now remain a spot of existence, bright, happy, and useful to the end. God grant that this new stage may come anywhere near it in proportion!'[95]

---

[w] Stanley described these encounters in 'Recollections of Philaret, Archbishop and Metropolitan of Moscow', *Macmillan's Magazine*, January 1867; reprinted in A. P. Stanley, *Essays on Church and State*, pp. 489ff.

[x] A. J. C. Hare included him after Stanley in his *Biographical Sketches*.

7
'The Rays of Regal Bounty Shine'
1858–1863

STANLEY'S APPOINTMENT as regius professor was especially unpopular at Christ Church which preferred to promote its own. Stanley's predecessor had come to the college from Westminster School in 1821, and resided there for the rest of his life. Stanley's liberal views were also uncongenial at a predominantly High Church, Tory college. However, it was the fact that Stanley had been secretary to the Oxford Commission, and principal author of its report, that caused most suspicion and resentment. Christ Church had refused to have anything to do with the commissioners, and regarded their recommendations (broadening the social background of undergraduates, for instance; opening scholarships and fellowships to competition; relieving fellows of the obligation to take orders) as destructive of the college's traditions and independence.

Christ Church's resistance to reform had its roots in the college's own peculiar history, character and constitution. The original foundation was Thomas Wolsey's Cardinal's College, a characteristically ambitious project that necessitated the suppression of twenty-two monasteries and the ruin of several university buildings. When Wolsey fell from grace in 1529, the college, with all Wolsey's property, passed to the Crown. Henry VIII seized the opportunity and re-founded a college named after him. Ten years later the Reformation had happened, monastic wealth was available, and the English Church was being reorganised. The King dissolved his first foundation, and in 1546 founded it again as Christ Church,[a] a unique dual arrangement of college and cathedral. Henry died before statutes could be devised, and it remained without a written constitution for 300 years. Cathedral of the diocese of Oxford, university college, and royal foundation[b] – three aspects that lend Christ Church an unrivalled and munificent character.

---

[a] Originally called *Ecclesia Christi*, *Aedes* soon replaced *Ecclesia* and the college is referred to as 'the House'.
[b] The reigning monarch is the Visitor. Charles I resided at the deanery during the Civil War.

Until the nineteenth century Christ Church comprised 101 students.[c] The term 'student' in Christ Church's peculiar parlance referred to both the sixty fellows (senior students) and the forty scholars (junior students). Twenty of the senior students were in orders, and forty were bachelors or masters of arts, occasionally in orders. Only some of the senior students were engaged in teaching, by no means all were resident, and many were preparing for careers in the Church, law or medicine. Although the emoluments were less than those of fellowships at many other colleges, and though governance of Christ Church resided with the chapter, a senior studentship remained a source of considerable pride and privilege, with access to powerful patronage.

Apart from three junior studentships reserved for Westminster pupils, all the rest were free of the usual restrictions to schools, dioceses, counties or founders' kin. This was an advantage, and allowed Christ Church to appoint tutors and undergraduates of genuine intellectual ability. However, since nominations rested solely in the hands of the cathedral's dean and chapter, they were vulnerable to nepotism. Canon Frederick Barnes (known ironically as 'Brains), who died, aged eighty-eight, the year after Stanley arrived, is reputed to have exclaimed: 'I don't know what we're coming to! I've given Studentships to my sons, and to my nephews, and to my nephews' children, and there are no more of my family left. I shall have to give them by merit one of these days!'[1]

For all its anomalies, Christ Church worked satisfactorily for nearly three centuries, and achieved a social and academic pre-eminence. A blend of custom, and pride in belonging to a college of such scale and grandeur, invested Christ Church with bonds of community and common purpose which made statutes unnecessary. The college escaped much of Oxford's eighteenth-century stagnation, and indeed led the university in academic distinction during the first thirty years of the nineteenth century. The commission's evidence revealed that between 1821 and 1830, Christ Church achieved fifty-one firsts compared to Balliol's eleven, an impressive statistic, even allowing for the fact that Christ Church had twice as many undergraduates. But then the tables turned. In the next decade, Balliol's firsts increased to twenty-two while Christ Church's declined to thirty-one, and from 1841 to 1850, Balliol maintained its twenty-two but Christ Church's fell to thirteen.

---

[c] See fn. on p. 193 for this Christ Church use of 'student'. Every evening at 9.05 p.m., 'Great Tom', the college bell, tolls 101 strikes (one more student was added to the original 100 at the Restoration).

There were a number of reasons for this reversal of fortune. By 1830 Balliol had opened its fellowships and scholarships to competition and increased their value, creating a college of clever undergraduates and effective tutors. Other colleges started to lag behind, though the size of Christ Church, and its freedom from closed fellowships, meant that it was still relatively well served by a sufficient number of good tutors. It could certainly cope with the demands of the examination honours system, introduced in part by Cyril Jackson, who was dean until 1809. Christ Church's difficulty was that Thomas Gaisford, his learned and defiantly conservative successor, actively discouraged undergraduates from competing for honours. Another reason for decline was the deterioration of Westminster School, which sent its most able pupils to Christ Church, many of whom became tutors. Eton and Harrow were also on the wane, and they supplied the majority of undergraduates. Furthermore, the college's royal associations made it fashionable, favoured by the sons of the nobility[d] and gentry. Since many had no need to work for a living, they squandered their time on drink and cards, and either left early, or read (very little) for a pass degree.[e]

The Oxford Commission's report, published in 1852, caused Christ Church fifteen years of conflict and confusion, as it tried to come to terms with reform. When Stanley arrived in the spring 1858, an ordinance for Christ Church was being finalised, after much disagreement. This was required to implement the Oxford University Act (1854), which pursued the commission's report and recommendations. Studentships were to be reduced from 101 to 80, and divided into two groups: 28 senior (9 of which were to be laymen), and 52 junior. The senior students were to be appointed by open examination; and of the junior students, twenty-one were to be elected by examination from Westminster, and the rest were open. The two canonries not annexed to professorships were to be suppressed, and their revenues used to raise the clerical students' stipends. These were far-reaching changes, and given Christ Church's peculiar constitution, the ordinance had to produce new administrative machinery. This had the effect of reducing the autonomy of the dean and chapter, though only in some areas, and

---

[d] Noblemen ranked as doctors and were granted the best rooms, and until 1862 places at high table.

[e] As an undergraduate, Stanley had written to Julius Hare: 'The Gentlemen Commoners of Christ Church being almost universally idle, generally profligate, and hardly ever rising into the highest society of Christ Church, even though it, like the rest of the college, is remarkable for its deference to mere aristocracy and mere gentlemanly manners.'

of giving new but limited powers to the senior students. To the authors of *Christ Church and Reform*, 'it was a system which might have been designed to promote conflict'.[2] Though the powers and stipends of senior students were increased, they remained inferior to those of fellowships in other colleges, and more tensions were created between students and chapter. What began as an argument about educational reform became at Christ Church an argument about its constitution. The argument continued until the passing of the Christ Church Oxford Act in 1867. This provided statutes and an enlarged governing body that included senior students.

By then Stanley had been Dean of Westminster for nearly four years. He had, of course, been largely sympathetic to these reforms; they were, after all, the result of his work for the commission. But he had found himself in an uncomfortable minority on the chapter. Professor Pusey had spoken for most of the canons when he lamented of the draft ordinance that 'Old Christ Church with its good and its defects is by this Ordinance among the things which have been'.[3] Henry Liddell, who had succeeded Gaisford as dean three years before, had also been an active member of the commission, and shared Stanley's liberal, reforming views. A former student, he was now in a difficult position as head of both chapter and college, and became cautious and conservative – though not always enough for the chapter, who thought him highhanded.[4] Liddell was also suffering from an acute bronchial condition (brought on by insanitary conditions at Westminster where he had been headmaster), and he spent long periods away, convalescing in Madeira. This too caused resentment among the canons. 'Certainly', Stanley told his mother, 'the Chapter here contains very explosive elements.'[5]

* * *

Liddell welcomed Stanley's understanding and loyalty. 'No other friend', wrote Liddell's biographer, 'exercised so much influence as did Stanley over Liddell's opinions, or had so great a share of his confidence and affection.'[6] His only other supporter in the chapter was William Jacobson, who had followed Hampden as Regius Professor of Divinity. Jacobson was learned, pious and liberal, and much admired by Stanley and Liddell. Five months before Stanley was appointed to the ecclesiastical history chair, Liddell had written to him from Bamburgh Castle to declare that 'mitres are flying about', and would he consider succeeding Jacobson if he too was made a bishop?[7] Jacobson, however, remained in post until 1865 when he was appointed Bishop of Chester.

The other canons were united in their conservatism. Edward Pusey had been Regius Professor of Hebrew for thirty years. Since his wife's death in 1839, he had lived the life a penitent recluse, often fasting and clad in haircloth. In his twenties he had been a fellow of Oriel with Newman and Keble, and was drawn, cautiously at first, into the Oxford Movement. After Newman's secession in 1845 he became its leader. Pusey was vehemently opposed to almost any liberalising trends in both Church and university, and regarded Stanley and Jowett with animosity, if not contempt.

Canon Richard Jelf began a lifelong friendship with Pusey at Eton, and he too had been a fellow of Oriel. For thirteen years he had been tutor to the future King of Hanover. In 1830 he married Countess Schlippenbach, the Queen of Hanover's lady-in-waiting, and was appointed a canon of Christ Church. Despite his friendship with Pusey, Jelf exerted a moderating influence on the Oxford Movement, though he was determined in his opposition to liberal theologians. In 1844 he succeeded the father of Stanley's Balliol contemporary, James Lonsdale, as Principal of King's College, London (which he held in plurality with his canonry), and was instrumental in depriving F. D. Maurice of his professorship.[f]

Charles Ogilvie had been a fellow and influential tutor at Balliol and, as Archbishop Howley's chaplain, had preached at Stanley's father's consecration when Howley refused the pulpit to Arnold. In 1842 he was appointed Oxford's first Regius Professor of Pastoral Theology, and succeeded to a canonry at Christ Church seven years later. Though a radical influence at Balliol, Ogilvie 'was now quite without enthusiasm for reform, and inclined to resent all novelties'.[8] He was a close friend of Martin Routh, the notoriously anachronistic President of Magdalen.

These older canons tended to keep aloof from the students, and more so as their powers were threatened by reform. Stanley tried to bridge this gap, and was assiduous in entertaining students, junior and senior, to breakfast and dinner, and introducing them to a wider circle than Christ Church and Oxford provided. One student was Charles Dodgson (*nom de plume*, Lewis Carroll) who had been appointed mathematical lecturer three years before Stanley arrived. There is no record in Stanley's correspondence of a friendship or otherwise with this shy, brilliant and eccentric young man. But Dodgson had been in

---

[f] On the grounds that Maurice had included unorthodox views on eternal punishment in his *Theological Essays* (1853).

School House at Rugby under Tait and, like Stanley, had won all the prizes, and this must surely have encouraged Stanley to take an interest in him. He was a Broad Churchman too, and had been influenced by Coleridge and Maurice. And given Stanley's close friendship with the Liddells,[g] it is more than likely that he was made aware of what was happening between Dodgson and their daughter, Alice.

Dodgson bought one of the first cameras in 1856, and was soon photographing the four-year-old Alice, and her two sisters, Lorina, seven, and Edith, two, who had recently moved into the deanery. This was the start of a lifetime's obsession with photographing little girls, often scantily dressed, sometimes in the nude. Dodgson delighted in their company, and was evidently infatuated with Alice: he called her his 'ideal child friend'.[9] He would take her and her sisters on long summer boat rides up and down the Isis, complete with picnics, songs and fairy-tales. It was on one of these expeditions that 'Alice in Wonderland', the most celebrated and enchanting of children's stories, was conceived. 'On the afternoon of 4 July 1862, in the Long Vacation, a minute expedition set out from Oxford up the river to Godstow. It returned laden with a treasure compared with which that of the *Golden Hind* was but dross.'[10] At Alice's request, Dodgson wrote down and illustrated the story he had told her that afternoon, and called it *Alice's Adventures Under Ground*. This he expanded for publication in 1865 as *Alice's Adventures in Wonderland*.[h]

A year after that 'golden afternoon'[11] there was a falling-out between Dodgson and the domineering Mrs Liddell, and he was forbidden from entertaining the children. What had happened remains a mystery: Mrs Liddell burned Dodgson's letters to Alice, and four volumes of his diaries have disappeared, including two which coincided with Stanley's time at Christ Church, when Dodgson's intimacy with Alice was intensifying. Furthermore, in another volume, the three days at the end of June 1863, when Mrs Liddell finally terminated Dodgson's friendship with Alice and her sisters, and banned him from the deanery, have been cut out with a razor.

*   *   *

---

[g] Liddell had been at Charterhouse with Stanley's brother Owen. Stanley was godfather to the Liddells' son, Albert Edward Arthur, who died in infancy in May 1863. The Prince of Wales was another godfather.
[h] The sequel, *Through the Looking-Glass, and What Alice Found There*, was published six years later.

Stanley was installed in Christ Church Cathedral on 13 March 1858. Under Liddell's direction, the cathedral had recently completed the first stage of its reconstruction, with the removal of the organ to the south transept, and the stalls of the dean and chapter from the choir to the nave.[i] 'Considering the immense inferiority to Canterbury,' wrote Stanley, 'it is still an interesting cathedral, and the very peculiar sight of the students in their white surplices somewhat makes up for the other losses.'[12] Stanley enjoyed the prestige of his new position: 'There is a pleasure in finding oneself at the top of the tree ...', he wrote, ' – everything open to one's view, great persons civil and kind, small persons grateful for notice.'[13]

Stanley's house was the first on the left after entering Peckwater from the Great Quadrangle. It was a substantial and elegant three-storey house, built in the seventeenth century, and provided another comfortable home for Kitty and Mary. Arthur's and Mary's cousin, Augustus J. C. Hare, lodged with them for a while, and wrote the following account:

> ... the greater portion of Stanley's days was spent in his pleasant study on the ground floor ... looking upon his little walled garden, with its miniature lawn and apple-trees, between which he was delighted to find that he could make a fountain; attended to by his faithful butler and house-keeper ...
>
> Here he was always to be found standing at his desk, tossing off sheet after sheet, the whole floor covered with scraps of papers written or letters received, which, by habit that nothing could change, he generally tore up and scattered around him.[14]

Stanley's life was subject to the routines of both cathedral and university, a combination of Canterbury and University College. He usually dined at home, but if in hall, dinner was at six, and at five on Sundays after evensong at four. The college held its own services in the cathedral, and attendance by undergraduates was strictly enforced. Latin prayers were said at eight every morning and at nine-fifteen every evening: in Stanley's third year Latin gave way at last to English. Holy communion was celebrated on the first Sunday of the month at the conclusion of matins, which began at eight; a weekly celebration was not introduced until 1865.

---

[i] Fifteen years later, the architect George Gilbert Scott was employed to design a complete restoration.

The chapter met regularly and often acrimoniously. Stanley found some of the business (leases, rents, and the like) as dull as he had at Canterbury. Of more interest to him at Christ Church were appointments to college offices, and the election and admission of students. The junior students and his professorial lectures gave Stanley most pleasure, and convinced him that he had been right to return to Oxford. Though he had made the most of the respite that Canterbury provided, his real work was in teaching and guiding the next generation, which he hoped would be free of the dogmatism or agnosticism that marred his own. 'I never cease', he wrote in 1863, 'to be thankful for the seven years in that green island; but I feel that it was good to take to sea again.'[15] Stanley liked to quote Clough's parody of Wordsworth's poem, 'My heart leaps up when I behold', with its substitution of 'an undergraduate' for 'a Rainbow in the sky'.[16]

'Stanley's lectures were always interesting', wrote Prothero –

Every character or incident with which he dealt was made alive to his hearers. In addressing large classes he combined the written lecture with simpler, unwritten illustration, or even with questioning, in a manner that might be commended to modern teachers. The questions were enforced by touches, sometimes, in his unskilful hands, by pokes with a long stick which was intended to indicate the quarter whence an answer was expected. Once, as a pupil remembers, he addressed a very ordinary question about the parent of a patriarch to one of those who were sitting near him. The stick touched the head which was leaning forward over a note-book. The head rose, and disclosed the blushing features of a well-known Oxford tutor, who could *not* answer the question. After this incident the use of the stick was discontinued.[17]

Stanley used his preaching, at Christ Church and at St Mary's, the university church, to reach a wider audience of undergraduates than those who attended his lectures, many of whom were reading for ordination. Like Arnold's, his sermons were usually ethical not doctrinal, as he strove 'to make religion a life rather than a creed'.[18] But the tone of the sermons was different from Arnold's, and instead of dwelling on sin, Stanley's emphasis was more positive and practical, exhorting his hearers to follow the example of Jesus and live good and useful lives. Henry Thompson, Liddell's biographer, recalled Stanley's preaching when he was a an undergraduate at Christ Church:

> He used to direct men's thoughts to the duty and manliness of earnest work; and those who were aroused by him from a frivolous and purposeless life, and found themselves led, by the very change, to think about the vital questions of religious doctrine, were by no means slavish followers of his opinions. He had given them a purpose by urging them to work; and then they were led to think, and to think for themselves.[19]

In the chapter 'The End of the Freshman's Year' in *Tom Brown at Oxford*, Tom and Hardy attend a service at St Mary's, and find Stanley in the pulpit, preaching on the parable of the prodigal son. Hughes quotes from a university sermon given by Stanley in 1859:

> So we heard the prodigal's confession this morning. So may the thought well spring up in the minds of any who in the course of this last year have wandered into sin, and found themselves beset with evil habits of wicked idleness, of wretched self-indulgence. Now that you are indeed in the literal sense of the word about to rise and go to your father, now that you will be able to shake off the bondage of bad companionship, now that the whole length of this long absence will roll between you and the past – take a long breath, break off the yoke of your sin, of your fault, of your wrong doing, of your folly, of your perverseness, of your pride, of your vanity, of your weakness; break it off by truth, break it off by one stout effort, in one steadfast prayer; break it off by innocent and free enjoyment; break it off by honest work.[20]

* * *

During Stanley's second year at Christ Church, his brother-in-law, Charles Vaughan, Headmaster of Harrow, resigned suddenly and unexpectedly after fifteen years, and aged only forty-three. The true reason for his resignation reveals a scandalous tale of hypocrisy and concealment.

Stanley and Vaughan had been friends at Rugby and had spent three years together as the devoted stars of Arnold's sixth form.[j] Vaughan went up to Trinity, Cambridge (where his distinctions in classics equalled Stanley's), and they regularly visited and corresponded. Stanley introduced Vaughan to his younger sister, Catherine, and they

---

[j] For Vaughan's reminiscences of Stanley at Rugby see Prothero, *Life of A. P. Stanley*, i, pp. 103ff.

married in 1850. Thirty years later Stanley chose Vaughan to preach at his funeral in Westminster Abbey.

In 1844, after a catastrophic eight-year rule, Christopher Wordsworth[k] resigned as Headmaster of Harrow. The need for a new headmaster happened to coincide with the publication of Stanley's *Life of Arnold*, and its broadcast of the great reforming work he had achieved at Rugby. The governors of Harrow wanted a man in Arnold's mould, and who better than Vaughan, the recipient of eight of Arnold's admiring letters reproduced in Stanley's biography, including one in which Arnold mentioned the possibility of persuading Vaughan to join the Rugby staff.[21] Two years later Vaughan applied to succeed Arnold but missed out to Tait 'by the narrowest of margins'.[22] Now, armed with printed testimonials from Mrs Arnold, Stanley and George Cotton, and a manifesto which declared that 'however arduous the task set before me, I shall always have one firm ground of encouragement and hope … in my affectionate and lively recollections of the example and instructions of Dr. Arnold',[23] Vaughan could not fail to be unanimously elected.

Vaughan modelled his headmastership on Arnold's, making himself chaplain and preaching earnest, moralising sermons every Sunday afternoon, maintaining a predominantly classical curriculum. and delegating responsibility for discipline to carefully directed prefects. 'Harrow', announced *The Times*, three months into Vaughan's reign, 'is now under the direction of one who is able and willing to carry out the Arnold system of education.'[24] The system proved highly successful, with the school doubling in size in 1845 and again the following year, the appointment of some outstanding men to the common room,[l] the opening of new boarding houses, and the rebuilding of the chapel, designed by George Gilbert Scott. Arnold's influence apart, Vaughan proved an astute and determined headmaster and, according to Harrow's most recent historian, 'in fifteen years [he] established Harrow on a pinnacle of renown and respectability.'[25]

But there is a very different story to be told, of a sordid sub-culture which was not just tolerated by the headmaster, but engaged in, and concealed beneath an outward veneer of moral condemnation. Though

---

[k] He had examined Stanley and Vaughan at Rugby for the leaving exhibitions.
[l] These included B.F. Westcott, later Regius Professor of Divinity at Cambridge and Bishop of Durham; F.W. Farrar, successively Master of Marlborough, Archdeacon of Westminster and Dean of Canterbury; and R.B. Hayward who was elected a fellow of The Royal Society.

there had been rumours from the start, the truth about Harrow and Vaughan only became known in 1964 with the publication of Phyllis Grosskurth's biography of the writer and aesthete, John Addington Symonds, followed twenty years later by her edition of Symonds's memoirs. The memoirs had been deposited in the London Library in 1926 on the death of Symonds' first, highly discreet, biographer, H. F. Brown, and with instructions from Symonds that they were not to be published in full for fifty years.

Symonds came from a Nonconformist background and his father was an eminent and cultured physician. He was sent to Harrow in 1854 after Vaughan had been headmaster for nearly ten years, and when the school's reputation was riding high. Symonds's memoirs suggest that, as a schoolboy, he was rather like Stanley: sensitive and scholarly, and disliking games. But while Stanley said he had been unaware of the rough and tumble of boarding school life that Thomas Hughes describes, Symonds recalled a culture of vicious sexual abuse. 'Every boy of good looks had a female name, and was recognized either as a public prostitute or some bigger fellow's "bitch" ... The talk in both the dormitories and the studies was incredibly obscene ... There was no refinement, no sentiment, no passion; nothing but animal lust in these occurrences. They filled me with disgust and loathing.'[26] Symonds describes one boy in his house who had been abused by three older boys, and who was then, for some reason unknown to Symonds, ostracised and bullied: '...after they had rolled upon the floor with him and had exposed his person in public – they took to trampling on him. Whenever he appeared in that mean dining room ... Currey and Clayton and Barber and the rest of the brood squirted saliva and what they called gobs upon their bitch, cuffed and kicked him at their mercy, shied books at him, and drove him with obscene curses whimpering to his den.'[27]

Symonds then relates that in his last year a friend, Alfred Pretor ('a vain light-headed and corrupt lad'),[28] informed him in a note that he and Vaughan were having an affair. He showed him a series of passionate letters that the headmaster had written to him. Despite his own nascent homosexual feelings, Symonds was 'disgusted to find [this species of vice] in a man holding the highest position of responsibility, consecrated by the Church, entrusted with the welfare of six hundred youths – a man who had recently prepared me for confirmation, from whose hands, kneeling by the side of Alfred Pretor, I received the sacrament, and whom I had become accustomed to regard as the pattern of my conduct.'[29] Symonds recorded the occasion when Vaughan had summoned the whole school after an obscene note from one boy to another had been intercepted by the form master. Vaughan had 'read the letter aloud, strongly condemned the use of female names for boys, and pronounced sentence on the culprits'[30] – a punishment (caning for one boy and lines for the other) which Symonds thought inadequate. He also confessed that he 'used to take essays and verses at intervals to Vaughan in the study, which was the scene of his clandestine pleasures ... I remember once that, while we sat together reading Greek iambics, he began softly to stroke my right leg from the knee to the thigh.'[31]

Symonds explains in his memoirs that he considered telling his father, and wondered whether he should confront Vaughan. But he also felt some sympathy for him, and did not want to betray Pretor's trust. In the end he kept everything to himself until 1859 when, during his third term at Balliol, he informed John Conington, the Corpus Professor of Latin, and a pupil of Arnold's at Rugby and Stanley's at University College, where they were later colleagues. Conington persuaded Symonds that it was his duty to tell his father, and to show him Pretor's note and his own Harrow diaries.

> What eventually happened was this. My father wrote to Vaughan, intimating that he possessed proofs of his correspondence with Alfred Pretor. He promised not to make a public exposure, provided Vaughan resigned the headmastership of Harrow immediately and sought no further advancement in the Church. Otherwise the facts would have to be divulged. On the receipt of my father's ultimatum, Vaughan came down to Clifton where he inspected Pretor's letter. He accepted the terms dictated to him. Mrs. Vaughan followed after a few days and flung herself at my father's knees. 'Would Dr Symonds not withhold the execution of his sentence? Her husband was subject to this weakness, but it had not interfered with his usefulness in the direction of the school at Harrow.' My father remained obdurate though he told me he suffered keenly at the sight of this unhappy woman – a Stanley – prostrate on the ground before him. He judged it would be wrong to hush up such a matter of such grave importance to a great public school. In this view of his duty, he was supported by Conington, and also by the friends whom Vaughan employed in the transaction – his brother-in-law Arthur P. Stanley and Hugh Pearson, afterwards Canon of Windsor.[32]

It was customary in the nineteenth century for headmasters to be made bishops, and the Prime Minister, Lord Palmerston, happened to be an Old Harrovian and chairman of the Harrow governors. Although there is some confusion in Symonds's memoirs, it seems certain that Vaughan was offered Rochester, which after two days' consideration, he accepted, but then withdrew four days later after receiving a telegram from Dr Symonds. Worcester was offered next, followed by grander sees – all of which he declined. Instead Vaughan was appointed to the humdrum benefice of Doncaster, where he lived for nine years before becoming Master of the Temple Church in London. In both places he exercised an accomplished ministry, and trained a succession of young men preparing for ordination, including a future Old Harrovian Archbishop of Canterbury, Randall Davidson.

What is to be made of Stanley's role in the affair, and of his attitude to Vaughan and what had happened at Harrow? There is no reference to any of this in Prothero's biography (which was published during Vaughan's lifetime), and Vaughan himself left instructions that all his papers were to be destroyed and no biography written. There appear to be no extant letters on the matter. So answers to these questions can only be a matter of informed guesswork.

Stanley was always close to Vaughan, and – after Pearson – he seems to have been his most intimate friend, a relationship strengthened by his marriage to Catherine. Though Vaughan seems to have found Stanley physically attractive at Rugby,[m] there is no reason to suppose that Stanley was even aware of this. His astonishment at the picture of Rugby in *Tom Brown's Schooldays* shows what an innocent Stanley was as a schoolboy.

Symonds claims that Stanley and Pearson (another Harrovian) were engaged by Vaughan to negotiate with his father. What did this entail? There can be no doubt that Stanley would have been horrified when he learned what Vaughan had done. He was bound to think it right and proper (however regrettable) that Vaughan should resign, and exclude himself from future advancement. Given Stanley's friendship with Vaughan, it is easy to assume that he played a part in supporting, or perhaps persuading, Dr Symonds not to expose him to public disgrace, and that he sanctioned Vaughan's reason for resigning that fifteen years was a long enough tenure for any headmaster.

It is understandable too that Stanley should have wished to keep the

---

[m] See p. 51.

truth from his family, and from his and Catherine's mother especially. In a letter to *The Spectator* apropos of Vaughan's death in 1897, Lionel Tollemache[n] claimed that 'Vaughan's mother-in-law, Mrs Stanley, told my father that she herself did not *quite* understand why he first accepted and then declined Lord Palmerston's offer. There seems to have been an element of *inscrutability* in him, which he, perhaps, thought it wise to encourage.'[33] And Stanley's cousin by marriage, Lady Henrietta, whose patience with Vaughan had already been tested by her troublesome son Johnny, wrote in exasperation to her mother-in-law when she heard about Rochester. Vaughan's act of declining preferment, she declared, was due to 'a morbid tenderness of conscience & want of moral courage to face all the difficulties of the position, which doubtless he would exaggerate ... Aunt Kitty has taken the event very well, full of tenderness for Catherine & determined to make the best of it. The Bishop of London naturally much annoyed as people do not like to be made fools of, he having taken much trouble about it; but some people are overwhelmed when responsibility comes near them.'[34] It is difficult to believe that Tait had not discussed this appointment with Stanley. We must presume that Stanley withheld the truth from him, and allowed the offer of Rochester to be made and then turned down.

Symonds recounts that Stanley went out of his way to keep in touch with him, inviting him to Christ Church and later to Westminster. He accepted these invitations because his father 'wished that appearances should be kept up and, in case of public exposure, that my recognition by the Dean should be a matter of notoriety'.[35] Understandably, Symonds found these encounters uncomfortable, and said that he 'could neither act nor talk with freedom'.[36]

*   *   *

The year after Vaughan's resignation, 1860, Stanley found himself arbitrating again in three notorious controversies. The first concerned a disgraceful case of ritualism, the growing trend in the Church of England to introduce Roman Catholic ceremonial. Its roots were in the Oxford Movement, but its shoots would not have appeared unless they had been fed and watered by Newman's conversion to Rome. This prompted further secessions among his followers or, for those who remained in the Anglican fold, at least a deep admiration for Rome, and a desire to adopt its sacramental rites and practices. The trend was

---

[n] Hon. Lionel Tollemache was a contemporary of Symonds at Harrow and Balliol.

particularly strong among clergy working in the slums, where ornament, music and drama offered a useful contrast to drab, impoverished surroundings, and arguably a more accessible means of communication than preaching or Bible study. But these priests' good intentions were sometimes vehemently resisted by congregations which shared a deep-seated English hostility to popery.

St George's in the East in Stepney was just that kind of parish church. 'It was the land of docks and sailors, of drinking-saloons and filthy bars, of public houses offering squads of harlots.'[37] Since 1842 the vicar, Bryan King, had been trying step by step to add colour to the Hawksmoor church and its services, but in the face of stubborn opposition. The last straw came in 1856 when King introduced eucharistic vestments. The vestry (church council) had the right to nominate a 'lecturer', who was allowed to preach after a Sunday afternoon service conducted by the vicar. In 1859 an Evangelical clergyman known for his anti-Romanising views was appointed, and the congregation split into two antagonistic groups. Those of Protestant persuasion would arrive early for the lecturer's sermon in order to disrupt the vicar's service, and with shameful results. 'Sunday afternoons at St. George's were the zoo and horror and coconut-shy of London.'[38] 'The whole service', wrote the vicar, 'was interrupted by hissing, whistling, and shouting. Songs were roared out by many united voices during the reading of the lessons and the preaching of the sermon; hassocks were thrown down from the galleries, and after the service, cushions, hassocks, and books were hurled at the altar ... I myself, and the other officiating clergy, had been spat upon, hustled, and kicked within the Church...'[39]

Tait had never had time for Tractarians, and now, as Bishop of London, he showed no sympathy to ritualists. But he was also horrified by the vicious and sacrilegious protest at St George's, and in September 1859 he wrote a long letter to the senior churchwarden. He required the churchwardens to notify him immediately 'if any clergyman so officiate in the Church, as to give reasonable offence by this childish mimicry of antiquated garments, or by so dressing himself up that he may resemble as much as possible a Roman Catholic priest'. But at the same time he begged all concerned, 'for the sake of the many ignorant and thoughtless souls in this parish of St. George's, not to allow another day to pass without taking such steps towards Christian reconciliation as may by God's blessing end the present miserable disturbances'.[40]

The letter was to no avail, the riots continued, and the bishop's authority had been challenged. Tait had consulted Stanley as examining chaplain before writing his letter, and in May 1860, having done all he could, he asked Stanley to intervene. Stanley's sympathetic nature and reputation for breadth and tolerance lent him credibility with both sides.º He convinced the vicar that he should take a year's leave while his place was filled by a curate-in-charge of Stanley's choosing. The man appointed was the Trollopian sounding Septimus Hansard, an Old Rugbeian who had useful experience ministering to an Irish neighbourhood near the Edgware Road. Stanley promised his and Thomas Hughes's support. 'You would', wrote Stanley persuasively, 'restore the parish to peace. You would win a crown of glory for yourself and many souls to God. By the end of the year you would have proved what you could do, and be rewarded accordingly.'[41] '"Trust in the Lord," as Cromwell said, "and keep your temper dry," was Stanley's final advice.'[42] Though Hansard resigned before the year was finished, he managed to quell the mob, and begin the process of restoring the services to Anglican form and order. The vicar did not return, and with Tait's help was appointed rector of Avebury in Wiltshire.

The publication in 1860 of a collection of disturbing theological papers with the bland title *Essays and Reviews* provoked violent and prolonged explosions.ᵖ Pusey even described it as 'the greatest crisis the Church of England has ever gone through'.[43] Much of this was due to unfortunate timing. Darwin's *Origin of Species* had been published just the year before, and though it took time for its revolutionary thesis to be absorbed, rumours were soon abroad that the Bible's authority was facing a new and devastating threat. Four months after the appearance of *Essays and Reviews*, Bishop Wilberforce of Oxford and the agnostic T. H. Huxley (Owen Stanley's junior surgeon on the *Rattlesnake*) had their famous quarrel at a meeting of the British Association for the Advancement of Science. 'Is it through your grandfather or grandmother that you claim to be descended from a monkey?' asked Wilberforce. 'I would rather be descended from a miserable ape', Huxley replied, 'than from a man highly endowed by nature and possessed of great means of influence who yet employs these faculties and that influence for the mere purpose of introducing ridicule into a grave discussion.'ᑫ

º Nonetheless, Stanley made clear his strong disapproval of ritualism in an article in the *Edinburgh Review* (April 1866).
ᵖ The book was reissued in thirteen editions in five years.
ᑫ There are various versions of what was said but this is the gist.

Biblical authority was already under fire from the historical critical approach pioneered in Germany, and introduced into England by Coleridge and his disciples – not least, Thomas Arnold and Julius Hare. George Eliot's translation of D. F. Strauss's *Leben Jesu* (1835–6) had been published in 1846. Its mythical interpretation of the gospels and rejection of miracles had caused widespread concern. Jowett's and Stanley's editions of Paul's epistles, and Stanley's sermons on the apostolic age, had taken their cue from the German approach in trying to get back to the original (or at least earliest) text, context and meaning. Even this was contentious because most British Christians still regarded every story and statement in the Bible as timelessly true, and in the most literal sense. New discoveries in science and the advent of Biblical criticism were raising questions which were profoundly disturbing. '1860 was a bad moment to produce a book deprecating the importance of the Bible and Church.'[44]

Essays and Reviews is a hotchpotch of independent and opinionated essays written by six Anglican clergymen and one layman. The short prefatory notice explains their common purpose: 'The Volume, it is hoped, will be received as an attempt to illustrate the advantage derivable to the cause of religious and moral truth, from a free handling, in a becoming spirit, of subjects peculiarly liable to suffer by the repetition of conventional language, and from traditional methods of treatment.' Frederick Temple, Headmaster of Rugby,[r] contributed an expanded university sermon on 'The Education of the World'. Rowland Williams, vice-principal of Lampeter's theological college, wrote on the Biblical scholarship of Baron von Bunsen; and Oxford's Savilian Professor of Geometry, Baden Powell,[s] on the evidences of Christianity. Charles Goodwin, a lawyer and Egyptologist, dealt with the conflict between natural science and Christian faith; Mark Pattison, fellow of Lincoln College, Oxford, wrote on 'Tendencies of Religious Thought in England, 1688–1750', and Henry Wilson,[t] vicar of Great Staughton, on the national Church.

Benjamin Jowett's essay 'On the Interpretation of Scripture' is the last and longest in the book, and arguably the best and most important. It had been written for inclusion in his Pauline commentaries, and in

---

[r] Temple had been an undergraduate and fellow at Balliol. After six years as Principal of Kneller Hall teachers training college in Twickenham, he succeeded Tait as Headmaster of Rugby in 1857.
[s] Father of Robert Baden-Powell, founder of the Scout Movement.
[t] Wilson had been, with Tait, a signatory to the four tutors' letter attacking Tract XC.

tune with their approach, argues that reason must be employed in interpreting the Bible, just as it would in explaining the meaning of a classical text. It was, in short, an attempt to establish in Britain the historical study of the Bible which had been pursued in Germany for fifty years. Jowett summarised his argument as follows:

> Scripture, like other books, has one meaning, which is to be gathered from itself without reference to the adaptations of Fathers or Divines; and without regard to *a priori* notions about its nature and origin. It is to be interpreted like other books, with attention to the character of its authors, and the prevailing state of civilization and knowledge, with allowance for peculiarities of style and language, and modes of thought and figures of speech.[45]

If there is a common theme in the collection it is most clearly expressed in Jowett's essay: 'The time has come when it is no longer possible to ignore the results of criticism, and it is of importance that Christianity should be seen to be in harmony with them.'[46] In a letter to Stanley written in 1858, Jowett had explained that 'the object is to say what we think freely within the limits of the Church of England ... We do not wish to do anything rash or irritating to the public or the University, but we are determined not to submit to this abominable system of terrorism, which prevents the statement of the plainest facts, and makes true theology or theological education impossible.'[47]

Though Stanley was in favour of the liberal theology in *Essays and Reviews*, he was against the book from the start, and refused to contribute. Writing to a former pupil in 1859, he had advised that he did not think any book on the interpretation of Scripture was necessary, and recommended instead Arnold's essay on the subject at the end of the second volume of his sermons, as well as some of the sermons themselves.[48] Furthermore, Stanley did not approve of the composite nature of the project, which he called 'a decided blunder'.[49] He was unimpressed by the quality of the essays, apart from Temple's, Pattison's and Jowett's, but even then he thought Temple's inexpedient, Pattison's 'imperfectly cooked',[50] and Jowett's too antagonistic. But it was the book's disparaging tone that most concerned him, as well as 'the absurdity of endeavouring to produce an effect on a public already terrified by throwing together a number of names which gather, not strength, but weakness, not attractiveness, but repulsiveness, from this concatenation'.[51]

The fuse was lit with publication but it took several months before the bomb exploded. An article in the *Westminster Review* in October 1860, followed by Bishop Wilberforce's anonymous attack in the *Quarterly Review* (January 1861), 'gave the signal for wild and panic-stricken agitation'.[52] As with Ward, Hampden and Gorham, Stanley was more incensed by the vicious reaction than he was by its cause, and was quick to defend the book and its contributors against charges of heresy or atheism. He did so in a long and measured article in the April edition of the *Edinburgh Review*.

In February the two archbishops and twenty-four bishops, all of whom had been overwhelmed by protests from thousands of clergymen, met at Lambeth Palace. Egged on by Wilberforce, they agreed to issue a public reply. The Archbishop of Canterbury (John Bird Sumner) announced that the bishops 'cannot understand how these opinions can be held consistently with an honest subscription to the formularies of our Church', and that a prosecution in the ecclesiastical courts or a synodical condemnation was under consideration.[53] Stanley regarded the bishops' declaration as an intolerant and unjust attack on the liberties of the Church, and as supporting the indiscriminate and insulting charges being made against the essayists. Tait and (ironically) Hampden were two of the signatories. Stanley and Temple wrote a series of pained letters to Tait, challenging his involvement.[54] They and Jowett had been his pupils and friends at Balliol, and had been given the impression that Tait was in broad agreement, at least with the essays of Temple, Jowett and Pattison. Tait defended himself by explaining that it was the book as a whole that he found unorthodox.

It seemed likely that Temple would have to resign his headmastership. J. B. Lightfoot was 'unable to conceive a greater calamity, happening just at this crisis, not only to Rugby, but to the English Church in general'.[u] It was an exaggeration typical of Arnold's followers, but Lightfoot added a perceptive observation: 'It is very much to be apprehended, I fear, that the agitation about "Essays and Reviews" will have the effect of dividing men into two well defined and extreme parties, the one consisting of irrational champions of so-called orthodoxy, the other of men who, under the pressure of opposition, will be driven into a position of reckless scepticism, from which they would have been quite safe if left to themselves.'[55]

---

[u] Joseph Barber Lightfoot was Hulsean Professor of Divinity at Cambridge and later Bishop of Durham. He had been a pupil of James Prince Lee at King Edward's School, Birmingham; Lee had taught at Rugby under Arnold.

The battles dragged on through 1862 until in December Williams and Wilson were sent for trial at the court of arches on the familiar grounds that their views were not consistent with subscription to the Thirty-Nine Articles. They were condemned and suspended, before being acquitted in February 1864 by the judicial committee of the Privy Council (which included Tait). Stanley had given generously to the fund set up to pay for their defence.

Jowett was disillusioned by the uproar. He lost confidence in the prospects of liberal theology in the Church of England, and devoted the rest of his life to Balliol and Plato. He was especially disappointed by Tait's failure to support the book, and by Temple's withdrawal of his essay in 1869 when he became Bishop of Exeter. Jowett came to the cynical view that 'really great men are never Clergymen'.[56] In other words, it is impossible to think and inquire critically and independently (as great men do) while submitting to inherited dogmas and creeds. Westcott had made much the same point in a letter to Stanley: 'It is acknowledged by all that men of high intellectual culture have for some years shrunk from taking Orders ... Now I fear this must be, and in fact is already the case, from the belief that all free criticism, however reverent, is banished from questions of theology.'[57] Kitty Stanley recognised with relief that her son's defence of the unorthodox in his article in the *Edinburgh Review* had 'put out of the question your ever being a Bishop'.[58]

In 1860, the year *Essays and Reviews* was published, Stanley began to bring to an end a long and unedifying row over Jowett's stipend as Regius Professor of Greek. He had been appointed five years before on the death of Thomas Gaisford, who had occupied the chair for forty-three years, twenty-four of which alongside the deanery of Christ Church. The £40 p.a. stipend for the professorship had remained the same since it was founded by Henry VIII. This had not been a problem for Gaisford because a succession of cathedral canonries and then the deanery of Christ Church provided ample remuneration: indeed he is renowned for concluding a sermon in the cathedral by recommending the study of Greek literature which, he explained, 'not only elevates above the vulgar herd, but leads not infrequently to positions of considerable emolument'.[59] Jowett took a different view, and his income was limited to the money he received as a fellow and tutor at Balliol. Furthermore, and unlike Gaisford, Jowett worked hard to fulfil his obligations.

Stanley was elected a professorial member of the hebdomadal board in November 1860, and this enabled him to bring the matter of Jowett's salary to the attention of the university. Unfortunately Pusey was re-elected at the same time, and it was Pusey who was most determined to prevent the university from getting involved. He detested Jowett's liberal theology, and had taken exception to his commentary on the epistles, and in particular an essay on the atonement which Jowett included. Indeed it was Pusey who had insisted that Jowett subscribe again to the Thirty-Nine Articles in the presence of the vice-chancellor (who happened to be Pusey's brother-in-law)[v] before being allowed to take up the professorship. Jowett signed: 'It seemed to me', he told Stanley, 'that I could not do otherwise without giving up my position as a Clergyman.'[60] Though Jowett made light of it to Stanley, and gave a comic account of what happened,[61] he was hurt and humiliated. It was soon after this that Jowett withdrew from Balliol's hall and common room, though this is more likely because he had failed to be elected to the mastership the year before.

Pusey took the view that the university's endowing the chair while Jowett was professor would imply support for his theological views, and Oxford's Anglican orthodoxy made this impossible. At the same, time Pusey recognised the difficulties of his own position, and was aware of accusations of mean-spiritedness. In October 1861 Stanley raised the matter again with the hebdomadal board. A statute endowing the Greek chair was submitted to congregation but was narrowly rejected. While planning his next step Stanley gave another generous donation, this time to a compensatory fund set up by Jowett's friends, and which raised £2,000. Jowett was touched by their kindness but he was a proud man and refused to accept the money. 'It does not do,' he wrote, 'and is not consistent with the dignity of a human being, to receive about £20 from everybody you meet at dinner.'[62]

At the end of 1862 Jowett's opponents tried to have him prosecuted in the vice-chancellor's court on the grounds that his essay on atonement (re-written and re-published in 1859), and on the interpretation of Scripture in *Essays and Reviews*, contradicted the articles. In a university sermon preached on 8 February 1863, Stanley attacked 'the hatred of Christians by each other for their theological opinions', and set out plainly his own rules to avoid the evils of *odium theologicum*:

---

[v] R. L. Cotton, Provost of Worcester College.

Never condemn a book unless we have read it ...

Let us determine never to condemn in one man the same sentiment which in another we forgive or applaud ...

Let us never judge one side of the question without hearing or reading the other side ...

Let us never impute to our opponents, whether Churches, sects, or individuals, intentions which they themselves disclaim, nor fasten upon them opprobrious names which they themselves repudiate ...

Let us never attack anyone without first making out deliberately, carefully, seriously, all the points when we agree; and then, and not till then, stating the points wherein we disagree ...[63]

The case against Jowett collapsed in May, and Pusey and his allies withdrew their charges.

In autumn 1863 Pusey proposed a statute which would allow the university to increase Jowett's salary tenfold, but 'on the understanding that the University shall be held to have pronounced no judgement upon his writings, insofar as they touch the Catholic Faith'.[64] This arrangement had been suggested by Keble and was accepted by Stanley. The measure received a sound majority in congregation and was submitted to convocation in March 1864. In scenes in the Sheldonian Theatre reminiscent of Ward's degradation a decade before, the statute was defeated to 'loud cheers from the opponents ... and violent hissing from the undergraduates' gallery'.[65] The Lord Chancellor introduced a bill in the House of Lords which proposed that the next cathedral canonry in his gift to become vacant should be annexed to the professorship of Greek, but this was thrown out in committee on the grounds that it would exclude the appointment of a layman. Then the university's vice-chancellor proposed another statute which would increase the stipend to £400, while reserving judgment on the professor's theological opinions. Pusey supported this, but it was lost by one vote in the hebdomadal board.

Now Edward Freeman, later Regius Professor of Modern History, published a letter that had first appeared in October 1864 in the *Daily News*. In it he brought to light a letter of 1854 which had been addressed by the dean and chapter of Christ Church to the Prime Minister in response to the Oxford Commission. The letter had explained that endowing the Greek chair was Christ Church's preferred way to dispose of further college funds for academic purposes.

However, Christ Church responded to Freeman's letter by explaining that five canonries were already endowing professorships, and, furthermore, that the commissioners had asked for two more canonries to be suppressed in order to provide for studentships. A fellow of Queen's College, Charles Elton, then discovered that lands had been granted by Henry VIII, first to the chapter of Westminster and then to Christ Church, for the support of professors of divinity, Hebrew and Greek. Now at last the dean and chapter, worn down by years of pressure to correct an injustice, 'agreed to take measures as might be necessary for increasing the yearly salary of the Regius Professor of Greek to the sum of £500'.[66]

*   *   *

Stanley's association with the court as Prince Albert's chaplain now began to extend and deepen, and to focus on the Prince of Wales. When the Prince was six, Stanley had been considered as a tutor, but Albert's mentor, Baron von Stockmar,[w] had advised against a clergyman, and Henry Birch, a young Eton master, was appointed instead. Bertie's education began then in earnest, and earnest it remained.

Stockmar had convinced Albert that the misdemeanours of Victoria's Hanoverian uncles, the sons of George III, were due to their lack of education. This must not to be repeated, and instead Bertie was to be fashioned by a strict and strenuous education into a model prince, ready to fulfil Albert's ideal of monarchy. From the time the Prince was eight, every weekday, including Saturday, was divided into five hourly or half-hourly lessons, during which Birch instructed him in arithmetic, geography and English. Religion, German, writing, drawing and music were taught by specialists. Albert was given a daily report on Bertie's industry and progress. Only a few days in the year were free of lessons, and the Prince had to work harder than any schoolboy. Furthermore, it was an education in isolation: the Prince was kept apart from his contemporaries lest they should corrupt him, or presume a relationship of equals. When he was older, Bertie was taken occasionally to Eton to visit various sons of the nobility, but these excursions often ended in embarrassment because the Prince had no idea how to socialise. He had a quick temper, and was at times so rude and aggressive that the headmaster had to complain.

---

[w] Stockmar (1787–1863) trained as a doctor but devoted his life to serving the Saxe-Coburg-Gotha family.

Albert decided that when the Prince was eighteen he should spend a year or more at Oxford and then at Cambridge, but not in a college like other undergraduates. Instead at Oxford he lived in Frewin Hall on New Inn Hall Street, with his governor, General Robert Bruce, and an equerry, Major Christopher Teesdale, who had won a Victoria Cross in the Crimea. The vice-chancellor insisted that Bertie should have at least a college association, and Christ Church was chosen on the grounds that it was a royal foundation, and Liddell, the dean, was one of the Prince Consort's chaplains. Nonetheless, Albert insisted to Bruce that 'he belongs to the whole University and not to Christ Church in particular, as the Prince of Wales will always belong to the whole nation'.[67]

Bertie came into residence as a nobleman in October 1859 at the start of Stanley's second year. According to Liddell's account, he matriculated with pomp and ceremony:

> He came down in a royal carriage (not by special train) at about four o'clock. I received him on the platform, and followed him to his house. The Vice-Chancellor and Proctors then called to pay their respects; then the Mayor and two Aldermen with an address; I standing by and introducing them. Then I went down to Christ Church, where we had the gates shut, and all the men drawn up in the Quadrangle. At five he came, and the bells struck up as he entered. He walked to my house between two lines of men, who capped him. I went out to meet him, and as we entered the house there was a spontaneous cheer. All through the streets, which were very full, the people cheered him well. Then I took him up to the drawing-room, and entered his name on the buttery book. He then retired with his Tutor, Mr. Fisher, and put on a nobleman's cap and gown in the gallery, and returned to receive greetings as the first Prince of Wales who had matriculated since Henry V.[68]

Stanley was one of a small group of professors chosen to deliver special courses of lectures to the Prince and six other Christ Church undergraduates, handpicked to be his companions. Lady Stanley wrote to her husband: 'I hear Arthur is to give private lectures to the Prince of Wales on Ecclesiastical History: at the request of Prince Albert. I am very glad of it. Arthur long ago wished to have something to do with the instruction of the Prince, & it will set him up with some of the people who cry him down.'[69] Stanley found the Prince courteous and attentive, though more, he thought, because of a sense of obligation than genuine interest or enthusiasm. But Bertie did well enough in his examinations, and his father even went so far as to inform the Princess Royal that he 'does what he *has to do* very well'.⁷⁰

After spending most of the summer vacation on an official tour of Canada and America, the Prince returned to Oxford for his fourth and final term. In January 1861 he joined Trinity College, Cambridge but was again lodged outside college, this time at Madingley Hall, a large country house four miles from the town. Bertie had now set his heart on joining the army, and Albert agreed to his spending the summer on a course of infantry training, attached to the Grenadier Guards, at the Curragh near Dublin. There he found the drill difficult and command impossible, and was not promoted as fast as Albert had expected.

It was at the Curragh that the Prince's fellow cadets smuggled a vivacious young actress called Nellie Clifden into his quarters, and with predictable results. The incident remained secret until rumours began to circulate in the clubs of St James's. By November, and the Prince's twentieth birthday, Prince Albert had been informed by Stockmar, and he wrote to his son 'with a heavy heart upon a subject which has caused me the greatest pain I have yet felt in this life'.⁷¹ On 25 November he travelled by special train to see Bertie at Cambridge. There they took a long walk in the rain which seems to have exhausted Albert, already worn down by years of work and worry. Within days typhoid fever was diagnosed, and, after collapsing at Windsor, the Prince Consort died on 14 December 1861, aged forty-two.

Stanley was staying with Tait at Fulham Palace when he heard the news. He told Pearson that 'No *public* death could have affected me so much ... so long as he lived I felt sure that there was a steady support to all that was most excellent in the English Church.'⁷² As another of Albert's chaplains, Stanley attended the funeral in St George's Chapel at Windsor, two days before Christmas. *The Daily Telegraph* promised a 'grand Gothic fane ... completely draped and carpeted with black', and a hearse 'drawn by plumed and mantled steeds and hung with escutcheons of the illustrious deceased'.⁷³ Stanley described it as 'a profoundly mournful and impressive sight. Indeed, considering the magnitude of the event and of the persons present all agitated by the same emotion, I do not think that I have ever seen, or shall ever see, anything so affecting.'⁷⁴ On Christmas Eve he wrote a letter to Mary which implies that he was aware of the Clifden affair: 'I still cling to the hope that the Prince of Wales may be converted by his death; and, if he is not, then to the consolation that his father had been spared the bitter grief of the next 20 years, for if he is not steadied by this, he will never be steadied at all.'[75]

Just as when Arnold died, Stanley collected every detail of Albert's illness and death, this time from members of the royal family and household, and from those who had been in attendance. He then wrote a private account in the form of a journal,[76] with a plan of the Prince's rooms and lists of the pictures on the walls and books on the tables. And like his description of Arnold's dying in the biography, Stanley's narrative is tragic, weaving a sense of divine destiny into the awful sadness and waste of a hero's death.[x]

*   *   *

Queen Victoria blamed Bertie and 'that dreadful business at the Curragh'[77] for what had happened to his father, and could not bear the sight of him. It was decided to send him on the journey to Palestine that Prince Albert had planned as 'the crowning feature of his son's formal education'.[78] A month after Albert's death, Stanley received a letter from General Bruce summoning him to Osborne House.[79] Albert had intended to consult Stanley about the details of the tour, but now Bruce persuaded him to accompany them, telling him that 'the Prince Consort has often said, "What would it be if Professor Stanley could go with you?" I fear it is impossible. The Queen has said the same thing to me since you came, and this morning the Prince of Wales has said the same thing from himself.'[80] Stanley was gratified by the proposal but (as was invariably the case when new challenges were offered) he was filled 'with vast reluctance and misgivings',[81] not to mention his usual reluctance to visit the same places more than once. And what about his theological opinions, he asked Bruce, and the reactions of those who regarded him 'with terror and aversion'?[82] Then there were two personal objections: the inconvenience of deserting his work in Oxford, and his reluctance to leave his mother who was now in poor health.

Jowett wrote a letter to Kitty to persuade her to let him go, and a long letter to Stanley giving reasons why he should accept 'a most interesting mission', concluding: 'I have heard the stories about the Prince. I should not hesitate on that account. In years to come if the Prince's character were to take a worse turn it might be painful not to have tried to avert such a calamity.'[83] When Kitty urged her son to accept on the grounds of rendering a service to a household in trouble, he agreed to

---

[x] See Introduction, pp. 9–10.

meet the Prince and his party at Alexandria, ascend the Nile with them, and accompany them through the Holy Land. 'I am perfectly satisfied,' he told Pearson at the end of January 1862, '(and so is the dear mother), that it was necessary to go. It may end in smoke, or even in gall and wormwood; but it may also be full of interest, and may be productive of some good.'[84] In a letter from Osborne, Stanley told Mrs Arnold that he had walked to Arnold's childhood home near East Cowes, and the equerry who had accompanied him had told him that the Prince possessed a copy of Arnold's sermons. 'God grant that in these months which lie before me I may have something of the spirit and power which I first learned to know from that source!'[85]

Stanley left England on 12 February en route to Marseilles from where he was to take a steamer to Malta, and from there to Egypt. He spent a few days in Paris at the house in the Rue du Bac where Madame Mohl held her famous salon.[y] The brilliant philologist Ernest Renan was there. He was writing his controversial *Vie de Jésus*, with its assertions that the life should be written like that of any other man, and that the Bible should be subject to the same critical scrutiny as other historical documents.[z] Stanley told his mother: 'He showed a curious mixture of interest and want of interest; had not been to Damascus because there were no monuments there; and was disappointed in Jerusalem, because there were so few monuments ... On the other hand, he gave most invaluable information about the ruins in Galilee and Phoenicia.'[86]

Stanley reached Alexandria on 24 February and was joined five days later by the Prince, who arrived from Trieste on the royal yacht, HMS *Osborne*, accompanied by Bruce and Teesdale. Also in the party were the Prince's physician, Dr Minter, and two other equerries, Captain Keppel and the Hon. Robert Meade, the son of an Irish peer. Stanley referred to them as 'the two boys of the party':[87] like the Prince and Teesdale, they were in their twenties. Bruce was the second son of the 7th Earl of Elgin, famous for bringing the Parthenon frieze from Athens to London. He had served in the Grenadiers and as military secretary to his elder brother when he was Governor-General of Canada. He was dour and earnest, and Stanley had already come to respect his single-minded devotion to his duties. Stanley found Teesdale 'the most courtly

---

[y] Julius Mohl was a German orientalist. Mary's salon was one of the most popular intellectual centres in Paris.

[z] Surprisingly, Jowett disapproved of the book and its '"French" Christ with some traits taken from Renan's own character'.

of the whole party – never encouraging any approaches, usually silent ... as a general rule, veiled in mystery.'[88] Dr Minter was 'a thoroughly sound, good man – plain spoken'.[89] But it was with Meade and Keppel that he felt most at ease: 'We confide our mutual grievances to each other. They were both excellent, open hearted, intelligent youths – who would be excellent fellow travellers under any circumstances.'[90] Stanley enjoyed the company of young men, and the three of them shared the advantage of being outside the intimate entourage of governor and senior equerry. Stanley told Kitty at the start of the journey that 'the only plan for one's own comfort is to consider oneself as part of a machine – and now and then one may act as a flywheel or the like. But the whole affair is an *institution* like Oxford, or the Church, – or the House of Commons – to be dealt with accordingly ... So you may rest in good spirits. I was a little discouraged at first – But I have found my place now – and shall keep to it.'[91]

Stanley spent the next three months retracing some of his steps of a decade ago. But this time he journeyed in regal luxury, cheered by crowds and fêted by dignitaries. The party travelled by royal barges (with a cabin each), carriages and camels 'with velvet saddles, and silken trappings and gilt and silver ornaments'.[92] They stayed in embassies and palaces, waited on by servants and slaves, and were subject to 'almost the same formality as if [the Prince's] father or mother had been present. Not only has every dinner been full evening dress, but no one speaks at dinner above their breath. A remark or two across the table is all that is ventured upon ... We dine at 7.30 and get to bed by 11 – breakfast at nine – lunch at one. The luxury is beyond all bounds.'[93] Stanley was bemused at first and rather enjoyed the attention, but 'in other respects, the grandeur of royalty sadly shore away the glories of the visit. A troop of horses, with awkward saddles and stirrups, were a poor exchange for the pleasant flight of donkeys. A long expectation of a long repast of many dishes carried on camels from the steamer ludicrously took the place of the familiar luncheon of dates and oranges under the palm trees. The Nubian population had lost all their originality by putting on their Sunday best.'[94]

The chief challenge of the tour for Stanley was how to interest the Prince (and his companions) in the sights and scenes of Biblical history. Bertie had definitely not inherited his father's intellectual inquisitiveness, and would have preferred to spend his days shooting every bird and beast in sight. Stanley and Bruce seemed to have handled this wisely, allowing plenty of time for hunting (though not on Sundays), while encouraging any signs of archaeological enthusiasm. 'Oddly enough, much as he dislikes going to tombs and temples, he has a passion for collecting relics and antiquities.'[95] Stanley was also ready to humour him and recognise his strengths. On one occasion, early in the journey, every one of the party went to view the tombs at Giza, but the Prince stayed behind, 'sitting in front of the tent, smoking, and reading *East Lynne*'.[96] This popular novel by Mrs Henry Wood had been published the year before, and told the story of a young woman who deserts her husband and children to elope with an aristocrat. Predictably the plot appealed to Bertie, but it was hardly Stanley's choice of reading matter. Nonetheless, 'At his request, I am reading *East Lynne* – which will while away this – even in a steamer – most uninteresting portion of the Nile.'[97] The next day Stanley added: 'H.R.H.[A] is perfectly friendly and easy. He has set his mind on my reading *East Lynne* – which I did in three sittings yesterday, and stood a tolerable examination in it. It is impossible not to like him. And to be constantly with him certainly brings out his astonishing memory of persons and names.'[98]

Some of the absurdities of the veneration accorded the royal party amused Stanley, Meade and Keppel. Indeed they appear to have enjoyed a good deal of irreverent laughter, made all the more intense by the required formalities, and the seriousness of Bruce and Teesdale. Before visiting Dendera, the last temple of the Ptolemiac kings, Stanley announced at breakfast ('as an inducement to the Prince')[99] that the colossal face of Cleopatra they were to see carved on the outer wall of the temple bore a remarkable likeness to a distinguished person they all knew. When they reached the figure, Teesdale guessed it. 'Would the Bishop of Oxford[B] have been gratified or not to see us all standing before the gigantic Queen and speculating on the resemblance of her features to his?'[100] The following day an ostrich that had been presented to the Prince (along with two gazelles and a monkey) by the Governor of Keneh collapsed and died. '"It is even sooner that I had hoped," said the general. Meade entirely enters into the excessively ludicrous side which it presents – and I am sure you wd. enjoy the roars of laughter which ring thro' our cabin. He, Keppel and I visit each other first thing every morning – and the General from time to time administers a playful rebuke.'[101]

[A] Stanley also refers to the Prince as Telemachus, the son of Odysseus and Penelope.
[B] 'Soapy Sam' Wilberforce.

Stanley's mother was nearly seventy and had been unwell for several months. Stanley received news at Thebes that she was now gravely ill. When the Queen was told, she wanted Stanley to be recalled. Lady Augusta Bruce, her most trusted lady-in-waiting, and General Bruce's sister, wrote to Mary Stanley to say that 'it was only when Mrs. Stanley's own wishes were made clear that the Queen, deeply touched and affected, desired me to express all she felt for you, for her, for Mr. Stanley, and to say that nothing should be done but what Mrs. Stanley decided.'[102] Stanley's loyalties were painfully torn but he determined not to return unless sent for. Back home in Alderley, the dowager Lady Stanley thought he had made the right decision but would always regret not seeing his mother before she died. She was also sceptical about the Prince: 'I cannot help many doubts whether he *can* do *much* good in the main object. There is not the material to work on.'[103]

In a long letter to Mary, Stanley described in detail how in Cairo on 23 March he learnt that Kitty had died more than two weeks before:

> The carriages came round – and I was as usual going in the second carriage – General Bruce called me to go in the first – with the Prince, Teesdale and himself. It was a long drive – The General looked very sad – but I tried to persuade myself that it was finding the Duke[C] here – but there was an immovable gravity in Teesdale's countenance and kindness in the Prince's manner, which kept me on constant anxiety. We arrived at the Palace here – entered the large Hall. General Bruce at last said 'Will you come into this room – I want to ask you a question.' The moment we were alone, he said 'Mr. Calnot has, I am afraid, received some bad news – Your Mother has been very ill – ' I interrupted him at once – and said '*She is dead*'.
>
> I found the letters piled up on the divan. But I could not bring myself to open them. At last I called for General Bruce. He immediately came ... In short nothing could have been more considerate than the conduct of everyone, from H.R.H. downwards. I forget whether it was then or afterwards that I had my first outpouring of bitter grief ...[104]

Stanley goes on to say that his sorrow had drawn the party closer

---

[C] They had already met the Duke of Saxe-Coburg (Prince Albert's brother) at Thebes, on his way to shoot wild boar in Abyssinia. Stanley and the rest of the party found him rude and objectionable.

together, and 'will (as the General most truly and considerately urged) lessen the levity and frivolity of the journey.'[105]

Despite the snub he had received when he wrote after Stanley's father's death, Jowett (who was fond of Mrs Stanley) wrote another tender and encouraging letter of condolence. 'I know that she was father, mother, brothers and friends to you all in one. Considering her extraordinary ability and intense affection it was most natural. And now perhaps there is only one thing that she would have cared for on earth, or does care for if the spirits departed retain the memories of such things: – that the end of your life should answer to the beginning of it and be consecrated, not without the thought of her, to the service of God and mankind ... Please write to me, if you are able, to tell me whether there is anything you would like me to do for you.'[106] This time Stanley wrote a grateful and courteous reply, concluding with a request to let him know how his sisters were, and what was being said about his mother.[107]

Stanley convinced himself that Kitty would have wanted him to continue the tour, though he confided to Jowett that it was 'a cruel pang' not to be present at her funeral, and 'to enter into the full tide of grief of all those who knew and loved and revered her.'[108] Kitty was buried in the churchyard at Alderley beneath an ancient yew tree. Her grave is marked by a simple white marble cross mounted on a rough block of local sandstone.[D] Inside the church, Stanley and his sisters placed a commemorative tablet alongside those of their father and brothers:

> TO THE DEAR MEMORY OF HER
> WHOSE FIRM FAITH, CALM WISDOM, AND TENDER SYMPATHY,
> SPEAKING THE TRUTH IN LOVE,
> COUNSELLED, ENCOURAGED, COMFORTED
> ALL WHO KNEW HER

It is difficult to exaggerate Stanley's love for his mother. He had been close to her since childhood, and they shared a bond and sympathy which neither enjoyed with Stanley's father. Stanley inherited his mother's intelligence, sensitivity, and broad, tolerant views. He had always shared with her his interests and ideas, seeking her advice and often reading her his writings, anxious for her opinions and approval.

[D] Kitty had seen crosses like this at Meran in the Tyrol in 1860 and had asked for something similar for herself.

Their easy companionship seems to have satisfied Stanley, and banished any wish for intimate relationships with either sex. Stanley's bereavement was prolonged and agonising. 'His sorrow', his sister Catherine told their aunt, Maria Hare, 'is of that deep, silent kind which does not admit of any relief. One sees that it never leaves him, and that it is a long, continuous suffering that has fallen upon him.'[109] When staying at Fox How with Mrs Arnold, Stanley wrote: '*Now*, for the first time, Arnold's death, and all that relates to it, is pushed back beyond another range. You will not wonder that I find life very dull – a burden ... which I would gladly lay down.'[110] From the same place, a year later, he wrote to Jowett: 'Nothing that has happened, nothing, I trust, that can ever happen, can make her memory other than the greatest gift I have received – a gift greater even than that which the *genius hujus loci* was in its time to me.'[111]

The Prince and his suite arrived at Jaffa on the royal yacht on 31 March and set off two days later on horseback for Jerusalem. A troop of 100 Turkish cavalry and 50 servants escorted the first heir to the English throne to visit Jerusalem since Edward Longshanks, 600 years before. Whether here on the Mount of Olives or in the Garden of Gethsemane, or at Bethlehem, Nazareth or the Sea of Galilee, Stanley tried hard to bring alive the gospel stories and quicken Bertie's interest. 'I bade the Prince look round to the only detail which wd. have been worth noticing on such an occasion – a flock of white sheep and black goats feeding on the mountainside, the framework of the great Parable delivered also from this hillside – on the Day of Judgment.'[112] Though Stanley had been chosen to accompany the Prince primarily because he was the author of *Sinai and Palestine* and knew the Holy Land at first hand, he also had an important role as chaplain. Indeed Stanley saw the journey as a divinely ordained opportunity to teach the Prince about the Bible and the Christian religion, and to strengthen his faith. Stanley did this not just through his explanations of the sites, but also through Sunday sermons delivered to the Prince and his entourage, and to anyone else who happened to be present.

The moralising tone, especially the first three sermons, indicates that at the start Stanley was intent on challenging the Prince's worldliness. In the first sermon, preached on a royal barge on the Nile, he points out that it is Abraham who is remembered, not the Pharaoh. 'So it is in the world at large ... Who is that, when years are gone by, we remember with the purest gratitude and pleasure? Not the learned, or the clever, or the rich, or the powerful. But those who, like Abraham, have had the force of character to prefer the future to the present – the good of others to their own pleasure.'[113] Stanley must have had Prince Albert in mind in the third sermon in which he praises the virtues of 'innocence – purity of life – simplicity and truthfulness of character – regard to our nearest and dearest relations'.[114] 'Those who have passed out of the family circle into the world beyond the grave are, in God's sight, and before our own hearts, still one with us ... Their wishes are now commands; their lightest desires now become sacred duties for us who remain.'[115] Stanley learned of his mother's death the next day.

As the weeks passed, and Stanley got to know the Prince better and to like and respect him, the sermons concentrated more on the meaning and significance of places, and the people and events associated with them. Stanley used his extensive knowledge and gift for description and story-telling, and produced short, vivid addresses which focused on central Christian truths. He certainly enjoyed preaching them, not least the freedom they allowed from having to engage in theological dispute. 'It was one of the blessings of my journey in the East,' he told Augusta Bruce, 'that I had to fix my attention on those parts of Christianity which were at once the most important and the most clear of any of these modern controversies. These I knew would be most useful for the Prince of Wales, as they were also most useful to me.'[116] Looking back, Stanley thought the sermons 'contain my thoughts on the most sacred and spiritual subjects more truly than anything else that I have written'.[117]

The Prince seems to have appreciated the sermons, and asked to have all thirteen privately printed on his return to England. The following year, at the Queen's request, they were published (with notes on some of the localities visited) as *Sermons in the East*. The book's preface, and dedication to the Prince of Wales on the eve of his wedding, strike an ingratiating note, in contrast to the polite but avuncular relationship Stanley describes in his letters. Phrases like 'in compliance with the desire, kindly expressed by His Royal Highness', 'the offering of this little volume', and 'the good of One whose future is so dear to us'[118] might have been written by the obsequious Mr Samgrass of All Souls in *Brideshead Revisited*. Some of this language, of course, was a matter of convention, but it is also indicative of a new courtly demeanour that Stanley adopted as his royal associations increased.

Most of the dedication's four pages describe General Bruce, who had died, aged forty-nine, two weeks after their return to England on 13 June 1862. He had been weakened at the start of the journey by a fall from a donkey which had then rolled over him, but the cause of death was assumed to be a debilitating fever caught in the marshes of the upper Jordan. Stanley's eulogy is designed to remind the Prince of 'the noble figure of our beloved and gallant Chief', and 'the example, which he has left to all, of an unfailing and lofty sense of duty, and of entire devotion to the charge committed to him'.[119] Stanley was with Bruce when he died ('the very first time I had seen a human soul pass with full consciousness from this world to the world beyond')[120] and assisted at the Presbyterian funeral at Dunfermline.

*   *   *

Stanley was summoned to Windsor in Bruce's place to give the Queen a private account of the tour. He arrived on 14 June and met his sister Mary whom the Queen had invited. Stanley preached the following day in the private chapel, and this address on 'The Breadth of God's Commandment' is included in *Sermons in the East*. It is more theological than the others, and reflects on divine revelation and the doctrine of the Trinity. Stanley's description of a comprehensive Church of England is typical, and would have appealed to the Queen's aversion to both ritualists and Evangelicals, and their insistence that they alone represented the true English Church. 'No single Church can claim for itself the graces of the whole [of Christendom]. No single creed has exhausted the whole of Christian truth. We may dwell with pleasure, with comfort, on the goodness and the truth which prevail in each. When we return to our own Church, we may thank God that it is large enough and generous enough to have a place for all who love the Lord Jesus Christ and wish to serve him faithfully.'[121]

The Queen was grateful to Stanley for dutifully continuing with the journey after his mother's death, and for the changes she now found in Bertie. Stanley had won her confidence and trust, and the foundations of friendship were laid. The Queen's 'good, excellent Dr. Stanley'[122] now became a regular visitor to Windsor and Osborne. At the start of the expedition he had been appointed an honorary chaplain to the Queen (as he had been to the Prince Consort), and on his return he was made a deputy clerk to the closet, with responsibility for the college of royal chaplains. But the deepest (and most demanding) of all compliments was paid when Stanley was commanded to spend a week at Windsor in December to mark the first anniversary of the death of Prince Albert. 'Such a week of various mournful, moving scenes as I never passed.'[123] On the anniversary itself, Sunday 14

December 1862, Stanley conducted two special services in the Blue Room where Albert had died, and which, apart from the addition of a garlanded bust and portrait of the Prince, was to remain exactly as it had been left until Victoria's death forty years later.[E]

> In the morning I went at 9.45 to Mrs Bruce's[F] room, and with her and Lady Augusta to the fateful room. I went in first. There was the valet who had been with him at his death. There was a table placed for me. In a few moments they came in. I began by kneeling down and reading two prayers, chiefly made up from the Burial Service. I then sat down and read from John xiv ... and upon these verses read about five pages of reflections, which I had written in the morning. Then two more prayers and the Lord's Prayer, and an enlarged form of the Blessing. The Queen then rose from the bedside, where she had been kneeling, kissed the Princesses (I think the Princes kissed her hand), kissed the Bruces, and then came across to me. I knelt and kissed her hand, and she passed away with all the others.[124]

The Queen told Stanley that 'it seemed like a birthday', to which he replied 'It *is* a birthday in a new world.'[125] She asked Stanley to read his address again at ten in the evening, the time of Albert's's death. At the end he appealed to her reliance on Albert to raise her spirits: 'He, too, like his Saviour, speaks to us from that unseen state. He, too, bids us to be of good cheer; for he, in that better state, has overcome, and conquered, and subdued under his feet the passing, shifting world of sin, and trial, and suffering, and we, too ... are called also to overcome and conquer, and subdue under our feet the same world, with all its trials, sorrows, cares, perplexities, temptations ...'[126]

The next day Stanley was joined by the Bishop of Oxford and the Dean of Christ Church (both also chaplains to Prince Albert) at the consecration of the new mausoleum at Frogmore. Albert's marble effigy was already in place and the royal family and household placed wreaths around it. 'I could not see,' Stanley told Mary, 'indeed, I did not venture to look at, the Queen.'[127] Albert's coffin was received the following morning.

Three months later Stanley was at Windsor again for the marriage of

---

[E] The Queen gave orders for Albert's dressing gown to be laid every evening on his bed, and for a jug of hot water to be placed on his washstand.

[F] Katherine Bruce, widow of General Bruce, was another woman of the bedchamber.

the Prince of Wales to Princess Alexandra of Schleswig-Holstein-Sonderburg-Glucksburg, daughter of Prince Christian of Denmark. The Queen and the Prince Consort had wanted the marriage to happen as soon as Bertie came of age, and the Nellie Clifden affair had made them more determined. Negotiations had been taking place since early in 1861, and Bertie had met the Princess for the first time in the autumn. He liked what he saw, as did his parents. Alexandra was seventeen, slim, graceful, unaffected, and with a beautiful complexion. Once Bertie had returned home from the tour, 'so improved in every respect (thought the Queen), so kind and nice to the younger children, more serious in his ways and views, and most anxious for his marriage',[128] there had been no need to wait, and an engagement followed in September 1862.

Though the Queen had ruled out a grand State ceremony at Westminster Abbey, the wedding in St George's Chapel on 10 March 1863 was a lavish affair, with mourning black set aside for the day. The Prince was dressed in his velvet Garter mantle, worn over the uniform of a general, and the Princess wore an ornate white satin gown trimmed with garlands of orange blossom, and with a long watered silk train carried by eight bridesmaids. Most of the men wore uniform and the women full court dress. 'The beauty of the scene was enhanced by the medieval costumes of attendant beefeaters and heralds, and by the coats of cloth of gold worn by the State trumpeters who announced the arrivals of the separate processions of the clergy, knights of the Garter, royalties, the bridegroom and the bride.'[129] But like the Coronation, there were mishaps. The bride arrived ten minutes late, the Archbishop of Canterbury made heavy weather of repeatedly announcing all six of her Christian names, the Garter knights rushed down the aisle in a gaggle, and (in Lady Somerset's opinion) the bridesmaids were 'eight as ugly girls as you could wish to see'.[130] Most awkwardly, though, the Queen herself remained dressed in black crepe, with a widow's cap and Albert's Garter ribbon. She had walked unseen from the deanery via a specially constructed covered walkway to a private closet overlooking the altar.[G] There she sat throughout the service with her ladies-in-waiting. Mary Stanley had been invited to the wedding and had what her brother described as 'the very best view of the Queen that was possible'.[131] Mary wrote an account of the service that was almost as detailed and valuable as her brother's description of the Coronation

---

[G] Added by Henry VIII so that Catherine of Aragon could watch the Garter ceremonies.

(Appendix I). 'The Queen was agitated and restless,' she observed, 'moving back her chair, putting back her long streamers, asking questions of the Dss. of Sutherland. Her expression was profoundly melancholy, but I only saw her in tears once.'[132] Mary also noticed the bad behaviour of the four-year-old future Kaiser Wilhelm II. 'Afterwards I heard that in answer to the Queen's enquiry if he had been good, the answer was "Oh no, he was *biting* us all the time!"'[133]

After the wedding, the Prince presented Stanley with a beautifully bound Bible with the inscription 'From Albert Edward in remembrance of the 10 of March'. He invited him to his new home at Sandringham to celebrate holy communion on Easter Sunday, and to remember the Easter before when they were together in Tiberias. 'The Princess', he told Mary, 'was more charming and beautiful even than I had expected: something so winning and graceful, and yet so fresh and full of life. I was there from Saturday afternoon, to Tuesday evening, and saw them every day. It was a delightful visit and sent me away rejoicing.'[134]

* * *

The extraordinary royal favour Stanley now enjoyed meant that ecclesiastical preferment was certain to follow. When the Archbishop of Canterbury, John Bird Sumner, died in September 1862 there had been much gossip in Oxford about who would succeed him, and who would be chosen to fill any consequent vacancies. Stanley's name was mentioned in connection with various bishoprics, but he determined that if he had to move (and he would rather not) it would only be to the archbishopric of York, or the deanery of Westminster or St Paul's. The Queen was pressing the Prime Minister, Lord Palmerston, to recommend him for a mitre, but he was opposed to the appointment on the grounds that Stanley's liberal views would cause inconvenient controversy. In September 1863 his name was being mentioned for the archbishopric of Dublin.[H] Jowett thought it a bad idea but Tait urged Stanley to accept if offered, on the grounds that it would allow him more leisure than an English diocese, and more independence from theological wrangles. But Stanley was convinced that he should decline. 'An English see', he replied, 'I should feel it my duty to take; because in the Church of England I have a real interest.'[135] Furthermore, leaving England would mean leaving the Queen. However, it was soon being rumoured that Dr Trench, the Dean of Westminster, was likely to be

---

[H] Archbishop Richard Whately, Arnold's friend at Oriel, was dying.

Part Three: Canterbury and Oxford 1851–1863   235

appointed to Dublin, and that Stanley would be in the running for Westminster.

Stanley was about to experience a much greater change in his life than this, and one he would never have predicted. His sister Mary and the general's widow, Katherine Bruce, had convinced themselves that Stanley should marry the general's sister, Lady Augusta, the Queen's favourite lady-in-waiting. They were not alone in thinking this an excellent match. 'They suit each other perfectly,' Katherine wrote to Mary in October 1863, 'know each other thoroughly and being both of mature years, shd. lose no more time.'[136] In a letter to her younger sister Lady Frances[I] a month before, Augusta confided that while out walking, 'Kath. suddenly tells me that she has been commissioned to find out if there will be any insuperable barrier to that which the world so confidently announced in Summer. Darling, if she had asked me to become Queen I could not have been more startled and unprepared. Miss S. had corresponded with her on the subject ... Then K. told me how dearest Robert had from their first acquaintance wished it and *his* Mother in Paris! She spoke of his goodness, his charm, his talent, his piety – and the atmosphere of his home, in which he thought I should feel so happy.'[137]

Stanley and Augusta had met in 1856 at Madame Mohl's salon.[J] Their paths crossed again through Augusta's contact with Mary Stanley during the Crimean War. Augusta had written to Stanley on behalf of the Queen during the eastern tour, and her brother's illness and death, soon after his mother's, had drawn them together. Now they saw each other whenever Stanley was at court. Augusta had come to regard him as 'the most valued, trusted and admired friend'.[138] Stanley's surviving letters to friends do not reveal any feelings or opinions he may have had about Augusta, but he cannot have failed to notice the sympathy, humour and charm which Augusta's own correspondence reveals. She had served selflessly at court for eighteen years, first as a lady-in-waiting to the Queen's mother, the Duchess of Kent, and then since 1861 as woman of the bedchamber to the Queen. The Duchess had treated her as a daughter, the Queen was hugely dependent on her (she had been present when both her mother and Prince Albert had died), and the Princes and Princesses adored her.

[I] Lady-in-waiting to the Duchess of Edinburgh. Frances married Evan Baillie in 1855. Their son, Albert, was Dean of Windsor and (with Hector Bolitho) edited Augusta's letters and wrote a memoir of Stanley, *A Victorian Dean* (1930).
[J] Augusta had spent her early years in Paris where her widowed mother, Lady Elgin, entertained the city's intelligentsia in her own salon in the Rue de Lille.

Encouraged by others, and after much agonising, Stanley summoned the courage to propose. Augusta accepted and they were engaged on 6 November 1863: Stanley was forty-seven and Augusta forty-one. There is no doubt that his mother's death was a major factor in Stanley's decision. He missed her dreadfully and needed someone to replace her, and give him the support and advice on which he depended. Augusta was aware of this, and in a letter written from Balmoral on 11 October she told her sister: 'In his dedication of his last book^K to the Memory of his Mother, he says "whose calm judgement, firm faith and tender sympathy" had sustained and cheered and guided him – I thought how ever could I replace that?'[139] But, for all her misgivings, Augusta told Frances that she was delighted: 'It is *Yes* that I have said, darling. I could not refuse ... Oh! my darling, it is like a dream!'[140]

Of course, the Queen had been informed and her permission sought. Katherine Bruce had spoken to her first in September, and she indicated then that she would not interfere where Augusta's happiness was at stake. Indeed in October it seemed to Augusta that she had 'quite come round to K's idea that it would be an advantage for Her to have this tie to such a person as Dr. S.'[141] However, the seventeen-year-old Princess Helena told Augusta that her mother thought the marriage foolish, and that the kind of companionship Augusta was hoping for could only spring out of a long and early marriage.[142] Indeed the Queen informed her uncle Leopold, the King of the Belgians, that she had thought Augusta would never leave her. 'It has been my greatest sorrow and trial since my misfortune!'[143]

The Queen also told Leopold that despite Augusta's first duty being now to another, 'she will remain in my service and be often with me.'[144] It is no coincidence that two days after the engagement Stanley received the following letter from the Prime Minister: 'The Deanery of Westminster is about to become vacant by the promotion of Doctor Trench to the Archbishopric of Dublin, and I have been authorised by the Queen to ascertain whether it would be agreeable to you to accept the Deanery when it becomes vacant. I shall have great pleasure in receiving an affirmative answer.'[145] Stanley accepted immediately. 'It was', he told Jowett, 'the one change my dear mother desired for me.'[146] The engagement and the deanery were announced together on 8 November. As always at important moments in his life, Stanley craved Arnold's approval. The day before the announcements he had written to Mrs Arnold:

---

^K *Lectures on the History of the Jewish Church*, i (1863).

From no one else must you hear
- (1) That the marriage so long talked of without foundation is to be. Lady Augusta consented yesterday to become my wife.
- (2) That to-day I hear, on authority which I cannot doubt, that I am to have the Deanery of Westminster.

Oh, my dear friend of blessed days gone by, give your blessing to me in the great crisis of my life. It is my comfort to believe that my dearest mother would have given it her entire sanction.[147]

* * *

Many of those who wrote to Stanley to congratulate him (and especially his university friends) expressed delight at the prospect of marriage, and pleasure that his talents had been recognised, but disappointment that he would be leaving Christ Church and Oxford. Stanley seems to have predicted this response, and had written (somewhat disingenuously) to Liddell before the offer was made, saying that such a change would be 'full of pain and repugnance', but that he felt ('however reluctantly') that he ought not to decline it.[148] Liddell was certain that Stanley should refuse. He had found being Headmaster of Westminster School frustrating, and he was convinced that Stanley would be of more use in Oxford. 'Life in London, no doubt, has its bright side; but *to live perforce for eight months in* WESTMINSTER is *(experto crede)* not an enviable lot. Preaching in the Abbey will give you a wider scope of influence; but I know not how far your physical powers will be adequate to fill that vast space; and I much question whether any influence you may there exert will, in reality, be nearly so great as that which you have at Oxford.'[149] The day after the announcement, Liddell repeated his disapproval: 'Neither for you, nor for us, nor for any one, can I look with pleasure on your leaving your living work here for the dead mass that will meet you at Westminster.'[150] Seven years before, Jowett had told Stanley that 'nothing could be more delightful and suitable'[151] than his appointment to Westminster. Now he had changed his mind, believing (typically) that 'the London clergy cannot be influenced like young men at Oxford'.[152] ... 'I am grieved beyond measure', he told Lady Stanley, 'that such a joyful occasion as his marriage, should be spoilt and undone by such a fatal error.'[153]

Stanley's friends' disapproval and his own natural antipathy to change combined to give Stanley some genuine regrets. Though he was relieved at the prospect of leaving behind the acrimony of Oxford's theological disputes he feared that he was deserting the liberal cause. He was afraid too of the vanity and stuffy conservatism that can accompany high ecclesiastical office, 'and destroys all that was sincere and natural in the former self'.[154] 'My dear father', he told Augusta, 'was far more useful as a bishop from carrying into the office qualities so unlike what are usually found there. May I be able to follow in his footsteps!'[155]

Stanley was cheered by what Augusta regarded as a vision. She was, she told him, alone in her rooms at St James's Palace:

> I did not sleep very well, and happening to wander into my darling brother's sitting room, which I now occupy,[L] at an unnaturally early hour, I was startled by the picture which suddenly offered itself to my gaze. The sky was crimson, and against it, in the clear atmosphere of early morning, the towers of Westminster and the whole group of those beautiful buildings stood out in the most perfect distinctness ... There was something so mysterious and impressive and solemn in the silent beauty of the scene that it seemed more like a vision of the Holy City than anything earthly or material.[156]

Stanley preached his farewell sermon to the university in Christ Church Cathedral on Advent Sunday, 29 November 1863. His theme was 'Great Opportunities', and he wanted to summarise what Oxford and Christ Church meant to him, where he felt they had lost their way, and where the next generation should take them. He appealed to the undergraduates to 'be as free, be as liberal, be as courageous as you will; but be religious, *because* you are liberal; be devout, *because* you are free; be pure, *because* you are bold; cast away the works of darkness, *because* you are the children of light; be humble and considerate and forbearing, *because* you are charged with hopes as grand as were ever committed to the rising generation of any Church or of any country.'[157] That characteristic call for a confident faith, inspired by freedom of thought and expression, clashed yet again with Oxford's narrow dogmatic conservatism. The decision was taken to remove Stanley's name from the list of select preachers authorised to address the university.

Nine days before the sermon, Augusta's eldest brother, James, 8th Earl of Elgin, died in India, aged fifty-two: he had been appointed

---

[L] General Bruce had stayed with Augusta when he was ill and died in her rooms.

Viceroy the year before.ᴹ Augusta felt the loss, though her brother was eleven years older, and had been serving abroad for twenty years in a number of distinguished colonial posts – Governor of Jamaica, Governor-General of Canada, Plenipotentiary to the Emperor of China, and Viceroy of India. The wedding, planned for 16 December, had to be postponed for a week and made private, with 'all music and show dispensed with, and as few as possible present'.[158] Stanley and Augusta asked Liddell to marry them, though in Westminster Abbey not Christ Church. The marriage was, after all, the start of a new life together which was to be lived in London. Stanley had written to Augusta a few weeks before to say that he had told the Queen that he thought that 'marriage is the only event in modern life which corresponds to what baptism was in the ancient church – a second birth, a new creation, all things passing away, all things becoming new. Oh, let us look forward to the new flight upwards! All things, indeed, will not pass away, but they will be transfigured.'[159]

ᴹ Stanley's memoir was published in *The North British Review*, May 1864.

PART FOUR
Westminster
1864–1881

8
'That Temple of ... Reconciliation'
1864–1870

THE STANLEYS SPENT Christmas and then New Year 1864 at Christ Church before moving to Westminster. Augusta loved the house with its views of the Great Quadrangle, and told Frances that she found it 'so quiet and homelike, so like old houses I remember in my youth – everything is so quiet, so methodical, so gentlemanlike'.[1] 'We have been twice at early Church, but in general have prayers at nine and breakfast after. Then Church at 10 or not and we write or occupy ourselves till luncheon at one – at 2 we walk or drive, today to where Amy Robsart[a] was murdered, – come home at 4 or 5 if we go to Service, tea and a quiet time till dinner.'[2]

Stanley was installed in Westminster Abbey on Saturday 9 January. As before, he began his new work with a heavy heart. 'I cannot but feel', he told a friend, 'that the day may have come when the shades of failure and disappointment are to close round me, as they have closed round so many others.'[3] The most influential canon had published a pamphlet protesting against Stanley's appointment, preached against it from the Abbey pulpit, and then refused to attend the installation. This was Christopher Wordsworth, the poet's nephew and Vaughan's predecessor at Harrow. He was a traditional High Churchman and Tory, who disapproved of Stanley's liberalism and distrusted his friendship with Vaughan. Typically, Stanley refused to answer his objections, and told Augusta that the best reply would be 'an invitation to dinner on the first opportunity'.[4] He went out of his way in the sermon delivered on the day after his installation to praise Wordsworth's work in Westminster. 'Dr. Wordsworth', Stanley later explained, 'published a protest against my appointment filled with the most reckless misrepresentations. I thought that the only notice that it was fitting for me to take of this attack was to pronounce an eulogy upon that part of his conduct

---

[a] Wife of Elizabeth I's favourite Robert Dudley, Earl of Leicester, who was rumoured to have had her murdered in 1560 at Cumnor House near Oxford.

which really deserved it.'5 Stanley's irenic approach soon won Wordsworth's enduring regard and friendship.

The installation was followed immediately by a chapter meeting with the same tiresome agenda of rents, leases and conveyances that Stanley had loathed at Canterbury and Christ Church:

> I confess that I felt no elation, nothing but depression, at the prospect before me. It seemed to me as if I were going down alive into the sepulchre.
>
> I had a long conversation with Lord J. Thynne, very courteous and sensible, but opening a vista of interminable questions of the most uninteresting kind, for the discussion of which I felt totally incapable. I repeat that, as far as the actual work of the Dean is concerned, it is far more unsuited to me than that of a bishop. To lose one's time in Confirmations is bad, but to lose it in leases and warming-plans is worse.
>
> However, the deed is done, and my useful life I consider to be closed, except as far as I can snatch portions from the troubles of the office.[6]

Despite Stanley's depressing introduction to Westminster's capitular affairs, John Thynne proved a loyal and dutiful ally. Liddell had found him the same when he was Headmaster of Westminster, describing him as 'a *real* gentleman, a most agreeable, kind, good man'.[7] Thynne was the third son of the Marquis of Bath and elder brother of Charles, who had been a canon with Stanley at Canterbury before converting to Rome. Appointed Westminster's sub-dean in 1831, aged thirty-three, John Thynne remained in post for fifty years, and acted as dean during five interregna. He also held three livings in Wiltshire and Somerset, and had a country seat near Bedford. He was in many respects a Georgian cleric, but not where industry and dedication were concerned. 'He was one of those rare men who are content (perhaps we should say, who can afford to be content) to be permanently second-in-command – and do the job superbly, neither shirking responsibility when it must be taken, nor resenting it when the time comes to surrender their power again.'[8]

Thynne's friendship and willingness to shoulder many of the Abbey's administrative burdens, together with the devoted support of Augusta ('the good Angel whom I have always at my side'),[9] lifted Stanley's spirits, and helped him to appreciate the wonders and potential of the Abbey as well as his own peculiar suitability for the responsibilities of dean. His experience as a canon of two cathedrals, his royal connections, his love of English history, and his idealistic belief in the national Church – this singular combination helped to convince Stanley that, for all his initial misgivings, Westminster Abbey was God's calling as well as the Queen's.

*   *   *

The Abbey, like Christ Church, is a complex religious, scholastic and royal foundation. Tradition has it that it started life in the seventh century as the chapel of a Benedictine monastery, dedicated to St Peter. But what is certain is that King Edward the Confessor adopted and endowed a monastery founded by St Dunstan in c. 960. He rebuilt the church and a palace close by, which became the main residence of English monarchs until Henry VIII.[b] In 1066 King Edward was buried in the Abbey, the first of twenty-eight kings and queens. Later in the same fateful year, William the Conqueror was crowned there on Christmas Day.[c] In the twelfth century Edward was canonised, and in the next century his remains were removed to a new magnificent tomb which served as the shrine of a saint. Also under Henry III, and in St Edward's honour, the Abbey was rebuilt again in a striking mixture of French and English Gothic styles – the start of what is essentially the glorious building we see today. Early in the sixteenth century Henry VII added the magnificent perpendicular chapel at the east end. Henry VIII dissolved the monastery and made the Abbey the cathedral of a new diocese of Westminster, with a dean and chapter and a grammar school. Under Edward VI, the diocese was absorbed into the see of London until Queen Mary's reign when the monastery was restored. Elizabeth I dissolved it a second time, and in 1560 she reinstated and lavishly endowed her father's collegiate foundation, and made the Abbey a royal peculiar.[d]

Intimate association with the monarchy ensured the Abbey's place at the heart of national life. Proximity to the king's palace meant proximity to the seat of Government. Parliaments had met in the palace since the thirteenth century, and its massive hall was still the chief law court

[b] King Canute is said to have built the first palace before 1035 and from there rebuked the waves of the Thames.

[c] Every English monarch since has been crowned in the Abbey except the two who were never crowned, Edward V and Edward VIII.

[d] Like St George's Chapel, Windsor, the Abbey is independent of any ecclesiastical jurisdiction other than that of the Sovereign.

when Stanley became dean.ᵉ Westminster Abbey's role then as now was to provide the nation's shrine, the 'theatre of national commemoration',¹⁰ and the 'pantheon of the illustrious dead'.¹¹ Kings and queens, poets in their corner, statesmen in their aisle, writers, soldiers and scientists – the nation's great and good are entombed and memorialised by a panoply of inscriptions, busts and statues.

Stanley came to rejoice in all this. He relished the unrivalled focus of England's story, and valued the daily order of services, with its origins in the devotion and discipline of the monastery. And a religious building whose life was interwoven with that of the nation and its affairs, secular and religious, made the Abbey an embodiment and symbol of Stanley's understanding of the Church, and the liberal theology that lay behind it. It was the perfect place for him to exercise a distinctive ministry that was rooted in two cardinal convictions: first, that all the world, and all human enterprise, belong to the good and loving God revealed in the character of Jesus Christ; and second, that the Church exists to witness to this fact, and to embrace the widest possible community of Christian believers. Stanley told Pearson that he had been 'greatly struck' by the oath he had taken at his installation to labour 'for the enlargement of the Christian Church'.¹² It was the vow that inspired almost everything Stanley accomplished at the Abbey. His mission, he believed, was to extend both the Abbey's service to the State and the English people, and its Christian borders, making it 'the centre of religious and national life in a truly liberal spirit'.¹³

Stanley's ideals and ambitions for the Abbey were to encounter fierce opposition, as he discovered early in 1864 when he invited clergy with a wide range of theological opinions to preach at the Abbey. His impatience exacerbated what in any case was bound to be contentious, especially at a time when religious feelings were running high. On 8 February, a month after Stanley's installation, the Lord Chancellor, on behalf of the Privy Council, delivered his long-awaited judgment on two of the contributors to *Essays and Reviews*, Rowland Williams and Henry Wilson. Both had been accused of denying the inspiration of the Bible, and Wilson was also charged with denying the doctrine of eternal punishment. They had been condemned by the court of arches but had appealed to the Privy Council, whose judicial committee reversed the

---

ᵉ Thomas More, Guy Fawkes and Charles I were tried there. It had survived the fire of 1834 and remained a court until 1870 when those in the Strand were completed. Sir Charles Barry's New Palace of Westminster was not fully completed until 1867.

decision on the grounds that the men's opinions were not inconsistent with the Thirty-Nine Articles. Stanley was present at the acquittal and thought 'the panic of "Essays and Reviews"'[14] was over, but he was mistaken. At once Pusey wrote a letter to the fervent Evangelical journal, *The Record*, in a bid to form an alliance between Churchmen High and Low. At a meeting in Oxford, a declaration of faith was devised, stating that the Church of England, in common with the whole catholic Church, maintained the inspiration and authority of Scripture, and taught that the punishment of the 'cursed' is everlasting. The document was sent to every clergyman, with a letter entreating him to sign 'for the love of God'.

While this was in the air, Stanley was writing to Keble, Pusey and Liddon;[f] as well to Evangelicals, and liberals like Tait, Temple and Maurice, inviting them to preach at the Sunday evening special service in the nave.[g] The chapter protested against Temple's invitation, and the three High Churchmen declined. The long correspondence between Pusey and Stanley illustrates the fundamental divisions between them, and the grave disapproval with which Stanley and other liberals were viewed by Tractarians (and Evangelicals). In his reply to Stanley's invitation, Pusey pointed to the antagonism between those like him, who had recently reaffirmed the doctrines on which the *Essays and Reviews* judgement had thrown doubt, and those like Stanley who were rejoicing in that judgement. 'I believe the present to be a struggle for the life and death of the Church of England, and what you believe to be for life I believe to be for death; and you think the same reciprocally of me.'[15] Although Pusey had never before been offered 'the privilege of preaching to all those souls in the Abbey',[16] he was certain that to accept Stanley's invitation would only cause confusion because it would imply that there were no radical differences between them. Stanley replied to explain that he wanted to give every eminent preacher the opportunity of the Abbey pulpit to express his opinions, but not to attack or contradict each other. Instead he hoped 'they might edify the congregation as far as possible in the truths which we all hold together'.[17] 'You appeal to me kindly in the name of "our common Christianity",' Pusey replied.

---

[f] Henry Liddon (1829–90) was Pusey's pupil at Christ Church and his biographer. He was a canon of St Paul's for twenty years, and a famous preacher.

[g] The service was 'special' as distinct from the statutory daily services of morning and evening prayer, and was the dean's responsibility. It had been started in 1851 for foreign visitors to the Great Exhibition, and had been revived by Dean Trench, Stanley's predecessor.

'Alas! I do not know what the common Christianity of myself and Professor Jowett is. I do not know what single truth we hold in common, except that somehow Jesus came from God, which the Mohammedans believe too.'[18] While Pusey remained courteous throughout this exchange, Stanley's letters became increasingly peevish, concluding: 'It is a matter of sincere sorrow that you should think it right thus to isolate yourself from the great mass of your fellow-Churchmen, and to deprive our congregation of the benefit of hearing you preach.'[19]

A more public and bitter controversy was provoked six years later when Stanley went further by inviting a Unitarian to receive holy communion in the Abbey. This was Dr George Vance Smith, one of many distinguished Biblical scholars commissioned to revise the Authorised Version of the New Testament. By the mid-nineteenth century, the growth of Biblical studies and changes in English usage were causing dissatisfaction with the translation of 1611. Scholars were becoming increasingly aware of its errors and additions, whether in the original text or in translation. In 1870, the Convocation of the province of Canterbury[h] was persuaded by a special sub-committee (Stanley was a member) to appoint a company of scholars to revise the King James Bible. It was not an easy decision because the version was widely cherished and revered. The revisers were instructed therefore to introduce as few alterations as possible, and to ensure that, in any changes, they followed the style of the authorised version. Christopher Wordsworth (who had left Westminster in 1868 to become Bishop of Lincoln) warned Convocation: 'Beware lest. by altering the text ... you shake the faith of many, especially of the vast multitudes of our poorer brethren ...'[20]

Convocation decided after much debate that the revisers should not be limited to Anglican scholars, nor even to Christians. What mattered most was expertise. Jewish scholars should therefore be invited to help with the Hebrew of the Old Testament, and since the Authorised Version was sacred to all English Christians, it was also important that representatives of other Churches should be encouraged to share in the work. Newman was asked to represent the Roman Catholics, but declined. The Unitarian minister, Vance Smith, was invited, albeit by a majority of one mistaken vote on the selection committee.

---

[h] Convocation is the provincial assembly (synod) of the clergy of the Church of England and is divided into upper (bishops) and lower (other clergy) houses. It had been suspended in 1711 and revived in 1851 (Canterbury) and 1860 (York). Members of the lower house are known as proctors.

Part Four: Westminster 1864–1881

The revisers[i] met for the first time on 22 June 1870 in the Jerusalem Chamber which was part of Stanley's deanery. Stanley invited them to take communion together in Henry VII's Chapel in the Abbey before their inaugural meeting. Almost all the revisers accepted, including Vance Smith. The communion was vehemently attacked by the High Church press as a blasphemous act of desecration, and Stanley was accused of 'casting pearls before swine, and giving that which is most holy to the dogs'.[21] Liddon wrote to Bishop Wilberforce, chairman of the revision committee, to complain that Stanley had replaced a divine mystery with a vacuous service 'to be offered to those with whom we differ on fundamental questions, when we wish to be on good terms with them'.[22] Under pressure from Wilberforce (newly translated from Oxford to Winchester) a resolution was carried in the upper house of Convocation 'that no person who denies the Godhead of our Lord Jesus Christ ought to be invited to join the company to which is committed the revision of the Authorised Version of Holy Scripture; and that it is further the judgement of this House that any such person now on the company should cease to act therewith.'[23] The resolution was sent to the lower house for adoption.

Stanley was incensed at the insult levelled at Vance Smith by the bishops. He concluded his speech in Convocation with an impassioned repudiation of the arguments that had been used to justify this breach of faith:

> It is put forward, I am grieved to see, in the Upper House, that while the resolution is fully acknowledged to be a breach of good faith, it is nevertheless desirable that this breach of good faith should be made for the honour of – of whom? the honour of the All-wise, the All-holy, the All-true, our Lord and Saviour Jesus Christ. Alas! and has it come to this? that our boasted orthodoxy has landed us in this hideous heresy! ... Can we believe that anything but dishonour can be conferred on Him by making His name a pretext for inconsistency, for vacillation, for a breach of faith between two contracting parties? ... I for one lift up my voice against any such detestable doctrine as that our Lord and Saviour can be honoured in any way but by a strict adherence to the laws of honour, integrity, and truth.[24]

Stanley's speech convinced the lower house which refused to endorse

---

[i] They included the Cambridge triumvirate of Biblical scholars, Westcott, Lightfoot and Hort, as well as Scott of the Greek lexicon. Pusey refused to join because of Vance Smith.

the resolution, though it still insisted on recording 'deep regret' that one who 'has publicly declared his rejection of the Nicene Creed'[25] should have been allowed to receive the sacrament.

* * *

Battling (often single-handedly) in Convocation in the cause of a comprehensive and tolerant Church of England absorbed a good measure of Stanley's energy and patience during his early years at Westminster. His predecessor, Richard Chenevix Trench, had spoken only once during his eight years as dean, and that was to put a stop to an especially loquacious proctor. Stanley was even less enthusiastic about Convocation than Trench, and thought it should never have been revived. 'There is engendered', he wrote, 'a fantastic and mischievous atmosphere throughout the whole body which renders it almost impossible for common sense to make itself appreciated.'[26] But sometimes important matters were discussed when Stanley felt duty bound to speak up for just the same essential principles that inspired his work in the Abbey.

Stanley's opinion of the limited powers of Convocation was made clear in the course of debates about ritualism. In February 1866 a committee was appointed to report on this growing and contentious movement. In subsequent debates Stanley explained his own view that, while ritualism could lead to the defiance of both the authority of bishops and the wishes of congregations, the adoption of Roman Catholic vestments and liturgical practices ought to be tolerated. There were two reasons for this: they were 'trifling' and insignificant, and more important, 'a national Church ought to contain the largest breadth both of practice and opinion, that can be included'.[27] Stanley supported Parliament when the Public Worship Regulation Bill was introduced in 1874. High Church proctors, on the other hand, who regarded Convocation as a means of asserting the Church's independence of the State, objected to the bill because they thought regulating the ceremonial habits of the clergy was their responsibility, not Parliament's. Stanley took the opposite view. Convocation's business was to debate not to legislate, and it was only when such matters were considered 'not in the heated atmosphere of partisan theologians, but by the dry daylight of English law'[28] that good sense could prevail. Stanley had argued the same during the Gorham controversy,[j] and he

---

[j] See p. 160.

remained consistent in upholding the supremacy of Parliament, and resisting any convocational pretensions:

> I do not acknowledge, and I do not think the clergy outside this House will acknowledge, any resolution passed by this House as binding upon them ... and I am more anxious to say this because there is no person in this House who is more eager on all occasions to conform to what I have the best reasons for knowing to be the law of this country, and therefore the law of this Church, than I am ... It is for that reason that I do deprecate most strongly, and have deprecated often before, the tone which runs through all these debates of endeavouring to set up the decrees and the resolutions of this House, either in temporal or spiritual matters, as having the binding force of, or as in any sense superior to, the acts of the Imperial Legislature.[29]

Convocation's sense of independent self-importance meant that it refused to be satisfied with the Privy Council's judgment on *Essays and Reviews*. Indeed Pusey regarded it as 'a miserable and soul-destroying judgment',[30] and the greatest crisis through which the Church of England had ever passed. As far as Stanley was concerned, the decision of the judicial committee, as the highest court of appeal, was final, and should have guaranteed an end to the heretics hunt.[31] Instead, the archbishops (who were both members of the committee) published pastoral letters explaining their dissent, and Pusey and his allies despatched their declaration of faith. In April 1864 Wilberforce brought the book to the upper house for censure, and two months later a synodical condemnation was carried in both houses. In the final debate, Stanley spoke up again, and at length, for toleration in the Church, and for the supremacy of the law which had defended it. His analysis of the condemnation (that it was 'an ambiguous, an indiscriminate, an unfair, and therefore iniquitous judgment')[32] was incisive and persuasive: the condemnation was carried in the lower house of 149 members by only 39 votes to 19.

One last after shock from *Essays and Reviews* occurred nearly a decade after the book's publication, when Gladstone nominated one of the contributors, Frederick Temple, as Bishop of Exeter. Stanley was delighted because he was a friend and a vigorous Headmaster of Rugby who reminded him of Arnold. Indeed Stanley was astonished at the opposition: 'I consider it so far the best appointment, and so inevitable if Gladstone was to make any Liberal bishops, that I cannot conceive anyone being surprised.'³³ The protest, however, was loud and intense, and recalled the appointment of Hampden to Hereford in 1847. Again Pusey 'went so far as to assert that it was the most frightful enormity that had ever been perpetrated by a Prime Minister'.³⁴

Though Temple's Devon roots were welcome in the diocese, he had the misfortune to succeed Henry Phillpotts, the strict and traditional High Churchman who for the past forty years had tried to exclude clergy like Gorham, and fill his diocese with disciples. The dean and chapter of Exeter were urged to vote against the nomination, but a majority of seven (including Phillpotts's son, the archdeacon) voted for Temple. However, Temple's consecration in Westminster Abbey on (many thought fittingly) Doubting Thomas's day, 21 December, was a fraught occasion, with the bishops meeting beforehand in the Jerusalem Chamber to express their objections. The Bishop of London (on behalf of Tait, the new Archbishop of Canterbury, who was unwell) resisted them all, but nonetheless the service was delayed, and in the end only four bishops attended. 'When we entered,' wrote Stanley, 'the darkness was something beyond all precedent. It was difficult even with all the lights in the Abbey, to discern one person from another; and so in the language of a High Church newspaper, "on that darkest day in the whole year was perpetrated the darkest crime which had been perpetrated in the English Church".'³⁵

Stanley's convictions about the supremacy of the law in settling disputes in the national Church, and in safeguarding its inclusiveness, were engaged again in the battles over Colenso. So too was his passion for justice, and his commitment to the freedom of theological inquiry. John William Colenso was Stanley's direct contemporary. From an impoverished Evangelical family, he had been a sizar and wrangler,[k] and then a fellow and tutor at St John's College, Cambridge. He had taught mathematics for four years at Harrow under Christopher Wordsworth, and was the author of popular textbooks on arithmetic and algebra. After seven years as an incumbent in Stanley's father's diocese, Colenso was appointed the first Bishop of Natal in 1853. A stubborn and imprudent man, Colenso was nonetheless an energetic colonial bishop with a zealous sense of mission and ambitious educational ideals, in the spirit of which he freely translated much of the Bible and Book of Common Prayer into Zulu. In 1861, a year after *Essays*

---

[k] Like a servitor at Oxford, a sizar was an undergraduate who waited at table in return for reduced fees. A wrangler is a Cambridge student who gains a first in mathematics.

and Reviews, he published a commentary on Romans that again questioned the doctrines of atonement and eternal damnation, and brought him to the anxious attention of the orthodox. A year later, Colenso produced the first part of a book that took him seventeen years to complete and was entitled *The Pentateuch and Book of Joshua Critically Examined*. Prompted by the Zulus' questions about events like Noah's flood ('Is all that true?'), Colenso decided to publicise his own doubts about the historical accuracy of the Old Testament. His detailed approach to the minutiae of the narrative was quirkily arithmetical. He calculated, for example, that 6 men are assumed to have had 2,748 sons between them, and that every priest was compelled to eat an indigestible 88 pigeons a day. Colenso concluded that Moses was a figure of dubious historicity, while Joshua was a hero of legend. In short, 'the narrative, whatever may be its value and meaning, cannot be regarded as historically true'.[36]

In Februrary 1863 a letter was sent to Colenso from all but one of the English bishops[1] advising him to resign. Colenso refused. Six months later, Robert Gray, the Bishop of Cape Town and metropolitan of Africa, and a moderate Tractarian, summoned him to be tried on a charge of heresy. Colenso refused to accept Gray's jurisdiction and ignored the summons. Gray went ahead and passed a sentence of deposition, and eventually excommunicated him. Colenso appealed to the judicial committee of the Privy Council which had to consider whether or not Gray's trial and deposition were legal. They concluded in March 1865 that, for various technical reasons, the Bishop of Cape Town had no coercive jurisdiction, and that the judgment of deposition was therefore null and void in law. Despite the almost total opposition of his clergy, Colenso resumed his duties. Meanwhile, Gray consecrated another Bishop of Natal, causing a fourteen-year schism with two rival bishops.

Stanley had much the same mixed feelings about Colenso as he had about *Essays and Reviews*. On the one hand, he was supportive of his challenge to traditional insistence on the literal accuracy of every word of Scripture. He agreed, for instance, that the Mosaic authorship of the Pentateuch was not essential to revelation. Furthermore, he was offended by 'the indiscriminate outcry against an evidently honest and single-minded religious man'.[37] On the other hand, Stanley objected to Colenso's provocative approach, and urged him to write his book

---

[1] Connop Thirlwall of St David's refused to sign.

'more like a defence and less like an attack ... No man ought ever to write himself down as a heretic.'[38] Stanley also found Colenso's arithmetical analysis mystifying and misguided. Stanley was, for a start, innately innumerate,[m] but more important, his own approach to Biblical history was entirely different. He was mindful of recent Biblical criticism, not least the more radical work of German scholars, and he was taking some of this into account in the Jewish history he was compiling.[n] But Stanley never lost sight of a Biblical narrative that was at least in essence verifiable, and which, regardless of factual accuracy, was the means of divine revelation. 'My object for twenty years,' he told Colenso, 'and my object in my forthcoming book, is to draw forth the inestimable treasures of the Old Testament, historically, geographically, morally and spiritually. To fix the public attention on the mere defects of structure and detail is, to my mind, to lead off the public mind on a false scent and a false issue.'[39]

Nonetheless, Stanley was determined to defend Colenso's writings and the judgement of the Privy Council against the attacks of Convocation. He did so in speeches that reached new heights of advocacy and persuasive power. On 28 June 1865 the lower house was asked to concur in an address of the bishops expressing 'hearty admiration of the courage, firmness, and devoted love of the truth of the Gospel' with which the South African bishops had opposed 'heretical and false doctrine'.[40] Stanley strongly opposed the resolution by pointing to its implications: 'Are we prepared to say that it is unlawful for any clergyman who holds that any portion of the early chapters of Genesis is to be taken in any other than a strict historical meaning to retain office in the Church of England?'[41] A year later, and without notice, similar resolutions were brought before Convocation, and the lower house was asked to agree to hold communion with an alternative Bishop of Natal if duly elected and consecrated. Stanley was vehement in his opposition, and in an impromptu speech, his finest to Convocation, Stanley explained the legal impossibilities of such a course of action, and then, in a final and

---

[m] There are various stories of Stanley's numerical handicap. For example, the poet Frederick Locker (Augusta's brother-in-law) told him that the musician Hallé's cook had won a sum of money in a lottery with the number twenty-three. Hallé asked her how she decided on this lucky number. 'I had a dream', she replied. 'I dreamed of 7 three times, and as three times 7 makes twenty-three, I chose that number.' Stanley did not understand the joke, and after a puzzled pause replied: 'Ah, yes, I see; yes, I suppose three times 7 is *not* twenty-three.'

[n] *Lectures on the History of the Jewish Church.*

courageous twist, he exposed the injustice and theological narrowness involved in the condemnation of Colenso:

> I have mentioned several prelates, I might mention many obscure clergymen. I might mention one whom you all know, who certainly on some of these matters has openly expressed the same opinions, I mean in principle, as the Bishop of Natal. I might mention one who, although on some of these awful and mysterious questions he has expressed no direct opinion, yet has ventured to say that the Pentateuch is not the work of Moses; has ventured to say that there are parts of the Sacred Scriptures which are poetical and not historical ... and that individual is the one who now addresses you. If you pronounce against the Bishop of Natal on grounds such as these, you must remember that there is one close to hand whom, perhaps even with the Bishop of Oxford, certainly with Jeremy Taylor and with Athanasius in former times, you will be obliged to condemn. I am not unwilling to take my place, if so be, beside the distinguished Prelate who presides over the great diocese in which I once resided. I am not unwilling to take my place with Gregory of Nyssa, with Jerome, and with Athanasius. But in that same goodly company I shall find the despised and rejected Bishop of Natal. At least deal out the same measure to me that you deal to him; at least judge for all a righteous judgment.[42]

The Colenso controversy raised important new issues about the relation of the expanding colonial Church to the Church in England, and in turn to the Crown. The Bishop of Cape Town, for instance, thought he had the right to ignore the Privy Council's judgement in defence of Colenso, and to consecrate an alternative bishop without royal mandate. As a consequence, the Canadian Church requested a gathering of Anglican bishops for consultation and advice. The suggestion was accepted by the Canterbury Convocation, and in February 1867 Archbishop Longley invited the entire episcopate to meet for the first time at Lambeth Palace. Stanley, with the Archbishop of York and bishops of the northern province, was anxious that the conference would support Gray against Colenso, and the northern bishops declined the invitation. Of 144 invitations, 76 were accepted. The question of Colenso was raised at the preliminary meeting, and on the fourth day of the conference Gray made a determined effort to rally support for the consecration of a new bishop. After heated debate, a resolution was adopted, declaring that the consecration would not sever communion between the home and the colonial Church, which Gray interpreted as approval.

Stanley could only observe the Lambeth Conference from across the Thames but he made his mark by exercising his rights as dean of a royal peculiar, and refusing to allow the bishops to hold a service in the Abbey. In a letter to Longley he explained his rule which allowed the Abbey to be used as widely as possible, but only for purposes co-extensive with the Church of England, or with 'a definite object of usefulness or charity, apart from party or polemical considerations'.[43] Instead Stanley offered a service relevant to but unrelated to the conference itself – for the Society for the Propagation of the Gospel, for example, or for another home or foreign mission. Stanley's refusal was greeted with anger and consternation by the bishops and his offer was firmly rejected.

*   *   *

In contrast to the quarrels of Convocation, Stanley's domestic life appears to have been blissfully contented. He and Augusta enjoyed the advantages of living at the deanery, a large and elegant house behind the Abbey's west cloister. It had once been the abbot's lodgings and is one of the oldest private houses still inhabited. Stanley's previous house had been arranged and furnished by his mother and now Augusta did the same, but in a more contemporary and comfortable style. The Jerusalem Chamber (where the lower house of Convocation held its meetings) was restored by Stanley. Henry IV had died there and Stanley placed his and Henry V's busts in the chamber, and repanelled its walls with cedarwood from Lebanon.

Stanley's marriage was unusual but no less loving and devoted. He was close to fifty and Augusta six years younger when they married, and neither had been engaged or even attached before. Despite the seriousness of his mind and the strength of his convictions, Stanley had retained a childlike quality, and with it an emotional dependency on his mother whom Augusta now replaced. After a visit to Windsor ten weeks after the wedding, the Queen wrote jaundicedly to the Princess Royal: 'He runs after her like a little Boy and looks at her whenever he speaks!! – Both were rather embarrassed.'[44] Stanley was open about his dependency, and in a letter written before they were married, he told his good angel Augusta: 'You must be my wings. I shall often flag and be dispirited; but you, now, as my dear mother formerly, must urge me on, and bid me not despair.'[45] Augusta's qualities of sympathy, affection and kindness fitted her well to be Stanley's wife. In exchange for his companionship and intellectual stimulation, and the position the deanery gave her in society, Augusta helped and supported him, and shared his many interests and responsibilities. Their letters to each other, and the testimony of friends, point to a strong friendship and a delight in being together.

Stanley was eccentrically unpractical and needed assistance with even the most basic things like dressing and eating. He never wore the gaiters he was entitled to as dean because of his difficulty with buttons. At breakfast he would scarcely eat or drink anything but tea, his favourite drink, and his favourite food of buttered toast. Occasionally he would eat a hard-boiled egg but only if Augusta peeled the shell. Stanley could not remember ever having any sense of taste or smell (or ear for music), and if left to himself he would eat almost nothing but toast.

Augusta shared and protected Stanley's daily routine. After breakfast at nine she would spend the morning with him in his library: she wrote letters while he worked at his standing-desk, surrounded by piles of discarded paper. He would constantly seek her advice and approval, especially when writing sermons – exactly as he had his mother. Lunch was another frugal meal, often eaten in the library while he continued working. After evensong at three they would go for a walk together, but not just for exercise. Stanley insisted on a purpose for the excursion – a friend to visit, a part of London to be explored, or a picture or statue to be seen. Tea at five was Stanley's favourite meal (more buttered toast), and after tea he returned to the library to work from six until dinner at eight.

Stanley's houses in Canterbury and Christ Church had often accommodated friends and guests, but never so many as the deanery. Augusta's experience at court and at home in Paris had taught her the arts and pleasures of entertaining, as well as giving her the social contacts and confidence to invite all kinds of interesting people. She created a salon, as her mother had done in Paris, where clergy mixed with writers, scientists and politicians. Augusta's nephew, Albert Baillie, left the following account:

> Never has there been a house in London where such a variety of people were collected.... You would see statesmen and ecclesiastics, men of science, distinguished foreigners, poets, writers, people of position in the great world, indeed, almost every one

who stood for anything in the life of England at that time. But, mixed with them, quite naturally and easily, some simple country clergyman or woman from the nursing home or some parish worker, or just ordinary relations and friends. All were equally welcome, and all felt [Augusta's] gift of bringing everybody into the circle ...

There were dinners and luncheons where she did carefully select the company, but, as a rule, the whole of the hospitality gave the feeling of being accidental. People were asked to lunch just because they called, or because they happened to be in London ... The evenings at the Deanery stand out most vividly in my memory. The Dean would stand near the tea table, drinking endless cups of tea, pouring out a conversation so vivid that it illuminated every subject he touched and drew in all those various intellectual forces. I can see him now. There would be Tyndal [*sic*] or Owen talking science. Kingsley or Bishop Temple or Bishop Wordsworth or some of his great antagonists in Convocation, like Archdeacon Denison, or Gladstone or Foster (*sic*) or any of the politicians. Renan might be the centre of one group and a Greek Archimandrite of another. Matthew Arnold and Locker would bring lightness and grace into the talk, or Carlyle pour out his fierce denunciations. Tennyson might stand, impressively and unquestionably, representing poetry, while Browning wandered round, deliberately inconspicuous as a man of the world. There came Jenny Lind, Christine Nilsson or Florence Nightingale or Madame Mohl. I hardly ever see a name distinguished in the mid-nineteenth century without its recalling some scene at the Deanery.[46]

The Queen came to tea in March 1869, and again a year later when she visited the Abbey to see the restored monument of Henry VII. On the first occasion she met, at her request, Thomas Carlyle ('a strange-looking eccentric old Scotchman, who holds forth, in a drawling melancholy voice'), the historian George Grote, and the geologist Sir Charles Lyell and their wives, and Robert Browning ('a very agreeable man'). 'It was, at first,' the Queen confided to her journal, 'very shy work speaking to them ... but afterwards, when tea was being drunk, Augusta got them to come and sit near me, and they were very agreeable, and talked very entertainingly.'[47] The Prince of Wales would call into the deanery uninvited, and Vicky, the Princess Royal, was usually asked when she was in England.º 'I did *so* enjoy the dinner and the party – ,' she wrote to Augusta, 'so kindly and so beautifully arranged. – I *wish* I could have stayed longer for how can one feel tired in such charming society.'[48]

Stanley was obliged to be in residence at the Abbey for eight months of the year. Unlike the canons, who generally preferred a pattern of two months on and one month off, Stanley took all his leave from August to November in order to travel. It was fortunate that Augusta was accustomed to life on the Continent, and shared Stanley's enjoyment of foreign tours. She was a prolific letter writer and sent home detailed accounts of the places and people they visited.

Augusta was fluent in French, and France was almost always included in their itineraries. Their first holiday together in August 1864 consisted mainly of visits to French country houses. They began at Provins where they stayed at the residence of the Counts of Champagne who (Stanley noted) had been zealous crusaders. The tour was cut short in September by news that Stanley's butler, Benjamin Waters, and one of his young daughters were dangerously ill with scarlet fever, and another daughter had died. Stanley hurried back to Westminster to find that Waters and both daughters were now dead. Stanley was horrified. Waters had been 'a faithful and familiar friend'[49] as well as a servant. He and his family had lived with Stanley at Christ Church, and Waters had accompanied him on the tour of Palestine with the Prince of Wales. 'I loved him like a brother,' Stanley told Maria Hare, 'and he was doubly endeared to me by his companionship through all those trying days in 1862.'[50] Waters's widow and her two surviving children were allowed to stay on at the deanery until after Stanley's death.

The Stanleys felt no desire to resume their tour abroad. At the end of October he travelled to Birmingham to preach and to visit Newman at his oratory. Newman was now sixty-three and it was nearly twenty years since his conversion to Rome, and just a few months after publication of *Apologia Pro Vita Sua*, his spiritual autobiography. In a fascinating letter to Shairp, Stanley describes Newman's features, voice and manner as unaltered: 'the same appearance of simplicity and tenderness, and yet, withal, something of weakness'.[51] They spoke about Biblical criticism (Newman said he regretted his ignorance of German) and whether or not it was barred by the Council of Trent.ᵖ Newman

---

º Victoria's eldest child who had married Frederick, the Crown Prince of Prussia, in 1858.
ᵖ Summoned in 1537 by Pope Paul III in response to the spread of Protestantism.

showed Stanley his library, where in the reading-room he met Tom Arnold. He had joined the Roman Catholic Church, and was about to leave it before rejoining a decade later. 'What was the upshot of the whole? It left the impression, not of unhappiness or dissatisfaction, but of a totally wasted life, unable to read, glancing at questions which he could not handle, rejoicing in the caution of the Church of Rome, which had (like the Privy Council) kept open question after question that he enumerated as having been brought before it; also, although without the old bitterness, still the ancient piteous cry, "O my mother! Why dost thou leave us all day idle in the market-place?" Studiously courteous, studiously calm.'[52]

The following August the tour started at Herzogenbosch with a visit to Queen Sophia of Holland. Stanley thought 'her consideration and her intelligence are, for her position, very remarkable'.[53] They travelled north to Amsterdam, where Augusta persuaded him to view the galleries: 'saw the pictures'[54] was his only recorded comment. At Utrecht Stanley visited the Jansenist archbishop. Jansenism, with its pessimistic belief in determinism, had been condemned by Pope Innocent X in the seventeenth century but was tolerated in Holland. 'The whole position of their Church is so singular', commented Stanley, 'that I am very glad to have seen them, and to have verified with my own eyes that they really existed.'[55] From Holland the Stanleys travelled to Baden-Baden to stay with Augusta's sister Frances and her husband Evan Baillie, the British chargé d'affaires. They went to tea with Queen Victoria's half-sister, Princess Feodore.[q] She and Augusta had become friends when they were trying to support the Queen after Albert's death. Feodore subjected Stanley to some serious questioning: how old is the world? what is the difference between Jews in Palestine and Jews in Europe? are there any likenesses between the Jewish religion and the Egyptian? 'When she had finished', Stanley told Mary, 'she rose and bade us an affectionate farewell. During the whole of the time (I think it must have been nearly two hours) no one spoke except the questioner and the answerer.'[56]

From Baden they travelled through the Dolomites to Venice, and returned home at the start of October through northern Italy, Switzerland and France. Later in the month they went to Wales to visit Connop Thirlwall, the Bishop of St David's. Thirlwall had been a friend and

---

[q] Daughter of the Duchess of Kent from her first marriage to the Prince of Leiningen; married the Count of Hohenhoe-Langenburg.

colleague of Julius Hare, who had introduced him to Stanley thirty years before. He had been a brilliant fellow, tutor and classical history lecturer at Trinity, Cambridge, and had been appointed Bishop of St David's by Melbourne in 1840. 'It is charming', Stanley wrote to his cousin Louisa, 'to see him surrounded by his books of every kind, and always with one of them in his hands, going every evening to feed his swans and ducks in the pond at the bottom of the garden.'[57] From Wales they travelled to Scotland where they learnt that the Prime Minister, Lord Palmerston, had died suddenly, aged eighty, and they had to return immediately to Westminster.

Palmerston's was Stanley's first funeral of national significance: 'very grand', he wrote, 'with ten cabinet ministers standing by the open vault',[58] including Stanley's cousin Lord Edward Stanley, who was Postmaster-General and a personal friend of Palmerston. Stanley was obliged to preach about Palmerston on the Sunday after the funeral, and was faced for the first time at Westminster with the dilemma of how to praise famous men without ignoring the less laudable side of their lives. Stanley found this sermon 'a very difficult and delicate task'[59] because, despite his popularity and considerable political achievements, Palmerston had been a notorious womaniser, with the nickname 'Lord Cupid'. Indeed he had tried to seduce Lady Stanley, Edward's wife, soon after their marriage. Perhaps Stanley had this especially in mind when he said that he would not inquire into the things that Palmerston had done 'in the unseen world which were known to God alone',[60] and when he described him as 'an Englishman even to excess'. 'It was England rather than any special party in England ... that fired his imagination, and stimulated his efforts, and secured his fame. To England, and to no lesser interest, the vast length of that laborious life, with whatsoever shortcomings, was in all simplicity and faithfulness devoted.'[61] Palmerston's marble statue stands in the Abbey's statesmen's aisle in the north transept.

Rome after Florence was the Stanleys' destination in 1866, and again in 1869 when they went to observe preparations for the famous council of bishops (Vatican I), called to 'receive with joy the proclamation of the dogmatic infallibility of the sovereign pontiff'.[62] Stanley was firmly on the side of the few anti-infallibilists and their brave resistance to the spread of ultramontanism under Pope Pius IX. In 1866 their visit coincided with the Gladstones' ('he is so extremely enjoying his liberty'),[63] and they dined together every evening. Stanley was granted a private and somewhat comic audience with the Pope:

> I went in full decanal costume. He observed and took hold of the cassock which I wore. He said, 'I have seen something of this kind before. It is the same as an English clergyman once wore in coming to see me. His name was Thompson.' We spent one or two minutes in endeavouring to ascertain who Thompson could be. It turned out to be Townsend, who had come in former years on a mission for converting the Pope. The Pope said, with shouts of laughter, 'And what do you suppose he came to do? – the most ridiculous thing in the world, to attempt the fusion of the two Churches. What nonsense!' ...
>
> When we got up to go away, and I knelt to kiss his hand, he again dwelt on the fact that the cassock was the same which he had seen worn by 'Thompson'; and so we parted.[64]

The only dream Stanley seems to have thought worth recording involved himself being elected Pope, and discussing with friends at the Athenaeum the name he would take. He had thought of Paul but the Bishop of Chester suggested his own name, Gulielmus.[65]

*   *   *

Stanley's energy was always extraordinary. On top of his duties as dean, his involvement in wider ecclesiastical affairs, and as much as a third of the year abroad, he continued to write and edit a prolific range of books, reviews and essays. He regarded the work of expanding his Oxford lectures on Jewish history as especially important. The first volume of *Lectures on the History of the Jewish Church* had been published in 1863, just before the move to Westminster, the second appeared in 1865, and the third eleven years later in 1876. In all three volumes Stanley manages to use the methodology of modern historical criticism while retaining confidence in the essential historicity of the Old Testament stories, and their important role in the drama of divine revelation. This is a balance missing in Colenso's peculiar work on the Pentateuch, where arithmetical errors were said to nullify historicity, and reduce revelation to a compendium of religious ideas.

Stanley's approach was influenced most by the work of the German scholar Heinrich Ewald whose *Hebrew Grammar*, published in 1827, had already introduced a new era in Biblical philology. His immense *Geschichte des Volkes Israel* (1843–59) was based on a learned and detailed critical examination of all available documents. Nonetheless, it describes the history of Israel in traditional terms as the way in which the one true religion came into the possession of mankind. His work stands comparison with Barthold Niebuhr's on Roman history, which Arnold had followed in writing his own three-volume *History of Rome*. Also akin to Arnold is Stanley's understanding of the unity and continuity of history, and the parallels between past and present, with the moral lessons to be learnt. Arnold's influence can be seen too (as in *Sinai and Palestine*) in the interdependence of history and geography.

Stanley's imaginative and descriptive power, however, is his own, and he paints in words the kind of vivid, idealised pictures of people and events that illustrate Victorian family Bibles.[r] 'All the charm and grace of his style are devoted to the picturesque illustration of the Scriptural narrative,' wrote Prothero. 'He clothes with new life and meaning the story of the Patriarchs, or of Israel in Egypt. He paints, with exquisite feeling and with the inward eye of the poet, the scenery of Sinai and the march through the Wilderness. He traces the effect of the wanderings on the ritual and character of the Israelitish race, and demonstrates, whether Moses was or was not the chronicler, the substantial reality of the facts. He gives to portions of the Jewish history which before were dim, obscure, confused ... a new clearness, a fresh interest, and a deeper significance.'[66]

Stanley's volumes of thoughtfully researched and imaginative narrative are impressive achievements. They are not, however, without their faults or detractors. The history was not critical enough for some liberals, but too critical for orthodox conservatives. The prose, despite the author's redrafting, can still read like a lecture, and there are errors and inaccuracies that suggest haste or distraction. Stanley can mistake later conceptions of historical events for the events themselves, and it is sometimes difficult to know what he believes to have actually happened. Most problematic though is his desire to draw moral lessons from the facts of history. In his review of volume ii, Matthew Arnold (here the son of his father) praised a book that fulfils 'the indispensable duty of edifying at the same time that it informs'.[67] But the fact is that the very different roles of historian and preacher become confused, and with adverse effects on both Stanley's homiletics and his historiography.

The same historical and scientific criticism was also being applied at the time to the New Testament, and with contentious results. The quest was on to discover the true historical Jesus by looking critically at the gospels, and stripping the Church's idealised, other-worldly Jesus of his

---

[r] For an example see Appendix III: Stanley's account of David and Goliath.

white robes and golden halo. The French philosopher and lapsed Roman Catholic Ernest Renan (whom Stanley had first met in Paris in 1862) was the pioneer, as Ewald had been with the Old Testament. Renan had been influenced by D. F. Strauss's *Leben Jesu*, though that was not so much a biography of Jesus as an investigation of sources, and a theological reflection on the consequences. Renan's *Vie de Jésus*, published nearly thirty years later in 1863, strikes something of the same balance as Stanley's in his *History of the Jewish Church*. Renan carefully examined all the sources available, retained his confidence in Jesus as a historical human being, but described him imaginatively as still in possession of idealised qualities: 'an original genius; a great soul; a superior person; an incomparable artist; a lovable character; an idyllic and gentle nature'.[68]

In December 1865 a life of Jesus with the title *Ecce Homo* was published by Macmillan. It was the first attempt at such a biography by an English author, and was published anonymously. Rumours spread as to the authorship. Stanley was mentioned, as were Jowett, Newman and Gladstone. Stanley rejoiced that it could be assumed that men of such different theological views might have written the same book about the heart of Christianity. It showed, he argued, that the essence of the Christian religion lay in doctrines held in common, and not in differences that divided. The author was in fact John Seeley, Professor of Latin at University College, London. He had been influenced by Renan, though his book was amateur by comparison, and gave the impression of someone thinking aloud. The title is misleading because the book is not so much a biography as a study of the foundations of Christian morality. 'Christ is portrayed as the moralist, almost as the new Moses, who founded a society whereby his moral principle should serve the nations.'[69]

With what must surely have been hyperbole, Lord Shaftesbury condemned the book as the 'most pestilential book ever vomited, I think, from the jaws of hell'.[70] The phrase became famous and Seeley regarded it as a favour, helping to sell 10,000 copies and earn him £1,000! There were some unfavourable reviews but others welcomed it. Gladstone, writing in *Good Words*, thought it would lead men to faith; Newman praised it as remarkable,[71] and Richard Church, the historian of the Oxford Movement, as 'a warning against trusting what is worn out';[72] and though *The Record* attacked it, some Evangelicals approved. Stanley enthused in his review in *Macmillan's Magazine* in June 1866, commending a brave attempt to write a description of what

Christ was and is for human history. He had already sketched out his views on the book in a letter written four months before:

> It had to me the same rare interest that was excited by Renan's book, namely, the feeling that here was an attempt, in one case as the other, by a mind of undoubted power, to grasp the vital points of the greatest subject in all history. As regards the appreciation of the character and the teaching of the Gospel as a whole, I need hardly say that it is all, and more than all, that Renan has achieved ...
>
> The style and the mode of delineating the character appear to me to have struck with marvellous tact and feeling the true historical chord, without losing a sense of the infinite possibilities and capacities wrapped up in the character; and to maintain the sense of reverence, without merging it in that cloud of conventional generalities which have so fatally obscured all ordinary representations of the subject.[73]

Stanley's other substantial tome written during his first seven years in London was his *Historical Memorials of Westminster Abbey*, published in 1868. The 800th anniversary of the Abbey's foundation by Edward the Confessor was celebrated at the end of 1865, and Stanley explains in the book's preface that it was this occasion that prompted friends and colleagues to urge him to write a volume along the lines of his *Memorials of Canterbury*.[74] He told Max Müller that he had agreed to do so with some reluctance, because it required considerable research which would take him away from 'the vital questions of the age'.[75] On the other hand, Stanley recognised that a book like this would help to fulfil his wish to draw attention to the Abbey's unique role in English national and religious life, and bring it to a wider audience. He was encouraged in this by the large numbers who attended the services for the anniversaries of the foundation, and a year later, of the coronation of William the Conquerer. There was evidently 'an interest that is felt by all classes in the history of this great institution',[76] and his *Memorials* was designed to meet and extend it.

Stanley dedicated the book to the Queen, 'with every sentiment of loyal and respectful gratitude'. In six 100-page chapters of detailed history and wide learning, Stanley describes the foundation of the Abbey, the coronations and royal tombs, the monuments, and the history of the Abbey before and after the Reformation. 'Crowded with information, and teeming with anecdote and illustration, the Memorials form a biographical dictionary without its dullness. To the personal interest of the building it is a copious guide, and its composition is marked by all Stanley's nice discrimination of analogies and contrasts, his mastery of facts and details.'[77] Among the most interesting passages is Stanley's description of the Abbey as both coronation church and royal mausoleum. He quotes the Caroline poet, Edmund Waller:

> That antique pile behold,
> Where royal heads receive the sacred gold:
> It gives them crowns, and does their ashes keep,
> There made like gods, like mortals there they sleep;
> Making the circle of their reign complete,
> These suns of empire, where they rise they set.[78]

The nearest to this, Stanley explains, is the cathedral at Cracow, where the kings of Poland were crowned and interred beside the shrine of St Stanislaus; and the Kremlin in Moscow, with its three cathedrals, the first where the tsars are crowned, the second where they are married, and the third where (before Peter the Great) they were buried.[79]

Stanley's *Memorials of Westminster Abbey* differs from the Canterbury version for which he had chosen four key events in the cathedral's history, and was able then to give free rein to his gift for dramatic and imaginative story-telling. Stanley found the Abbey's history too rich and various to make the same kind of selection. The result is an admirably comprehensive history and guide which is still authoritative today, but which in form is more like a reference book or encyclopaedia. Stanley did not rate it a good book. 'But my position here made it necessary, and therefore it has been written.'[80]

9
'To Dust and Ashes Turned'
1870–1876

ANOTHER BOOK Stanley thought duty-bound to compile was his *Essays Chiefly on Questions of Church and State*, published in 1870. He told Jowett that 'all I am really anxious for ... is that I should not be misunderstood'.[1] 'It is not a volume to which I am much attracted', he wrote to his cousin Louisa, 'but I trust that by degrees it will form a soil for the peaceful olive, the sustaining corn, the cheering vine.'[2] Stanley explains in the preface that, although most of the essays were written in response to the transitory theological disputes of the last twenty years, they 'involve permanent principles, and have a continuous purpose'.[3] The collection includes Stanley's articles on *Essays and Reviews*, the Gorham controversy, ritualism and Colenso; essays on 'The Connection of Church and State' and the 'Theology of the Nineteenth Century'; shorter biographical pieces on Julius Hare, Dean Milman, John Keble, and Philaret Drozdov, the Metropolitan of Moscow; and a description of the passion play at Oberammergau, which Stanley saw in 1860. The common theme is Stanley's familiar apologia for his ideal of the national Church. His intention in republishing these essays 'has been to maintain the advantages which flow from the Church as a national institution, comprehending the largest variety of religious life which it is possible practically to comprehend, and claiming the utmost elasticity which "the will of our Lord Jesus Christ and the order of this realm" will permit'.[4]

Stanley was always aware of the unique ways in which Westminster Abbey embodied and expressed the life and spirit of the Church of England. He valued the fact that the Abbey's history and functions were inseparable from the State. He regarded the beauty and order of its building and services as models for Anglican architecture and liturgy. He understood its unrivalled capacity to express the religious beliefs of the English people as exhibiting at a national level the responsibility of every parish church. It was an appreciation that informed almost everything Stanley tried to achieve as dean.

Dealing with the dead absorbed much of Stanley's time. His researches for *The Memorials* had stimulated his interest in the mass of monuments in and around the Abbey, and drawn his attention to many cases of decay and careless arrangement. With Stanley ancestry in mind, he had the recumbent portrait effigies of Henry VII and his Queen, Elizabeth of York, and the King's mother, Lady Margaret Beaufort, cleaned and repaired.[a] All three had been carved by the Florentine sculptor Pietro Torrigiano, the rival of Michelangelo. Stanley restored and moved the resplendent portrait of Richard II from the Jerusalem Chamber to the Abbey's sanctuary. It is the earliest known contemporary portrait of an English monarch. New monuments were added to commemorate John Keble who died in 1866, and John and Charles Wesley. The original request for the latter had come from the president of the Wesleyan Conference, who had asked for a monument in Poets' Corner to Charles Wesley. Stanley insisted that his brother John, the founder of Methodism, should also be commemorated, 'as the greater genius, and the greater spirit of the two'.[5] He placed the joint memorial in the south choir aisle, close to that of Isaac Watts, the Congregational poet and divine.

Stanley was anxious to discover exactly where particular corpses were buried, and he gained a macabre reputation as a tomb-raider.[b] He had the grave of Richard II opened in order to determine whether or not the murdered King was actually interred there, and was disappointed to find no traces of violence in the remains. He found by accident the place in the south aisle of Henry VII's Chapel where lie in a row the bodies of Queen Anne, Prince George of Denmark, William III, Mary II and Charles II. The discovery of James I's remains, however, was the reward for a long and careful search which also unearthed other hidden treasures: James's Queen, Anne of Denmark, was found alone in a large vault, and the coffin of Elizabeth I was discovered lying on top of that of her half-sister, Mary Tudor. The missing coffin of James I was found beside that of Henry VII and his Queen in the vault immediately beneath their monument:

> We returned to the head of Henry VII.'s tomb, and there, after much pushing, the wall suddenly yielded, an aperture was found, and there, in the most majestic tranquillity, lay, side by side, the

---

[a] Sir Thomas Stanley married Edmund Tudor's widow, Margaret Beaufort, mother of the future King Henry VII: see p. 29.
[b] Queen Victoria referred to him as 'that body snatcher Arthur Stanley'.

two dark-grey, leaden coffins of Henry VII. and Elizabeth of York – and a shade newer and lighter, James I. I need not describe my thoughts. The vaults were closed this morning, and so the mystery is solved, and my three weeks' intense interest and anxiety are over. It has been more of both to me than an outside observer can easily imagine, haunting me with agitating and magnificent visions both by day and night.[6]

Archbishop Tait was in the Jerusalem Chamber at the time, presiding over a meeting of the ritual commission.[c] George Scharf, the first director of the National Portrait Gallery, was present at the discovery, and described how he was dispatched by Stanley to tell the archbishop that he desired his presence. When Tait arrived at the tomb, Stanley 'made a motion with his hands, as if asking for space to be cleared, and said in his peculiar tone of short breath, "Stand back! Stand back! And let the first Scottish archbishop look upon the first Scottish king of England."'[7]

Fifteen illustrious corpses were interred in the Abbey during Stanley's seventeen years as dean, including Lord Palmerston, Charles Dickens, the astronomer Sir John Herschel, the historian George Grote, the geologist Sir Charles Lyell, and the missionary-explorer, Dr David Livingstone.[d] A request for burial had to come either from the family or, in Palmerston's case of a State funeral, from the Government, and Stanley's consent was then required.[e] In each case he consulted specialists who had to sign a requisition, and agreement had then to be reached as to exactly where to place the coffin. Dickens's burial in June 1870, however, was exceptional.

Stanley had met the great man three times that year – at a private party, a Royal Academy banquet where Dickens was speaking, and, just a few weeks before he died, at the deanery.[8] Stanley let it be known that if he received an application for burial, he would gladly consider it. Dickens though had always been scathing about funereal pomp, and had given strict instructions in his will that he was to be buried simply and privately. He had expressed a wish for this to happen in the precincts of Rochester Cathedral. However, on 13 June, four days after his death, a leading article in *The Times* strongly recommended a

[c] Royal commission appointed in 1867 'to inquire into the Rubrics and Ritual of the Church of England'.
[d] The others were the Duke of Northumberland, George Peabody, Sir George Pollock, Lord Lytton, Sir William Sterndale Bennett, Bishop Thirlwall, Lord Lawrence, Sir Rowland Hill and Lord Henry Percy.
[e] The Sovereign's permission is required for a burial in Henry VII's Chapel.

funeral in Westminster Abbey, 'the shrine of English genius', and the only place fitting for so celebrated an author: 'The present Dean is distinguished for his appreciation of the national character of the Abbey over which he presides, and will, we are sure, be as anxious as any to add this great name to those it already enshrines.'[9] At eleven the same morning, John Forster, Dickens's friend and first biographer, arrived at the deanery, assuming that Stanley had been behind *The Times* leader. Stanley explained that this was not the case, but that he would certainly consent to the burial if requested.

> Mr Forster replied, 'Do not consent till you hear what are the conditions on which alone I can allow it.' I answered, 'Let me hear them.' Mr. Forster said, 'The first condition is, that there shall be only two mourning-coaches, with mourners sufficient to fill them.' 'That,' I said, 'is entirely an affair for the family, do as you like.' 'The second condition is, that there shall be no plumes, trappings, or funereal pomp of any kind.' 'That,' I replied, is a matter between you and the undertaker, and is of no concern of mine.' 'The third condition is, that the place and time of the interment shall be unknown beforehand.' I replied, 'To this condition I am perfectly willing to consent so far as I am concerned. But look at the circumstances: a leading-article in the 'Times' requesting his burial; a public – by this, as well as by their own feelings – on the tiptoe of expectation; the remains, now at Rochester, to be removed to London. How is it possible, under these circumstances, to preserve the secret?'[10]

The body was brought that night from Kent. As soon as the last sightseer had left the Abbey, the grave was dug in Poets' Corner, close to Thackeray's bust. At nine the following morning, a hearse and two black coaches drove into Dean's Yard. Stanley and five other members of the Abbey's clergy were waiting as the coffin was carried into the south transept, accompanied by just twelve mourners, and lowered into the grave. Stanley read the committal sentences, and when the short service had ended, the organ played a dead march. 'It was', wrote Stanley, 'a beautiful summer morning, and the effect of the almost silent and solitary funeral, in the vast space of the Abbey, whose interment, had it been known, would have drawn thousands to the Abbey, was very striking.'[11] Rumours soon spread, however, and thousands of people did arrive to see the grave, and Stanley gave orders for it to be kept open for two days. 'Every class of community was present, dropping flowers, verses, and memorials of every kind, and, some of them quite poor people, shedding tears.'[12]

Five days after the funeral, Stanley preached a sermon about Dickens and quoted a passage from his will: 'I commit my soul to the mercy of God, through our Lord and Saviour Jesus Christ; and I exhort my dear children humbly to try to guide themselves by the teaching of the New Testament in its broad spirit, and to put no faith in any man's narrow construction of its letter here or there.'[13] This might have been written by Stanley himself, and illustrates how he made use of eulogies to convey his own liberal convictions. In his sermons on Herschel and Lyell he defended science as a source of truth, and 'as no subtraction from any theology which deserves the name'. 'It is giving new meaning to its words, new bounds to its domain, new life to its skeleton.'[14] On Grote, Stanley argued for a religious interpretation of all history: 'On the great scale of the world's movements, we see impressed the "unceasing purpose" of the Creator; on the smaller scale of the lives of heroes, saints, and sages, we see the highest efforts of the Creature.'[15] Beside the grave of Livingstone, Stanley quoted the explorer's words that he never, as a missionary, 'felt himself bound to be either Presbyterian, Episcopalian, or Independent, or called upon in any way to love one denomination less than another'.[16]

Although Stanley was obliged as dean to preach in the Abbey only three or four times a year, he did so as often as he was able. His sermons at a new service he started on Sunday afternoons attracted hundreds of people, crowded into the nave, standing or squatting on the steps of the monuments.[17] 'One can see the little Dean still, ambling up to the pulpit with his short steps close behind the shoulders of his tall, handsome verger, apparently oblivious of his surroundings. His strained, harsh yet not unpleasant voice would break the silence with a short prayer and then he would give forth of his best for half an hour.'[18] Stanley's sermons were not long by Victorian standards, and this comparative brevity, as well as their picturesque language and anecdote, generosity of spirit, and practical application, help to explain their popularity. Not surprisingly for a man who preached so often, the quality of the sermons varies. Stanley was at his best and most engaged when preaching a new sermon written for a particular occasion, but too often he repeated old sermons, sometimes several times. Manuscripts show new passages scribbled in every corner and between the lines of the original text, with marks in red ink where they were to be inserted. Prothero records that 'the result was that at times the preacher either lost his way, or was so absorbed in finding it as to lose his energy of delivery'.[19]

Stanley never flaunted his learning, and usually managed to pitch his sermons at a level that at least the majority of his congregation could understand. This included children, to whom he always enjoyed talking, whether from the pulpit or when taking them on tours of the Abbey. In December 1871 he started a service especially for the Westminster children, to be held annually on Holy Innocents' Day. The psalms and Bible readings were carefully chosen, and Stanley's short, simple sermons were addressed to the parents as well as the children:

> Little children give an idea of what man, who was born in the image of God, was meant to be. No doubt there are bad children – naughty children; and even in good children, there is something which may become very bad. Still, in children there is an innocence, a lightness of heart, an ignorance of evil, a joyousness and a simplicity, which ought to be refreshing to every one. It was this which made our Saviour so fond of them – taking them up in His arms and saying, '*Of such is the kingdom of heaven;*' and it is this which is well expressed by a good English poet who says, as he looks back regretfully to his childhood:
>
> > Happy those early days, when I
> > Shined in my new angel-infancy;
> > Before I taught my tongue to wound
> > My conscience with a sinful sound ... [20]

After the service Augusta entertained the children to tea in the deanery, and after tea there were games of charades and hide-and-seek. Stanley kept up a correspondence with many of the children, sending them verses on the deaths of their pets, or ideas for the plays they were planning. Among the treasured objects on his study mantelpiece Stanley kept a Christmas card from a boy who was a particular favourite.

Another of Stanley's innovations was an annual service and lecture on missionary work, delivered at the end of November. Tait had appointed the feast of St Andrew as a day of intercession for missions, and this gave Stanley an excuse to invite Nonconformists to speak in the Abbey, an almost unprecedented and arguably illegal initiative. But Stanley wanted them 'to take their part in showing that they too, joined, on various grounds, in this common work of ours, and that, at least in this place, the heathen world should not be scandalised by the echoes of a disunited Christendom'.[21] Stanley had criticised the Church of England's disparagement of Dissenters in his essay on 'The Connection of Church and State',[22] and had pleaded for their ministers to be admitted to preach in Anglican pulpits. 'Dissenting brethren', he wrote, should be treated 'as our friends, our equals, our allies – in one word, as "Nonconforming members and ministers of the National Church".'[23] Furthermore, by also inviting laymen to lecture, Stanley gave expression to his Arnoldian view that the laity were as much the Church as the clergy, and shared responsibility for proclaiming the Christian message. He consulted the Lord Chief Justice as to the legality of the lectures, and he agreed that they could go ahead. Stanley was careful though not to cause offence: 'The service was in the nave, not in the choir; the lecture was delivered from the reading-desk, not from the pulpit; the garment which I wore was my black Geneva gown, not my surplice; a few hymns and prayers were substituted for the ordinary service.'[24]

Max Müller, Professor of Comparative Philology at Oxford, was invited to give the inaugural lecture in 1872, but he hesitated, and his place was taken by a missionary who had recently returned from India. Müller lectured the following year on science and religion, followed in 1874 by Richard Caird, Principal of the University of Glasgow. It was, thought Stanley, 'the most impressive address I have ever heard within Westminster Abbey'.[25] Canon Charles Kingsley[f] was so enthusiastic that he could not help standing up and crying 'Bravo!'. He was taken ill soon after and never recovered: a sad loss to Stanley because he and Kingsley were friends, and he was a welcome ally on the chapter. There were four more lectures, the last given by John Tulloch, Principal of St Andrews University, and Moderator of the General Assembly of the Church of Scotland. Stanley decided to end the lectures because of lack of interest, and the difficulty he had in finding suitable speakers.

The introduction of grand choral and orchestral music into the liturgy was an innovation of Stanley's which survived, and became a widespread practice. Early in 1871 the Abbey's precentor suggested using Bach's *St Matthew Passion* as a setting for a special service, just as the composer had intended. Surprisingly for someone with no interest in music, Stanley was enthused by the idea, and took on both the cost

---

[f] Christian socialist and author of *Westward Ho!* and *The Water Babies*. Kingsley was rector of Eversley, Hampshire, from 1844, and also a canon of Westminster from 1873 until his death in January 1875. Stanley officiated at his funeral in Eversley parish church.

and responsibility for the experiment. Before 1871 musical festivals had been held in cathedrals but the liturgical element was missing. 'It was Stanley who first invested the performance of great musical works in this country with the solemn religious character which was their most appropriate setting.'[26] A platform was erected in the nave for 50 instrumentalists and a choir of 250, conducted by Joseph Barnby.[g] A vast congregation gathered for the service on Maundy Thursday. It began with the usual order for evening prayer, but instead of the psalms, the first part of the passion music was performed. Stanley then preached a sermon on the propriety of devoting man's highest gifts to God the creator, and the second part followed. Some of the religious press was critical, but *The Times* warmly approved of the innovation, and *The Guardian* praised 'the liberality and large-mindedness of Dean Stanley, to which we are indebted for a hearing of the work in its proper place – in church'.[27] Liturgical oratorios became an annual event in the Abbey.

Stanley took considerable pleasure in showing visitors around the Abbey, and enthusing them with his knowledge of its history, tombs and monuments. Some of these were distinguished foreign visitors (Queen Emma of the Sandwich Islands, the Shah of Persia and the Emperor of Brazil), but most were members of the public. Dean Trench had made the nave and transepts available to sightseers free of charge, and Stanley went further by opening the Abbey's many chapels on Mondays and bank holidays. He wrote to Mary in April 1870: 'Easter Monday was the great trial for the opening of the Abbey on Mondays. We had 4,000 the week before, and were therefore prepared with additional policemen. I do not think there were quite as many as we expected – about 9,000. I went in and out several times. Of all the people that I asked, only one had been there before. They all expressed the deepest gratitude.'[28] On Saturday afternoons, Stanley and Augusta conducted parties of workmen, and afterwards gave them tea in the Jerusalem Chamber.[29] To Stanley, this was 'one of the most useful purposes to which the Abbey can be turned',[30] and the appreciation seems to have been mutual. In 'A Working Man's Recollections of the late Dean and Lady Augusta Stanley', Geoffrey Humphery describes his first encounter with the Stanleys in May 1870:

> Having introduced himself and Lady Augusta Stanley to us, and expressed his great pleasure in meeting us, he drew me to one side,

---

[g] Conductor of 'Mr Joseph Barnby's Choir', which gave popular oratorio concerts until 1872, when it was amalgamated to form the Royal Albert Hall Choral Society.

and said, 'Are there any Roman Catholics in your party?' I replied, 'Not that I am aware of; but there are a few of no Church.' 'Because,' he added, 'in any description I may give I should not like to hurt the feelings of anyone.' I at once concluded that none but a great man would be so thoughtful of the feelings of others, or so candid in expressing his solicitude for the same. This was my brief introduction to one of the best friends of the working-classes, and a friend my class can ill afford to lose. We spent the afternoon with the Dean and her Ladyship, each of whom vied with the other in contributing to the enjoyment and adding to the information of our party, and few of those present will forget their kindness.[31]

People and ideas interested Stanley more than buildings, and his Broad Churchmanship made him impatient with what he disparagingly called 'the materialism of the Altar and the Sacristy'.[32] Nonetheless, he relished the beauty of the Abbey, and did what he could to enhance it. In 1873 the sanctuary and the screen behind the high altar were finally restored after many years of planning and discussion. Stanley took a keen interest in the ornate designs by Sir George Gilbert Scott, the Abbey's architect, and paid for the expensive porphyry used in the paving of the steps in front of the altar. Preaching at the thanksgiving service on Easter Day, Stanley affirmed: 'Everything that there is of beauty in sculpture, poetry, painting or architecture, everything that there is of skill and mechanical contrivance, has its religious side, has the link, if it can be found, which binds it round the throne of God and the gates of heaven.'[33]

The thirteenth-century octagonal chapter house was also restored in Stanley's time. For many years it had been used by the Government as a public record office. Scott managed to persuade the authorities to let him investigate what lay beneath the wooden floor, and behind the cupboards, shelves and false ceiling, and found the original interior with its brightly-coloured tiles and mural paintings of the Apocalypse. Stanley persuaded the Government to return the building to the Abbey's care (though it remained a Government possession), and to make a substantial grant to complete its repair and restoration.

*   *   *

Outside the Abbey, Stanley's same commitment to a more comprehensive Church of England (and the elasticity of belief required) was engaged in a bitter battle in Convocation over the Athanasian Creed. One of the tasks of the royal commission on ritual (of which Stanley was a member) had been to inquire into 'the varying interpretations put upon the rubrics, orders, and directions for regulating ... the order of services contained in the Book of Common Prayer'.[34] Respect for rubric was a feature of the Oxford Movement, and one controversial consequence was the revival of the Athanasian Creed. The relevant rubric directed that the creed should be said or sung at morning prayer on important feast days, but the instruction has often been ignored, and by the nineteenth century it was followed in less than half the parishes. The creed was unwelcome for two reasons: first, the philosophical language of its doctrinal definitions was difficult to comprehend; and second, and more important, its damnatory clauses[h] were unpalatable, not only because they condemned to eternal perdition all members of, for example, the Eastern Orthodox Church,[i] but also because they seemed to contradict Christian faith in a loving and forgiving God.

Stanley was most certainly of this view, and for him the issue of the creed also expressed in painful form his long-held misgivings about subscription. The eighth of the Thirty-Nine Articles states that the Nicene, Apostles', and Athanasian Creeds 'ought thoroughly to be received and believed: for they may be proved by most certain warrants of Holy Scripture'. It was precisely this article in relation to the Athanasian Creed that had caused Stanley such heartsearching at his ordination. Since then he had been consistent in his opposition to subscription, and in campaigning to have the legal obligations abolished. In almost all the theological controversies in which Stanley had been involved, the issue of subscription to the articles, 'these vexatious and useless barriers of ancient party warfare',[35] had played an essential part: Hampden, Tract XC, Ward's degradation, Gorham, *Essays and Reviews*, Jowett's stipend. In each case, one side judged another's doctrine as heretical on the grounds that it contradicted the teaching of the articles to which the persons in question had subscribed. To Stanley's mind, all that *odium theologicum*, all that persecution and prosecution, could have been avoided if only men were not required, at

---

[h] 'Which Faith, except every one do keep whole and undefiled: without doubt he shall perish everlastingly.'
[i] The creed affirms: 'The Holy Ghost is of the Father, and of the Son.' The latter phrase (*filioque*) was added to the earlier Nicene Creed by the western Church but not the eastern. This became a major cause of controversy between the two Churches.

ordination or in taking their degree, to declare that 'all and every XXXIX Articles are agreeable to the Word of God'.

Stanley's *Essays on Church and State* includes the long letter 'on the State of Subscription in the Church of England and in the University of Oxford' that he had written to Tait in April 1862 when he was Bishop of London. Stanley described how the articles had often been used 'as weapons of bitter recrimination and exclusion',[36] and asserted that many intelligent and thoughtful young men were being deterred from ordination by the continuing imposition of subscription. He adopted his usual historical approach, and conceded that the articles were 'a valuable index to the chief points of controversy which engaged the attention of the English Reformers'.[37] But as such they could have no use as definers or guardians of contemporary orthodoxy. 'They consist of a number of complicated propositions ... drawn up by men who lived three hundred years ago, in the heat of vehement struggles which have long since passed away.'[38]

Tait needed no persuading, and in his second charge to his diocese in 1862, he had already indicated his own desire to revise the terms of subscription. A bill was twice introduced into Parliament, but defeated, provoking a pamphlet war and heated debates in Convocation. Stanley discussed the matter with Gladstone at Cliveden, the home of the Duchess of Sutherland, and found that they were largely in agreement. A royal commission was appointed to break the deadlock, and was surprisingly quick to agree a unanimous recommendation that subscription should be reduced to a simpler and less stringent form. The Clerical Subscription Act was passed in 1865, requiring at ordination a declaration of assent to the articles rather than subscription, a subtle but significant reform. Stanley would have preferred abolition, but he accepted that 'this was not the choice submitted to the clergy or the legislature', and welcomed 'a declaration as bare and general as it was possible to be'. It was, he acknowledged, 'an advance in the direction of freedom, of enlargement, and of comprehension'.[39]

The ritual commission's fourth and final report dealt with the Athanasian Creed, and was published in September 1870. The commissioners had discussed re-translating, shortening or omitting the creed, but instead they recommended retaining its place in the Book of Common Prayer, but adding a rubric to explain that the anathemas were not in fact condemnations to eternal damnation of those who failed to assent to every doctrinal statement in the creed, but were instead 'a solemn warning of the perils of those who wilfully reject the

Catholic Faith'.⁴⁰ Of the twenty-seven commissioners who signed the report, seventeen (including Stanley and Tait, now Archbishop of Canterbury) appended their names to a protest. Stanley published no fewer than twenty reasons for his doing so.⁴¹ This time he was unwilling to compromise: in his view the new declaration of assent could not mitigate the grave errors of this creed. He would accept nothing less than the omission of the the creed from all services. Tait would have preferred this but knew that it would be unacceptable to the majority. In December 1871 he gave notice that the expediency of adopting a slightly altered explanatory rubric would be put to Convocation in February.

Party battle-lines were drawn. On the one side, Broad Church latitudinarians like Stanley and Thirlwall, who would accept nothing less than omission; on the other, equally intransigent High Church conservatives like Pusey and Liddon, both of whom threatened to retire from the ministry if even an explanation was added. Stanley gave another rousing speech in Convocation. First he defended the doctrinal statements in the creed as containing sacred Biblical truths. 'But when we come to the (damnatory) clauses ... it is exactly the reverse ...

> These clauses belong to a state of mind which prevailed no doubt in the seventh, eighth, and ninth centuries, and, we must confess with sorrow even perhaps in one or two centuries preceding. They belong to that state of belief which maintained that error on these theological subjects was the greatest of crimes. They belong to that wretched system which regarded heresy as a crime which the Church, and the State, and all the powers of the earth, were bound to extirpate, in the same way as murder or theft, or any of the other great moral or social evils which pollute mankind. I hold that this opinion, which is thus incorporated in the Damnatory Clauses, is absolutely false, and I will venture to say, not only is it absolutely false, but it is believed by every single member of this House to be absolutely false.⁴²

Stanley's position may seem commendable today, but the forces of conservatism in the Victorian Church were domineering and vociferous. Stanley's chief protagonist in Convocation, George Denison,ʲ stormed out of the Jerusalem Chamber in disgust. Stanley's speech was denounced by another opponent as 'scarcely reconcilable with the most

---

ʲ Archdeacon of Taunton and a traditional High Churchman.

fundamental principles of morality',[43] and he and his followers were called on 'to go out instantly from the Church, of which such men proclaim themselves disaffected and disloyal members'.[44] Stanley was accused of committing a graver offence than 'the tutor who corrupts his pupil's mind, or the trustee who robs the widow and the orphan of their property'.[45]

Tait wisely withdrew the discussion from Convocation, and appointed a committee of both houses to consider the question in the light of recent debates, and in a spirit of compromise. Stanley persisted in his opposition to any explanatory rubric, which, he told the committee, he regarded as 'an endeavour, not to relieve the scruples of those aggrieved, but to retain the use of the creed in spite of the objections felt for it'.[46] But moderation prevailed, and a synodical declaration was agreed which was to take the place of a rubric in the Book of Common Prayer. The declaration was brought before the lower house in February 1873 and was carried, in spite of Stanley's sombre warning:

> I know that if we continue in the course which was initiated by Tract 90, that if we continue in this constant system of making anything mean anything, it is very possible, nay, it is more than probable, that the same process will be applied to the other Creeds ... It is this danger which I have seen with regret constantly growing in the Church of England since the time to which I have alluded, thirty years ago. It is that danger constantly growing, that disregard of the plain meaning of English words, that makes me look on these explanations with more than a passing emotion of melancholy.[47]

The move to end subscription had not been confined to the Church. Stanley's letter to Tait also addressed itself to subscription at Oxford, and the University Tests Act was passed at last in 1871. Every man at Oxford was now free to take degrees and hold office without even assenting to the articles. This opened the university to Roman Catholics and Nonconformists, as well to those of other faiths and none. To Pusey, Oxford was 'lost to the Church of England';[48] for Stanley, the act meant peace, liberation, and a promising future, as he proclaimed in an excited sermon in St Mary's in February 1872:

> There is the glorious prospect now for the first time revealed to Oxford of becoming not the battle-field of contending religious factions, but the neutral, the sacred ground, where the healing

genius of the place and the equal intercourse of blameless and generous youth shall unite the long estrangements of Judah and of Ephraim, of Jerusalem and Samaria. There are the chances for the teachers and the students of the nineteenth century, such as have not been known in any previous age, for the reconcilement of the holy claims of both science and religion, of the love of truth and the love of goodness.[49]

When Stanley left Christ Church his name had been removed from the list of those trusted to preach at university services. Liddell became vice-chancellor in 1870 and was determined to redress this injustice. He nominated Stanley to preach the university's annual sermon on the Jewish interpretation of prophecy. Liddell recalled 'a noble sermon'. 'The church was crowded. Stanley began by saying that he should not enlarge on the *Principles* of such interpretation, because he had spoken on that subject the last time he had addressed a University audience, *nine years ago!*'[50] In December 1872 Stanley was nominated as a select preacher for the following year, and Liddell gave his enthusiastic approval. But the nomination had to receive the sanction of the university's convocation. A letter was sent to the vice-chancellor to say that Stanley's name would be opposed. It was signed by five senior members of the university, including John Burgon, the vicar of St Mary's, and Montagu Burrows, the Chichele Professor of Modern History. All disliked what Burgon called Stanley's 'negative and cloudy Christianity',[51] and blamed him for the ending of subscription. Many of Stanley's High Church opponents ignored the meeting on 11 December, taking the view that, since the university's convocation was no longer composed entirely of members of the Church of England, it was in no position to decide on the orthodoxy of a clergyman. On the other hand, a pleasing number of Stanley's supporters made the effort to travel to Oxford to vote, and Stanley's nomination was carried by 349 votes to 287. 'I can truly say,' Stanley told Liddell, 'that even if there had been any personal annoyance – which there was not – it would have been a hundred-fold repaid by the kindness of my friends. Even the single vote of Dr. Lushington[k] will be to me "a joy for ever." I wish that I could find some means of expressing my gratitude. I fear there is none, except to do the best I can to justify the appointment.'[52]

But Stanley resented the resignation as a select preacher of Edward

---

[k] Stephen Lushington was 91 and travelled to Oxford from Surrey; he had been dean of the court of arches.

Goulburn, his Balliol friend and former Headmaster of Rugby, now Dean of Norwich. He had written to Liddell: 'If the pulpit of the University is to be turned into a vehicle for conveying to our youth a nerveless religion, without the sinew and bone of doctrine, a religion which can hardly be called faith so much as a mere Christianised morality, I for one must decline to stand there.'[53] Goulburn was an Evangelical, and he summarises here the charge against Stanley's theology shared by many Low and High Churchmen alike. Stanley's core belief, that all humankind is loved by God who in Jesus Christ sets an example of love for men and women to follow, was to him so natural and unshakeable that it often blinded him to the value and importance to others of more specific and robust Christian convictions – that people are fallen and sinful, for instance, and in need of salvation, whether through personal conversion and repentance, or by means of the dogmas, sacraments and rituals of the Church. Goulburn took the trouble to write to Stanley to say that he hoped that his resignation would not interrupt their friendship. Stanley's reply was defensive and self-righteous, and indicated a liberal mind that could at times be paradoxically closed to other points of view:

> ... it has been so long my fate to encounter misunderstanding and opposition that I cease to consider it as a subject either of surprise or annoyance ...
>
> I only regret that excellent persons like yourself should feel it your duty to thwart the efforts of those who, no doubt with many imperfections, are striving to bring out the treasures of the Bible, to enter into the spirit of the Gospels, and to show that religion and science need not be opposed to each other, and that reason is the means which God has given us for arriving at the knowledge of His will ...
>
> This regret is increased by the reflection that meanwhile little discouragement – I might say much encouragement – is given to the return of the grossest superstitions, and to expressions of unchristian uncharitableness.
>
> This, however, only makes it more evidently incumbent on those who value the maintenance of pure Christianity in England to pursue their own course, as best they can, in the hope of better days, and in the faith that truth will at last prevail.[54]

* * *

Marriage to Augusta drew Stanley to Scotland every autumn. They stayed with various members of the Bruce family in and around Dunfermline, but travelled widely. This was a delight for Stanley because he had been captivated by the country and its history since devouring the novels of Walter Scott as a child. Scott remained Stanley's favourite author: he even considered him 'a second Shakespeare'.[55] Prothero discerns similarities:

> Both men pursued the same broad, tolerant method of regarding open questions; both adopted the same historical and synthetical, rather than philosophical and analytical, treatment of character. Both loved to dwell in the past, and both possessed the power of revivifying its scenes and figures till they lived again in the present ... Both treasured tales of Scottish superstition, popular legends, and any anecdotes which illustrated the national peculiarities, social or theological ... In both there was the same love of the grandiose, of pageantry, romance, and of chivalry ... Both men sympathised deeply with conflicting schools of opinion and feeling, and both held the balance evenly between contending parties.[56]

Scott had inspired Stanley's boyhood imagination with a vision of a magic country with wild scenery, haunted castles, and a romantic history. 'Whatever of early romance England has had to show', he wrote, 'pales before the stories of Robert Bruce and James the Fifth.'[57]

Scott also stimulated Stanley's interest in Scotland's religious history, and his own broad, tolerant approach helped to reinforce Stanley's understanding. He found the country's Christian events and legends full of dramatic characters and events, and not least in his own century. Stanley had paid his first visit to Scotland in 1843, the year of the 'great disruption', when, in a dispute over patronage, over 470 out of 1,200 ministers left the Presbyterian Church of Scotland to form the Free Church.

In January 1872 Stanley delivered four lectures to the Philosophical Institution of Edinburgh on the history of the Church of Scoland, from St Ninian in the fourth century to the present Kirk. Though Stanley does not profess to give a complete narrative of the history, the lectures are detailed and knowledgeable, and focus on leading figures and episodes which serve, he explains, as 'landmarks to the whole'.[58] Typically, Stanley's overriding aim is to vindicate the established Church of Scotland as a national Church. He singles out for praise men of moderate opinion who have worked to broaden the Church, tempering the Calvinistic fervour of Presbyterianism, and 'grafting on its characteristic virtues that catholicity, elasticity, variety, and sympathetic adaptation which found little room in its fiery, though contracted, heart'.[59] 'Throughout its whole existence – from John Knox to the present day – [Stanley] found that the softer and more harmonious tones of saintly charity, and reasonable faith, and hopeful aspiration, were blended with the excesses of a harsher and more violent colouring.'[60]

On the Sunday before the opening lecture, Stanley preached at Old Greyfriars' in Edinburgh, his first sermon in a Presbyterian church. It serves as an introduction to the theme of the lectures, and is prefixed to the published *Lectures on the History of the Church of Scotland*. It is a masterly summary of Stanley's fundamental Christian convictions. He tells the story of Samuel Rutherford, the minister of the parish of Anworth in the seventeenth century. One evening, when he was catechising his children and servants, a stranger knocked at the door of the manse, seeking shelter for the night. Rutherford invited him in to join the family. The next question in the catechism was 'How many commandments are there?' The stranger answered, 'Eleven.' 'What do you mean?', asked the surprised minister, and the stranger replied: '"A new commandment I give unto you, that ye love one another; As I have loved you, that ye also love one another."'[61] The stranger turned out to be the Irish archbishop and scholar, James Ussher.[l]

Stanley takes these words from John's Gospel as his text.[m] He begins by criticising the false eleventh commandment invented by sects and parties, and sometimes by Churches: 'Thou shalt do something for this particular community, which none else may share. Thou shalt maintain the exclusive sacredness of this or that place, this or that word, this or that doctrine, this or that party, this or that institution, this or that mode of doing good.' 'For some commandment like this men have fought and struggled and shed their own blood and the blood of others.' 'But', Stanley explains, 'the true new commandment which our Saviour gave was ... peculiarly characteristic of the Christian religion.' '"Love one another", was the doctrine of Jesus Christ, "as I have loved you."' This was the doctrine too of the apostles Paul and Peter, and of St John. Stanley argues that obedience to the eleventh commandment

---

[l] Known for teaching that the world was created in 4004 B.C. He was buried in Westminster Abbey.
[m] John 13.34.

has three consequences: first, 'ceremonies, doctrines, ordinances' are 'altogether of secondary importance'. Second, the reconciliation of Churches, 'for which the whole civilised world is longing', is a Christian duty. And third, Christian union demands 'temperance in theological argument', and 'better sense of proportion in theological statements'.[62]

The Stanleys were in Scotland in August 1870 when the Franco-Prussian War was reaching its denouement. Stanley had been in Paris soon after the revolution in 1848, and would have liked to be there again to witness the collapse of the Second Empire, but he would not have been allowed to enter the country. He took a keen interest in what was happening, and regarded it as so much more important than his own battles at the time over Vance Smith. 'Surely,' he wrote to Pearson, 'this, like many other ridiculous things, must be withered up in the presence of this terrible catastrophe of the war.'[63] The Stanleys took the German side – partly because they regarded France's declaration of war as 'most wicked and causeless',[64] and partly because of their friendship (through Augusta) with the Crown Prince of Prussia who was married to the Princess Royal. Stanley and Augusta were visiting the battlefield of Culloden when they heard news of France's crushing defeat at Sedan on 1 September.[n] Though Stanley was glad for the Prussians, 'it is impossible', he wrote, 'not to feel pity for the bitter mortifications which this unhappy Emperor and this vainglorious nation must now be enduring.'[65]

The following September the Stanleys returned to France to inspect the battlefield, just as his parents had done at Waterloo fifty-five years before.[o]

> Sedan we reached at 11, and took a carriage, in which we drove incessantly until 4 P.M. over every part of the field. It was most interesting – as if five or six battles had been fought. Everywhere were graves marked by white crosses with garlands. The general features are clear enough: the vast plain enclosed by the hills which the Germans surrounded, and the Belgian frontier coming down on two sides ...
>
> We finished by seeing, first the little house where the Emperor of the French had his interview with Bismarck, and the larger

---

[n] 20,000 Frenchmen were killed; 84,000 men, 2,700 officers, 39 generals and the Emperor Napoleon III surrendered.
[o] See pp. 32–3.

Château of Bellevue, where he made the final capitulation with the King ... The woman who was present at the scene took us up by a small back stairs the same way which the Emperor and the Bismarck had mounted, into two very small rooms. In the inner of these they sat down for a few minutes at a table with two chairs ... one of which had been carried off by Bismarck, the other by a Prussian officer.[66]

From Sedan they travelled via Metz and Strasbourg to Potsdam to stay for three days with Prince Frederick and Princess Vicky and their six children, who 'were most tender to us – ', noted Augusta, 'so delightful to talk to, so bright and interested in everything'.[67] 'The battlefields furnished endless topics of conversation with the Prince. No one could be more modest or frank about them, and we were able from him to get many questions answered which were suggested to us on the spot, and which no one else could have answered.'[68]

The Stanleys' itinerary took them from Potsdam to Berlin, then Oberammergau (where Augusta was enthralled by the passion play), and finally Munich, to allow Stanley to observe the congress of the Old Catholics.[p] He did the same the following September, 1872, but this time in Cologne. Stanley admired the Old Catholics, not just for their resistance to ultramontanism, but for the vague and tentative nature of their separation from Rome, and their reluctance to create a schism and a new sect. When Stanley was invited to attend the Cologne congress he published his letter of acceptance in *The Times*,[69] and described the discussions in two further letters from 'An Occasional Correspondent'.[70] One question discussed was that of the celibacy of the clergy. This had been raised by the recent marriage of the former superior of the Carmelite convent at Passy, a man with the charmingly fragrant name of Père Hyacinthe.[q] Stanley admired the stance Hyacinthe had taken at the Vatican Council two years before, and had invited him to stay at the deanery. He disapproved of Hyacinthe's marriage because he thought it provocative, but was present nonetheless as a friend. He told Mary that 'he certainly is one of the most interesting and elevated characters I ever saw'.[71]

While they were in Cologne, Augusta received a telegram from the

---

[p] A group of small national Churches which separated from the Roman Catholic Church in 1870 over the proclamation of papal infallibility.
[q] Hyacinthe Loyson was renowned for his Advent sermons in Notre-Dame. He joined the Old Catholics and later founded L'Eglise Gallicane in Paris.

Queen informing her that her half-sister, Princess Feodore, was dying of cancer. The Stanleys hastened to Baden-Baden but arrived too late. 'The light gone from those glorious eyes, the loving welcome, the bright kindling response silent,' Augusta wrote to the Queen. 'The only sister and such a sister! A life long love and tenderness and sympathy and support which nothing on earth can ever replace. Dearest, dearest Madam, my own sore aching heart aches for Your Majesty with an unspeakable bitterness.'[72] Though Feodore was twelve years older than Victoria, they had been companions when they were young, and the recently widowed Feodore had helped Augusta to provide consolation when Albert died. Augusta represented the Queen at the funeral and wrote afterwards: 'It is indeed really the greatest loss almost that she could sustain.'[73]

*   *   *

Sadly during this period, death featured almost as often in Stanley's personal life as it did in his life as dean. In November 1870, Kitty Stanley's sister, Maria Hare, died, aged seventy-one, after being taken ill in Italy. She had been a loving and affectionate aunt to Stanley, and since her death, an important link to his mother. The funeral was at Herstmonceux where she had lived after her husband's death with his brother Julius. 'The day', Stanley told Louisa, 'was wild and stormy... Poor Augustus![r] For him it is the end of a blessed service of more than a son's affection. To me, it is the uprooting of a thousand memories ... the last of our dearest mother's family. How far we seem on our way to join them!'[74]

1873 was an especially mournful year, with the deaths of several of Stanley's oldest friends. Mrs Arnold died in September. She was eighty-two and had been a widow for over thirty years. Stanley had always felt a responsibility for her, visiting her at Fox How and writing to her regularly, and always on the anniversary of Arnold's death. She had remained a central figure in the lives of her nine children, and had shown admirable sympathy when, in their various ways, they reacted to their father's enduring influence. Matthew described her as having 'a clearness and fairness of mind, an interest in things, and a power of appreciating what might not be in her own line, which were very remarkable, and which remained with her to the very end of her life'.[75] Stanley wrote to him in similar vein to say 'what

---

[r] Augustus J. C. Hare, Maria's adoptive nephew.

to me was so impressive was not merely that she rose instead of sinking under the blow which we all feared would crush her, but that she retained the life-long reverence for your father's greatness, without a blind attempt to rest in the form and letter of his words.'[76]

Sir Henry Holland, physician-in-ordinary to the Queen, died a month later. He lived in Lower Brook Street, close to the Stanleys' London home, and Stanley wrote to Mary to remind her of how he had crossed the street 'to ask what we had heard of Arnold's death when the news came in 1842'.[77] 'He was a most faithful friend, and did truly rejoice in all our joys, and mourn in all our sorrows.'[78] Holland shared the Stanley family's Whiggery. He had been part of the Holland House set, and his second wife was the daughter of Sydney Smith, the wit and canon of St Paul's. Holland was as enthusiastic a traveller as Stanley, and had visited every capital city in Europe. In the autumn of 1873 he journeyed with his son Francis (a canon of Canterbury) from Russia to southern Italy. He returned to London on 25 October feeling unwell, and died two days later, aged eighty-five.

The ecclesiastical lawyer, Dr Lushington, died at the start of the year, and Stanley told Mary in the same letter that Holland had 'said to me with tears in his eyes that that was just the end which he should desire for himself'.[79] Lushington and Holland had become friends in 1820 when a bill was introduced in the House of Lords to dissolve the marriage of King George IV and Queen Caroline, on the grounds of her alleged adultery. Lushington was one of the counsel for the Queen; Holland was the Queen's physician, and was asked to testify at the inquiry which sought evidence to grant the divorce. Lushington was another Whig and a reformer, and had been influential in the campaign to abolish the slave-trade. But he was conservative in Church matters, and as dean of the court of arches he had condemned Williams and Wilson for their contributions to *Essays and Reviews*. Though he did not share Stanley's Broad Church views, he respected the courteous but critical position he had taken over the symposium, and had been determined to travel to Oxford to vote for him in the election for the select preacher. Lushington was ninety-one, was exhausted by the winter journey, and died four weeks later on 19 January. Stanley officiated at his funeral in Ockham parish church.

Richard Bethell died on 20 July. He had been appointed Lord Chancellor in 1861 and took the title Baron Westbury. When Wilson and Williams appealed to the Privy Council against Lushington's decision, it was Westbury who found in favour of the appellants. Wilson had argued in his article that the punishment of the wicked might not be for eternity. In response to Westbury's judgment, it was wittily suggested that an appropriate epitaph for him would be that 'he took away from orthodox members of the Church of England their last hope of everlasting damnation'.[80] Bishop Wilberforce, however, was not amused by Westbury's judgment, and proposed a synodical condemnation of the book which was passed by convocation. The Lord Chancellor ridiculed Wilberforce's action, which (like Stanley) he regarded as taking the powers of Convocation far beyond their proper limits. With a famous swipe at Wilberforce's sobriquet, 'Soapy Sam', he told the bishops that the synodical judgment was 'simply a series of well-lubricated terms – a sentence so oily and so saponaceous that no-one could grasp it'.[81]

Antagonists in the 1860s, Westbury and Wilberforce were united in death in 1873 when Wilberforce died after a riding accident, the day before Westbury. Stanley described the news 'as the shock of an earthquake'.[82] Wilberforce was sixty-eight and, like Mrs Arnold, had been widowed for over thirty years. He had been a staunch, if at times clumsy, defender of orthodoxy, and he and Stanley had often clashed. But Stanley admired his determination, and his innovative and invigorating work as Bishop of Oxford, and they were always friendly to one another. Indeed it was said that they had agreed to love one another in private, but to do each other as much mischief as possible in public. Stanley made a point of visiting the spot where Wilberforce had fallen from his horse, and said that his death 'shakes me to the centre'.[83] He preached a sermon in the Abbey on both men with the text 'How are the mighty fallen!', describing them as two of the most distinguished men of their generation.

The winter of 1871–2 had been marred by anxiety that another death might occur which would bring catastrophic results for the nation, as well as personal sadness for the Stanleys. At the end of November the Prince of Wales was taken ill with typhoid fever, and by the beginning of December he was thought to be dying. It seemed a bitter irony that Prince Albert had died of the same illness ten years before, and the Queen was still in mourning. Almost every day Augusta received letters or telegrams from Sandringham with the latest bulletin. On 10 December the Duchess of Roxburgh wrote to say that she did not 'feel there is any hope', and Augusta told her sister Frances that 'this dreadful news on Friday knocked us down'.[84] The Prince's illness reached its crisis on 13 December, the day before the anniversary of his father's death. But on the dreaded day itself he began to recover. 'The

Queen', wrote Augusta, 'was allowed to go up to his bed – he did not quite know her at first – but soon did and said he was glad to see her.'[85] The next day Augusta wrote to Frances again: 'You are by this time rejoicing with us – I can hardly keep my hope below confidence for the dear Patient has shewn such a good will to recover ... that I cannot but rejoice and anticipate good ... How it touches one to read of the dear Queen sitting holding the P. of W.'s hand! Is it not affecting?'[86]

The Prince's dangerous illness did much to heal the lingering rift between mother and son, at least for the moment. Though the Queen was not enthusiastic about the Government's proposal of a thanksgiving service, she played her part, and told Gladstone afterwards that she had been deeply touched by 'the immense enthusiasm and affection displayed towards her dear son and herself'.[87] St Paul's was chosen for the service on 27 February, and was attended by a congregation of 13,000, including the Stanleys. Victoria and Bertie drove past cheering crowds from Buckingham Palace to the cathedral in an open carriage, with the now ubiquitous John Brown sitting behind on the box.

Stanley had preached three times in the Abbey on the Prince's illness, twice in December, and then on 3 March at a more private thanksgiving service. He was keen for Bertie to attend, and went to Marlborough House to invite him. 'He consented at once,' Stanley told Louisa, 'and it was agreed that he, the Princess, and the Crown Prince of Denmark, and, if in town, Prince Alfred, should come. I kept it a secret, except from the Canons. We met them at the great Western door ... They walked in with me, and took their places on my right.'[88] Stanley took considerable trouble over his sermon on the mutual duties of throne and people. 'It was', he thought, 'one of those rare occasions on which I was able to say all that I wished to say.'[89]

*   *   *

In July 1873 the engagement was announced between Queen Victoria's second son, Prince Alfred, Duke of Edinburgh, and the Grand Duchess Marie Alexandrovna, only daughter of Tsar Alexander II. The Queen wrote to Augusta a fortnight later to say that she was desirous that Stanley should perform the English part of the marriage service in St Petersburg, and that Augusta should attend on her behalf. 'You travel so much, and dread cold so little, that, as in January the Russian climate is said to be healthy, I hope you may be able to undertake a mission which will require great discretion, and which will be a comfort to me.'[90] Stanley and Augusta were delighted to oblige, and they were both to write long and excited letters from Russia, describing in detail the extravagant pomp and circumstance of the imperial court. They were evidently thrilled and impressed by the ways they were honoured as the Queen's envoys and distinguished guests of the Tsar.

They sailed from England on Friday 9 January 1874, and headed first to Berlin to stay with the Prince and Princess of Prussia. In Stanley's first letters to Mary he describes the same regal treatment he had received when travelling with the Prince of Wales. 'The moment we touched the shores of Calais began the change from ordinary travelling. The Consul and Vice-Consul appeared on board, took us instantly to a private room in the station, and placed us in a *coupé*, in which we remained, unchanged and uninvaded, the whole way to Cologne.'[91] They arrived in Berlin the following evening, and were met by Sir Odo Russell, the British ambassador, and driven to the palace. 'It is impossible to imagine anything more splendidly comfortable. A whole suite of rooms, all warmed, and with blazing fires – real open fireplaces. They are the rooms which the First Napoleon occupied on his invasion of Berlin.'[92] Two days later the Prince and Princess of Wales arrived with Prince Arthur. At a dinner that evening, attended by the Empress of Prussia, Stanley met Prince Bismarck and found him more gracious than he had expected. Bismarck expressed his approval of the marriage, and told Stanley that it was 'very important that the two countries which *we* regard as friends to *us* should be friends to one another'.[93] Stanley sat between Princess Vicky and Princess Marie, whom he found 'a very simple, innocent, pleasing girl'.[94]

The Stanleys reached St Petersburg early in the morning of 16 January. 'Never', Stanley told Mary, 'had we seen such a disembarkation before. There was red cloth laid down into the station, servants dressed like the doges of Venice in red embroidered cloaks and white ruffs.'[95] They were given luxurious rooms in the winter palace looking out on to the Neva. A letter was brought from the British ambassador to say that Stanley was to be presented to the Tsar the next day. He called first on the Russian Prime Minister, who told him that he had been to Westminster Abbey to attend the coronation of George IV. The Tsar spoke about his sadness at losing his only daughter. 'The Emperor's eyes filled with tears', Stanley wrote to Queen Victoria, 'and he said: "Yes. It is true. She has been the constant joy of our lives."'[96] On Sunday morning the Stanleys attended the liturgy in the imperial chapel, together with the Tsar, the Russian and English princes, two metropolitans, two bishops, six archimandrites, and an array of army officers in full dress uniforms. After the service they watched the waters of the Neva being blessed to celebrate the Epiphany. In the afternoon Stanley preached on the wedding at Cana at a service in the English chapel. It was, Stanley admitted to the Queen, much the same sermon he had preached in the chapel in Whitehall on the Sunday after Bertie's marriage.[97] The Tsarina sent a message to say that she desired to have Stanley read the sermon to her.

On Tuesday Stanley travelled by sledge drawn by reindeer to visit the three metropolitans of St Petersburg, Moscow and Kiev, and the chaplain of the imperial family, who was to perform the marriage. The Russian Orthodox service began at noon on Friday 23 January in the imperial chapel. Stanley sat dressed in his red doctoral robes close to the chancel rails, and followed the service in a French translation. Augusta wore a satin gown with a brocade train, trimmed with velvet and lace, and all the diamonds she had managed to borrow from family and friends. Stanley thought the ceremony 'was much more like a family gathering than anything in Western Churches.

> The bride and bridegroom were closed round by four groomsmen (for there are no bridesmaids), as if protecting them, and the crowns are held over their heads so long as to give the impression of a more than fugitive interest. Walking round and round the altar, with these four youths pacing with them, had quite the effect of what originally it must have been, a wedding dance. The sunshine, which after a dull, gloomy morning had gradually crept into the dome, at this moment lighted up the group below and gave a bright, auspicious air to the whole scene. The singing was magnificent. The Lord's Prayer again struck me as the most beautiful vocal music I had ever heard.[98]

The English service happened immediately after in the Alexander Hall of the palace. 'It was a thrilling moment', Stanley told Mary, 'when, for the first and last time in my life, I addressed each by their Christian name – "Alfred" and "Marie" – and looked each full in the face, and they looked up into mine.'[99] Stanley added a prayer he had written especially for the occasion, and in which he struggled to avoid any hint of precedence between the two families. The wedding was followed by a sumptuous banquet (with men and women separated) and a ball with 800 guests. 'I sat by the Danish Minister;' wrote Stanley, 'opposite me were the Emperor and the whole line of Princes and Princesses. The four heirs of England, Russia, Denmark and

Germany, all so different, each from each, but, of all, certainly none to compare with the last.'[100]

During another ten days at the winter palace the Stanleys attended more dinners, a concert of sacred music, the Hermitage museum, a monastery, a review of troops, the imperial library (which Stanley had visited on his last visit to Russia in 1857), the house of Peter the Great, and a play about Ivan the Terrible. The court travelled next on the imperial train to Moscow, accompanied by the English princes and the Stanleys (who had to stay this time in a modern hotel because there was no room for them in the Kremlin). There followed another week of celebratory services, ceremonies and banquets, with sightseeing in between. Stanley and Augusta returned to St Petersburg for five days of still more banqueting before setting off to Berlin. 'The glorious dream is over,' he wrote, 'and the most splendid certainly, and one of the most interesting, passages of my life.'[101]

*   *   *

The Stanleys arrived home in Westminster on 25 February. They had been away for seven weeks, and though on their journey back they had been able to rest for a few days in Germany and France, they were both exhausted. Stanley had suffered from a heavy cold in Moscow, and Augusta went down with something similar on their return, but severe enough in her case to confine her to bed. She had already complained of a sharp pain in her forehead, caused, she assumed, by the freezing temperature.[102] But the demands of royal duty continued with the arrival of the Duke and Duchess of Edinburgh at Windsor in March, followed in May by the visit of the Tsar.

Augusta had worn herself out. She was devoted to Stanley and always ready to answer his many needs. She took seriously her responsibilities as the dean's wife, in the Abbey and the deanery, and in philanthropic work for the sick and poor in Westminster. And she was subject to relentless demands from the Queen, who relied on her as if she were still at court, requiring her to be in attendance at Windsor and Osborne, and to write to her regularly with sympathy, gossip and advice. Augusta had always been a voluminous correspondent and now she often had to stay up late at night to write her letters. The last ten years had taken their toll, and the rigours of Russia had undermined her health to such an extent that she was never to recover.

Stanley had to carry on with his duties despite his worries about Augusta and the time he devoted to caring for her. An encounter characteristic of his kindness and tolerance occurred in April 1874 when Annie Besant visited the deanery to ask him to give communion to herself and her mother. Besant was a determined freethinker, though at twenty-seven she had not yet gained her notoriety as a socialist and theosophist.[s] In her teens Besant had been a fervent Tractarian, but at twenty she had married an Evangelical clergyman who was twice her age. The marriage was unhappy from the start. Annie blamed God for not sparing their second child from a near fatal bout of whooping cough, and abandoned her faith. She turned for sympathy to the Reverend Charles Voysey, with whom Stanley had been corresponding for a decade.[103] Voysey's opinions were essentially Unitarian, and amounted to a rejection of the creeds, Biblical inspiration and the divinity of Christ. His appeal in 1871 to the Privy Council against the judgment of an ecclesiastical court was rejected, and Voysey was deprived of his living. He introduced Besant to the freethinker Thomas Scott, who encouraged her to write a sceptical pamphlet 'On the Deity of Jesus of Nazareth by the Wife of a Beneficed Clergyman'. Mr Besant issued Annie with an ultimatum: she must either take communion regularly at the altar of his church, or she must leave. 'Hypocrisy or expulsion,' she wrote, 'I chose the latter.'[104] She moved to London in 1874.

In 1884 Besant published her account of what happened ten years before when she visited Stanley.[105] She explained that her mother was dying and had a longing to take the sacrament, but refused to do so unless her daughter took it with her: 'I would rather be lost with her than saved without her.'[106] Besant went to a clergyman she knew well, explained the situation, but he refused. The same happened with another parson, and she was in despair. 'At last a thought struck me: there was Dean Stanley, my mother's favourite, a man known to be of the broadest school within the Church of England; suppose I asked him?'[107] Besant went nervously to the deanery and put her request to Stanley. After listening to her account of her position, he agreed. 'I could barely speak my thanks,' she wrote, 'so much did the kindly sympathy move me ... Well was I repaid for the struggle it had cost me to ask so great a kindness from a stranger when I saw the comfort that gentle, noble heart had given to my mother.'[108]

Two months later, on Wednesday 10 June 1874, Augusta was well enough to accompany Stanley to Bedford where she had been invited

---

[s] The Theosophical Society was founded in New York in 1875. Its members believe in reincarnation and deny immortality and a personal God.

to unveil a bronze statue of John Bunyan, and at which Stanley was to give an address.[109] This was a welcome assignment for Stanley because he held Bunyan and his *Pilgrim's Progress* in high esteem. In his speech he explained that, in early youth, he had identified a passage which, if he ever became professor of ecclesiastical history, he would quote at the start of his inaugural lecture. He had kept that promise in his first lecture as regius professor in 1857.[110] Now, seventeen years later, Stanley emphasised the common ground between Churchmen and Nonconformists, and cited Bunyan and his universally admired story as an example. 'It is', he stated, 'one of the few books which acts as a religious bond to the whole of English Christendom.'[111]

> Protestant, Puritan, Calvinist as he was, yet he did not fear to take the framework of his history and the figures of his drama, from the old mediaeval Church, and the illustrations in which the modern editions of his book abound give us the pilgrim with his pilgrim's hat, the wayside cross, the crusading knight with his red-cross shield, the winged angels at the Celestial Gate, as naturally and as gracefully as though it had been a story from the 'Golden Legend',[t] or from the favourite romance of his early boyhood, 'Sir Bevis of Southampton'.[u] Such a combination of Protestant ideas with Catholic forms had never been seen before, perhaps never since.[112]

Stanley wrote to the Queen afterwards to express his hope that she would not disapprove of their involvement in the unveiling. 'The Dissenters are at this time very unreasonable and uncharitable. But the Dean thinks that this is an additional reason for trying to soften their prejudices by taking part in anything where he can express sympathy with them, whilst at the same time it gives him the opportunity of saying to them a few words of wholesome truth.'[113]

From Bedford the Stanleys travelled to Leicester where Arthur preached for Charles Vaughan's younger brother, who had succeeded him as vicar of the family living in the town. After Leicester they went to Rugby where Stanley was to address the school on the thirty-second anniversary of the death of Thomas Arnold.[114] It was, of course, a moving occasion for him, and an opportunity to pay tribute, and describe his still vivid memories of Arnold, and the influence he had exerted:

---

[t] Medieval manual containing lives of saints, published by Caxton.
[u] Popular verse romance (early 14th century).

The sermons which I heard from his lips in this place are still, through the vicissitudes of an often stormy and eventful time, as fresh in my memory as when I first listened to them in this chapel, with a mixture of admiration and delight. The effect of his character, and the lessons of his teaching, have been the stimulus to whatever I may have been able to do in the forty years since I left school; and his words constantly come back to me as expressing better than anything else my hopes and fears for this life, and for the life to come.[115]

In explaining Arnold's teaching about religion, Stanley summarised the profound and lifelong effect Arnold's views had on his own central convictions that the Christian religion is more a matter of ethics than doctrine or ritual, and embraces sacred and secular alike:

He made us understand that the only thing for which God supremely cares, the only thing that God supremely loves is goodness – that the only thing which is supremely hateful to God is wickedness. All other things are useful, admirable, beautiful in their several ways ... But Religion, the true Religion of Jesus Christ, consists in that which makes us wiser and better, more truthful, more loving, more tender, more considerate, more pure. Therefore, in his view, there was no place or time from which Religion is shut out – there is no place or time where we cannot be serving God by serving our fellow-creatures.[116]

It is entirely true that Stanley's religion 'grew, but never changed its character from the day when he sat under the pulpit and heard Arnold preach at Rugby'.[117]

*   *   *

Augusta's health had rallied but her excursions had weakened her, and she was required to rest. Later in 1874 the Queen asked her to edit and preserve extracts from her mother's journals before destroying them. Augusta was the obvious choice because she had been the Duchess of Kent's lady-in-waiting for fifteen years, and had lived with her almost as a daughter. But Victoria also wanted to provide Augusta with something to distract her. Whether or not Augusta's editing was biased is impossible to tell, but the picture of the duchess that emerges is certainly kinder than that of popular history. What remains of the journals suggests a close and affectionate relationship between mother and daughter, at least after Victoria became Queen and dismissed the duchess's adviser, Sir John Conroy. Augusta wrote to the Queen on 19 August:

> It has been so great an interest and so affecting a pleasure to trace the outline of that dear life, able as I am, to fit in so much of the detail and live over again so many happy years ... It must comfort and soothe Your Majesty to feel how entirely the tenderness of Your Majesty and the Prince brightened the declining years of that loving Mother ... It will be a terrible wrench to destroy the Volumes, but Your Majesty will be strengthened if it is carrying out a wish.[118]

In the same letter Augusta complained about 'that stupid lameness for which warm sea baths are recommended'.[119] Augusta's doctor was the Queen's physician, Sir William Jenner, and he advised a holiday in France. The Stanleys crossed the Channel in September, and spent three weeks staying at various locations along the coast, as far south as La Rochelle. They landed first at Dieppe where they were guests of the Marquess of Salisbury[v] and his family at their house on the cliffs. From there they travelled to Rouen, and then back to the coast to stay at Fécamp and Etretat, which was excellent for bathing. But despite the sea water, Augusta's knee, which she described as 'rheumaticky',[120] was causing discomfort.

Stanley could not resist his usual historical excursions, and he wrote to the Queen on 4 October to say that he had made a point of revisiting the Abbey at Fontevraud in Anjou to see the tombs and statues of Henry II and Eleanor of Aquitaine, Richard I, and the second wife of King John. Stanley reminded Victoria that the Emperor (Napoleon III) had offered to remove the tombs to England (and therefore to Westminster Abbey), but had withdrawn his offer after the French antiquaries objected.[121]

Before returning home, Stanley and Augusta stayed in Paris with Madame Mohl. Augusta was feeling better, and for a moment it seemed that the baths and the rest were working. But on 13 October, when out walking in the Champs Elysées, she collapsed with a fever. Stanley managed to get her back to the apartment where she remained in bed for a month. She was showing some signs of recovery at the start of November, and was able to sit up for two or three hours each day. But

---

[v] Prime Minister, 1885, 1886–92, 1895–1902.

she remained weak, and Stanley felt unable to break the news to her that Frances's husband, Evan Baillie, had died on 9 November. 'It is heart rending', he wrote, 'to see her so incessantly treasuring up her little experiences, and sending messages to Fanny, and to have to keep up a cheerful countenance about it; but so it must be.'[122] The Queen was concerned, and wrote with inquiries and sympathy. On 12 November Augusta managed to reply: 'Flowers are showered upon me as if at Midsummer and everything I can think of is bought or lent. Your Majesty sees how kind Providence is to me, and how thankful I ought to be for all the blessings I have.'[123]

The day before Stanley had written:

> The Queen asks what is the nature of the malady. It is, the Dean presumes, not typhoid, but something exactly of the nature of a Roman fever. It came on in the same way – in a moment, from a chill caught on the day after our arrival here, and having overheated herself before she got into the carriage. What she now suffers from is extreme weakness and sensitiveness to the slightest agitation.[124]

Exactly what was wrong with Augusta has never been explained. The Victorians were quick to find causes of illness in chills or changes of temperature, and the fear of typhoid fever was always present. Indeed Dr Jenner was an expert on the disease, and had diagnosed it in Prince Albert and the Prince of Wales.[w] Roman fever is a severe form of malaria which seems unlikely. It appears that Augusta may have been suffering from some kind of chronic infection. Tuberculosis is a possibility. So too, perhaps, is rheumatic fever, which can affect the joints as well as the heart, and can be fatal. Given Augusta's symptoms, the most likely diagnosis is motor neurone disease, which damages the nervous system, causing the muscles to waste, and inducing fatigue, muscle pains and weakness in arms and legs. It also affects speaking, swallowing and breathing.

Augusta was well enough to start the journey home on 19 November. They travelled by train from Paris to Boulogne in a private carriage arranged for them by the embassy, and took the steamer to Dover. As soon as they were home Stanley wrote to Mary with a mixture of relief and regret: 'Here she is, safe, and, I trust, recovering; but very different

---

[w] The diagnosis of typhoid as the cause of Prince Albert's death has been challenged. Most recently, Helen Rappaport argues in *Magnificent Obsession* (2011) that Albert died of Crohn's disease.

from that indefatigable, indomitable dispenser of all good influences which has hitherto shared all my labours.'[125]

Welcome news followed that Stanley had been elected Rector (chancellor) of the University of St Andrews. Stanley received seventy votes and the Marquess of Salisbury sixty-six. Augusta was delighted because of the honour and the link with Scotland. The duties were light and included an annual address to the university to be delivered before Easter. Stanley gave his first on 31 March 1875 on 'The Study of Greatness', and praised 'this secluded sanctuary of ancient wisdom, with the foam-flakes of the Northern Ocean driving through its streets, with the skeleton of its antique magnificence lifting up its gaunt arms into the sky'.[126] He argued that the special duty of education in an age of mediocrity was to fix the minds of students on all that is great in men, books, ideas and institutions. He singled out theology as the most profitable subject for the contemplation of greatness, and placed in the first ranks of Scottish theology the 'wise humour' and 'tender pathos' of Robert Burns, and 'the lofty sense of Christian honour, purity, and justice' of Walter Scott.[127] Of course, Augusta was unable to accompany him, but the university's principal, Stanley's friend John Shairp, wrote to her to say that 'during his three days here he was at his brightest and best, with but one thing wanting to make all perfect – your presence ... His presence has been like a bright angel visit, that has sweetened many a heart not used to such things ... Before the term of his Rectorship expires we shall hope to see him here again, and you with him, restored to health, as before.'[128]

The visit to St Andrews was almost Stanley's only break from Westminster in 1875. His decanal duties continued unabated, though he spared as much time as he could to be at Augusta's bedside. 'I resign myself to six months of this stranded existence,' he had told Max Müller in February. 'If at the end of that time my dear wife is anything like what she was before in activity and strength, I shall be satisfied.'[129] But in June he wrote a weary letter to Mary Mohl to say that 'our life is sadly changed – a mere ghost of its former self'.[130] Stanley found solace in working on the third volume of his lectures on the Jewish Church, much of which he wrote in Augusta's room, reading extracts to her and asking her opinion, just as he had done before. These lectures cover the five centuries between the Babylonian captivity and the beginning of the Christian era. Stanley thought this comparatively obscure period less interesting than that covered in the first two volumes. Furthermore, he was afraid that 'the whole work will bear the marks of the terrible calamity under the weight of which it was composed'.[131] But he was unnecessarily anxious. The final part may share the defects of its predecessors, but it also contains some of Stanley's most graphic descriptions and vigorous portraiture (the golden city of Babylon and the character of the mighty Judas Maccacbaeus, for instance). 'The scattered threads of Hebrew history are gathered together; the tangled skeins of intrigue, discord, and controversy are unravelled, and the whole material is woven together into the fabric of picturesque, vivid narrative, which is often powerful and always interesting.'[132]

On 10 October 1875, the Prince and Princess of Wales called at the deanery to see Augusta. Bertie was embarking the next day on a four-month tour of India, the first heir to the British throne to visit the subcontinent. They arrived in the afternoon with all their children. Augusta was delighted, and 'talked with all her usual animation'.[133] Alix looked, thought Stanley, 'inexpressibly sad':[134] whether this was because of anxiety about Augusta's illness or the forthcoming trip is unclear. Stanley told Mary that 'Augusta was very much gratified, and none the worse for the exertion'.[135] It was almost exactly a year since her collapse in Paris.

Augusta rallied a little towards the end of the year, and at the start of December, Jenner thought her better than at any time since her return from France. But the recovery was short-lived. The Queen sent a letter to Stanley on his and Augusta's wedding anniversary, 22 December, explaining why Augusta was so dear to her:

> I know your beloved one so well, and love her so truly. She was with me on those two fearful nights in my life when my darling mother and when my precious husband were taken. She was so much with me during those two dreadful first years of loneliness, and was always so kind and helpful, that to think of her now as so suffering, or at least as so helpless, is terrible. May our Heavenly Father, who has sent this fearful trial, support, comfort, and sustain you![136]

On New Year's Day 1876 Stanley informed Pearson that 'my angel wife' was much worse.[137] 'I sometimes doubt', Stanley confided to Pearson, 'whether, when I see her so constantly suffering, I ought to wish her stay in this world to be prolonged. And yet to have her, even in this state, is so inexpressibly precious and consoling that I cannot endure to think that she may be lost to me.'[138] But Stanley began to lose hope, and to pray for a speedy release from her sufferings. As for himself, 'I live on, and sleep. I perform my indispensible duties. But the sunshine, the spring, the energy are gone.'[139] He wrote to Liddell on 16 January:

> I knew that you would feel for us. *You* joined our hands in one, and gave us the blessing which has been fulfilled a hundredfold into our bosoms. To have had such a mother and such a wife was, perhaps, too much for one man's existence. I have two most loving sisters, and many faithful friends, who will, I know, sustain me when the blow at last falls. But the glory of my life will have departed ... [140]

By the start of February, Augusta was finding it difficult to speak or swallow, and there was nothing more the doctors could do for her. But she struggled hard to remain cheerful and uncomplaining, and never lost her characteristic concern for others. Stanley was reminded of a line in a sonnet by Michelangelo: 'The more the marble wastes, the more the statue grows.'[141] On 7 February the Queen came to the Deanery to visit Augusta, and instructed Stanley to post a notice in Dean's Yard: *The Queen has decreed that, in order not to disturb Lady Augusta Stanley in her present suffering condition, and as a mark of respect, the bells of Westminster Abbey, and of S. Margaret's Westminster, shall not be rung, as usual, on the occasion of Her Majesty's procession to the opening of Parliament.*[142] Victoria returned three weeks later, and recorded in her journal that she had entered 'poor dear Augusta's bedroom, and I saw her sleeping heavily, but peacefully, not looking much altered. I then sat a little while with the Dean, who was much upset at first. He said he only lived from day to day.'[143]

Augusta's end came at last on Ash Wednesday, 1 March. She was fifty-three and had been married for twelve years. Stanley told George Bradley that the night before she had spoken his name. 'This morning, for the last time, in answer to my urgent appeal, she opened those dear eyes upon me.'[144] He read to her throughout the day until in the evening she drifted silently and peacefully into unconsciousness. Stanley's mother had also died on Ash Wednesday, a coincidence he found full of painful pertinence. 'On this same dark day', he told Pearson, 'the two great lights of my life have gone out.'[145] Two years later, Stanley composed a five stanza lament:[146]

> O Day of Ashes! – twice for me
> Thy mournful title hast though earned,
> For twice my life of life by thee

Has been to dust and ashes turned.
No need, dark day, that thou shouldst borrow
The trappings of a formal sorrow:
In thee are cherish'd fresh and deep
Long memories that cannot sleep.

A flood of letters of sympathy and condolence poured into the deanery. The Prince of Wales sent a message from India by electric telegraph: 'No words can adequately express how deeply I feel for you in the terrible and irreparable loss you have sustained. May God give you strength to bear it.'[147] Stanley arranged every detail of the funeral which was to take place in the Abbey at noon on Thursday 9 March. Augusta had asked to be buried there, rather than with her family at Broomhall, Dunfermline, and the Queen had already bestowed the honour of interment in the vault beneath Henry VII's Chapel. 'Thank the dear Queen,' she had written. 'I shall be near him now. I shall be with him whenever he takes people round the Abbey, whenever he is at his duty.'[148] It was Stanley's responsibility as dean to choose the exact spot for the memorial, and he decided on the bay in the far south-east corner of the chapel, next to the monument to the Duc de Montpensier.[x] Stanley thought this appropriate because of Augusta's affection for France.

The Queen broke with protocol and attended the funeral in person. She sat with the Princesses Alice, Louise and Beatrice in the abbot's pew, the wooden gallery at the south-west corner of the nave which adjoins the deanery. The pall-bearers included Archbishop Tait, the Duke of Westminster, Lord Shaftesbury, Henry Campbell-Bannerman[y] and Robert Browning. Tait described seeing Carlyle[z] and Gladstone, Stanley's Rugby and Oxford friends, a crowd of Westminster poor, and 'every shade of Christians and a good many whose Christianity is doubtful – certainly a wonderful testimony to the extended influence of the Dean and Lady Augusta in every sphere'. He thought it 'the most strange and touching gathering that has probably ever been assembled in the Abbey'.[149] Two sermons were preached, by Charles Vaughan and Henry Liddell, not at the funeral but on the following Sunday. Liddell described Augusta as 'a woman of truly catholic spirit, of all-embracing

---

[x] Brother of Louis Philippe, King of the French. He died in 1807 when in exile in England.
[y] M.P. for Dunfermline; Prime Minister, 1905–8.
[z] Carlyle (who was 80) is described by A. J. C. Hare as acting strangely at the funeral, running along beside the coffin, and 'making the strangest ejaculations at intervals through the service'.

sympathies'[150] – the perfect match for Stanley. The inscription on Augusta's black marble monument, composed by Stanley, commemorates: 'the beloved wife of Arthur Penrhyn Stanley ... for 30 years the devoted servant of Queen Victoria and the Queen's mother and children, for 12 years the unwearied friend of the people of Westminster, and the inseparable partner of her husband's toils and hopes.' The Queen erected her own memorial at Frogmore, close to her mother's mausoleum. 'For me,' wrote Stanley,

> there is a consolation in the full tide of sympathy which flows in from every rank, and every country, and every Church. But the sad future still remains of my work to be carried on without the support which hitherto carried me through all obstacles ... Was ever mortal man so blessed with such a mother and with such a wife? Was ever a union of twelve years so rich in incidents of extraordinary interest and happiness? May God give me grace to use the few years that may still be granted worthily of such a past – worthily of the hope of reunion with two such angelic spirits![151]

10

'Of Slowly Ebbing Powers'

1876–1881

HUGH PEARSON HAD been unable to attend the funeral. Stanley described the service to him as 'the crowning honour of our dear angel ... I gave the blessing at the end, beginning this weary life again without the sunshine which made it tolerable.'[1] Stanley was never to recover from his loss. He told the Queen that 'all the anxieties, and cares, and hopes, and fears of the last year and a half seem to me like unmixed happiness, compared with that desolation and sorrow which have now fallen upon me'.[2] To Edward Lear[a] he wrote: 'I have now crossed the summit of my life. All that remains can but be a long or short descent, cheered by the memories of the past.'[3]

A long-ingrained habit of unrelenting work allowed Stanley a welcome solace and refuge. He knew that this would be the case, and he deliberately intensified his efforts in order to relieve his disappointment and loneliness. Writing, preaching, lecturing and travelling were all increased, as well as his work at Westminster, which now included taking on some of Augusta's initiatives to relieve the sick and poor. 'I am trying', he wrote in October 1876, 'by incessant occupation, not to banish grief – for mine is always at home – but to carry on the work which my dear wife has left for me to accomplish, and to console me in her absence.'[4] His first sermon in the Abbey after the funeral was on Easter Day. He knew it would be a trial but he told the Queen: 'I must begin some time; and I could not have a better day than that which speaks of immortality and hope.'[5]

Stanley determined to finish the third and final volume of his *History of the Jewish Church*, which he had been writing at Augusta's bedside. In a letter to Liddell (in which he had offered ideas for his address at the funeral) Stanley quoted Augusta's urging him to '"work on and go to the very bottom of things, and leave work that shall be imperishable". And in speaking of my forthcoming volume, which I said I

---

[a] Artist and author of the *Book of Nonsense* (1846).

would dedicate to her, and ... would try to make it worthy, she said with emphasis: "make it ... *perfect*."[6] Stanley set about revising and rewriting some of the lectures, aware that Augusta had rebuked him for being satisfied with the superficial. He had dedicated the first volume thirteen years before to his mother: the third, published in September 1876, he dedicated 'to the beloved memory' of his wife, 'the inseparable partner in every joy and every struggle of twelve eventful years'.

Stanley was less active and passionate in Convocation than before but he continued to speak in most sessions, usually to defend the national Church and to promote its comprehensiveness. He continued to contribute articles and obituaries to *The Times*, the *Edinburgh Review*, *Macmillan's Magazine*, and *Fraser's Magazine*. He was still an active member of the committee for the revision of the New Testament. The revisers' work was completed on Stanley's sixty-third birthday, 13 December 1878, and the new text was published in 1881. It was unfavourably received, as Stanley had warned. He had taken a generally conservative approach to the revision, and argued, often in vain, for the retention of understandable archaisms. Objections were indeed raised that the translation contained many irritating and unnecessary alterations to familiar passages.

Family and friends rallied to provide Stanley with necessary practical help and support. Augusta's cousin, Mrs Drummond of Megginch Castle near Perth; her recently widowed sister, the vivacious Lady Frances Baillie; and Stanley's sister, Mary, all took it turns to run the household. 'There are', Stanley used to say, 'two things I cannot do: one is to understand arithmetic, the other is to take care of myself.'[7] The Queen had views on Mary's living at the deanery. She had disapproved of her falling out with Florence Nightingale, and certainly of her conversion to Roman Catholicism. 'And now I come to the last and *most* important subject,' she wrote to Mrs Drummond, 'viz: our dear little Dean ... Of *all* those *now* living, *you* are his greatest earthly comfort. His Sister is *no real comfort* in any way – it is only a *feeling* of duty & affection towards her, wh. makes him speak and act as he does.'[8]

Whoever was with him did her best to maintain Stanley's daily routine. *The Times* was read to him at breakfast, as Augusta had done, so that he was sure to eat his bread and butter and not be distracted by the news. His companion was never far from his library when he was working, in case she was needed to check a reference, or find a quotation or lost sermon, or correct a proof for the printer. Augusta had

9 Portrait of Stanley by Lowes Cato Dickinson

10 The Great Quadrangle (Tom Quad) at Christ Church, with Wren's Tom Tower; Mercury in the foreground

11 Lewis Carroll's photograph of Stanley at Christ Church

12a (left) The Prince of Wales's wedding – with Queen Victoria intent on a bust of Prince Albert   12b (right) Lady Augusta Stanley by George Richmond

12c Some Oxford liberals associated with *Essays and Reviews*: Jowett, Pattison, Temple, Kingsley and Stanley

13a Westminster Abbey and St Margaret's Church, 1753

13b Stanley at his standing-desk in the Deanery

13c The entrance to the Deanery

14 Portrait of Stanley by G. F. Watts, RA, 1866–7

15 Portrait of Stanley by Heinrich von Angeli, showing insignia of the Order of the Bath

16 'Philosophic Belief', *Vanity Fair*, September 1872

shared the library with Stanley and now he placed her bust on the desk next to his where she used to write her letters. 'You must see it as you pass through,' Stanley told Arnold's youngest daughter, Fanny, to whom (after her mother had died) he wrote every year on the anniversary of her father's death. 'The marble face expresses so much more than I could ever have expected; and as I see it by sunshine and shadow, by moonlight and lamplight, it seems to live over again through the changes of this solitary state, and to encourage me to persevere.'[9] Stanley often lunched at the Athenaeum and one of the ladies would walk with him past Horse Guards to Pall Mall. After lunch she might accompany him on his walk or drive or visit to friends, again just as Augusta had done. Stanley's happiest visits were to the Temple Church to see his sister Catherine and his oldest friend, Charles Vaughan, who had been master (incumbent) since 1869. In the evening Stanley worked again, or talked, or read aloud to his companion – Matthew Arnold, Walter Scott and Keble's *Christian Year* were favourites. He hosted occasional dinner parties, but on a smaller scale than before, and only with guests he found congenial.

Stanley still had confidence that travel would provide the interest and energising relief it had in the past, and in September 1876 he set off for a month in Portugal. He thought this would be the best place to start because he had not been there with Augusta. He wrote to Mary Mohl to say that he might return through Paris, though he doubted he could face the prospect of staying again in the rooms he had shared with Augusta. 'I agree with you that there is no place where I am really happy – if happiness it can be called – except in this, her own home, with her presence constantly before me.'[10] Stanley did not enjoy Portugal, which he found a 'marvellously uninteresting country',[11] and the charm of seeing new places seemed to have vanished. He decided to return via Spain, and to visit Cordoba for the first time, and Seville and Granada after thirty years. Spain cheered him but the absence of Augusta was inescapable. On looking at the tomb of Isabella, wife of Ferdinand, the first King of Spain, he wanted instead to stand before Augusta's grave in Henry VII's Chapel. He found the journey empty, and looked forward to picking up 'the chain of associations with *her* at Madame Mohl's'.[12] 'How many remembrances', he told the Queen, 'were stirred as I walked alone up the staircase in the Rue du Bac, which we had left in such agonising anxiety in the November of 1874.'[13]

Stanley tried but could not escape his grief, and need to sense that

Augusta was present. These feelings were intensified as he approached the first wedding anniversary and Christmas without her. On the anniversary, 22 December, he wrote to Mrs Drummond to say that he will 'try to think that the future may be less dreary than it seems to be'.[14] At Christmas he asked to dinner some of what he called his 'poorer neighbours': 'It pleases me, as a continuation of her good work.'[15] Three days after Christmas, Stanley preached at the service on Innocents' Day. It was, he said, 'attended by hundreds of children. I was glad, for it was a service in which my Augusta took the greatest delight.'[16] The following year, 1877, Stanley took comfort in two tangible commemorations. In April the Queen invited him to plant a tree at Osborne in Augusta's memory. A juniper was chosen and Stanley noted with approval that in China and Japan it was regarded as an emblem of everlasting life. And with the Queen's permission, he had commissioned a stained-glass window to be placed above Augusta's grave. It was completed on the day of their anniversary. One section depicted episodes in the life of her famous ancestor, Robert the Bruce, and scenes associated with the lives or deaths of three of her brothers, James, 8th Earl of Elgin; General Robert Bruce, the Prince of Wales's governor; and Sir Frederick Bruce, who had been the British envoy in Washington. The rest of the window represented the 'six acts of mercy so suitable to her – tending the hungry, the thirsty, the poor, the sick, the stranger, the oppressed'.[17] Stanley wrote to the Queen on Christmas Day to say that 'there is now nothing further to be done in that sweet spot, which Your Majesty has given to her, till I join her.'[18]

In March 1877 Stanley returned to St Andrews to deliver his second rectorial address.[19] Despite his title, 'The Hopes of Theology', he struck a very different and jaded note. He admitted as much to the Queen, describing it as 'less inspiring'[20] than his inaugural lecture. Whether this was due to his bereavement or his disenchantment with the Church of the time, is difficult to tell, and indeed the former may well have aggravated the latter. 'The face of Providence', he told Max Müller, 'seems set against a reasonable progress of Christianity.'[21] Stanley's disappointment had been growing during the last ten years or so, and it was focused on the Churches' stubborn refusal to move away from their narrow, dogmatic enmities towards what Stanley called in his address 'the catholic, comprehensive, discriminating, all-embracing Christianity',[22] which he had spent most of his life championing and defending. Stanley had once hoped that the theological changes in his own century promised a new Reformation,[b] but he realised now that 'the day, the year, may perchance belong to the destructives, the cynics, and the partisans'. It has to be to the future, he concluded, 'the times that are yet to be',[23] that those who shared his enlightened vision must look.

* * *

Stanley was taken ill in January 1878, found it hard to recover, and spent three weeks in March convalescing in Torquay. He was wearing himself out with his incessant occupation, and was already looking old and frail. Nonetheless, by the summer he felt well enough to try the tonic of travel again, and decided, not without some misgivings, to accept an invitation to visit the east coast of America and Canada. Augusta had wanted to visit her brother Frederick, but his death in 1867 had set the plan aside. Stanley wrote to the Queen at the end of August:

> My dear Augusta had often wished that we should accomplish the voyage to America, and I feel that the change of scene would be better for me than anything else. It is a long journey; but I enjoy the sea, and I have often felt that I could never quite understand Europe till I had seen America. My old and tried friend, Mr. George Grove,[c] goes with me, and also a young medical man, Mr. Gerald Harper, a friend of my sister, Mrs. Vaughan, who is much in favour of my going.[24]

Two weeks before, Jowett had advised against the visit: '1. Because it is a loss of time, and at our age we cannot afford to lose time: 2. Because it is a great risk to health: 3. Because you will learn nothing useful from it & will, I believe, derive no pleasure from it, for you have little sympathy with the Americans: 4. Because you can hardly avoid being lionised & if it were possible, vulgarised: 5. Because all your friends seem to be opposed to it.'[25] But Stanley was not to be dissuaded, and left Liverpool on 6 September on board the steamship *Siberia*.

The voyage took ten days. Stanley spent the time reading books on American history and the novels of Nathaniel Hawthorne and James

---

[b] See Stanley's essay on 'Theology of the Nineteenth Century' (*Fraser's Magazine*, February 1865, and *Essays on Church and State*). Stanley points to German influences as the main impulse for theological change which is 'hardly less universal and important than that involved in the Reformation itself'.

[c] Musicologist and editor of *Macmillan's Magazine* which is how Stanley knew him. He was one of Stanley's literary executors, and Stanley wanted him to write his biography.

Fenimore Cooper. One of the fifty passengers was the Bishop of Western New York, whom Stanley found 'full of information and very agreeable'.[26] 'I can now', he wrote to Mary, 'repeat the names of all the Presidents, and explain the meaning of Democrat and Republican.'[27] Stanley started by missing Augusta, and wishing she were there, but by the time Boston harbour was in sight, he found himself distracted by the same enthusiasm and excitement he had invariably experienced when seeing places for the first time. Those feelings were strengthened throughout the visit which lasted seven weeks. The warmth of his reception, the vibrancy of his hosts, and the freedom and openness of the young Churches revived Stanley's hopes for the future. He was busy from start to finish, sightseeing but mostly attending meetings, services and receptions, at which he usually spoke or preached. He already had a reputation in America as Arnold's biographer and the author of *Sinai and Palestine*. His position as Dean of Westminster, and his personal associations with the royal family, gave him prestige, especially among Episcopalians. Furthermore, he was regarded (as his obituary in *The New York Times* put it) as 'a leader of the Broad Church Party. He may fairly be regarded to have been the head of the latitudinarian element in the Church of England.'[28] Wherever he went, people wanted to meet him and hear him speak. Some of his engagements had been planned in advance, but many came from spontaneous invitations which Stanley gladly accepted when he could, and at which he spoke almost unprepared.

Three days after his arrival, Stanley gave a speech at a luncheon in Salem to mark the 250th anniversary of the landing of John Endecott, the first governor of the colony at Massachusetts Bay. He was surrounded by guests and speakers who were descendants of the earliest settlers. 'It was as if one were sitting at table far back in the opening of European or English history, with the grandsons or great-grandsons of Hengist and Horsa, or of Clovis and Pepin.'[29] Stanley replied to the toast of 'our old homes', and described 'the pleasure which an Englishman feels when, after long waiting and long desiring, he visits for the first time the shores of this new home of his old race'.[30] Stanley told the Queen that his speech had been well received, and that he had been 'much struck by the fact that there was no topic of conversation about which people here are so eager as details of the life of Your Majesty and the Royal Family'.[31]

The Reverend Phillips Brooks was present and had arrived from New York. He was rector of Trinity, the main Episcopal church in

Boston, and was famous as a preacher and author of the popular carol, 'O Little Town of Bethlehem'. He and Stanley became friends, though they made an odd sight together since Brooks was almost a foot taller than Stanley. Stanley preached for him three days later before a large congregation. 'No one who heard it', enthused Brooks, 'will ever forget the benediction which Dean Stanley uttered at the close of the service ... He was for the moment the representative of English Christianity. And as he spoke the solemn words, it was not a clergyman dismissing a congregation, it was the Old World blessing the New; it was England blessing America.'[32]

The following day, 23 September, Stanley gave a brief address to a group of clergy at a breakfast in Boston hosted by Brooks. His subject was 'The Prospects of Liberal Theology', and though he begins by saying that 'it is not altogether a view of unmixed rejoicing',[33] the address was noticeably more positive and confident than that at St Andrews on much the same subject. Stanley defined liberal theology as 'a theology which, whilst comprehending all the wholesome elements of thought at work in the world, yet holds that the Christian belief is large enough to contain them; which insists not on the ceremonial, the dogmatic, or the portentous, but on the moral side of religion; which insists on the spirit, not on the letter – on the meaning, not on the words – on the progressive, not on the stationary character of Christianity'.[34] After describing the progress of 1. Biblical criticism, 2. a liberal appreciation of the national Church, 3. doctrinal understanding, and 4. the relations of theology to literature, Stanley concluded with a rallying call: 'I am persuaded that what is called Liberal Theology is the backbone of the Church of England, and will be found to be the backbone of its daughter Church in America. The fact that a large proportion of the world and the Church is against us ought not to alter our conviction that, in the main, we are right. We must still hold by our colours.'[35]

En route from Newport to Philadelphia Stanley spent just three hours in New York to meet the American Bible revisers. In Philadelphia he stayed in 'a white marble palace with blue-satin rooms, our host and hostess letting us do whatever we wished, asking everyone to meet us that they thought we should like to meet, or that they thought would like to see us'.[36] He preached at Michaelmas, 29 September, at St James's church. In his sermon Stanley mentioned 'the most majestic divine of the English Church, Richard Hooker'[37] and his meditations on the number and nature of angels. The newspaper reporters, however, 'expressed a particular wish to have precisely the passage in which I had referred to Joe Hooker, one of the generals in the war of 1862'.[38] On the same Sunday, Stanley attended a negro Methodist meeting-house, and a very different service it was from matins at Westminster Abbey. 'The preacher was a mulatto, not wholly illiterate, but with a rant and raving beyond anything I have ever heard, to which from time to time the negroes responded by loud shouts ... At every expression of sulphurous torments the old negroes absolutely screamed for joy. It was, I must say, a most hideous exhibition.'[39]

The next day Stanley was in Baltimore to address the students of the Johns Hopkins University, and from there he travelled to Washington. He found the capital 'rough and unfinished, yet with all the appearance of an imperial city'.[40] On Sunday 6 October Stanley was back in New York to preach on 'The Perplexities of Life' at Calvary church. Sightseeing filled every moment between engagements, including, a week later, the Niagara Falls, which Stanley thought 'the climax of our tour'.[41] He painted for Mary a vivid picture of the 'barrier of rock and earth saturated like a sponge, with springs and streams bursting forth in every direction. But on what a scale!'[42]

From Niagara Stanley journeyed to Montreal to meet the Governor-General, who accompanied him to Quebec where he preached in the cathedral. Then to Ticonderoga, Saratoga, Concord and Stockbridge, before spending a week in New York before returning home:

> On Wednesday, October 29th, a reception of the Baptists. On Friday, a sermon at All Saints, the Mother-Church of New York, in the morning, and a reception of the Methodists in the evening. On Saturday, a reception at the Century Club, with speeches, and another at a small club in the afternoon. On Sunday, a sermon at Grace Church, the fashionable church, in the morning, and at Holy Trinity – popular and Low Church – in the evening. On Monday, a reception of the Baptists, and then a reception and a breakfast of the clergy, with speeches; in the afternoon, the autumn reception at the American Museum; in the evening a large party at the Fields'. On Tuesday, a visit to the Episcopal College, and to the fair in the Roman Catholic Cathedral, and an immense reception at the Fields' in the evening. On Wednesday, a visit to the schools, and our embarkation on the *Bothnia* at 2 P.M.[43]

'So the splendid dream is over!', Stanley told Mrs Drummond, 'not one single day that did not teem with interest.'[44] *The New York Times* described the departure, and Stanley on the quarter-deck waving goodbye to friends, wearing a shabby cloak, a broad-brimmed felt hat (even more shabby than his cloak), and a black shawl wound about his neck.[45]

There had been moments of exhaustion during the tour, but the vitality and generosity of Stanley's American hosts had revived and cheered him, and he returned to England invigorated, and over at least the first, traumatic phase of mourning. What was left was the lingering pain of loneliness revealed in a poem, 'Absence and Presence', that Stanley wrote soon after his return:

> I feel her absence, as I move
>   Stumbling in ways untried, unknown,
> Without the word of warning love
>   To guide my path, uncertain and alone.[46]

There was a demand from America for the publication of Stanley's sermons and addresses and he set to work to revise scripts and write up notes. The volume was published in 1879 and then in England by Macmillan in 1883.[d] Bradley thought it contained 'almost everything characteristic of the man, and some gems of a kind not to be found in his earlier writing'.[47]

The book certainly includes in summary the main themes of Stanley's theology. First, there is the emphasis on morality not doctrine which he had learned not least from Arnold. What mattered to Stanley was the Bible, and especially the teaching and example of Christ, and not later metaphysical dogmas. Precise formulations of the person of Christ or the Trinity were of little interest or worth to him, except as history. He had something of the quality the poet Keats called '*Negative Capability*, that is, when a man is capable of being in uncertainties, mysteries, doubts, without any irritable reaching after fact and reason'.[48] To Stanley, doctrines were divisive distractions from the true mission of the Church, which is to inspire and enable the world to follow Christ. 'Religious doctrine,' he told the congregation of Holy Trinity, New York, 'religious ordinances, are of no value unless they produce in our lives justice, integrity, honesty, purity, gentleness, modesty.'[49] In another address in New York, at St Paul's Methodist Church, Stanley described the principle of John Wesley's life as 'not the promotion of any particular dogma or any particular doctrine, but the elevation of the whole Christian world in the great principles of Christian

---

[d] *Addresses and Sermons delivered during a visit to the United States and Canada in 1878.*

holiness and morality'. 'Let us keep to this,' urges Stanley, 'leaving a thousand disputable points to those that have no better business than to toss the ball of controversy to and fro.'[50]

The second theme, tolerance, follows from the first. Doctrinal differences are not themselves of great importance. 'It is astonishing how vast a loss we sustain in our spiritual life by thinking only how we can destroy, attack and assail, instead of thinking how we can build up, define, or edify.'[51] Disputes and disagreements strangle spiritual growth. What matters to Stanley are the simplest elements of Christianity, with which all Christians, and even unbelievers, can agree, and here again he emphasises moral truths. And third, Stanley's goodwill towards all Christian denominations does not in the least diminish his loyalty to the Church of England. In his American addresses he extols the history and features the Episcopalians share with their mother Church. He refers to 'the glow of historical and national life'[52] of the Church of England, exemplified in Westminster Abbey. He praises Anglicanism's 'large and comprehensive associations', its 'union of secular and religious influences', and its 'diversity of gifts'.[53] Being a national, comprehensive Church makes it more wholesome than a narrow religious sect, and furthermore, allows it the confidence to be open to the secular world, and to new ideas and modes of inquiry.

* * *

Stanley returned to his decanal duties with new energy and, with Mary's help, he set to work to edit his mother's letters and journals. This was to be published with a revised edition of his memoir of his father (1851).[e] Stanley also included a brief tribute to his brother Owen. In his preface, Stanley refers to Sydney Smith's description of Kitty's 'porcelain understanding', and explains that 'it is in this "porcelain" delicacy of intelligence that the main interest of these extracts consists'.[54] They were written from the time of Kitty's marriage to the end of her life, and reveal many of the same occupations, opinions and characteristics of her favourite son: wide reading and intellectual interests; liberal theology and Whiggish politics; sympathy, gentleness and tolerance. But also evident is a practical worldliness and personal insight lacking in Stanley.

The memoirs were published in 1879, at the same time as a comparable volume edited at the request of the Archbishop of Canterbury.[f]

---

[e] *Memoirs of Edward and Catherine Stanley*.
[f] *Catherine and Crauford Tait: A Memoir*, ed. W. M. Benham.

This commemorated Tait's only son, Crauford, who had died aged twenty-nine in May 1878, and Tait's wife Catherine, who never recovered from her grief, and died six months later. Twenty-three years before, five of the Taits' six daughters had died of scarlet fever. The memoirs include their mother's moving account of their deaths, and of the parents' heroic faith and courage. Crauford became their idol, and everything he did – Eton, Christ Church, ordination, his father's domestic chaplain[g] – filled them with doting pride. His memoir is a cloying panegyric, and a contrast to Stanley's memoirs, as he explained in a letter to the Queen:

> I venture to send to Your Majesty a book something of the same kind, yet very different ... It is the very opposite to the Archbishop's book, for there is in it hardly anything personal. I had not the nerve, even if I had wished it, to go into details, and the same feeling still further withheld me from adding anything of my dear Augusta ...[55]

Depression and fatigue returned in the summer of 1879 when Stanley's secretary, Henry Montgomery, moved to what was then a suburban parish. Montgomery had been at Harrow after Vaughan, though Vaughan had prepared him later for ordination. He was appointed curate of St Margaret's, Westminster in 1876, and became a friend of the rector, Frederick William Farrar,[h] and married his daughter. Farrar and Montgomery shared Stanley's Broad Church views, and Montgomery became Stanley's confidant and efficient organiser of his affairs. 'I am staggering', Stanley informed Mrs Drummond in July, 'under the dreadful blow of Montgomery feeling himself constrained to accept the living of Kennington. I hardly knew before how indispensable he was to me.'[56] Montgomery recorded that Stanley had told him he felt like Abraham. 'I said, "Why?" He looked up at me, and took my hand, and burst into tears, saying, "My only son! My dearly beloved son!" and could not go on.'[57]

---

[g] He was succeeded as Tait's chaplain by his friend Randall Davidson who married Tait's daughter Edith in November 1878, and became Archbishop of Canterbury in 1903.
[h] Farrar taught at Marlborough under the Arnoldian George Cotton, and at Harrow under Vaughan. He wrote the moralising school story, *Eric, or, Little by Little* (1858). He was appointed Master of Marlborough in 1871, Canon of Westminster and Rector of St Margaret's in 1876, and Dean of Canterbury in 1879. Montgomery was consecrated Bishop of Tasmania in 1889; one of his sons was the future field marshal, Viscount Montgomery of Alamein.

Stanley told Mary that he felt as he had before he went to America: 'all my forces and powers are shattered and withered.'[58] In August he went to visit the Vaughans at Llandaff where Charles had been installed as dean. Dr Symonds, who had threatened to reveal the Harrow scandal if Vaughan accepted advancement in the Church, had died in 1871. After that, Llandaff Cathedral was the best, if not the only, preferment he was offered. Stanley enjoyed his stay, even describing Llandaff as 'Paradise'.[59] He travelled north to stay with the Drummonds at Megginch Castle and there again he found 'perfect rest and repose'.[60] From Scotland he made his way to Switzerland to join Mary. They travelled by train from Lucerne to Venice, a journey Stanley had made first with his sister Catherine, then with his mother, and last with Augusta. 'Now I feel that this is for the last time, and that I shall in all probability never again set eyes on those first scenes of my travels.'[61]

Mary found the travelling exhausting, and like her brother, seemed much older than she was (sixty-six). After the Crimea she had worked relentlessly for various philanthropic enterprises: supporting soldiers' wives and widows, organising a scheme for parish nursing and helping various sisterhoods. She received very little recognition and Stanley thought this 'cast something of shade over her life'.[62] On 24 November she collapsed at home in Grosvenor Crescent. Stanley hurried to her bedside, but she remained unconscious and died two days later. It was another serious blow. Stanley and Mary had been close from childhood, and he had remained loyal to her when her secession to Rome caused a rift with the family. 'I knew', he wrote, 'that this would be the next great shock. How, at such a separation, all "the things which are temporal" – all the frets and fumes and fears vanish away, and "the things which are eternal" – her surpassing love, her strong, almost excessive passion for justice, her widespread affection and sympathy, envelop the whole horizon.'[63] Mary's coffin was buried above her mother's in the churchyard at Alderley, and under the same unusual gravestone, a white marble cross fixed to a sandstone boulder. The inscription from Galatians reads: 'NEVER WEARY IN WELL DOING'.

'The fourth great calamity of my life is past,' Stanley told Mrs Drummond:[64] the first three were, of course, the deaths of Arnold, his mother and Augusta. Mary's left Stanley depressed and dispirited, and he was unwell again in the following spring. 'His frail figure shrank, his hair grew more white and silvery, his voice became enfeebled.'[65] In October he visited Oxford, but this time it filled him with sad thoughts and left him 'feeling a total estrangement from the world moving there – forgetting and forgotten'.⁶⁶ Stanley felt much the same when he returned to Rugby for an old boys' dinner in June 1881: 'I shall never go again ... I feel that I am losing interest in these special and youthful gatherings.'⁶⁷ 'Everything I do', he wrote, 'is sure to fail. The public have ceased to read or listen to anything I can tell them.'⁶⁸ Though only sixty-five, Stanley became acutely conscious of his own mortality, assuming that he was visiting places for the last time, and adding 'if I am alive' to any discussion of future plans.

After a visit to the Channel Islands with Gerald Harper and his sister Catherine in April 1880, Stanley returned to Westminster to face a storm of protest against a proposed monument to the Prince Imperial. Prince Napoleon, the twenty-three-year-old only son of Emperor Napoleon III of France, had been killed in action in southern Africa in June 1879 while fighting for the British in the Zulu War. Stanley had received a request to erect a monument in Henry VII's Chapel and had been pleased to consent, subject to approval of the Queen. He thought the appropriate place for the recumbent effigy was the chantry chapel at the south-east end which corresponded to the chapel where the Duc de Montpensier, and Augusta, were buried. Montpensier was the brother of the Bourbon King Louis Philippe, and had died while in exile in England: Prince Napoleon belonged to a rival dynasty, but he too had been exiled and had found refuge in England. Stanley was mindful too that Elizabeth I and her rival half-sister, Mary Tudor, were buried together in the same royal chapel.

At first the plan for the monument proceeded without difficulty. The Queen gave permission, though with some reluctance. But in the spring of 1880 smouldering opposition caught fire, fanned by the general election.ⁱ The protest was based partly on ignorance of the details, but mostly on a reaction against costly imperialist wars, and disapproval of the great-nephew of Napoleon Bonaparte being commemorated in the nation's mausoleum. It was rumoured that the effigy was to be placed over the grave of Oliver Cromwell, and that the French republic was insulted. Stanley started to receive deputations, petitions and even threatening letters. On 16 July the House of Commons voted against the memorial as inconsistent with the national character of the Abbey. Stanley was ready to withdraw his consent when the matter was taken out of his hands by the Napoleon

---

ⁱ The Midlothian Campaign had seen a series of passionate speeches by Gladstone, condemning the foreign and imperial policy of Disraeli's Government.

Memorial Committee. The chairman wrote to him five days after the vote to say that the committee had unanimously resolved to drop the proposal. Stanley replied by return:

> There are few acts of my official life at Westminster on which I look back with more satisfaction than the acceptance of the offer of the monument to the Prince Imperial.
>
> It was the response to a feeling of universal sympathy which at the time I believed to be permanent, and which I still believe to be genuine.
>
> It was in entire conformity with the best traditions of the Abbey, in the commemoration of an event most tragical, and, considering all the circumstances of the case, most historical. It expressed the sense of national reparation due for a single misfortune.[69]

Stanley had stuck fast to his conviction that the memorial was appropriate, and had done so in the face of unwarranted abuse, and with little support from the committee. He was personally disappointed that the brave death of the last of the Bonapartes was no longer to be commemorated. At least, he consoled himself, it 'show(ed) how deeply the English people love their Abbey'.[70]

August was spent again with the Vaughans in Wales and the Drummonds in Scotland, followed by three days on the Isle of Man where he had been asked to preach in Douglas. Stanley went then with Montgomery and Harper to Paris, where he reminisced about the decisive events he had witnessed there. From Paris the three travelled south to Chartres, Orleans, Tours and Blois, and then on to Biarritz. 'I shall end my travelling', he told Mrs Drummond, 'where I began it – with the Pyrenees.'[71]

*   *   *

Before his holiday Stanley had received an intriguing letter from Jowett, urging him to make the most of the rest of his life which, he seemed to infer, had so far been wasted. Jowett had been ambiguous about Stanley's marrying, though he admired Augusta and understood Stanley's need to replace his mother. (Jowett had decided fifteen years before that the only marriage he wanted was to Balliol.)[72] He had been outspoken, however, in his disapproval of Stanley's leaving Oxford and academia for Westminster, where he was certain his talents would be squandered. As Jowett observed Stanley's ministry to the Abbey and the

Court, he became convinced that his misgivings had been right. Jowett's letter is worth quoting in full:

> My dear Arthur, – I hardly like to offer you advice, because it is intrusive, and because it is so difficult for one friend to judge of another's character or circumstances. And please not to suppose that in giving it I think myself your superior in any way; the reverse is the truth.
>
> It always seemed to me that the last ten years of life are the most important of all (and for myself I build my hopes entirely on what I can do in them). I sometimes fear that you are allowing yourself to be crushed by personal misfortunes – some very real, like the loss of dear Lady Augusta which I shall never cease to lament, but others partly fanciful, like this matter of the Prince Imperial, which really does not affect you in any important manner. Will you not shake this off and fix your mind exclusively on high things? I really believe that this 'expulsive power' is necessary for your happiness. I am certain that your talents are as good as ever and your experience far greater. I am not flattering you when I say that you are the most distinguished clergyman in the Church of England, and could do more than any one towards the great work of placing religion on a rational basis. If you can accomplish this task you may effect more good and have a much more enduring fame than any Bishop or Archbishop of the English Church.
>
> What you have done has been good and valuable; but like other theological writings it has been transient, suited to our generation more than to another. But *this* work should be of a deeper kind – the last result of many theological thoughts and experiences, into which your whole soul and life might be thrown, all the better because the truths of which you speak had been realised by suffering.
>
> It may be objected that such a book could not be written by a person holding a leading position in the Church. But if it were, it would win the battle of freedom for other clergymen, and to fight such a battle would be a great interest and a legacy to leave to the Church if gained. Few things will rouse the laity; but that certainly would.
>
> Such a labour would require you to withdraw a good deal from society, from Convocation, and from Church agitation of other

sorts. But there would be nothing lost in this; you have gained all that you can possibly gain from society, and as for Convocation, your friends regret your going to a place where they are rude to you. And, whereas they do you harm, you can do these bigots no good, to say nothing of the whole affair being a great sham. You would return to the studies of your youth, the great religion of the world, the early Christian Church, its Gospels, the good in everything which is a mere vacant and unmeaning word, but may be made a power in the world. You would live among the thoughts which a wise and good man would wish to have familiarly haunting him during his last years. And you would be able to say after all, 'It is finished.'

Will you reflect upon the whole matter? Forty years ago we all expected you to be the most distinguished man among us, and you must not disappoint us. I would like you to plan out a course of study and writing, and to place yourself in circumstances in which you can carry it out, and allow nothing to interrupt it. The more you come to Oxford for the search of quiet reading, the more I shall be the gainer. You shall talk to us about the work or *not*, as you think best. You and I, and our dear friend Hugh Pearson, and Rogers,[j] and some others are rather isolated in the world, and we must hold together as long as we can.

Farewell; I shall not intrude upon you again in this way, but
    Believe me, ever your affectionate
                      B. JOWETT.[73]

Emphasising the supreme importance of rigorous academic work is typical of Jowett, who had devoted much of his own working life to translating and commenting on the works of Plato. The painful experience of *Essays and Reviews* had persuaded him to abandon theology, and his disappointment that Stanley had also failed to become a dedicated theologian suggests perhaps a sense of guilt on Jowett's part. There is also something here of the same frustration he had felt towards Tait and Temple, and the theological caution both men displayed after accepting high office in the Church. Jowett had decided that 'really great men are never Clergymen'.[74] Stanley's reply (if indeed there was one) has not survived. But it can be confidently assumed that he would have resented the letter's patronising tone, and its advice. First, Jowett

---

[j] The Revd William Rogers, rector of St Botolph's, Bishopsgate.

is unsympathetic to the fatigue and depression Stanley felt, and the painful reasons why; second, Jowett is unappreciative of over sixteen years of hard and often trying work for the Abbey and the Church; and third, Stanley would have recoiled, as he had in the past, from Jowett's schoolmasterly directives as to exactly what to do.

There was to be no great theological book of the kind Jowett demanded. Indeed there never had been because Stanley had neither the talent nor the inclination. He was an historian and ecclesiologist, not a theologian, and his cast of mind was not metaphysical, but imaginative and practical. There was, however, to be one more, final book. Stanley had started working on it at the end of 1879 and it was published in March 1881. It is a collection of his essays on ecclesiastical subjects with the title *Christian Institutions*. Subjects include baptism, the eucharist, vestments, the clergy, the creeds, the Lord's Prayer and the Ten Commandments. Stanley deploys his expert and detailed historical approach, and by tracing the origins of his subjects, he aims to distinguish between what was intended and what has been passed down, with all the accumulated accretions and distortions of a long tradition. In his preface Stanley criticises the 'reluctance to look the facts of history in the face', which, he says, 'has favoured the growth of a vast superstructure of fable'.[75] By identifying what they still held in common with the early catholic and apostolic Church, Stanley aims to show contemporary Christian denominations that what divides them is at best of only secondary significance. Take baptism, for example. Infant baptism may have largely superseded adult baptism, and the ceremony may no longer be conducted only by the bishop, but what remains from the beginning is the idea of passing from darkness to light, from uncleanness to purity, from evil to good, and it is this, argues Stanley, that baptism typifies. For Stanley (as for Arnold) it is moral and spiritual significance which matters, and not outward forms and expressions, whose sometimes mysterious nature Stanley regards as largely superstition (Arnold called it 'priestcraft'). In summary, 'The "Essays on Christian Institutions" urged the necessity of discriminating between things essential and things secondary, and of distinguishing the letter from the spirit; they showed the religious significance of many of the combats which have distracted, and still distract, the minds of religious men; they establish the groundlessness of many of the fears and forebodings by which they are agitated.'[76]

Stanley knew that this was his last book. The final essay on 'The Ten Commandments' closes with a section on the eleventh commandment, based on the sermon Stanley gave in 1872 at Old Greyfriars' in Edinburgh.[k] This section, and the book, close with a new page in praise of love. With echoes of Paul's great hymn in I Corinthians 13, it eloquently describes what Stanley held most dear, and had spent his life doing and preaching. It amounts to Stanley's last will and testament:

> Love one another in spite of differences, in spite of faults, in spite of the excesses of one or the defects of another. Love one another, and make the best of one another, as He loved us, who, for the sake of saving what was good in the human soul, forgot, forgave, put out of sight what was bad – who saw and loved what was good ... Make the most of what there is good in institutions, in opinions, in communities, in individuals. It is very easy to do the reverse, to make the worst of what there is of evil ... By so doing we shall have no difficulty in making estrangements more wide, and hatreds and strifes more abundant, and errors more extreme ... But this was not the new love wherewith we are to love one another. That love is universal, because in its spirit we overcome evil simply by doing good. We drive out error simply by telling the truth. We strive to look on both sides of the shield of truth ... And, in proportion as we endeavour to do this, there may be a hope that men will see that there are, after all, some true disciples of Christ left in the world, 'because they have love one to another'.[77]

*   *   *

In the first four months of 1881, Stanley preached obituary sermons on two national figures, Thomas Carlyle and Benjamin Disraeli. Carlyle died on Saturday 5 February, aged eighty-five. Stanley went immediately to his home in Chelsea to persuade his niece that her uncle should be buried in the company of other great men of letters. She refused, knowing that Carlyle would not have approved, and had in any case left instructions that his body was to be interred at Ecclefechan in Scotland, where he had been born. Stanley gave his sermon the following morning. He recalled an occasion during the Crimean War when he had encountered Carlyle in St James's Park, and walked with him to his home in Cheyne Row. Stanley asked him what he thought was the duty of a canon of Canterbury. 'Whatsoever thy hand findeth to do,' he replied, 'do it with all thy might.'[78] Stanley compared him to Socrates,

---

[k] See pp. 283–4.

St Paul, Luther and John Wesley: like them, he said, Carlyle was 'one of the gifted few' who had been ' a new light in the world'.[79] Carlyle was a prophet, and 'a prophet most of all in the emphatic utterance of truths no-one else, or hardly anyone else, ventured to deliver, and which he felt to be a message of good to a world sorely in need of them'.[80]

Disraeli died ten weeks later on 19 April. As soon as the news reached Hawarden, Gladstone telegraphed the executors to offer a State funeral, and the same morning Stanley went to Disraeli's London house in Curzon Street to offer the Abbey. But again directions had been left in the will for a simple funeral, at Hughenden, followed by burial beside his wife in their vault in the churchyard. The Queen sent two wreaths, one of fresh primroses, which she claimed were Disraeli's favourite flowers.[1] The last letter Stanley received from the Queen was written two days after Disraeli's death:

> Thank you very much for your sympathy in the loss of my dear, great friend, whose death on Tuesday last completely overwhelmed me.
>
> His devotion and kindness to me, his wise counsels, his great gentleness combined with firmness, his *one* thought of the honour and glory of the country, and his unswerving loyalty to the Throne, make the death of my dear Lord Beaconsfield a national calamity. My grief is great and lasting.[81]

In his sermon on 1 May Stanley spoke of 'the extraordinary career which led the alien in race, the despised in debate, the romantic adventurer, the fierce assailant, the eccentric in demeanour ... to reach the highest summits of fame and splendour'.[82]

Since June 1880 the Abbey had faced grave fabric and finance problems which added considerably to the strain on Stanley, who was already exhausted. To what extent Stanley's indifference and incompetence in such matters had contributed to the crisis is difficult to tell: they certainly did not help.

In 1849 Edward Blore had been replaced by George Gilbert Scott as the Abbey's Surveyor of the Fabric. For the next thirty years, Scott was occupied with the seriously decayed condition of the exterior stonework. 'It was like trying to maintain a crumbling sea wall; before the gap was fully plugged the water began to come through somewhere

---

[1] When Disraeli was dying he declined a visit from the Queen: 'No, it is better not. She'd only ask me to take a message to Albert.'

else at an astonishingly alarming rate.'[83] The result was that, for all Scott's efforts, much of the essential work had not been done. Scott died in March 1878 and his son, J. Oldrid Scott, took over his work, though he was not the surveyor. J. L. Pearson was appointed in July 1879 and set to work to survey the entire building. A year later he submitted his report, with an estimate for the cost of immediate external repairs and restorations of £49,000, or over £3,500,000 today.

The dean and chapter were faced, not just with a severe problem with the building, but also with how to pay it. Parliament was no longer willing, as in previous centuries, to grant public money to the Abbey, and as a result of various cathedrals and ecclesiastical commissioners acts, the chapter had commuted most of the resources with which they might once have been able to finance the restoration. The problem had been long in the making but had not been addressed. Ten years before, in March 1870, John Thynne, the sub-dean, had warned of financial difficulties ahead.[84] The great agricultural depression which followed meant that tenants of the farms the chapter still held were unable to pay their rents in full. In March 1880 the treasurer reported that the chapter's credit balance had fallen to little more than £1,000, and their tenants were in arrears of almost £3,000. A year later, the balance had sunk to £358, and the arrears were now over £3,000.

Thynne died in February 1881 aged eighty-three, and after fifty years as sub-dean. As senior canon he had lived for most of his tenure in Ashburnham House, and had spent considerable amounts of his own money on repairs and alterations. The house was one of the finest in London, and contained part of the oldest structure connected with the Abbey. Its garden adjoined the Abbey's south cloister and was on the site of the ancient refectory which the dean and chapter intended one day to restore. However, the 1868 Public Schools Act insisted that three capitular houses should be transferred to Westminster School as and when each became vacant. This was the first do so, but was the last house the dean and chapter wanted to lose. In difficult negotiations they tried to bargain with the governing body of the school by offering alternatives, but without success, causing bitter feelings between the Abbey and its neighbour. This Stanley took to heart, and it may even have hastened his death.

* * *

In June and July 1881, Stanley introduced services on Saturday afternoons with short, simple sermons on the beatitudes in the Sermon on the Mount. These were designed again to attract people who might not otherwise attend the Abbey. Stanley's aim in the sermons was to select one or two illustrious persons commemorated in the Abbey to illustrate each of the beatitudes, and so to give 'a glimpse of what is meant by the "pure in heart," by the "merciful," by the "poor in spirit," by the "peacemakers" ...'[85] The examples chosen included Edward the Confessor, Henry V, Sir Isaac Newton, John Milton, William Wordsworth and Charles Dickens. The fourth sermon was to be preached on 9 July, at the end of a scorching hot week. In the morning Stanley drove with Frances Baillie to the Athenaeum and walked home alone. He lunched with another sister-in-law, Charlotte, who was married to the poet Frederick Locker. After lunch, as Stanley was preparing to leave the deanery for the service, Frances noticed that his hand was shaking violently. He left the room and Frances followed him to the library, where he was walking up and down, his face drawn and pale, and his hands cold as ice. She sent for Stanley's doctor and friend, Gerald Harper, and tried to dissuade Stanley from going to the Abbey. He resisted, but returned ten minutes later feeling faint and sick. He revived, returned to the Abbey, and managed to preach his last sermon on 'Blessed are the pure in heart, for they shall see God'. Purity of heart was perhaps the virtue which most distinguished Stanley's own character. 'The words', he explained, 'may bear a two-fold meaning – pure, disinterested love of truth, and pure and clean aversion to everything that defiles.'[86]

On returning to the deanery Stanley went straight to bed and slept most of the next day. He rallied on Wednesday and managed to correct the proofs of an article for *Macmillan's Magazine*.[m] He also wrote a preface for the twelfth edition of his *Life of Arnold*. His temperature rose again in the afternoon and Harper ordered him back to bed. The condition deteriorated on Thursday, and the Queen's physician, Sir William Jenner, was called. The next day Jenner diagnosed erysipelas, a skin infection known as Saint Anthony's Fire, which causes a bright red, burning rash, mainly on the face.[n] In Stanley's case the inflammation spread rapidly, extending down the neck to the chest and right shoulder. On Sunday, 17 July, Hugh Pearson was sent for, and Archbishop Tait was asked to tell Stanley how serious matters were. Again he rallied and Tait left without seeing him. By dawn the next day

---

[m] 'The Westminster Confession of Faith', *Macmillan's Magazine*, August 1881, xliv.
[n] The rash is usually preceded by symptoms of fever, fatigue and vomiting, as in Stanley's case. Erysipelas is caused by streptococcus bacteria and would be treated today with antibiotics.

Stanley was worse again. Tait himself was not well enough to be summoned so early, and Pearson had missed the last train from Sonning. Canon Farrar was sent for to read prayers, and Stanley's sister repeated his favourite hymns.

The disease had attacked Stanley's throat and he now found it almost impossible to speak. Nonetheless, he made himself heard. 'I always wished', he said, 'to die at Westminster. The end has come in the way that I most desired that it should come. I could not have controlled things better.'[87] He expressed his hope that Vaughan would preach his funeral sermon: 'I have been so very intimate with him. He has known me longest.'[88] He then asked to send a message to the Queen: 'As far as I understood what the duties of my office were supposed to be, in spite of every incompetence, I am yet humbly trustful that I have sustained before the mind of the nation the extraordinary value of the Abbey as a religious, national, and liberal institution.'[89]

According to Harper's account, Stanley's last hours had all the quiet, ordered, selfless drama of a classic Victorian death. He sent an affectionate message to his friends the Drummonds. He asked to see his housekeeper, Mrs Waters, his butler and housemaid, and to each he spoke a few appropriate words of farewell. Farrar administered the sacrament to the dying man and to those gathered around his bed. At the end Stanley interrupted him and summoned what strength he had to give the final blessing. There was a slight improvement later in the morning but by noon he was exhausted, and gradually lapsed into unconsciousness. The Queen's assistant private secretary° was sent from Windsor to inquire as to the state of the dean. Pearson had arrived by now, and during the evening he and Grove sat at Stanley's bedside, joined later by Vaughan and then Tait, who could only stay for a while. Stanley's face had been covered by the doctors, and Jenner advised Pearson not to see him. 'He was quite unrecognisable,' wrote Pearson, 'and he said the sight would haunt me.'[90] By eleven Stanley's breathing was becoming increasingly laboured, until at twenty to twelve on the night of Monday 18 July, it ceased altogether.

The suddenness of Stanley's death came as a painful shock to those who were close to him. 'The light has gone out of my life,' wrote Pearson in the same letter. Liddell told his wife that 'out of my own dear family no death could so rend my heart ... I cannot bear to think that I

° Captain Arthur Bigge had served with the Prince Imperial in the Zulu War. Later Baron Stamfordham, private secretary to King George V.

shall never again press his hand, or be greeted by his friendly smile, or listen to the charm of his words.'[91] The Queen was reminded of Albert's death: 'I could not restrain my tears, and when I went into the dear sacred Blue Room, I thought of how the Dear Dean had stood by me and comforted me on that first anniversary of the 14th of December. How beautifully he spoke! I remember thanking him, and his kneeling down to kiss my hand.'[92] Gladstone wrote to her to offer his deep and cordial sympathy on the loss of 'one who was capable of the deepest and widest love, and who received it in return, and who unsparingly devoted his entire life and all his faculties ... towards promoting the honour of his Maker, and the welfare of mankind'.[93]

The funeral in the Abbey was arranged for Tuesday 26 July. The Prince of Wales wished to attend in person but was not willing to miss the racing at Goodwood, and the service had to be moved to the day before. This provoked an angry letter from the Queen, praising Stanley as 'more than any Bishop or Archbishop', and deploring her son's frivolity.[94] The Prince had already provoked the Queen's ire in refusing to postpone a ball at Marlborough House until after the funeral.

Eulogies were delivered in the Abbey on the Sunday before the service, with Farrar preaching at matins and Vaughan at evensong. Vaughan had agreed to Stanley's dying request and Liddell had been invited by the chapter: both men had spoken on the Sunday after Augusta's funeral. However, Liddell reluctantly declined, telegraphing: 'The distance and the heat I could not well bear.' He told his wife that 'I COULD not have gone through a sermon in the Abbey – I am sure I could not.'[95] Vaughan concentrated on memories of his friend at Rugby, and dwelt on Arnold's enduring influence. His character, he explained, had 'fostered itself on this young disciple with a force and tenacity which yet, in him, was destructive neither of individuality, nor of grace, nor of freedom'.[96]

The service began at four, though the crowds started to queue at the doors at eleven-thirty in the morning. In addition to the Prince of Wales, Gladstone, the Prime Minister, was present, with the Duke of Argyll and the Marquess of Salisbury. Among the pall-bearers were the Duke of Westminster, Frederick Temple, the President of the Royal Society, Jowett and Westcott representing Oxford and Cambridge, Matthew Arnold and his brother-in-law, William Forster, representing the House of Commons and the Government.[p] The Queen sent a

---

[p] W. E. Forster had married Thomas Arnold's eldest child Jane in 1850, after her broken engagement to Cotton.

wreath with a card inscribed in her own hand: 'A mark of sincere affection and high esteem: from Victoria R.' Vaughan was the chief mourner: Catherine, the last remaining member of Stanley's family, was too distressed to accompany him.

Archbishop Tait gave the blessing and read the prayers at the graveside. Most bishops of the Canterbury province were present and robed, together with a host of lower clergy and representatives of nonconforming congregations. 'The old Abbey full from end to end:' recorded Tait, 'all the genius of the country – princes, peers, prelates, Cabinet ministers, and the poorest of the people of Westminster. All felt they should never see his like again.'[97] What struck the American poet and ambassador, James Russell Lowell, as most remarkable, 'was seeing all ranks and conditions of men equalised, all differences of creed obliterated, all animosities of sect and party appeased by the touch of that common sympathy in sorrow'.[98] It was this most of all that made Stanley's funeral so fitting.

The Queen had already given permission for Stanley to be buried in the same grave as Augusta's in Henry VII's Chapel. This was not only a comfort to him but also a source of familial pride because his ancestor, Sir Thomas Stanley, had been the King's stepfather.[q] Beneath the detailed inscription on Augusta's monument were added, at Stanley's request, simply his names and dates, and a quotation from Psalm 119: 'I see that all things come to an end: but thy commandment is exceeding broad.' The canons, however, and Stanley's successor as dean, were determined that he should be better commemorated than this, and commissioned a more splendid tomb than that of any Dean of Westminster before or since. It was designed in the classical tradition by Pearson, the Abbey's surveyor. It consists of a chest of brown marble decorated with heraldic shields. The Viennese sculptor, Edgar Boehm, was engaged to carve a recumbent effigy in white marble. Stanley wears his decanal robes and Bath badge and ribbon,[r] with his right hand resting on his chest.

A slightly altered copy of Boehm's figure was placed in 1884 in Rugby School chapel. It was positioned in the north transept immediately beneath that of Arnold, forming a single tomb. It makes for a curious (if peculiarly appropriate) combination, and was soon nicknamed 'the bunk-bed' memorial. Matthew Arnold also brought schoolmaster

[q] See p. 29.
[r] The Dean of Westminster is ex officio Dean of the Order of the Bath.

and scholar together in death in 'Westminster Abbey', his poetic tribute to Stanley:

> I would not break thy rest, nor change thy doom.
>   Even as my father, thou –
> Even as that loved, that well-recorded friend –
>   Hast thy commission done; ye both may now
> Wait for the leaven to work, the let to end.

Arnold had admired Stanley since his childhood at Rugby, but he was out of practice as a poet and his threnody is turgid and contrived.[s] He draws on the legend that St Peter had appeared to an Anglo-Saxon fisherman on the Thames and shown him a vision of the Abbey ablaze with light. This allows him to celebrate Stanley as a 'bringer of heavenly light' after centuries of darkness:

> What! For a term so scant
>   Our shining visitant
> Cheered us, and now is passed into the night?
>   Couldst thou no better keep, O Abbey old,
>   The boon thy dedication-sign foretold,
> The presence of that gracious inmate, light?
>   A child of light appeared;
> Hither he came, late-born and long-desired,
>   And to men's hearts this ancient place endeared;
> What, is the happy glow so soon expired?

The Queen was exercised about who might follow Stanley. Three days before the funeral she wrote to the Dean of Windsor, Gerald Wellesley, 'about the successor to our beloved friend, a duty and a thought too painful almost for me to contemplate, and yet for his own sake and for that of the Abbey and the Church he loved and served so well, it is necessary'. She mentioned Farrar, whom she said she liked and admired, though she thought him 'too vehement and violent in his expressions' and 'a strong political partisan'.[99] She preferred Montagu Butler, Vaughan's successor at Harrow, whom she thought Stanley's choice, and next to him Lord Compton, the Dean of Worcester. Ten days later she wrote to Gladstone to urge caution about appointing Alfred Barry, a new canon at Westminster, who 'has not the social

---

[s] Professor Kenneth Allott called it 'a deplorable piece of frigidity with classical embroidery in the manner of Alma-Tadema.'

position or superiority over others he should have'. She would 'infinitely prefer the Dean of Christ Church, for whom the Prince of Wales is also very anxious'.[100] Gladstone agreed to sound Liddell and the Queen wrote to urge him to accept 'Mr. Gladstone's proposal to recommend him to succeed our beloved and so deeply regretted friend, Dean Stanley'.[101] Liddell felt the honour, and the pressure of what was almost a command, but a combination of age (he was seventy), reverence for Stanley, and dislike of Westminster which had damaged his health when he was headmaster, convinced him that he should decline. Butler now became the Queen's first choice again, followed by Bradley, Stanley's devoted pupil at University College and now the master. Gladstone pushed for Edwin Palmer, Archdeacon of Oxford and brother of the Lord Chancellor, but the Queen insisted on Bradley after Butler decided that he was not ready to leave Harrow. 'The appointment of Dr. Bradley to Westminster is, I think, good …', wrote Tait. 'He is a man of real sterling worth, of ability and of wide reading, thoroughly trustworthy, with a humble estimate of himself.'[102]

* * *

Benjamin Jowett was in his eleventh year as Master of Balliol. He and Stanley had sat together at the scholars' table nearly half a century before, and though relations between them had often been strained, Stanley was one of Jowett's oldest friends. His death was 'the saddest loss I could have had,' he wrote, 'and alters a good deal the colour of my life.' In the same letter, Jowett described 'A.P.S.' as 'wonderfully good, with a natural kind of goodness – blameless, innocent, never going wrong in word, thought or act. He was not always trying to improve his character, but then he did not need it … Considering all that he did, and his simplicity and energy, I should call him a really great man, if greatness is not to be confined to force of will or great imaginative power.'[103]

Jowett had told Stanley in that letter written a year before that he considered him the Church's most distinguished clergyman. That was a personal, subjective view: Stanley may have been dean of a royal peculiar, but the Abbey was not a cathedral, and Stanley was not an archbishop or even a bishop. To Jowett he was distinguished not by the office he held, but for his enlightened liberalism, and his brave determination to defend and promote it – qualities Jowett had seen conspicuously lacking on the episcopal bench. In a sermon preached in Balliol chapel, Jowett explained that 'first of all he believed in toleration –

that is, comprehension – that is, charity, extending far and wide, the love of God and man shed abroad in the human heart. He thought that theological differences were much more differences of word than was usually allowed ... He could not believe that those whom we daily meet here, often our relations and friends, whom we hoped hereafter to meet in heaven, could be really divided from us by barriers of sects and churches ...

But it would be a mistake to suppose that he was lost in any dream of universal philanthropy, or that he held any theory about the salvation of all mankind ... The first principle of toleration needed to be supplemented by a second principle: 'the interpenetration of religion and morality, of holiness and truth, of the secular and religious life' ... To him Christianity was essentially of the nature of good.[104]

Stanley was a man of singular intelligence and natural virtue. His vision of a world created and loved by a God of goodness, in which the so-called secular is as important to God as the sacred, and in which members of the Church are called to demonstrate love one to another, is profoundly Christian. His, said Jowett, was 'the spirit of comprehensive charity, the spirit which makes men to be one mind in a Church, the spirit which calls them out of differences into unity, which raises them above their own miserable quarrels into the presence of the eternal and true ... No follower will take up his mantle, no sect will call itself by his name; but to him we look back as more than any one in the Church of England the apostle of this great and simple truth.'[105]

Appendices

APPENDIX I

Stanley's Eyewitness Account of the Coronation of Queen Victoria, 28 June 1838

MY BROTHER AND SISTER went to the upper galleries, the rest of us to the lower choir gallery, where to our utter dismay we found that none except the very front row could see anything. There was every prospect of our having to remain the whole day in a place where it was impossible to see anything but the persons immediately before us, the whole gallery being besides obstructed even to suffocation by enormous pillars, beams of wood, and a roof so low that we could not stand upright – In utter despair I wandered out into some of the dark passages below, with thoughts of escaping from the Abbey altogether, when to my infinite delight I stumbled upon Thornton, whose omnipotent goldstick conveyed him whithersoever he would. I pointed out our wretched state, and by his kind activity and through him, the arrival of my father, we were delivered. My mother and sister were deposited behind the Peeresses, and I was taken up to the vaultings to my brother and sister; this was the first view of the Abbey I had – most glorious – the dazzling splendour of the prodigious crowd all in their full dress, and literally 'living out' upon the walls. I saw everything but the nave and Peeresses, being very high up but with the widest possible view. It was perfectly easy to walk about in the hinder and therefore unoccupied parts of the Abbey where were refreshments &c. prepared with the most perfect convenience. At 9 the guns announced that the Queen had left the Palace. An electric shock ran visibly thro' the whole Abbey, and from that time to the end of all at 3½ P.M. the interest was so intense that I did not feel exhausted for a moment. At 10½ another gun announced that she was at the Abbey door, and in about ¼ of an hour the procession appeared from under the organ advancing up the purple approach to the Chancel, everyone leaning over, and in they came: first the great Dukes, struggling with their enormous trains, then Bishops, &c: and then the Queen with her vast crimson train outspread by 8 ladies all in white, followed by the great ladies of her court with delicate sky blue trains, trailing along the dark floor. When she came within the full view of the gorgeous Abbey, she paused, as if for breath, and clasped her hands. The Orchestra broke out into the most tremendous crash of music I ever heard. 'I was glad when they said unto me, let us go into the House of the Lord' – everyone literally gasped for breath from the intense interest – and the rails of the gallery visibly trembled in one's hands from the trembling of the spectators. I never saw anything like it – tears would have been a relief. One felt that the Queen must sink into the earth, under the tremendous awe; but at last she moved on – to her place by the Altar, and (as I heard from one of my cousins who had a place close by) threw herself on her knees, buried her face in her hands and evidently prayed fervently. For the first part the silence was so great that at my extreme point I could hear quite distinctly the tremulous but articulate voice of the Archbishop, afterwards it was quite inaudible. The great drawbacks were the feeble responses to the service, and feebleness of the acclamations; hardly at all at the Recognition, and only tolerable at the Coronation. That was the crisis of the ceremony, and the most striking part. The very moment the Crown touched her head, the guns went off, the trumpets began, and the shouts. She was perfectly immovable, like a statue. The Duchess of Kent burst into tears, and her lady had to put on her coronet for her. The Anointing was very beautiful from the cloth of gold – the homage, also, from the magnificent cluster in the very centre. It was a take off, though a necessary one I suppose, that, throughout, her face was turned from the spectators, towards the altar. All the movements were beautiful: she was always accompanied by her 8 ladies, floating about her like a silvery cloud. The House of Commons who were above, behaved very ill, and talked so much during the actual Administration of the Communion, that the Archbishop's voice was drowned, even to those who were close – and in general the behaviour of those who being in the very Theatre itself ought to have considered themselves as part of the congregation, as well as spectators, was very profane. Considering the distance of the galleries, I think they behaved very well there. The scrambling for the medals at the Homage was also very indecorous. It was over at 3fi, i.e. she went out then, with her Crown, her Orb and her Sceptre.

APPENDIX II

Extract from 'The Murder of Becket', Historical Memorials of Canterbury (1855)

THE VESPERS HAD already begun, and the monks were singing the service in the choir, when two boys rushed up the nave, announcing, more by their terrified gestures than by their words, that the soldiers were bursting into the palace and monastery. Instantly the service was thrown into the utmost confusion; part remained at prayer – part fled into the numerous hiding-places the vast fabric affords; and part went down the steps of the choir into the transept to meet the little band at the door. 'Come in, come in!' exclaimed one of them, 'come in, and let us die together.' The Archbishop continued to stand outside, and said, 'Go and finish the service. So long as you keep in the entrance, I shall not come in.' They fell back a few paces, and he stepped within the door, but, finding the whole place thronged with people, he paused on the threshold and asked, 'What is it that these people fear?' One general answer broke forth, 'The armed men in the cloister.' As he turned and said, 'I shall go out to them,' he heard the clash of arms behind. The knights had just forced their way into the cloister, and were now (as would appear from their being thus seen through the open door) advancing along its southern side. They were in mail, which covered their faces up to their eyes, and carried their swords drawn. With them was Hugh of Horsea, surnamed Mauclerc, a subdeacon, chaplain of Robert de Broc. Three had hatchets. Fitzurse, with the axe he had taken from the carpenters, was foremost, shouting as he came, 'Here, here, king's men!' Immediately behind him followed Robert Fitzranulph, with three other knights, whose names are not preserved; and a motley group – some their own followers, some from the town – with weapons, though not in armour, brought up the rear. At this sight, so unwonted in the peaceful cloisters of Canterbury, not probably beheld since the time when the monastery had been sacked by the Danes, the monks within, regardless of all remonstrances, shut the door of the cathedral, and proceeded to barricade it with iron bars. A loud knocking was heard from the terrified band without, who, having vainly endeavoured to prevent the entrance of the knights into the cloister, now rushed before them to take refuge in the church. Becket, who had stepped some paces into the cathedral, but was resisting the solicitations of those immediately about him to move up into the choir for safety, darted back, calling aloud as he went, 'Away, you cowards! By virtue of your obedience I command you not to shut the door – the church must not be turned into a castle.' With his own hands he thrust them away from the door, opened it himself, and catching hold of the excluded monks, dragged them into the building, exclaiming, 'Come in, come in – faster, faster!'

At this moment the ecclesiastics who had hitherto clung round him fled in every direction; some to the altars in the numerous side chapels, some to the secret chambers with which the walls and roof of the cathedral are filled. One of them has had the rashness to leave on record his own excessive terror. Even John of Salisbury, his tried and faithful counsellor, escaped with the rest. Three only remained – Robert, canon of Merton, his old instructor; William Fitzstephen (if we may believe his own account), his lively and worldly-minded chaplain; and Edward Grim, the Saxon monk. William, one of the monks of Canterbury, who has recorded his impressions of the scene, confesses that he fled with the rest. He was not ready to confront martyrdom, and, with clasped hands, ran as fast as he could up the steps ...

What has taken long to describe must have been compressed in action within a few minutes. The knights who had been checked for a moment by the sight of the closed door, on seeing it unexpectedly thrown open, rushed into the church. It was, we must remember, about five o'clock in a winter evening; the shades of night were gathering, and were deepened into a still darker gloom within the high and massive walls of the vast cathedral, which was only illuminated here and there by the solitary lamps burning before the altars. The twilight, lengthening from the shortest day a fortnight before, was but just sufficient to reveal the outline of objects. The transept in which the knights found themselves is the same as that which – though with considerable changes in its arrangements – is still known by its ancient name of 'The Martyrdom'. Two staircases led from it, one from the east to the northern aisle, one on the west to the entrance of the choir ... At the moment of [the knights'] entrance the central pillar exactly intercepted their view of the Archbishop ascending (as would appear from this circumstance) the eastern staircase. Fitzurse, with his drawn sword in one hand, and the carpenter's axe in the other, sprang in first, and turned at once to the right of the pillar. The other three went round it to the left. In the dim twilight they could just discern a group of figures mounting the steps. One of the knights called out to them 'Stay.' Another, 'Where is Thomas Becket, traitor to the King?' No answer was returned. None could have been expected by any who remembered the indignant silence with which Becket had swept by when the same word had been applied by Randulf of Broc at Northampton. Fitzurse rushed forward, and, stumbling against one of the monks, on the lower step, still not able to distinguish clearly in the darkness, exclaimed, 'Where is the Archbishop?' Instantly the answer came – 'Reginald, here I am, no traitor, but the Archbishop and Priest of God; what do you wish?' – and from the fourth step, which he had reached in his ascent, with a slight motion of his head – noticed apparently as his peculiar manner in moments of excitement – Becket descended to the transept. Attired, we are told, in his white rochet, with a cloak and hood thrown over his shoulders, he thus suddenly confronted his assailants. Fitzurse sprang back two or three paces, and Becket passing by him took up his station between the central pillar and the massive wall which still forms the south-west corner of what was then the chapel of St. Benedict. Here they gathered round him, with the cry, 'Absolve the bishops whom you have excommunicated.' 'I cannot do other than I have done,' he replied, and turning to Fitzurse, he added – 'Reginald, you have received many favours at my hands; why do you come into my church armed?' Fitzurse planted the axe against his breast, and returned for answer, 'You shall die – I will tear out your heart.' Another, perhaps in kindness, striking him between the shoulders with the flat of his sword, exclaimed, 'Fly; you are a dead man.' 'I am ready to die,' replied the Primate, 'for God and the Church; but I warn you, I curse you in the name of God Almighty, if you do not let my men escape.'

The well-known horror which in that age was felt at an act of sacrilege, together with the sight of the crowds who were rushing in from the town through the nave, turned their efforts for the next few moments to carry him out of the church. Fitzurse threw down the axe, and tried to drag him out by the collar of his long cloak, calling 'Come with us – you are our prisoner.' 'I will not fly, you detestable fellow,' was Becket's reply, roused to his usual vehemence, and wrenching the cloak out of Fitzurse's grasp. The three knights, to whom was now added Hugh Mauclerc, chaplain of Robert de Broc, struggled violently to put him on Tracy's shoulders. Becket set his back against the pillar, and resisted with all his might, whilst Grim, vehemently remonstrating, threw his arms around him to aid his efforts. In the scuffle Becket fastened upon Tracy, shook him by his coat of mail, and exerting his great strength, flung him down on the pavement. It was hopeless to carry on the attempt to remove him. And in the final struggle which now began, Fitzurse, as before, took the lead. But, as he approached with his drawn sword, the sight of him kindled afresh the Archbishop's anger, now heated by the fray; the spirit of the chancellor rose within him, and with a coarse epithet, not calculated to turn away his adversary's wrath, exclaimed, 'You profligate wretch, you are my man – you have done me fealty – you ought not to touch me.' Fitzurse, glowing all over with rage, retorted – 'I owe you no fealty or homage, contrary to my fealty to the King', and waving the sword over his head, cried 'Strike, strike!' ('Ferez, ferez'), but merely dashed off his cap. The Archbishop covered his eyes with his joined hands, bent his neck, and said, 'I commend my cause and the cause of the Church to God, to St. Denys the martyr of France, to St. Alfege, and to the saints of the Church.' Meanwhile Tracy, who, since his fall, had thrown off his hauberk to move more easily, sprang forward, and struck a more decided blow. Grim, who up to this moment had his arm round Becket, threw it up, wrapped in a cloak, to intercept the blade, Becket exclaiming, 'Spare this defence.' The sword lighted on the arm of the monk, which fell wounded or broken; and he fled disabled to the nearest altar, probably that of St. Benedict within the chapel. It is a proof of the confusion of the scene, that Grim the receiver of the blow, as well as most of the narrators, believed it to have been dealt by Fitzurse, while Tracy, who is known to have been the man from his subsequent boast, believed that the monk whom he had wounded was John of Salisbury. The spent force of the stroke descended on Becket's head, grazed the crown, and finally rested on his left shoulder, cutting through the clothes and skin. The next blow, whether struck by Tracy or Fitzurse, was only with the flat of the sword, and again on the bleeding head, which Becket drew back as if stunned, and then raised his clasped hands over it. The blood from the first blow was trickling down his face in a thin streak; he wiped it with his arm, and when he saw the stain, he said – 'Into thy hands, O Lord, I commend my spirit.' At the third blow, which was also from Tracy, he sank on his knees – his arms falling – but his hands still joined as if in prayer. With his face turned towards the altar of St. Benedict, he murmured in a low voice, which might just have been caught by the wounded Grim, who was crouching close by, and who alone reports the words – 'For the name of Jesus, and the defence of the Church, I am willing to die.' Without moving hand or foot, he fell flat on his face as he spoke, in front of the corner wall of the chapel, and with such dignity that his mantle, which extended from head to foot, was not disarranged. In this posture he received from Richard the Breton a tremendous blow, accompanied with the exclamation (in allusion to a quarrel of Becket with Prince William) 'Take this for love of my lord William, brother of the King.' The stroke was aimed with such violence that the scalp or crown of the head – which, it was remarked, was of unusual size – was severed from the skull, and the sword snapt in two on the marble pavement. The fracture of the murderous weapon was reported by one of the eye-witnesses as a presage of the ultimate discomfiture of the Archbishop's enemies. Hugh of Horsea, the subdeacon who had joined them as they entered the church, taunted by the others with having taken no share in the deed, planted his foot on the neck of the corpse, thrust his sword into the ghastly wound, and scattered the brains over the pavement – 'Let us go – let us go,' he said in conclusion, 'The traitor is dead; he will rise no more.'

APPENDIX III

Stanley's Account of David and Goliath, Lectures on the History of the Jewish Church, *ii (1865)*

The scene of the battle which the young shepherd 'came to see' was in a ravine in the frontier-hills of Judah, called probably from this or similar encounters Ephes-dammim, 'the bound of blood'. Saul's army is encamped on one side of the ravine, the Philistines on the other. A dry watercourse marked by a spreading Terebinth runs between them. A Philistine of gigantic stature insults the whole Israelite army. He is clothed in the complete armour for which his nation was renowned, which is described piece by piece, as if to enhance its awful strength, in contrast with the defencelessness of the Israelites. No one can be found to take up the challenge. The King sits in his tent in moody despair. Jonathan, it seems, is absent. At this juncture David appears in the camp, sent by his father with ten loaves and ten slices of milk-cheese fresh from the sheepfolds, to his three eldest brothers, who were there to represent their father, detained by his extreme age. Just as he comes to the circle of waggons which formed, as in Arab settlements, a rude fortification round the Israelite camp, he hears the well-known shout of the Israelite war-cry. 'The shout of a king is among them.' The martial spirit of the boy is stirred at the sound; he leaves his provisions with the baggage-master, and darts to join his brothers (like one of the royal messengers) into the midst of the lines. There he hears the challenge, now made for the fortieth time – sees the dismay of his countrymen – hears the reward proposed by the king – goes with the impetuosity of youth from soldier to soldier talking of the event, in spite of his brother's rebuke – he is introduced to Saul – he undertakes the combat.

It is an encounter which brings together in one brief space the whole contrast of the Philistine and Israelite warfare. On the one hand is the huge giant, of that race or family, as it would seem, of giants which gave to Gath a kind of grotesque renown; such as in David's after days still engaged the prowess of his followers – monsters of strange appearance, with hands and feet of disproportionate development. He is full of savage insolence and fury; unable to understand how any one could contend against his brute strength and impregnable panoply; the very type of the stupid 'Philistine', such as has in the language of modern Germany not unfitly identified the name with the opponents of light and freedom and growth. On the other hand is the small agile youth, full of spirit and faith; refusing the cumbrous brazen helmet, the unwieldy sword and shield – so heavy that he could not walk with them – which the king had proffered; confident in the new name of the 'Lord of Hosts' – the God of Battles – in his own shepherd's sling – and in the five pebbles which the watercourse of the valley had supplied as he ran through it on his way to the battle. A single stone was enough. It penetrated the brazen helmet. The giant fell on his face, and the Philistine army fled down the pass and were pursued even within the gates of Ekron and Ascalon. Two trophies long remained of the battle – the head and the sword of the Philistine. Both were ultimately deposited at Jerusalem; but meanwhile were hung up behind the ephod in the Tabernacle at Nob.

APPENDIX IV

Address Delivered in Rugby Chapel on 12 June 1874, Thirty-two Years after the Death of Arnold

IT IS NOW thirty-two years ago, since on Sunday morning, the 12th of June, the most famous Headmaster of this school, to whom we all look back as its second founder, Thomas Arnold, was called away by a death, of which the sudden shock was felt through every part of the country, wherever a Rugby scholar happened to be, and which to those who were engaged in their work at that time in the school, whether as masters or as boys, gave the feeling as if the whole place were passed away with one who had been in every sense its head. If any of you wish to have recalled to your minds what were the feelings of Rugby boys at that moment, read again the last chapter of 'Tom Brown's School Days.' That admirable book gives you the best idea of what Arnold was to Rugby; and that chapter especially gives you the best notion of what his scholars thought and felt when they heard of his death. I myself had, as many of you know, been under his care for six years, which I still cherish as amongst the most precious of my life. The sermons which I heard from his lips in this place are still, through the vicissitudes of an often stormy and eventful time, as fresh in my memory as when I first listened to them in this chapel, with a mixture of admiration and delight which I cannot describe. The effect of his character, and the lessons of his teaching, have been the stimulus to whatever I may have been able to do in the forty years since I left school; and his words constantly come back to me as expressing better than anything else my hopes and fears for this life, and for the life to come.

I have said thus much to you that you may know why it is that I have obeyed your Headmaster's wishes, and ventured (though a stranger whom many of you perhaps never heard of or saw before) to say a few words that may serve to make you know what Arnold was. Let me speak first of his teaching, and then of himself.

Of his teaching. A very distinguished schoolfellow of mine said to me some time ago, 'There are two words whose meaning we both learned from him – Religion and History.'

Religion. What was it that Arnold told us of Religion? It was that Religion – the relation of the soul to God – depends on our own moral and spiritual characters. He made us understand that the only thing for which God supremely cares, the only thing that God supremely loves is goodness – that the only thing which is supremely hateful to God is wickedness. All other things are useful, admirable, beautiful in their several ways. All forms, ordinances, means of instruction, means of amusement, have their place in our lives. But Religion, the true Religion of Jesus Christ, consists in that which makes us wiser and better, more truthful, more loving, more tender, more considerate, more pure. Therefore, in his view, there was no place or time from which Religion is shut out – there is no place or time where we cannot be serving God by serving our fellow-creatures.

History. No doubt he taught us much beside. But History, past and present, was his favourite study; and he made us feel that the dead men of Greece and Rome, the departed times of England and France, were full of living interest. He made us understand that much that we call ancient was really modern, much that we call modern was really ancient. He made us feel that there was a sequence in the events of history, and that it was through the knowledge of the successive forms which goodness and truth can take at different times that Religion itself can best be understood. He taught us how great a thing it was to be Englishmen – citizens of the kingly commonwealth of England. He taught us the value of Law – that there is in all moral matters only one authority, and that is the law of God; and in all other matters only one authority, and that is the law of our country. He made us understand the greatness of Christianity by making us feel the grandeur of Europe and the magnificence of Christendom.

I have just briefly touched on these two main points of his teaching because the more you look at them as he looked at them, the more you feel that they will bear all the weight of life, and all the sifting of inquiry. Many things which he said, no doubt, have been changed as times have changed, and knowledge has widened. But the essential spirit of his method remains still.

But most of all, we learned the meaning of those two words from himself. When we looked in his face, when we heard him speak from this pulpit, when we heard him in the Big School reading prayers, or heard him in the library teaching the Sixth Form, we saw that he was always acting, or trying to act, as in the presence of God, enjoying all the innocent pleasures of life because God had given them to him – turning away from everything base, or mean, or dishonourable because he knew that God abhorred it.

That we felt to be his religion. His presence made us also feel what history was. For we – any of us who could think at all – knew that he was like one of those great men of whom we read in history. We thought then, and, after having witnessed many famous events, and seen many famous men of our time, I think and know now, that he was one of the heroes of our age – one whom to have known and loved is an honour and a privilege, and a responsibility which will last as long as life endures.

One word I will say in conclusion. I remember that on the Sunday after his death one of the lessons read in this chapel was that chapter where Samuel takes leave of his people, and says, 'Behold, my sons are with you.' I remember being deeply affected by those words. I thought then chiefly of his actual children – those sons and daughters who are all, save one, living still, who for the thirty-two years since his departure were gathered round their dear and venerable mother, who only last year departed to join the husband whom she had so loved. But I will now take these words in a larger sense. 'Behold his sons are with us.' We are indeed all of us here, and in many and many a place besides, 'the sons of Arnold'. Your teachers, though some of them never saw him – the two most distinguished Headmasters of this place, though they had seen him only as it were but for a moment – were in this sense his sons. They felt, and they feel, that much of what was best and noblest within them and around them came from his example and his teaching. He who is now the Primate of the English Church, and he whose farewell words in this place four years and a half ago, I heard with a feeling that it was like hearing Arnold's voice again – are both the sons of Arnold.* But you also – you, the youngest amongst you, you to whom the name of Arnold is of one who lived and died long, long ago – you also are, without knowing it, his children. Whatever there is good and inspiriting and lofty and stimulating in this place, comes from him. You need not repeat his words, you need not share his opinions, you may perhaps never read his life, but so far as you sustain the honour of Rugby boys, setting to yourselves now and to your coun-

---

* Stanley refers to Archbishop Tait and Frederick Temple, Tait's successor but one as both Headmaster of Rugby and Archbishop of Canterbury.

try afterwards, the examples of upright, generous, truthful boys, and afterwards of fearless, energetic, noble-minded Englishmen; – so far you are Christians in Arnold's spirit; so far you carry on to future days the glory of him who sleeps in the midst of this chapel, and whose memory is its best inheritance.

Source Notes

INTRODUCTION

1. 16 October 1881; W. H. Fremantle (ed.), *Sermons Biographical and Miscellaneous by the late Benjamin Jowett, M.A.*, p. 141.
2. A. P. Stanley, *Life of Thomas Arnold, D.D., Head-Master of Rugby* (1844), 1904 edn, p. v.
3. Ibid., p. 49: the provost was Edward Hawkins.
4. See pp. 206–11.
5. 'A Funeral Sermon on Arthur Penrhyn Stanley, D.D. Preached in Westminster Abbey on Sunday Afternoon, July 24, 1881 by C. J. Vaughan, D.D.', p. 8.
6. Virginia Woolf, 'The Art of Biography', *The Death of the Moth* (1942), p. 121.
7. Harold Nicolson, *The Development of English Biography*, p. 125.
8. *Ibid.*, p. 113.
9. Lytton Strachey, *Eminent Victorians* (1918), Chatto and Windus, 1948, p. 7.
10. *Ibid.*
11. John Percival, quoted in the preface to the teachers' edn of Stanley's *Life of Arnold*, p. xiv: Percival was a master at Rugby and later headmaster.
12. Thomas Hughes, *Tom Brown's Schooldays* (1857), Nelson Classics, pp. 124–5.
13. Vaughan, *op. cit.*, p. 7.
14. Roland E. Prothero, *The Life and Correspondence of Arthur Penrhyn Stanley, D.D.*, i, p. 102.
15. Stanley, *op. cit.*, p. xviii.
16. George Granville Bradley, *Recollections of Arthur Penrhyn Stanley*, p. 36.
17. Letter to Hugh Pearson, 18 June 1842; Pusey House archive.
18. 15 June 1842; Roland E. Prothero (ed.), *Letters and Verses of Arthur Penrhyn Stanley, D.D.*, p. 75.
19. Woolf, *op. cit.*, p. 120.

20 Vaughan, *op. cit.*, p. 8.
21 Stanley, *op. cit.*, p. xv.
22 *Ibid.*, p. xvii.
23 *Ibid.*
24 *Ibid.*, p. xviii.
25 Edward C. Mack, *Public Schools and British Opinion, 1780 to 1860*, p. 308.
26 A. O. J. Cockshut, *Truth to Life: The Art of Biography in the Nineteenth Century*, p. 102.
27 Stanley, *op. cit.*, pp. 650ff.
28 Cockshut, *op. cit.*, p. 104.
29 Strachey, *op. cit.*, p. 165.
30 Nicolson, *op. cit.*, p. 110.
31 Cockshut, *op. cit.*, p. 89.
32 Stanley, *op. cit.*, p. 26.
33 *Ibid.*, p. 31.
34 *Ibid.*
35 1 November 1830; *ibid.*, p. 247: J. T. Coleridge was the poet's nephew, and became a friend of Arnold at Oxford.
36 Stanley, *op. cit.*, p. 171.
37 *Ibid.*, p. 170.
38 *Ibid.*p. 158.
39 26 April 1836; Cheshire Record Office, DSA/80/1.
40 Stanley, *op. cit.*, p. 382.
41 *Ibid.*, p. 1.
42 Cockshut, *op. cit.*, p. 14.
43 Stanley, *op. cit.*, p. 84.
44 *Ibid.*, p. 122.
45 *Ibid.*, p. xx: the 12th edn of the *Life of Arnold* was published in 1881, the year Stanley died.
46 Letter from Gerald Harper, *The Spectator*, 6 November 1897.
47 10 June 1857; Prothero, *Letters*, p. 262.
48 12 June 1874; *Macmillan's Magazine*, July 1874, xxx, p. 279: see Appendix IV.
49 T. W. Bamford, *Thomas Arnold*, p. 51.
50 Stanley, *op. cit.*, p. 154.
51 Hughes, *op. cit.*, p. 136: compare Stanley, *op. cit.*, pp. 203–4.
52 *Ibid.*, pp. 359ff.
53 Stanley, *op. cit.*, pp. 154–5.
54 *Macmillan's Magazine*, *op. cit.*, p. 279.

55 Hughes, *op. cit.*, pp. 329ff.
56 15 October 1881; *University College Record*, December 1963, p. 184.
57 Bradley, *op. cit.*, p. viii.
58 *Ibid.*, p. 58: the same eulogising is present in Bradley's introduction to Prothero's biography.
59 Prothero, *Life*, p. 17.
60 *Ibid.*, p. 18.
61 Cockshut, *op. cit.*, pp. 22–3.

CHAPTER I

Title: Jane Austen, *Pride and Prejudice* (1813).
1 Augustus J. C. Hare, *Biographical Sketches*, p. 3.
2 A. P. Stanley, *Memoirs of Edward and Catherine Stanley*, p. xi.
3 Hare, *op. cit.*, pp. 2–3.
4 Jane H. Adeane and Maud Grenfell (edd.), *Before And After Waterloo: Letters from Edward Stanley*, p. 16.
5 E. F. Jacob, *The Fifteenth Century, 1399–1485* (1961), The Oxford History of England, vi, p. 617.
6 Stanley, *op. cit*, p. 14.
7 *Ibid.*, pp. 15–16.
8 *Ibid.*, pp. 1–2.
9 Adeane and Grenfell, *op. cit*, p. 139.
10 *Ibid.*, pp. 260, 262–3.
11 Stanley, *op. cit.*, p. 8.
12 *Ibid.*, pp. 10ff.
13 *Ibid.*, pp. x–xi.
14 Hare, *op. cit*, pp. 4f.
15 *Ibid.*, pp. 6–7.
16 *The Carthusian*, September 1932, xv, p. 1080.
17 Adelaide Lubbock, *Owen Stanley R.N.*, p. 15.
18 *Ibid.*, p. 10.
19 *Ibid.*, p. 25.
20 *Ibid.*, p. 8.
21 *Ibid.*, p. 33.
22 Quoted by Hare, *op. cit.*, p. 7.
23 *Ibid.*, p. 8.
24 *Ibid.*, p. 9.
25 R. E. Prothero, *Life of Stanley*, i, pp. 8–9.

26 Hare, *op. cit.*, p. 12.
27 *Ibid.*, pp. 12–13.
28 Kitty's journal 1820–30, typescript, p. 19; Cheshire Record Office, DSA/195.
29 Hare, *op. cit.*, pp. 13–14.
30 Prothero, *op. cit.*, p. 21.
31 *Ibid.*
32 Hare, *op. cit.*, p. 18.
33 Prothero, *op. cit.*, p. 15.
34 Kitty's journal, *op. cit.*, p. 23.
35 17 November 1827; R. E. Prothero (ed.), *Letters of Stanley*, pp. 1ff: the letter is misdated 1829.
36 Prothero, *Life*, p. 19.
37 *Ibid.*, p. 22.
38 *Ibid.*
39 *Ibid.*, pp. 31–2.
40 *Ibid.*, p. 28.
41 *Ibid.*, p. 24.
42 Hare, *op. cit.*, p. 19.
43 *Ibid.*, pp. 19ff.
44 *Ibid.*, pp. 22–3.

CHAPTER 2

Title: Matthew Arnold, 'Rugby Chapel' (1857).
1 To W. A. Greenhill, December 1832; R. E. Prothero, *Life of Stanley*, i, p. 44.
2 T. Hughes, *Tom Brown's Schooldays*, p. 64.
3 Katharine Chorley, *Arthur Hugh Clough: The Uncommitted Mind*, p. 13.
4 Hughes, *op. cit.*, p. 157.
5 Christopher Hollis, *Eton: A History* (1960), pp. 236ff.: Gladstone said that if a boy could survive long chamber he could survive anything in life.
6 A. P. Stanley, *Life of Arnold*, p. 164.
7 Hughes, *op. cit.*, pp. 200–1.
8 H. G. Allen; Prothero, *op. cit.*, p. 41.
9 *Ibid.*, pp. 38 ff.
10 Rugby School archives.
11 16 October 1829; Prothero, *op. cit.*, p. 49.

12 Letter to Mary, 26 February 1829; *ibid.*, p. 42.
13 10 March 1829; *ibid.*, p. 43.
14 7 April 1829; *ibid.*, p. 44.
15 Prothero, *op. cit.*, p. 57.
16 27 September 1829; *ibid.*, p. 48: Sir Walter Scott's eponymous hero, Edward Waverley, is rejected by the Jacobite Flora MacIvor.
17 *Ibid.*
18 Prothero, *op. cit.*, p. 57.
19 *Ibid.*, p. 51.
20 *Ibid.*, p. 52: Stanley was always innumerate.
21 *Ibid.*, p. 44.
22 7 April 1829; *ibid.*, p. 43.
23 25 May 1829; *ibid.*, p. 45.
24 Prothero, *op. cit.*, p. 55.
25 *Ibid.*
26 *Ibid.*, p. 56.
27 'A Funeral Sermon on A. P. Stanley', 24 July 1881, p. 5.
28 Prothero, *op. cit.*, pp. 103–4.
29 Stanley, *op. cit.*, p. 148.
30 Appendix to 'A Sermon Preached in the Chapel of Rugby School on Sunday, August 14, 1842', pp. 28–9.
31 Thomas Arnold, *Sermons*, ii, p. 108.
32 *Ibid.*, p. 111.
33 Stanley, *op. cit.*, pp. 147–8.
34 Prothero, *op. cit.*, p. 64.
35 May 1834; *ibid.*, pp. 102–3.
36 Stanley *op. cit.*, pp. 121–2.
37 *Ibid.*, p. 116.
38 *Ibid.*, p. 107.
39 *Ibid.*, p. 132.
40 Katharine Lake (ed.), *Memorials of William Charles Lake, Dean of Durham*, p. 8.
41 Stanley, *op. cit.*, p. 123.
42 *Ibid.*, p. 136.
43 26 November 1832; Rugby School archives.
44 Lake, *op. cit.*, p. 9: Lake is quoting Stanley.
45 Arnold, *op. cit.*, p. 378.
46 *Ibid.*, p. 388.
47 Prothero, *op. cit.*, p. 99.
48 *Ibid.*, p. 69.

49 *Ibid.*, p. 89.
50 Lake, *op. cit.*, p. 11.
51 Stanley, *op. cit.*, p. 105.
52 *Ibid.*, pp. 105f.
53 27 September 1829; Prothero, *op. cit.*, p. 48.
54 Stanley, *op. cit.*, p. 104.
55 Prothero, *op. cit.*, p. 89.
56 Lake, *op. cit.*, p. 12.
57 Prothero, *op. cit.*, pp. 104–5.: Vaughan's transcribing suggests that Stanley's notoriously illegible handwriting was already in decline.
58 *Ibid.*, p. 64.
59 14 April 1832; R. E. Prothero, *Letters of Stanley*, pp. 7–8.
60 Letter to Mary, 26 April 1832; *ibid.*, p. 15.
61 *Ibid.*, p. 16
62 Letter, 11 November 1831; A. J. C. Hare, *Biographical Sketches*, p. 30.
63 A. P. Stanley, *Memoirs of E. and C. Stanley*, pp. 301–2.
64 *Ibid.*, p. 295.
65 Prothero, *Life*, p. 96.
66 *Ibid.*, pp. 99–100.
67 A. Lubbock, *Owen Stanley*, pp. 32–3.
68 Prothero, *Life*, p. 100.
69 Letter to Mary, August 1833; *ibid.*
70 *Ibid.*, p. 101.
71 Prothero, *Life*, p. 92.
72 Rugby School archives: the letter is undated.
73 Letter to J. E. Tyler, 10 June 1832; Stanley, *Life*, p. 278.
74 Stanley, *Memoirs*, p. 300.
75 Thomas Arnold, 'Principles of Church Reform', *The Miscellaneous Works of Thomas Arnold, D.D.*, ed. A. P. Stanley, p. 332.
76 Stanley, *Life*, pp. 44–5.
77 26 November 1832; Rugby School archives.
78 Letter from Augustus Hare (undated); Rugby School archives.
79 Hughes, *op. cit.*, p. 108.
80 27 November 1833; Rugby School archives.
81 Letter to Mary, 29 November 1833; Rugby School archives.
82 6 December 1833; Prothero, *Life*, p. 72.
83 *Ibid.*
84 Prothero, *Life*, p. 69.
85 *Ibid.*, p. 75.

86 *Ibid.*, p. 73.
87 5 April 1834; *ibid.*, pp. 73f.
88 Prothero, *Life*, pp. 76f.

CHAPTER 3

Title: William Wordsworth, 'The Prelude' (1805, published 1850).
1 R. E. Prothero, *Life of Stanley*, i, p. 108: see also A. P. Stanley, 'Archdeacon Hare', *Quarterly Review*, July 1855; reprinted in A. P. Stanley (ed.), *Essays Chiefly on Questions of Church and State from 1850 to 1870*, pp. 546–7.
2 9 September 1834; Pusey House archives.
3 Prothero, *op. cit.*, p. 117.
4 *Ibid.*, p. 109.
5 *Ibid.*, p. 110.
6 *Ibid.*, p. 113.
7 Letter to J. T. Coleridge, 12 October 1835; A. P. Stanley, *Life of Arnold*, p. 374.
8 Prothero, *op. cit.*, p. 111.
9 *Ibid.*, p. 114.
10 *Ibid.*, p. 112.
11 *The Dictionary of National Biography* (1917), xviii, p. 1082.
12 Prothero, *op. cit.*, p. 112.
13 A. J. C. Hare, *Biographical Sketches*, p. 38.
14 Stanley, 'Archdeacon Hare', *op. cit.*, p. 563.
15 Prothero, *op. cit.*, p. 118: Lake had another year at Rugby, and Vaughan was staying with the Arnolds before going to Cambridge.
16 10 October 1834; *ibid.*, p. 119.
17 11 October 1834; *ibid.*, p. 120: the Praetorium is School House where Arnold lived.
18 *Ibid.*
19 15 October 1834; Pusey House archives.
20 Prothero, *op. cit.*, p. 126.
21 James Boswell, *The Life of Samuel Johnson* (1791), Penguin Classics, 1986, p. 318.
22 M. G. Brock, 'The Oxford of Peel and Gladstone, 1800–1833', *The History of the University of Oxford*, vi, edd. M. G. Brock and M. C. Curthoys, p. 40.
23 Mark Pattison, *Memoirs*, p. 68.

24 Thomas Hughes, *Tom Brown at Oxford* (1861), Nelson Classics, p. 7.
25 *Ibid.*, p. 11.
26 Wilfrid Ward, *William George Ward and the Oxford Movement*, p. 431: the description is from Jowett's recollections in Ward's appendix d.
27 John Jones, *Balliol College: A History*, p. 187.
28 *Ibid.*, p. 186.
29 Prothero, *op. cit.*, p. 122.
30 *Ibid.*, p. 123.
31 *Ibid.*
32 *Ibid.*
33 Quoted by Pattison, *op. cit.*, p. 64.
34 Letter to Mary, 25 October 1834; R. E. Prothero, *Letters of Stanley*, p. 26.
35 Prothero, *Life*, p. 127.
36 *Ibid.*, pp. 124–5.
37 *Ibid.*, p. 125.
38 *Ibid.*, p. 129.
39 *Ibid.*, p. 130.
40 *Ibid.*, p. 135.
41 *Ibid.*, p. 131.
42 *Ibid.*, p. 135.
43 *Ibid.*, p. 136.
44 *Ibid.*, p. 137.
45 *Ibid.*, p. 116.
46 Edward Burton to Arthur Wellesley, 24 April 1834: P. B. Nockles, '"Lost causes and…impossible loyalties": the Oxford Movement and the University', Brock and Curthoys, *op. cit.*, p. 213.
47 10 August 1834; Prothero, *Life*, p. 107n.
48 Letter to Kitty, May 1835; *ibid.*, p. 144.
49 *Ibid.*, p. 145: the measure was defeated by 459 votes to 57.
50 *Ibid.*, p. 146.
51 Geoffrey Faber, *Oxford Apostles: A Character Study of the Oxford Movement*, pp. 251–2.
52 R. P. Flindall (ed.), *The Church of England 1815–1948: A Documentary History*, p. 40.
53 V. H. H. Green, *Religion at Oxford and Cambridge*, p. 269.
54 Prothero, *Life*, p. 123.
55 'The Oxford Counter-Reformation' (1883); Faber, *op. cit.*, p. 380.

56 R. D. Middleton, 'The Vicar of St. Mary's', *John Henry Newman: Centenary Essays* (1945).
57 K. Lake, *Memorials of W. C. Lake*, pp. 46–7.
58 September 1833; Prothero, *Life*, p. 134.
59 Lake, *op. cit.*, p. 47.
60 Prothero, *Life*, p. 142.
61 January 1835; *ibid*.
62 Undated; Rugby School archives.
63 February 1836; Prothero, *Life*, p. 160.
64 *Ibid.*, p. 161.
65 *Ibid.*, p. 158.
66 *Ibid.*, p. 159.
67 *Ibid.*, pp. 160–1.
68 Stanley, *Life of Arnold*, p. 381.
69 Prothero, *Life*, pp. 162f.
79 Letter to Mary, May 1836; *ibid.*, p. 164.
71 Prothero, *Life*, p, 164.
72 *Ibid.*, pp. 130–1.
73 July 1836; Ward, *op. cit.*, appendix i, pp. 461–2.
74 Randall Davidson and William Benham, *Life of Archibald Campbell Tait*, i, p. 102.
75 J. C. Shairp, *Studies in Poetry and Philosophy* (1868), pp. 240–1.
76 Ward, *op. cit.*, p. 33: Ward replied, 'I should like to know whose opinions, yours or mine, agree most with those of the founders of the college.'
77 Notes for a eulogy on Stanley (1881); Balliol College archives, I D18.
78 Peter Hinchliff and John Prest, 'Jowett, Benjamin (1817–1893)', *Oxford Dictionary of National Biography*.
79 Prothero, *Life*, p. 146.
80 *Ibid.*, p. 151.
81 *Ibid.*, pp. 152–3.
82 *Ibid.*
83 *Ibid.*, pp. 153–4.
84 *Ibid.*, p. 154.
85 *Ibid.*, p. 165.
86 *Ibid.*
87 28 August 1836, *ibid.*, pp. 165ff.
88 A. P. Stanley, *Memoirs of E. and C. Stanley*, p. 33.

89 *Ibid.*, p. 34.
90 Augustus J. C. Hare, *The Story of My Life*, i, p. 69.
91 Prothero, *Life*, p. 180.
92 Letter to Whately, 8 July 1836; Graham Howes, 'Dr Arnold and Bishop Stanley', *Studies in Church History*, ii, ed. C. J. Cuming, p. 323.
93 Stanley, *Memoirs*, p. 81.
94 22 September 1837; Prothero, *Life*, pp. 185–6.
95 Prothero, *Life*, p. 151.
96 Stanley, *Memoirs*, p. 63.
97 *Ibid.*, p. 66.
98 11 November 1834; Lake, *op. cit.*, p. 155.
99 Pattison, *op. cit.*, pp. 118–19: Pattison was a contemporary of Stanley; he was an undergraduate at Oriel, and a fellow and Rector of Lincoln College.
100 *Ibid.*, p.172.
101 Prothero, *Life*, p. 171.
102 *Ibid.*
103 *Ibid.*, pp. 172–3.
104 *Ibid.*, pp. 173–4.
105 *Ibid.*, p. 174.
106 *Ibid.*, p. 180.
107 *Ibid.*, p. 177.
108 Prothero, *Letters*, pp. 31–2.
109 Prothero, *Life*, p. 178.
110 W. Tuckwell, *Reminiscences of Oxford*, p. 98.
111 Prothero, *Life*, p. 185.
112 13 November 1837; *ibid.*, pp. 187–8.
113 Prothero *Life*, p. 188.
114 Undated; Pusey House archives.

CHAPTER 4

Title: Percy Bysshe Shelley, 'Prometheus Unbound' (1820).
1 Letter to Lady Henrietta Stanley, 5 November 1862; Balliol College archives, I F6.
2 R. E. Prothero, *Life of Stanley*, i, p. 191.
3 Undated; Pusey House archives.
4 27 February 1838; R. E. Prothero, *Letters of Stanley*, p. 44.

5   Letter to Vaughan, March 1838; Prothero, *Life*, p. 196.
6   Letter to Vaughan (undated); *ibid.*, pp. 210–11.
7   K. Lake, *Memorials of W. C. Lake*, p. 4.
8   David Williams, *Too Quick Despairer: A Life of Arthur Hugh Clough*, p. 30.
9   Letter to Mrs Clough; W. Ward, *W. G. Ward*, p. 108.
10 *Ibid.*, pp. 109–10.
11 Letter to Frederick Temple; *ibid.*, p. 111.
12 Ward, *op. cit.*, p. 107.
13 2 May 1838; Prothero, *Life*, p. 197.
14 *Ibid.*, p. 200.
15 Letter to Mary, 27 June 1838; Pusey House archives.
16 4 July 1838; Pusey House archives.
17 John Jones, 'Sound Religion and Useful Learning: the Rise of Balliol under John Parsons and Richard Jenkyns, 1798–1854', *Balliol Studies*, ed. John Prest, p. 110.
18 Prothero, *Life*, p. 201.
19 *Ibid.*, p. 211.
20 Robin Darwall-Smith, *A History of University College, Oxford*, p. 352.
21 *Ibid.*, p. 354.
22 T. Hughes, *Tom Brown's Schooldays*, p. 121.
23 15 October 1881; 'Master Bradley on Dean Stanley', *University College Record*, iv.3 (3 December 1963), pp. 184ff.
24 Prothero, *Life*, p. 364.
25 2 December 1839; Pusey House archives.
26 Prothero, *Life*, p. 217.
27 *Ibid.*, p. 216.
28 *Ibid.*, p. 219.
29 *Ibid.*
30 *Ibid.*, p. 222.
31 *Ibid.*
32 *Ibid.*
33 Appendix to ch. vii, Prothero, *Life*, pp. 230ff.
34 *Ibid.*, p. 231.
35 T. Arnold, *Sermons*, ii, pp. 121ff.
36 To Maria Hare, 15 February 1840; Prothero, *Letters*, p. 49.
37 Prothero, *Life*, p. 242.
38 *Ibid.*, p. 241.
39 *Ibid.*, pp. 225–6.

Source Notes

40 22 June 1839; Cheshire Record Office, DSA/88.
41 Prothero, *Life*, pp. 227ff.
42 *Ibid.*, pp. 229–30.
43 20 December 1839; Stanley, *op. cit.*, p. 526.
44 Prothero, *Life*, p. 243.
45 12 January 1840; Prothero, *Letters*, p. 47.
46 *Ibid.*
47 A. P. Stanley (ed.), *Addresses and Charges of Edward Stanley, D.D.*, p. 88.
48 Prothero, *Life*, p. 247.
49 27 July 1839; Pusey House archives.
50 Prothero, *Life*, p. 259.
51 *Ibid.*, p. 261.
52 *Ibid.*, pp. 264ff.
53 *Ibid.*, p. 253.
54 *Ibid.*, p. 254.
55 G. G. Bradley, *Recollections of Stanley*, pp. 51–2.
56 Prothero, *Life*, p. 255.
57 Bradley, *op. cit.*, p. 52.
58 Prothero, *Life*, pp. 268–9.
59 *Ibid.*, p. 275.
60 15 March 1841; *ibid.*, pp. 286–7.
61 John Henry Newman, *Apologia Pro Vita Sua* (1864), Fontana Books, 1972, p. 201.
62 Prothero, *Life*, pp. 293–4.
63 R. P. Flindall, *Church of England*, p. 88.
64 *Ibid.*, p. 83.
65 R. T. Davidson and W. Benham, *Life of Tait*, i, p. 76.
66 *Ibid.*, p. 81.
67 *Ibid.*, p. 82.
68 27 May 1841; Prothero, *Life*, p. 296.
69 31 May 1841; *ibid.*, p. 297.
70 Ward, *op. cit.*, p. 175.
71 31 May 1841, Prothero, *Life*, p. 298.
72 Letter to Edward Stanley, 24 August 1840; G. Howes, 'Dr Arnold and Bishop Stanley', *op. cit.*, p. 326.
73 Prothero, *Life*, p. 304.
74 *Ibid.*, p. 306.
75 29 September 1841; Stanley, *Life*, p. 613.
76 *Ibid.*, p. 614.

77 4 December 1841; Prothero, *Letters*, pp. 63–4.
78 Prothero, *Life*, p. 308: for Newman's account of the meeting see letter to Mrs J. Mozley, 31 October 1844; *Letters and Correspondence of John Henry Newman*, ii (1891), pp. 440ff.
79 Bernard Bergonzi, *A Victorian Wanderer: The Life of Thomas Arnold the Younger*, p. 24.
80 Stanley, *Life*, pp. 628–9.
81 Letter to Pearson, 18 June 1842; Pusey House archives.
82 14 June 1842; Prothero, *Letters*, p. 66.
83 15 June 1842; *ibid.*, p. 75.
84 Letter to Pearson, 18 June 1842; Pusey House archives.
85 15 June 1842; Prothero, *Letters*, p. 70.
86 Stanley, *Life*, pp. 658–9.
87 Prothero, *Life*, p. 312.
88 *Ibid.*, p. 313.
89 *Ibid.*

CHAPTER 5

Title: Alfred Tennyson, 'Break, break, break' (1842).
1 R. E. Prothero, *Life of Stanley*, i, p. 314.
2 15 June 1842; R. E. Prothero, *Letters of Stanley*, p. 75.
3 A. P. Stanley, *Life of Arnold*, p. 94: the capitals are Stanley's.
4 R. T. Davidson and W. Benham, *Life of Tait*, i, p. 117.
5 Prothero, *Life*, p. 315.
6 Davidson and Benham, *op. cit.*, p. 111.
7 Prothero, *Life*, p. 316.
8 29 July 1842; Davidson and Benham, *op. cit.*, pp. 113–14.
9 *Ibid.*, p. 114.
10 Letter to Mary; Prothero, *Life*, p. 317.
11 14 August 1842; *ibid.*, pp. 317–18.
12 Prothero, *Life*, p. 318.
13 *Ibid.*, p. 309.
14 M. C. Curthoys, 'The "Unreformed" Colleges', *History of University of Oxford*, vi, M. G. Brock and M. C. Curthoys, p. 149.
15 Cuthbert Bede, B.A., *Mr. Verdant Green: Adventures of an Oxford Freshman* (1857), Nonsuch Publishing, 2006, p. 97: Cuthbert Bede was the *nom-de-plume* of the Revd Edward Bradley.
16 M. Pattison, *Memoirs*, p. 130.
17 University College archives, S16/MS1/1–6.

18 G. G. Bradley, *Recollections of Stanley*, p. 57.
19 Prothero, *Life*, p. 359.
20 Bradley, *op. cit.*, pp. 59, 61.
21 A. G. Butler; Prothero, *Life*, p. 360.
22 *Ibid.*, p. 363.
23 *Ibid.*, p. 364.
24 11 June 1844; Pusey House archives.
25 Prothero, *Life*, p. 319.
26 *Rambler*, lx, 13 October 1750.
27 H. Nicolson, *Development of English Biography*, p. 124.
28 Prothero, *Life*, p. 321.
29 Peter Hammond, *Dean Stanley of Westminster*, p. 55.
30 Letter to Pearson; Prothero, *Life*, p. 323.
31 16 October 1881; W.H. Fremantle, *Sermons Biographical and Miscellaneous*, p. 141.
32 Prothero, *Life*, p. 323.
33 Letter to J. R. Bloxam, 25 March 1841; W. Ward, *W. G. Ward*, p. 194.
34 Ward, *op. cit.*, pp. 306–7.
35 'Religious Movements of the Nineteenth Century', *Edinburgh Review*, April 1881, p. 320.
36 Prothero, *Life*, p. 341.
37 Davidson and Benham, *op. cit.*, p. 128.
38 A. P. Stanley, 'Religious Movements', *op. cit.*, p. 322.
39 Ward, *op. cit.*, p. 340.
40 Prothero, *Life*, p. 336.
41 Ward, *op. cit.*, p. 343n.
42 Letter to B.C. Brodie; Evelyn Abbott and Lewis Campbell, *The Life and Letters of Benjamin Jowett, M.A.*, i, p. 95.
43 Prothero, *Life*, p. 327.
44 28 September 1844; Prothero, *Letters*, pp. 82–3.
45 Letter to Mary; Prothero, *Life*, p. 329.
46 Abbott and Campbell, *op. cit.*, p. 90.
47 Prothero, *Life*, p. 331.
48 Abbott and Campbell, *op. cit.*, p. 98.
49 Prothero, *Life*, p. 365.
50 Abbott and Campbell, *op. cit.*, p. 99.
51 A. P. Stanley, *Sermons and Essays on the Apostolical Age*, p. 3.
52 *Ibid.*, p. 1.
53 *Ibid.*, p. 9.

54 *Ibid.*, p. 8.
55 *Ibid.*, p. 19.
56 Letter to Mary, 9 February 1846; Prothero, *Letters*, p. 98.
57 Prothero, *Life*, p. 369.
58 *Ibid.*, p. 388.
59 *Ibid.*
60 See pp. 89–90.
61 See R. P. Flindall, *Church of England*, pp. 105ff: a royal licence (the *congé d'élire*) obliged the cathedral's dean and canons to elect the person nominated by the Crown to be bishop of the diocese.
62 Abbott and Campbell, *op. cit.*, p. 132.
63 Prothero, *Life*, pp. 347–8.
64 *Ibid.*, pp. 349–50.
65 *The Warden* (1855), Oxford World's Classics, 1988, pp. 100–1.
66 7 January 1848; Standish Meacham, *Lord Bishop: The Life of Samuel Wilberforce, 1805–1873*, p. 161.
67 Prothero, *Life*, p. 353.
68 *Ibid.*, p. 389.
69 *Ibid.*, p. 407.
70 *Ibid.*
71 Letter to Kitty; *ibid.*, p. 390.
72 Prothero, *Life*, p. 392.
73 *Ibid.*: the *garde mobile* was a new police force.
74 Letter to Mary, 13 April 1848; *ibid.*, p. 394.
75 *Ibid.*
76 *Ibid.*
77 *Ibid.*, p. 395.
78 Letter to Mary, 20 April 1848; *ibid.*, p. 400.
79 *Ibid.*, p. 401.
80 *Ibid.*, pp. 401–2.
81 Prothero, *Life*, p. 409.
82 A. P. Stanley, *Memoirs of E. and C. Stanley*, p. 103.
83 7 September 1849; Lady Maria Stanley to Henrietta Stanley, 9 September 1849; Nancy Mitford (ed.), *The Ladies of Alderley*, p. 212.
84 8 September 1849; Prothero, *Letters*, p. 133.
85 *Ibid.*, pp. 133–4.
86 A. P. Stanley, *Addresses of E. Stanley*, p. 142.
87 Mitford, *op. cit.*, pp. 187–8.
88 Stanley, *Memoirs of E. and C. Stanley*, pp. 106–7.
89 *Ibid.*, p. 91.

90 September 1849; Prothero, *Letters*, pp. 134–5.
91 15 September 1849; *ibid.*, pp. 135–6.
92 Balliol College archives, MS 410, Mynors' catalogue.
93 Prothero, *Letters*, pp. 160f.
94 23 October 1849; *ibid.*, pp. 139f.
95 A. J. C. Hare, *Biographical Sketches*, p. 55.
96 Prothero, *Life*, p. 414.
97 26 September 1849; *ibid.*
98 1 October 1849; Balliol College archives, MS 410, Mynors' catalogue.
99 3 October 1849; Balliol College archives, III S: the Dean of Wells was Richard Jenkyns who was also Master of Balliol.
100 Stanley, *Addresses of E. Stanley*, p. 31.
101 Mitford, *op. cit.*, p. 86.
102 Letter to Jowett, 27 October 1845; Balliol College archives, MS 410, Mynors' catalogue.
103 'A Sermon Preached in the Chapel of Rugby School on Sunday, August 14, 1842', pp. 6, 13f.
104 24 October 1849; Balliol College archives, MS 410, Mynors' catalogue.
105 A. Lubbock, *Owen Stanley*, p. 151.
106 Lady Maria Stanley to Henrietta Stanley, 27 October 1844; Mitford, *op. cit.*, pp. 83–4.: Emmy was Lady Stanley's 10th child.
107 Stanley, *Addresses of E. Stanley*, pp. 191ff.
108 Letter to Henrietta Stanley, 6 July 1850; Mitford, *op. cit.*, pp. 237–8.
109 Letter to Pearson, 21 September 1841; Prothero, *Life*, p. 301.
110 'The Gorham Controversy'; reprinted in A. P. Stanley, *Essays on Church and State*.
111 Owen Chadwick, *The Victorian Church*, i, p. 252.
112 Sidney Dark, *Five Deans*, p. 176.
113 Stanley, *Essays on Church and State*, p. 6.
114 *Ibid.*, p. 22.
115 *Ibid.*, p. 8: author's italics.
116 *Ibid.*
117 *Ibid.*, p. 27
118 *Ibid.*, pp. 43–4.
119 *Ibid.*, p. 20.
120 'Catholic Love': Stanley's favourite of Charles Wesley's hymns.
121 Prothero, *Life*, p. 419.
122 Balliol College archives, MS 410, Mynors' catalogue.

123 Letter to Pearson; Prothero, *Life*, p. 422.
124 *Ibid.*, p. 431.
125 *Mark Pattison and the Idea of a University*, p. 90.
126 W. R. Ward, 'From the Tractarians to the Executive Commission, 1845–1854', Brock and Curthoys, *op. cit.*, p. 323.
127 'The Recommendations of the Oxford University Commissioners, with Selections from their Report', p. 209.
128 Davidson and Benham, *op. cit.*, p. 170.
129 Prothero, *Life*, p. 434.
130 William Thackeray, 'May-Day Ode'.
131 Letter to Patrick Brontë, 7 June 1851; *The Brontës: Life and Letters*, ed. C. K. Shorter, ii (1908), p. 216.
132 Royal Archives, VIC/MAIN/QVJ/1851.
133 1 May 1851; Prothero, *Life*, pp. 423ff: c.34,000 people were present.

CHAPTER 6

Title: John Bunyan, *The Pilgrim's Progress* (1678).
1 1 May 1851; R. E. Prothero, *Life of Stanley*, i, p. 426.
2 *Ibid.*, p. 427.
3 23 October 1851; *ibid.*
4 Illustrations, p.
5 Prothero, *op. cit.*, p. 428.
6 *Ibid.*
7 Lady Maria Stanley to Lady Henrietta Stanley, 14 November 1852; Nancy Mitford, *The Stanleys of Alderley*, p. 54.
8 Prothero, *op. cit.*, pp. 428–9.
9 Derek Ingram Hill, *Christ's Glorious Church: The Story of Canterbury Cathedral*, pp. 77–8.
10 O. Chadwick, *Victorian Church*, ii, p. 369.
11 4 January 1852; Prothero, *op. cit.*, p. 431.
12 A. J. C. Hare, *Biographical Sketches*, pp. 57–8.
13 *Ibid.*, pp. 56–7.
14 4 January 1852; Prothero, *op. cit.*, p. 431.
15 E. M. Goulburn, *The Principles of the Cathedral System Vindicated* (1870), p. xxxiv.
16 26 September 1852; R. E. Prothero, *Letters of Stanley*, pp. 160ff.
17 29 September 1852; *ibid.*, pp. 168–9.
18 Prothero, *Life*, p. 438.

19 *Ibid.*, p. 436.
20 Letter to Pearson, 2 November 1852; Prothero, *Letters*, pp. 172–3.
21 Prothero, *Life*, pp. 439ff.
22 S. Dark, *Five Deans*, p. 177.
23 Prothero, *Life*, p. 443.
24 *Ibid.*
25 *Ibid.*, p. 444.
26 Letter to Mary, 5 February 1853; Prothero, *Letters*, p. 189.
27 Letter to Mary, 10 January 1853; *ibid*, p. 185.
28 *Ibid.*, pp 186–7.
29 Prothero, *Life*, p. 450.
30 *Ibid.*, pp 451.
31 *Ibid.*, p. 452.
32 *Ibid.*, p. 453.
33 Letter to Mary, Easter Eve 1853; Prothero, *Letters*, p. 201.
34 *Ibid.*, pp. 202–3.
35 *Ibid.*, p. 203.
36 *Ibid.*, pp. 204f.
37 Letter to Mary, 3 April 1853; *ibid.*, p. 207.
38 Letter to Mary, 8 April 1853; *ibid.*, p. 220.
39 Prothero, *Life*, p. 461.
40 Letter to Mary, Trinity Sunday 1853; Prothero, *Letters*, pp 242–3.
41 *Ibid.*, pp 243–4.
42 *Ibid.*, p. 245.
43 Prothero, *Life*, p. 462.
44 *Ibid.*, p. 463.
45 *Ibid.*, p. 464.
46 *Ibid.*, p. 491.
47 *Ibid.*, p. 492.
48 E. T. Cook, *The Life of Florence Nightingale* (1913), i, p. 234.
49 Cecil Woodham-Smith, *Florence Nightingale, 1820–1910* (1950), p. 192.
50 Gillian Gill, *Nightingales: The Story of Florence Nightingale and Her Remarkable Family* (2004), pp. 366–7.
51 18 February 1856; Mitford, *op. cit.*, pp. 134–5.
52 October 1855; Gill, *op. cit.*, p. 368.
53 19 December 1855; *ibid*, pp. 368–9.
54 Lady Henrietta to Lord Edward Stanley, 4 December 1851; Mitford, *op. cit.*, p. 25.
55 Lord Stanley to Lady Stanley, 8 December 1851; *ibid.*, p. 26.

56 Prothero, *Life*, p. 494.
57 *Ibid.*
58 *Ibid.*, p. 478
59 G. G. Bradley, *Recollections of Stanley*, p. 72.
60 20 February 1856; Prothero, *Letters*, p. 246.
61 A. P. Stanley, *Sinai and Palestine*, pp. 181–2.
62 *Ibid.*, pp. xix–xx.
63 Prothero, *Life*, p. 477.
64 28 February 1858; *ibid*, p. 484.
65 Letter to Stanley, 8 July 1856, and Stanley's reply, 10 July 1856; Prothero, *Life*, pp. 481ff.
66 Stanley, *op. cit.*, pp. xxi–xxii.
67 28 August 1856; Prothero, *Letters*, p. 252.
68 Prothero, *Life*, p. 496.
69 R. T. Davidson and W. Benham, *Life of Tait*, i, p. 198.
70 12 November 1856; *ibid.*, p. 208.
71 26 November 1856; *ibid.*, p. 209.
72 Prothero, *Life*, p. 497.
73 Bradley, *op. cit.*, p. 78.
74 W. Tuckwell, *Reminiscences of Oxford*, p. 155.
75 Prothero, *Life*, p. 499.
76 Henry Lewis Thompson, *Henry George Liddell, D.D., Dean of Christ Church, Oxford: A Memoir*, pp. 183–4.
77 Prothero, *Life*, p. 508.
78 *Ibid.*; p. 500: see also Jowett's letter to Kitty, December 1856; E. Abbott and L. Campbell, *Life of Jowett*, i, p. 285.
79 *Ibid.*
80 Prothero, *Life*, p. 502.
81 June 1857; *ibid.*, p. 503.
82 A. P. Stanley, *Lectures on the History of the Eastern Church*, p. 28.
83 *Ibid.*, p. 36.
84 *Ibid.*, p. 48.
85 *Ibid.*, p. 65.
86 *Ibid.*, pp. 213–14.
87 Prothero, *Life*, p. 517.
88 *Ibid.*, p. 520
89 *Ibid.*, p. 523.
90 *Ibid.*, p. 520.
91 *Ibid.*, pp. 526–7.
92 Letter to Kitty, 20 August 1857; Prothero, *Letters*, p. 276.

93   Prothero, *Life*, p. 529.
94   *Ibid*, p. 535.
95   *Ibid.*, p. 536.

CHAPTER 7

Title: Samuel Johnson, 'The Vanity of Human Wishes' (1749).
1   Tuckwell, *Reminiscences of Oxford*, p. 134: Barnes had been a canon since 1810.
2   E. G. W. Bill and J. F. A. Mason, *Christ Church and Reform 1850–1867*, p. 61.
3   *Ibid.*, p. 63.
4   Dean and Chapter minutes, 17 December 1862; Christ Church archive: Liddell is criticised for 'ordering certain repairs and alterations in and about the College without communication with the Chapter'.
5   R. E. Prothero, *Life of Stanley*, ii, p. 2.
6   H. L. Thompson, *Liddell*, p. 183: Thompson arrived at Christ Church (as a junior student) in the same year as Stanley.
7   23 July 1856; Christ Church archive.
8   Thompson, *op. cit.*, p. 137.
9   Letter to Alice (Liddell) Hargreaves, 1 March 1885; Morton N. Cohen (ed.), *The Letters of Lewis Carroll* (1979), i, p. 561.
10 Walter de la Mare, *Lewis Carroll* (1932), p. 45.
11 From the first line of the verse prelude to *Alice's Adventures in Wonderland*.
12 Prothero, *op. cit.*, i, p. 536.
13 Letter to Shairp, *ibid.*, ii, p. 3.
14 A. J. C. Hare, *Biographical Sketches*, p. 65; see also Hare, *The Story of my Life*, ii, pp. 153ff.
15 Prothero, *op. cit.*, p. 10.
16 G. G. Bradley, *Recollections of Stanley*, p. 82.
17 Prothero, *op. cit.*, p. 12.
18 *Ibid.*, p. 9.
19 *Ibid.*, p. 13.
20 Hughes, *Tom Brown at Oxford*, Nelson Classics, p. 333.
21 4 November 1840; Stanley, *Life of Arnold*, pp. 572–3.
22 Christopher Tyerman, *A History of Harrow School*, p. 247.
23 *Ibid.*, p. 248.
24 3 March 1845.

25 Tyerman, *op. cit.*, p. 274.
26 Phyllis Grosskurth (ed.), *The Memoirs of John Addington Symonds*, p. 94.
27 *Ibid.*, p. 95.
28 *Ibid.*, p. 91.
29 *Ibid.*, p. 97: there were in fact c.440 boys in the school.
30 *Ibid.*, p. 96: Stanley had been called 'Nancy' at Rugby.
31 *Ibid.*, pp. 97–8.
32 *Ibid.*, p. 112.
33 30 October 1897: Tollemache reiterates this in his *Old and New Memories*, p. 119.
34 2 March 1860; N. Mitford, *Stanleys of Alderley*, p. 237.
35 Grosskurth, *op. cit.*, p. 115.
36 *Ibid.*
37 O. Chadwick, *The Victorian Church*, i, p. 497.
38 *Ibid.*, p. 499.
39 R. T. Davidson and W. Benham, *Life of Tait*, i, p. 245.
40 5 September 1859; *ibid.*, pp. 241, 243.
41 3 June 1860; Prothero, *op. cit.*, p. 28.
42 24 July 1860; *ibid.*, p.29.
43 Letter to Tait; Davidson and Benham, *op. cit.*, p. 314.
44 A. O. J. Cockshut, *Anglican Attitudes: A Study of Victorian Religious Controversies*, p. 67.
45 *Essays and Reviews*, 10th edn, 1862, p. 490.
46 *Ibid.*, p. 453.
47 15 August; E. Abbott and L. Campbell, *Life of Jowett*, i, p. 275.
48 Prothero, *op. cit.*, p. 17.
49 A. P. Stanley, 'Essays and Reviews', *Edinburgh Review*, April 1861; *Essays on Church and State*, p 59.
50 Prothero, *op. cit.*, p. 31.
51 *Ibid.*
52 *Ibid.*, p. 30.
53 12 February 1861; Flindall, *Church of England*, p. 179.
54 Davidson and Benham, *op. cit.*, pp. 284ff.
55 Letter to Stanley; Prothero, *op. cit.*, p. 39.
56 1867 notebook; Geoffrey Faber, *Jowett: A Portrait with Background*, p. 136.
57 Prothero, *op. cit.*, p. 40.
58 *Ibid.*, p. 41.
59 Jan Morris (ed.), *The Oxford Book of Oxford* (1978), p. 237.

60 14 December 1855; Abbott and Campbell, *op. cit.*, pp. 239–40.
61 *Ibid.*, p. 240.
62 2 February 1862; *ibid.*, p. 307.
63 Prothero, *op. cit.*, pp. 134f.
64 Abbott and Campbell, *op. cit.*, p. 314.
65 *Ibid.*, p. 315.
66 *Ibid.*, p. 320.
67 27 October 1860; Philip Magnus, *King Edward the Seventh*, p. 31.
68 Letter to his father, 18 October 1859; Thompson, *op. cit.*, p. 177.
69 Lady Henrietta to Lord Edward Stanley, 28 November 1860; Mitford, *op. cit.*, p. 252.
70 Magnus, *op. cit.*, p. 32.
71 16 November 1861; *ibid.*, p. 51.
72 Prothero, *op. cit.*, pp. 60–1.
73 19 December 1861.
74 Prothero, *op. cit*, p. 61.
75 24 December 1861; P. Hammond, *Dean Stanley*, pp. 123–4.
76 Cheshire Record Office, DSA/85.
77 Lord Hertford's memorandum, February 1862; Christopher Hibbert, *Queen Victoria: A Personal History*, p. 299.
78 Magnus, *op. cit.*, p. 53.
78 13 January 1862; Prothero, *op. cit.*, p. 63.
80 Letter to Kitty; *ibid.*
81 *Ibid.*, p. 64.
82 *Ibid.*
83 Dated 1862; Balliol archives, III S99.
84 Prothero, *op. cit.*, p. 65.
85 20 January 1862; R. E. Prothero, *Letters of Stanley*, p. 317.
86 15 February 1862; *ibid.*, p. 318.
87 Letter to Kitty, 3 March 1862; A.V. Baillie and Hector Bolitho (edd.), *A Victorian Dean*, p. 117.
88 *Ibid.*, p. 116.
89 *Ibid.*, p. 117.
90 *Ibid.*
91 *Ibid.*
92 Letter to Kitty, 6 March 1862; *ibid.*, p. 118.
93 Letter to Kitty, 3 March 1862; *ibid.*, p. 116.
94 Letter to Kitty, 15 March 1862; *ibid.*, p. 127.
95 Letter to Kitty, 16 May 1862; *ibid.*, p. 90.
96 Letter to Kitty, 6 March 1862; *ibid.*, p. 120.

97 *Ibid.*, p. 121.
98 Letter to Kitty, 7 March 1862; *ibid.*, pp. 121–2.
99 Letter to Kitty, 20 March 1862; *ibid.*, p. 136.
100 *Ibid.*
101 *Ibid.*, pp. 136–7.
102 27 February 1862; Prothero, *Life*, p. 70.
103 Letter to Lady Henrietta Stanley, 4 April 1862; Mitford, *op. cit.*, p. 284.
104 24 March 1862; Baillie and Bolitho, *op. cit.*, pp. 137–8.
105 *Ibid.*, p. 138.
106 9 March 1862; Abbott and Campbell, *op. cit.*, p. 358.
107 25 March 1862; Prothero, *Life*, pp. 75ff.
108 *Ibid.*, p. 75.
109 Prothero, *Life*, pp. 95–6.
110 *Ibid.*, p. 97.
111 *Ibid.*
112 Baillie and Bolitho, *op. cit.*, p. 148.
113 A. P. Stanley, *Sermons in the East*, p. 4.
114 *Ibid.*, p. 21.
115 *Ibid.*, pp. 22–3.
116 May 1863; Prothero, *Life*, p. 122.
117 Letter to Hon. Lady Welby, 1875; *ibid.*, p. 123.
118 Stanley, *Sermons in the East*, pp. v ff.
119 *Ibid.*, p. xvii.
120 Prothero, *Life*, p. 93.
121 Stanley, *Sermons in the East*, p. 126.
122 Queen Victoria's journal, 15 February 1863; Hammond, *op. cit.*, p. 143.
123 Prothero, *Life*, p. 123.
124 Letter to Mary; *ibid.*, pp. 123–4.
125 Queen Victoria's journal, 14 December 1862; Helen Rappaport, *Magnificent Obsession*, p. 159.
126 'Service Held in Windsor Castle On the Anniversary of the Lamented Death of The Prince Consort', p. 17; Cheshire Record Office, DSA 89/4.
127 Prothero, *Life*, p. 125.
128 Queen Victoria's journal, 21 June 1862; Magnus, *op. cit.*, p. 57.
129 *Ibid.*, p. 67.
130 Hibbert, *op. cit.*, p. 304.
131 Baillie and Bolitho, *op. cit.*, p. 216.

Source Notes

132 14 March 1863; A.V. Baillie and Hector Bolitho (edd.), *Letters of Lady Augusta Stanley: A Young Lady at Court, 1849–1863*, appendix iii, p. 307.
133 *Ibid.*, p. 309.
134 Baillie and Bolitho, *A Victorian Dean*, p. 218.
135 Prothero, *Life*, pp. 131–2.
136 Baillie and Bolitho, *Letters of Lady Stanley*, appendix v, p. 319.
137 29 September 1863; *ibid.*, p. 291.
138 *Ibid.*, p. 292.
139 *Ibid.*, pp. 295–6.
140 6 November 1863; *ibid.*, p. 300.
141 Letter to Frances, 1 October 1863; *ibid.*, p. 294.
142 Letter from Augusta to Frances, 31 October 1863; *ibid.*, 298ff.
143 Hibbert, *op. cit.*, p. 315.
144 *Ibid.*
145 8 November 1863; Prothero, *Life*, p. 139.
146 *Ibid.*, p. 97.
147 7 November 1863; Prothero, *Letters*, pp. 338–9.
148 Prothero, *Life*, p. 133.
149 Thompson, *op. cit.*, p. 189: the letter was sent to Stanley in Italy where he was touring with Mary and Pearson. It miscarried and Stanley did not receive it until January 1864.
150 9 November 1863; Christ Church archive.
151 September 1856; Balliol College archives, III S.
152 8 November 1863; *ibid.*, III S110.
153 9 November 1863; *ibid.*, I F6/6.
154 Letter to Augusta; Prothero, *Life*, p. 144.
155 *Ibid.*
156 *Ibid.*, pp. 148–9.
157 'Great Opportunities: A Farewell Sermon' (1863), p. 21.
158 Prothero, *Life*, p. 150.
159 *Ibid.*, pp. 147–8.

CHAPTER 8

Title: Thomas Babington Macaulay, 'Warren Hastings' (1841).
1 A. V. Baillie and Hector Bolitho (edd.), *Later Letters of Lady Augusta Stanley, 1864–1876*, p. 29.
2 *Ibid.*
3 Letter to Shairp: R. E. Prothero, *Life of Stanley*, ii, p. 155.

4 A. V. Baillie and H. Bolitho, *A Victorian Dean*, p. 224.
5 Letter to de Circourt; Prothero, *op. cit.*, p 151.
6 Prothero, *op. cit.*, p. 154.
7 H. L. Thompson, *Liddell*, p. 89.
8 M. S. Stancliffe, 'Victorian Chapter', *A House of Kings: The History of Westminster Abbey*, ed. Edward Carpenter, p. 279.
9 Prothero, *op. cit.*, p. 156.
10 Richard Jenkyns, *Westminster Abbey*, p. 187.
11 *Ibid.*, p. 72.
12 Prothero, *op. cit.*, p. 156.
13 Stancliffe, *op. cit.*, p. 302.
14 Letter to Pearson; Prothero, *op. cit.*, p. 158.
15 23 February 1864; Henry Parry Liddon, *Life of Edward Bouverie Pusey*, iv, p. 63.
16 *Ibid.*, p. 64.
17 25 February 1864; Prothero, *op. cit.*, p. 161.
18 28 February 1864; Liddon, *op. cit.*, p. 65: Jowett was not asked to preach until 1866.
19 6 March 1864; Prothero, *op. cit.*, p. 165.
20 *Chronicle of Convocation,* Canterbury, upper house, 3 May 1870, p. 222.
21 R. T. Davidson and W. Benham, *Life of Tait*, ii, p. 65.
22 11 July 1870; S. Meacham, *Lord Bishop*, p. 304.
23 *Chron. Convoc.*, lower house, 15 February 1871, p. 143.
24 *Ibid.*, 16 February 1871, pp. 177–8.
25 *Ibid.*, 17 February 1871, pp. 243–4.
26 A. P. Stanley, 'Recollections as Dean' (unpublished typescript), p. 40; Westminster Abbey muniments.
27 *Chron. Convoc.*, lower house, 9 February 1866, p. 175.
28 A. P. Stanley, 'The Bennett Judgment', *Edinburgh Review*, July 1872.
29 *The Guardian*, 6 May 1874, pp. 358f.
30 Stanley, *Chron. Convoc.*, lower house, 24 June 1864, p. 1792.
31 A. P. Stanley, 'The Three Pastorals', *Edinburgh Review*, July 1864; reprinted in A. P. Stanley, *Essays on Church and State*, pp. 97ff.
32 *Chron. Convoc.*, lower house, 24 June 1864 p. 1792.
33 Prothero, *op. cit.*, p. 370.
34 Stanley, *Recollections,* p. 38: see also Stanley, *Essays on Church and State*, p. xxxii n.
35 Prothero, *op. cit.*, p. 372.

36 J. W. Colenso, *The Pentateuch and Book of Joshua Critically Examined*, p. xx.
37 Letter to Shairp, November 1862; Prothero, *op. cit.*, p. 100.
38 Letter to Jowett, August 1862; *ibid.*
39 Prothero, *op. cit.*, p. 104.
40 *Chron. Convoc.*, lower house, 28 June 1865, p. 2359.
41 *Ibid.*, p. 2383.
42 29 June 1866; Stanley, *Essays on Church and State*, pp. 329–30.
43 21 September 1867; Prothero, *op. cit.*, p. 199.
44 2 March 1864; Royal Archives, VIC/ADDU/32.
45 Baillie and Bolitho, *Later Letters*, p. 47.
46 *Ibid.*, pp. 16–17.
47 4 March 1869; P. Hammond, *Dean Stanley*, p. 179.
48 Baillie and Bolitho, *Later Letters*, p. 75.
49 Prothero, *op. cit.*, p. 338.
50 24 September 1864; *ibid.*, p. 339.
51 30 October 1864; *ibid.*, pp. 340ff.
52 *Ibid.*
53 Prothero, *op. cit.*, p. 349.
54 *Ibid.*
55 *Ibid.*, p. 350.
56 *Ibid.*, p. 351.
57 Baillie and Bolitho, *Later Letters*, p. 44.
58 Prothero, *op. cit.*, p. 353: the funeral took place on 27 October 1865.
59 *Ibid.*, p. 353.
60 Jasper Ridley, *Lord Palmerston*, p. 783.
61 Prothero, *op. cit.*, pp. 353–4.
62 Alec R. Vidler, *The Church in an Age of Revolution*, p. 155.
63 Letter to Mary; Prothero, *op. cit.*, p. 356: in 1866 Gladstone was Chancellor of the Exchequer.
64 Prothero, *op. cit.*, pp. 358–9.
65 *Ibid.*, pp. 359f.
66 *Ibid.*, p. 109.
67 *Essays of Matthew Arnold* (1904), p. 427: first published in *Macmillan's Magazine*, February 1863.
68 O. Chadwick, *Victorian Church*, ii, p. 63.
69 *Ibid.*, pp. 64–5.
70 *Ibid.*, p. 65: Shaftesbury was speaking at the annual meeting of the Church Pastoral-Aid Society, May 1866.

71 *The Month*, June 1866.
72 *The Guardian*, 7 February 1866.
73 Prothero, *op. cit.*, pp. 254–5.
74 A. P. Stanley, *Historical Memorials of Westminster Abbey*, p. vii.
75 Prothero, *op. cit.*, p. 261.
76 *Ibid.*, p. 259.
77 *Ibid.*, p. 260.
78 'On St James's Park'; Stanley, *Westminster Abbey*, p. 116.
79 *Ibid.*
80 Letter to Max Müller; Prothero, *op. cit.*, p. 261.

CHAPTER 9

Title: A. P. Stanley, 'O Day of Ashes!' (1878).
1 Prothero, *Life of A. P. Stanley*, ii, p. 271.
2 *Ibid.*
3 A. P. Stanley, *Essays on Church and State*, p. vi.
4 *Ibid.*, p. x: Stanley quotes from the ordination service.
5 Prothero, *op. cit.*, p 284.
6 Letter to J.A. Froude, February 1869; *ibid.*, pp. 285f: if Stanley had consulted the Abbey's burial register he would have discovered that it recorded James I's burial in Henry VII's vault.
7 Prothero, *ibid.*, p. 286: Tait's biography begins with a different account in which Stanley was sitting next to Tait at the meeting in the Jerusalem Chamber, at the end of which a messenger arrived to tell him that the coffin had been discovered.
8 Arthur A. Adrian, 'Charles Dickens and Dean Stanley', *The Dickensian*, 320 (1956), pp. 152ff.
9 *The Times*, 13 June 1870.
10 Prothero, *op. cit.*, pp. 322–3.
11 *Ibid.*, p. 323.
12 *Ibid.*, p. 324.
13 19 June 1870; *ibid.*, p. 317.
14 21 May 1871; *ibid.*
15 25 June 1871; *ibid.*, p. 318.
16 19 April 1874; *ibid.*
17 Ellen C. Clayton, 'A Sunday Afternoon in Westminster Abbey', *The Sunday Review*, i.4 (July 1877), pp. 223ff.
18 H. E. B. Arnold, 'Westminster Abbey in the Middle of the Nineteenth

Century', *Westminster Abbey Quarterly*, i.3 (1939), pp. 19ff: the author's father had been a minor canon.
19 Prothero, *op. cit.*, p. 316.
20 28 December 1876; Frances A. Humphrey, *Dean Stanley with the Children*, pp. 106ff: the poet is Henry Vaughan.
21 Prothero, *op. cit.*, p. 295
22 Essay viii in *Essays on Church and State*.
23 *Ibid.*, p. 369.
24 Prothero, *op. cit.*, p. 296.
25 *Ibid.*, p. 297.
26 *Ibid.*, p. 298.
27 *Ibid.*, p. 299.
28 *Ibid.*, p. 307.
29 William Boyd Carpenter, *Some Pages of My Life* (1911), pp. 195–6.
30 Prothero, *op. cit.*, p. 310.
31 *House and Home*, 19 May 1882; *ibid.*, p. 311.
32 M.S. Stancliffe, 'Victorian Chapter', *A House of Kings*, ed. E. Carpenter, p. 308.
33 *Ibid.*, p. 310.
34 R. T. Davidson and W. Benham, *Life of Tait*, i, p. 409.
35 Stanley, *op. cit.*, p. xx.
36 *Ibid.*, p. 168.
37 *Ibid.*, pp. 153–4.
38 *Ibid.*, p. 155.
39 *Fraser's Magazine*, December 1865; Stanley, *op. cit.*, pp. 213–14.
40 Davidson and Benham, *op. cit.*, ii, p. 128.
41 Prothero, *op. cit.*, appendix to ch. xxi, pp. 232ff.
42 *Chronicle of Convocation*, Canterbury, lower house, 24 April 1872, p. 353.
43 Prothero, *op. cit.*, p. 225.
44 *Ibid.*
45 *Ibid.*
46 *Ibid.*, pp. 229f.
47 *Chron. Convoc*, lower house, 12 February 1873, pp. 131–2.
48 H. P. Liddon, *Life of Pusey*, iii, p. 408.
49 25 February 1872; E. Abbott and L. Campbell, *Life of Jowett*, ii, p. 25.
50 H. L. Thompson, *Liddell*, p. 192.
51 Prothero, *op. cit.*, p. 226.
52 Thompson, *op. cit.*, p. 193.

53 Prothero, *op. cit.*, p. 228.
54 *Ibid.*, pp. 228–9.
55 *Ibid.*, p. 384.
56 *Ibid.*, pp. 384–5.
57 *Ibid.*, p. 386.
58 A. P. Stanley, *Lectures on the History of the Church of Scotland*, p. 19.
59 Prothero, *op. cit.*, 274.
60 *Ibid.*
61 Stanley, *Lectures on Church of Scotland*, p. 5.
62 *Ibid.*, pp. 3ff.
63 Prothero, *op. cit.*, p. 382.
64 Letter to Pearson, 12 August 1870; *ibid.*
65 Prothero, *op. cit.*, p. 383.
66 *Ibid.*, pp. 403f; see also A.V. Baillie and H. Bolitho, *Later Letters of Augusta Stanley*, p. 128.
67 Baillie and Bolitho, *op. cit.*, p. 132.
68 Quoted by Prothero, *op. cit.*, p. 405.
69 19 September 1872.
70 27 September and 2 October 1872.
71 Prothero, *op. cit.*, p. 412.
72 Baillie and Bolitho, *op. cit.*, p. 156.
73 *Ibid.*, p. 160.
74 Letter to Louisa Stanley, 21 November 1870; Prothero, *op. cit.*, p. 401.
75 A. L. Rowse, *Matthew Arnold: Poet and Prophet*, p. 189.
76 *Ibid.*
77 1 November 1873; R. E. Prothero, *Letters of Stanley*, p. 381.
78 *Ibid.*, p. 380.
79 *Ibid.*
80 J. B. Atlay, *The Victorian Chancellors* (1906), ii, p. 264.
81 S. Meacham, *Lord Bishop*, p. 312
82 Letter to Walter Hook, Dean of Chichester, 19 July 1873; Bodleian Library, MS. Eng. c. 3336, fols 65–6.
83 Prothero, *Life*, p. 416.
84 Baillie and Bolitho, *op. cit.*, p. 147.
85 *Ibid.*, p. 148.
86 *Ibid.*, pp. 148–9.
87 Giles St Aubyn, *Queen Victoria: A Portrait*, p. 388.
88 Prothero, *Life,* p. 408.

89 Ibid.
90 8 August 1873; Baillie and Bolitho, op. cit., pp. 187–8.
91 12 January 1874; Prothero, Life, p. 423.
92 Ibid.
93 Ibid., p. 424.
94 Ibid.
95 Ibid., pp. 425–6.
96 18 January 1874; Prothero, Letters, p. 384.
97 Ibid., p. 385.
98 Letter to Mary, 23 January 1874; Prothero, Life, pp. 432–3.
99 Ibid., p. 433.
100 Ibid., p. 434.
101 Letter to Mary; ibid., p. 442.
102 Letter to Frances, 10 February 1874; Baillie and Bolitho, op. cit., p. 232.
103 Prothero, Life, pp. 374ff.
104 A.W. Besant, Annie Besant: An Autobiography (1908), p. 99.
105 Our Corner; Prothero, Life, pp. 451ff.
106 Ibid., p. 451.
107 Ibid., p. 452.
108 Ibid., pp. 452f.
109 Macmillan's Magazine, July 1874.
110 See 6/29–30.
111 Macmillan's Magazine, op. cit., p. 276.
112 Ibid., p. 277.
113 14 June 1874; Royal Archives, VIC/MAIN/D/4/62.
114 Also published in Macmillan's Magazine, op. cit: see Appendix IV.
115 Ibid., p. 279.
116 Ibid.
117 Baillie and Bolitho, A Victorian Dean, p. xv.
118 Baillie and Bolitho, Later Letters, pp. 255–6.
119 Ibid., p. 257.
120 Ibid., p. 267.
121 Baillie and Bolitho, Later Letters, pp. 263–4.
122 Prothero, Life, p. 458.
123 Baillie and Bolitho, Later Letters, pp. 268–9.
124 Ibid., p. 269.
125 21 November 1874; Prothero, Life, p. 458.
126 Prothero, Life, p. 460.
127 Ibid.

128 *Ibid.*, pp. 461–2.
129 *Ibid.*, p. 464.
130 *Ibid.*
131 Letter to Comte Adolphe de Circourt; *ibid.*, p. 482: friend of Mary Mohl, his wife had also been mistress of a Paris salon.
132 Prothero, *Life*, p. 484.
133 Letter to Mary, 11 October 1875; Baillie and Bolitho, *Later Letters*, p. 271.
134 *Ibid.*
135 *Ibid.*
136 Prothero, *Life*, p. 467.
137 Baillie and Bolitho, *Later Letters*, p. 271.
138 Prothero, *Life*, p. 467.
139 Letter to de Circourt; *ibid.*, p. 469.
140 Prothero, *Life*, p. 470.
141 Letter to de Circourt; *ibid.*
142 Autograph of Dean Stanley; Bodleian Library, MS. Eng. d. 2566, fol. 15.
143 Queen Victoria's journal, 26 February 1876; G. E. Buckle (ed.), *The Letters of Queen Victoria*, ii, p. 448.
144 Prothero, *Life*, p. 472.
145 *Ibid.*
146 A. P. Stanley, *Memoirs of E. and C. Stanley*, pp. 332–3.
147 Quoted by Liddell in his sermon at Augusta's funeral; Bodleian Library, MS. Eng. d. 2566, fol. 9.
148 Prothero, *Life*, p. 471.
149 Davidson and Benham, *op. cit.*, pp. 317–18.
150 Bodleian Library, MS. Eng. d. 2566, fol. 9.
151 Letter to de Circourt; Prothero, *Life*, p. 474.

CHAPTER 10

Title: A. P. Stanley, 'The Perfect Death' (1880).
1   R. E. Prothero, *Life of Stanley*, ii, pp. 473–4.
2   March 1876; Prothero, *op. cit.*, p. 480.
3   Prothero, *op. cit.*, p. 475
4   Letter to de Circourt, *ibid.*, p. 491.
5   7 April 1876; *ibid.*, p. 481.
6   10 March 1876; R. E. Prothero, *Letters of Stanley*, p. 408.
7   Prothero, *Life*, p. 491.

8 4 June 1877; Royal Archives, VIC/ADDA/7/394.
9 11 June 1877; Prothero, *Letters*, pp. 411f: the bust was sculpted by Lady Lucy Grant, the daughter of Augusta's half-sister.
10 August 1876; Prothero, *Life*, p. 484.
11 *Ibid.*, p. 485
12 *Ibid.*, p. 486
13 *Ibid.*, p. 487.
14 Prothero, *Letters*, p. 409.
15 Prothero, *Life*, p. 490.
16 *Ibid.*
17 *Ibid.*, p. 487.
18 *Ibid.*, pp. 487–8; the window was destroyed in September 1940 by a bomb which exploded in Old Palace Yard.
19 Published in *Macmillan's Magazine*, May 1877.
20 Prothero, *Life*, p. 462.
21 *Ibid.*
22 *Ibid.*, p. 463.
23 *Ibid.*
24 31 August 1878; *ibid.*, p. 510.
25 16 July 1878; Balliol College archives, I F5/12.
26 Letter to Mary Stanley, 15 September 1878; Prothero, *Letters*, p. 420.
27 *Ibid.*
28 19 July 1881.
29 Prothero, *Life*, p. 519.
30 A. P. Stanley, *Addresses and Sermons delivered during a visit to the United States and Canada in 1878* (London, 1883 edn), p. 5.
31 Prothero, *Life*, p. 520.
32 *Atlantic Monthly Magazine*, October 1881.
33 Stanley, *op. cit.*, p. 8.
34 *Ibid.*, pp. 8–9.
35 *Ibid.*, pp. 13–14.
36 Prothero, *Life*, p. 523.
37 Stanley, *op. cit.*, p. 118.
38 Prothero, *Life*, p. 524.
39 *Ibid.*
40 *Ibid.*: the building of the Washington Monument, for example, had stalled during the Civil War and was less than a third of its final height. Work resumed in 1879, the year after Stanley's visit.
41 *Ibid.*, p. 526.

42 13 October 1878; Prothero, *Letters*, p. 429.
43 Letter to Mrs Drummond; Prothero, *Life*, p. 532.
44 *Ibid.*
45 7 November 1878.
46 Prothero, *Letters*, p. 433.
47 G. G. Bradley, *Recollections of Stanley*, p. 136.
48 Letter to George and Thomas Keats, 21 December 1817; Robert Pack (ed.), *Selected Letters of John Keats* (1974), p. 55: Keats thought this capacity helped to form 'a Man of Achievement'.
49 3 November 1878; Stanley, *op. cit.*, p. 254.
50 1 November 1878; *ibid.*, pp. 46–7.
51 Stanley, *op. cit.*, p. 86.
52 Prothero, *Life*, p. 540.
53 *Ibid.*
54 A. P. Stanley, *Memoirs of E. and C. Stanley*, p. xi.
55 Prothero, *op. cit.*, p. 543.
56 *Ibid.*
57 *Ibid.*
58 *Ibid.*, p. 544.
59 *Ibid.*
60 *Ibid.*
61 Letter to Mrs Drummond; *ibid.*, p. 545.
62 Quoted by Monica E. Baly, 'Stanley, Mary (1813–1879)', *Oxford Dictionary of National Biography* (2004).
63 Prothero, *Life*, p. 547.
64 *Ibid.*
65 *Ibid.*, p. 549.
66 *Ibid.*, p. 554.
67 *Ibid.*, p. 550.
68 Letter to Mrs Drummond, *ibid.*
69 21 July 1880; *ibid.*, p. 328.
70 Prothero, *Life*, p. 330.
71 *Ibid.*, p. 553.
72 Letter to Stanley, March 1865; G. Faber, *Jowett*, pp. 296–7.
73 14 July 1880; Balliol College archives, I F5/15.
74 Notebook, 1867; Faber, *op. cit.*, p. 136: see p. 217.
75 A. P. Stanley, *Christian Institutions: Essays on Ecclesiastical Subjects*, p. 6.
76 Prothero, *Life*, pp. 560–1.
77 Stanley, *Christian Institutions*, p. 353.

Source Notes

78 A. P. Stanley, 'Recollections of Events Connected with Westminster Abbey', (handwritten document), Westminster Abbey muniments.
79 *Ibid.*
80 *Ibid.*
81 21 April 1881; Prothero, *Life*, pp. 564–5.
82 A. P. Stanley, *Sermons on Special Occasions*, p. 282.
83 M. S. Stancliffe, 'Victorian Chapter', *House of Kings*, ed. E. Carpenter, p. 315.
84 Letter to treasurer, 1 March 1870; *ibid.*, pp. 321–2.
85 Prothero, *Life*, p. 303.
86 *Ibid.*, p. 567.
87 *Ibid.*, p. 569.
88 *Ibid.*
89 *Ibid.*, p. 570: according to Tait, Stanley's last words were similar.
90 *Ibid.*, p. 571.
91 H.L. Thompson, *Liddell*, p. 259.
92 Queen Victoria's journal, Osborne, 19 July 1881; Buckle, *op. cit.*, p. 225.
93 19 July 1881, Royal Archives, VIC/MAIN/A/54/4.
94 27 July 1881; Magnus, *op. cit.*, p. 172.
95 Thompson, *op. cit.*, p. 260.
96 'A Funeral Sermon on Arthur Penrhyn Stanley, D.D. Preached in Westminster Abbey on Sunday Afternoon, July 24, 1881 by C. J. Vaughan, D.D.', p. 7.
97 31 July 1881; R.T. Davidson and W. Benham, *Life of Tait*, ii, p. 541.
98 'Speech at the meeting in the chapter house of Westminster Abbey in commemoration of Dean Stanley, 13 December 1881'; James Russell Lowell, *Democracy and Other Addresses* (1887), pp. 57ff.
99 22 July 1881; Buckle, *op. cit.*, iii, p. 226.
100 2 August 1881; *ibid.*, pp. 227–8
101 2 August 1881; *ibid.*, p. 228
102 Letter to Wellesley, 27 August 1881; *ibid.*, p. 240.
103 Letter to Robert Morier, 10 August 1881; E. Abbott and L. Campbell, *Life of Jowett*, ii, p. 184.
104 16 October 1881; W.H. Fremantle (ed), *Sermons Biographical by Benjamin Jowett*, pp. 146ff.
105 Fremantle, *op. cit.*, p. 151.

Select Bibliography

Primary Sources

Balliol College, Oxford archives: Jowett papers.
Bodleian Library, Oxford: misc. correspondence.
British Library, London: misc. correspondence.
Canterbury Cathedral archives: chapter minutes, 1850–60.
Cheshire Record Office, Chester: Stanley of Alderley records.
Christ Church, Oxford archive: Liddell papers, dean and chapter papers.
Lambeth Palace Library: Tait papers.
Pusey House, Oxford archive: Stanley papers (uncatalogued), *Chronicles of Convocation*, Canterbury.
Royal Archives, Windsor Castle: Stanley correspondence, Lady Augusta Bruce correspondence.
Rugby School archives: Arnold papers, Stanley papers (uncatalogued).
University College, Oxford archives: Stanley papers.
Westminster Abbey library and muniments: Stanley papers, chapter books 1860–85.

Books by Stanley

His publications are listed in full in appendix to R. E. Prothero, *Life and Correspondence of A. P. Stanley*, ii).

The Life and Correspondence of Thomas Arnold, i, ii, 1844.
Sermons and Essays on the Apostolical Age, 1847.
Addresses and Charges of E. Stanley, Bishop of Norwich, 1851.
The Epistles of St Paul to the Corinthians, i, ii, 1855.
Historical Memorials of Canterbury, 1855.
Sinai and Palestine, in connection with their History, 1856.
Three Introductory Lectures on the Study of Ecclesiastical History, 1857
Lectures on the History of the Eastern Church, 1861.

Sermons in the East, preached before the Prince of Wales, 1863.
Lectures on the History of the Jewish Church, i, 1863.
Lectures on the History of the Jewish Church, ii, 1865.
Historical Memorials of Westminster Abbey, 1868.
Essays Chiefly on Questions of Church and State, from 1850 to 1870, 1870.
Lectures on the History of the Church of Scotland, 1872.
Lectures on the History of the Jewish Church, iii, 1876.
Addresses and Sermons delivered during a visit to the United States and Canada, 1879.
Memoirs of Edward and Catherine Stanley, 1879.
Christian Institutions: Essays on Ecclesiastical Subjects, 1881.

Secondary Sources

The place of publication is London unless otherwise stated.

Abbott, Evelyn and Campbell, Lewis, *The Life and Letters of Benjamin Jowett, M.A.*, i, ii, John Murray, 1897.
—— (ed.), *Letters of Benjamin Jowett, M.A.*, John Murray, 1899.
Adeane, Jane H. and Grenfell, Maud (edd.), *Before and After Waterloo: Letters from Edward Stanley*, T. Fisher Unwin, 1907.
Aglen, Anthony S. (ed.), *A Selection from the Writings of Dean Stanley*, John Murray, 1894.
Annan, Noel, *The Dons: Mentors, Eccentrics and Geniuses*, Harper-Collins, 1999.
Arnold, Thomas, *Sermons, with an Essay on the Right interpretation and Understanding of the Scriptures*, ii, B. Fellowes, 1832.
Baillie, Albert, *My First Eighty Years*, John Murray, 1851.
Baillie, Albert and Bolitho, Hector, *A Victorian Dean: A Memoir of Arthur Stanley, Dean of Westminster*, Chatto & Windus, 1930.
—— (edd.), *Letters of Lady Augusta Stanley: A Young Lady at Court, 1849–1863*, Gerald Howe, 1927.
—— (edd.), *Later Letters of Lady Augusta Stanley, 1864–1876*, Jonathan Cape, 1929.
Bamford, T. W., *Thomas Arnold*, Cresset Press, 1960.
Barnes, Malcolm, *Augustus Hare*, Allen & Unwin, 1984.
Barrett, Philip, *Barchester: English Cathedral Life in the Nineteenth Century*, SPCK, 1993.

Bede, Cuthbert (Edward Bradley), *Mr Verdant Green: Adventures of an Oxford Freshman*, Macmillan, 1857.
Beeson, Trevor, *The Bishops*, SCM, 2002.
——, *The Canons*, SCM, 2006.
——, *The Deans*, SCM, 2004.
Benham, William (ed.), *Catharine and Craufurd Tait: A Memoir*, Macmillan, 1879.
Bergonzi, Bernard, *A Victorian Wanderer: The Life of Thomas Arnold the Younger*, Oxford University Press, Oxford, 2003.
Best, G. F. A., *Temporal Pillars: Queen Anne's Bounty, the Ecclesiastical Commissioners, and the Church of England*, Cambridge University Press, 1964.
Bill, E. G. W. and Mason, J. F. A., *Christ Church and Reform 1850–1867*, Oxford University Press, Oxford, 1970.
Bolitho, Hector, *A Biographer's Notebook*, Longmans, 1950.
Bradby, G. F., *The Lanchester Tradition*, Smith Elder & Co., 1914.
Bradley, George Granville, *Recollections of Arthur Penrhyn Stanley*, John Murray, 1883.
Briggs, Asa, *Victorian People: A Reassessment of Persons and Themes 1851–67*, Odhams Press, 1954.
Brock, M. G. and Curthoys, M. C. (edd.), *The History of the University of Oxford*, vi, vii, Oxford University Press, Oxford, 1997, 2000.
Bryce, James, *Studies in Contemporary Biography*, Macmillan, 1903.
Buckle, George Earle (ed.), *The Letters of Queen Victoria, 1862–1885*, i-iii, John Murray, 1926–8.
Buckton, Oliver S, *Secret Selves: Confession and Same-Sex Desire in Victorian Autobiography*, Union of North Carolina Press, 1998.
Carpenter, Edward (ed.), *A House of Kings: The History of Westminster Abbey*, A. & C. Black, 1966.
——, *Cantuar: The Archbishops in their Office*, Cassell, 1971.
Cecil, David, *A Portrait of Jane Austen*, Constable, 1978.
Chadwick, Owen (ed.), *The Mind of the Oxford Movement*, A. & C. Black, 1960.
——, *The Victorian Church*, i, ii, A. & C. Black, 1966, 1970.
Chandos, John, *Boys Together: English Public Schools 1800–1864*, Hutchinson, 1984.
Chorley, Katharine, *Arthur Hugh Clough: The Uncommitted Mind*, Oxford University Press, Oxford, 1962.
Cockshut, A. O. J., *Anglican Attitudes: A Study of Victorian Religious Controversies*, Collins, 1959.

——, *Truth to Life: The Art of Biography in the Nineteenth Century*, Collins, 1974.
Collins, Irene, *Jane Austen and the Clergy*, Hambledon Press, 1993.
Copley, Terence, *Black Tom – Arnold of Rugby: The Myth and the Man*, Continuum, 2002.
Cox, G. V., *Recollections of Oxford*, Macmillan, 1868.
Curthoys, Judith, *The Cardinal's College: Christ Church, Chapter and Verse*, Profile Books, 2012.
Daniell, G. W., *Bishop Wilberforce*, Methuen, 1891.
Dark, Sidney, *Five Deans*, Harcourt, Brace & Co., New York, 1928.
Darwall-Smith, Robin, *A History of University College, Oxford*, Oxford University Press, Oxford, 2008.
Davidson, Randall Thomas and Benham, William, *Life of Archibald Campbell Tait, Archbishop of Canterbury*, i, ii, Macmillan, 1891.
Davis, H. W. C., *Balliol College*, F. E. Robinson & Co., 1899.
Dewey, Clive, *The Passing of Barchester*, Hambledon Press, 1991.
Dunn, Waldo H., *English Biography*, J. M. Dent, 1916.
Elliott, Sir Ivo (ed.), *The Balliol College Register 1833–1933*, Oxford University Press, Oxford, 1934.
Ensor, R. C. K., *England, 1870–1914*, Oxford History of England, xiv, Oxford University Press, Oxford, 1936.
Essays and Reviews, Longmans, 1860.
Faber, Geoffrey, *Jowett: A Portrait with Background*, Harvard University Press, Cambridge, Massachusetts, 1958.
——, *Oxford Apostles: A Character Study of the Oxford Movement*, Faber & Faber, 1933.
Flindall, R. P. (ed.), *The Church of England 1815–1948: A Documentary History*, SPCK, 1972.
Forster, John, *The Life of Charles Dickens*, iii, Chapman and Hall, 1874.
Fremantle, W. H. (ed.), *College Sermons by the Late Benjamin Jowett, M.A.*, John Murray, 1896.
—— (ed.), *Sermons Biographical and Miscellaneous by the Late Benjamin Jowett, M.A.*, John Murray, 1899.
Gardiner, John, *The Victorians*, Hambledon and London, 2002.
Green, V. H. H., *A History of Oxford University*, B.T. Batsford, 1974.
——, *Oxford Common Room: A Study of Lincoln College and Mark Pattison*, Edward Arnold, 1957.
——, *Religion at Oxford and Cambridge*, SCM, 1964.
Grenville, J. A. S., *Europe Reshaped 1848–1878*, Fontana, 1976.
Grosskurth, Phyllis, *John Addington Symonds*, Longmans, 1964.

—— (ed.), *The Memoirs of John Addington Symonds*, Hutchinson, 1984.
Hamilton, Ian, *A Gift Imprisoned: The Poetic Life of Matthew Arnold*, Bloomsbury, 1998.
Hammond, Peter, *Dean Stanley of Westminster*, Churchman Publishing, Worthing, 1987.
——, *The Parson and the Victorian Parish*, Hodder and Stoughton, 1977.
Hampden, R. D., *Sermons Preached Before the University of Oxford, 1836 to 1847*, B. Fellowes, 1848.
Hare, Augustus J. C., *Biographical Sketches*, George Allen, 1895.
——, *Memorials of a Quiet Life*, i–iii, Strahan & Co., 1872–6.
——, *The Story of My Life*, i–vi, George Allen, 1896–1900.
Haultain, Arnold (ed.), *Reminiscences by Goldwin Smith, D.C.L.*, Macmillan, New York, 1910.
Heffer, Simon, *Moral Desperado: A Life of Thomas Carlyle*, Weidenfeld & Nicolson, 1995.
James, Herbert, *The Country Clergyman and His Work*, Macmillan, 1890.
Heywood, J., *The Recommendations of the Oxford University Commissioners, with Selections from their Report*, Longmans, 1853.
Hibbert, Christopher, *Queen Victoria: A Personal History*, HarperCollins, 2000.
—— (ed.), *Queen Victoria in her Letters and Journals*, John Murray, 1984.
Hill, Derek Ingram, *Christ's Glorious Church: The Story of Canterbury Cathedral*, SPCK, 1976.
Hinchliff, Peter, *Benjamin Jowett and the Christian Religion*, Oxford University Press, Oxford, 1987.
——, *John William Colenso: Bishop of Natal*, Thomas Nelson, 1964.
Honan, Park, *Matthew Arnold: A Life*, Weidenfeld & Nicolson, 1981.
Honey, J. R. de S, *Tom Brown's Universe: The Development of the Victorian Public School*, Millington Books, 1977.
Hope Simpson, J. B., *Rugby Since Arnold: A History of Rugby School from 1842*, Macmillan, 1967.
How, F. D., *Six Great Schoolmasters*, Methuen & Co., 1904.
Howes, Graham, 'Dr Arnold and Bishop Stanley', *Studies in Church History*, ii, ed. G. J. Cuming, Nelson, 1965.
Hughes, Thomas, *Memoir of a Brother*, Macmillan, 1871.
——, *Tom Brown's Schooldays*, Macmillan, 1857.

——, *Tom Brown at Oxford*, Macmillan, 1861.
Humphrey, Frances A., *Dean Stanley with the Children*, D. Lothrop & Co., Boston, 1884.
Jenkyns, Richard, *Westminster Abbey*, Profile Books, 2004.
Jones, John, *Balliol College: A History*, Oxford University Press, Oxford, 1988; 2nd edn. revised, 2005.
Kenny, Anthony, *Arthur Hugh Clough: A Poet's Life*, Continuum, 2005.
Lake, Katharine (ed.), *Memorials of William Charles Lake: Dean of Durham 1869–1894*, Edward Arnold, 1901.
Liddon, Henry Parry, *Life of Edward Bouverie Pusey*, iv, Longmans, 1897.
Longford, Elizabeth, *Victoria R.I.*, Weidenfeld & Nicolson, 1964.
——, *Wellington: Pillar of State*, Weidenfeld & Nicolson, 1972.
Lubbock, Adelaide, *Owen Stanley R.N. 1811–1850: Captain of the 'Rattlesnake'*, Heinemann, 1968.
Mack, Edward C., *Public Schools and British Opinion, 1780 to 1860*, Methuen & Co., 1938.
McCrum, Michael, *Thomas Arnold: A Reassessment*, Oxford University Press, Oxford, 1989.
Magnus, Philip, *King Edward the Seventh*, John Murray, 1964.
Mallett, Charles Edward, *A History of the University of Oxford*, i–iii, Methuen, 1924–7.
Marsh, P. T., *The Victorian Church in Decline*, Routledge & Kegan Paul, 1969.
Meacham, Standish, *Lord Bishop: The Life of Samuel Wilberforce, 1805–1873*, Harvard University Press, Cambridge, Massachusetts, 1970.
Meadows Cooper, J., *The Lives of the Deans of Canterbury, 1541 to 1900*, Cross & Jackman, Canterbury, 1900.
Mitchell, Leslie, *The Whig World 1760–1837*, Hambledon and London, 2005.
Mitford, Nancy (ed.), *The Ladies of Alderley: Letters Between Lady Stanley of Alderley and Henrietta Maria Stanley 1841–1850*, Hamish Hamilton, 1938.
——, *The Stanleys of Alderley: Their Letters Between the Years 1851–1865*, Hamish Hamilton, 1939.
Morrow, John, *Thomas Carlyle*, Hambledon Continuum, 2006.
Newsome, David, *Godliness and Good Learning: Four Studies on a Victorian Ideal*, John Murray, 1961.

Nicolson, Harold, *The Development of English Biography*, Hogarth Press, 1927.
Oliver, Grace A., *Arthur Penrhyn Stanley: His Life, Work, and Teachings*, Sampson Low, 1885.
Oxford Dictionary of National Biography, Oxford University Press, Oxford, 2004.
Pattison, Mark, *Memoirs*, Macmillan, 1885.
Prest, John (ed.), *Balliol Studies*, Leopard's Head Press, 1982.
Prothero, Roland E., *The Life and Correspondence of Arthur Penrhyn Stanley, D.D.*, i, ii, John Murray, 1893.
—— (ed.), *Letters and Verses of Arthur Penrhyn Stanley, D.D.*, John Murray, 1895.
Quinn, E. V. and Prest, J. M., *Dear Miss Nightingale: A Selection of Benjamin Jowett's Letters 1860–1893*, Oxford University Press, Oxford, 1987.
Rappaport, Helen, *Magnificent Obsession: Victoria, Albert and the Death that Changed the Monarchy*, Hutchinson, 2011.
Reardon, Bernard M. G., *From Coleridge to Gore: A Century of Religious Thought in Britain*, Longmans, 1971.
——, *Religious Thought in the Nineteenth Century*, Cambridge University Press, 1966.
Ridley, Jasper, *Lord Palmerston*, Constable & Co., 1970.
Rouse, W. H. D., *A History of Rugby School*, Duckworth & Co., 1898.
Rowse, A. L., *Matthew Arnold: Poet and Prophet*, Thames and Hudson, 1976.
Rugby School Register, 1675–1874, i, ii, A. J. Lawrence, Rugby, 1886.
St Aubyn, Giles, *Queen Victoria: A Portrait*, Sinclair-Stevenson, 1991.
Sanders, Charles Richard, *Coleridge and the Broad Church Movement*, Duke University Press, New York, 1942.
Sandford, E. G. (ed.), *Memoirs of Archbishop Temple by Seven Friends*, i, ii, Macmillan, 1906.
Selfe, Lt Col. Sydney, *History of Rugby School*, A. J. Lawrence, Rugby, 1910.
Shannon, Richard, *Gladstone: Peel's Inheritor, 1809–1865*, Hamish Hamilton, 1982.
Slater, Michael, *Charles Dickens*, Yale University Press, New Haven, 2009.
Somerset, Anne, *Ladies in Waiting: From the Tudors to the Present Day*, Phoenix, 1984.

Sparks, Margaret, *Canterbury Cathedral Precincts: A Historical Survey*, Dean and Chapter of Canterbury, Canterbury, 2007.
Sparrow, John, *Mark Pattison and the Idea of a University*, Cambridge University Press, 1967.
Stanley, Lord Thomas of Alderley, *The Stanleys of Alderley 1927–2001*, AMCD Publishers, Cheshire, 2004.
Strachey, Lytton, *Eminent Victorians*, Chatto & Windus, 1918.
——, *Queen Victoria*, Chatto & Windus, 1921.
Symondson, Anthony (ed.), *The Victorian Crisis of Faith*, SPCK, 1970.
Thomas, Donald, *Lewis Carroll: A Biography*, John Murray, 1996.
Thompson, Henry Lewis, *Christ Church*, F. E. Robertson and Co., 1900.
——, *Henry George Liddell, D.D., Dean of Christ Church, Oxford: A Memoir*, John Murray, 1899.
Thomson, David, *Europe Since Napoleon*, Longmans, 1957.
Tollemache, Hon. Lionel A., *Old and Odd Memories*, Edward Arnold, 1908.
Trevor, Muriel, *The Arnolds: Thomas Arnold and His Family*, Bodley Head, 1973.
Trevor-Roper, Hugh, *Christ Church Oxford: The Portrait of a College*, Governing Body of Christ Church, Oxford, 1950.
Trowles, Tony, *A Bibliography of Westminster Abbey, 1571–2000*, Boydell Press, Woodbridge, 2005.
Tuckwell, Rev. W., *Reminiscences of Oxford*, Cassell and Co., 1900.
Tyerman, Christopher, *A History of Harrow School*, Oxford University Press, Oxford, 2000.
Vidler, Alec R., *F. D. Maurice and Company: Nineteenth Century Studies*, SCM, 1966.
——, *The Church in an Age of Revolution: 1789 to the Present Day*, Penguin, 1961.
Ward, Sir A. W. and Waller, A. R. (edd.), *The Cambridge History of English Literature*, xii, Cambridge University Press, 1970.
Ward, Wilfrid, *William George Ward and the Oxford Movement*, Macmillan, 1889.
Ward, William, *The Ideal of a Christian Church Considered in Comparison with Existing Practice*, James Toovey, 1844.
Ward, W. R., *Victorian Oxford*, Frank Cass & Co., 1965.
Westall, Roy, *Wilmslow and Alderley Edge: A Pictorial History*, Phillimore & Co., Chichester, 1994.

Willey, Basil, *Nineteenth-Century Studies: Coleridge to Matthew Arnold*, Chatto & Windus, 1949.
——, *More Nineteenth-Century Studies: A Group of Honest Doubters*, Chatto & Windus, 1956.
Williams, David, *Too Quick Despairer: A Life of Arthur Hugh Clough*, Rupert Hart-Davis, 1969.
Wilson, A. N., *God's Funeral*, John Murray, 1999.
——, *The Victorians*, Hutchinson, 2002.
Winchester, Simon, *The Alice Behind Wonderland*, Oxford University Press, Oxford, 2011.
Witheridge, John, *Frank Fletcher: A Formidable Headmaster*, Michael Russell, Norwich, 2005.
Woodward, Frances J., *The Doctor's Disciples*, Oxford University Press, Oxford, 1954.
Woodward, Sir Llewellyn, *The Age of Reform, 1815–1870*, Oxford History of England, xiii, Oxford University Press, Oxford, 1962.
Wymer, Norman, *Dr Arnold of Rugby*, Robert Hale, 1953.

Index

Adelaide, Queen, 95 and n
Albert of Saxe-Coburg (Prince Consort), biography of, 20 and n; APS chaplain to, 165 and n, 220, 222, 231; and Great Exhibition, 165–6; 188; and Prince of Wales's education, 220–1, 222, 223; 230; and Prince of Wales's marriage, 233; death, 222, 231–2 and n, 235, 286, 288, 297 and n; funeral, 222–3
Alexander II, Tsar, 197, 289, 290, 291, 292
Alexandra ('Alix', Princess of Wales), 233, 234, 290, 299
Alford, Henry, 197 and n
Alfred, Prince (Duke of Edinburgh), marriage to Marie Alexandrovna, 289, 290, 291–2
Anstey, Charles Alleyne, 47 and n, 50
Argyll, 8th Duke of (George Douglas Campbell), 325
Arnold, Frances ('Fanny'), 305
Arnold, Mary, and Arnold's death, 9 and n, 25, 127; commissions Arnold's biography, 3, 7–8, 47–8, 134; 15, 128, 136, 151, 189, 207, 229, 286
Arnold, Matthew, 'Rugby Chapel', 14 and n, 15, 17; 124–5, 134, 258, 286, 305; and father's death, 128; praises *Sinai and Palestine*, 263; at APS's funeral, 325; 'Westminster Abbey', 326–7 and n
Arnold, Dr Thomas, Introduction and ch. 1 *passim*; 71, 72, 85, 89, 93, 103, 104, 105, 106, 109, 111, 112, 144, 151, 216, 236; character, 6, 10, 11, 16; Headmaster of Rugby, 4, 12–14, 15–17, 46, 51, 58, 157, 206, 207, 209; influences APS, and APS devoted to, *see* Stanley, A. P.; his sermons, 6, 52 and n–54, 60, 73, 75, 91, 92, 102, 113–14, 130, 205, 215, 224, 295; teacher, 54–7, 99, 295; 'Oxford Malignants', 11–12, 89, 90 and n–91, 97; recommended by Augustus Hare, 43, 44; and Biblical interpretation, 56–7, 60, 73, 97; stays at Alderley, 60–1; *Principles of Church Reform*, 62–3, 83, 97; Coleridge's influence, 73, 214; APS visits, 74, 75; and Newman, 88, 104–5, 106, 125–6; Ward visits, 92; recommended for preferment, 97, 124; *History of Rome*, 112, 130, 263; on subscription, 115, 116; regius professor, 124–6, 194; APS compares to his father, 151; death, 3, 7, 17–18, 126–8, 129, 223, 229, 287, 314; anniversary of, 294, 305; portrait, 169, Illustrations 2c
Arnold, Thomas, jnr ('Tom'), 37, 61, 126, 127, 134, 260
Arthur, Prince (Duke of Connaught), 25n, 290
Athanasian Creed, 114–16, 276 and nn, 279–9
Austen, Jane, 25, 26, 77, 170, 185; *Emma*, 25; *Mansfield Park*, 72, 88

Bagot, Richard, Bishop of Oxford, 116, 122; ordains APS, 116; Bishop of Bath and Wells, 171 and n
Baillie, Albert, 235n, 257
Baillie, Evan, 260, 297
Baillie, Lady Frances (*née* Bruce), 235 and n, 260, 297, 304, 323
Balliol College, Oxford, ch. 3 *passim*; 76 and n, 78–9, 199, 214n, 216, 218; scholarships, 64, 200; firsts, 199; fellowships, 200; Illustrations 4c

Barnby Joseph (*later* Sir), 274 and n
Barnes, Frederick ('Brains'), canon of Christ Church, 199
Barry, Alfred, 327
Barry, Charles (*later* Sir), 165
Bathhurst, Henry, Bishop of Norwich, 96
Beaufort, Lady Margaret, 29, 268 and n
Becket, St Thomas (Archbishop of Canterbury, 1162–74), APS fascinated by, 173–4; his essay on, 195, Appendix II (335–9)
Bede, Cuthbert (Edward Bradley), *Verdant Green*, 132
Bekker, (August) Immanuel, 141
Besant, Annie, 293
Bigge, Capt. Arthur (*later* Baron Stamfordham), 324 and n
Birch, Henry, 220
Bismark, Prince Otto von, 284, 285, 290
Blomfield, Charles James, Bishop of London, 117, 159n 178, 191
Blore, Edward, 321
Boehm, (Joseph) Edgar (*later* Sir, 1st Bart), 326
Bolitho, Hector, 235n
Bonaparte, Napoleon (Emperor Napoleon I), 32, 55, 58, 88, 96, 179, 290, 315
Bonaparte, Louis Napoleon (Emperor Napoleon III), 179, 188, 296, 315
Boswell, James, *Life of Johnson*, 3, 13, 58, 134, 135
Bowdler, John, 53
Bradby, G.F. (Godfrey Fox), *Lanchester Tradition*, 157n
Bradley, Edward, *see* Bede, C.
Bradley, George Granville, 18–19, 109–10, 129, 134; APS's biographer, 19, 20, 119, 120, 132, 133; describes University College, Oxford, 110–11; succeeds APS at Westminster, 328
Bridgeman, Mother Frances, 186
Brontë, Charlotte, describes Great Exhibition, 165
Brooks, Phillips, 308–9
Brown, H.F., 208

Brown, John, 289
Browning, Robert, 258, 301
Bruce, Sir Frederick, 306, 307
Bruce, Katherine, 232 and n, 235, 236
Bruce, Maj. Gen. Hon. Robert, 224, 306; Prince of Wales's governor, 221, 223, 235; tour of Egypt and Palestine, 224–7; death, 230–1, 238 and n
Bull, Dr John, 197
Bunsen, Christian Charles Jonas, Baron von ('Chevalier Bunsen'), 111, 118, 147, 165n, 214
Bunyan, John, 294
Burgess, Sarah, 41, 173
Burgon, John William, 280
Burns, Robert, 298
Burrows, Montagu, 280
Burton, Edward, 89
Butler, Arthur Gray, 195
Butler, Montagu, 327, 328

Caird, Richard, 273
Campbell-Bannerman, Sir Henry, 301 and n
Canterbury Cathedral, ch. 6 *passim*; 172, 173, 196; Illustrations 6c
Carlyle, Thomas, 74, 258, 301 and n, 320–1
Carroll, Lewis (Charles Lutwidge Dodgson), 202–3
Charterhouse, praised by Duke of Wellington, 36; Owen Stanley attends, 36, 48, 203n
Christ Church, Oxford, ch. 7 *passim*; 65, 76, 79, 80, 82, 92, 219–20, 221; history, 198 and n–201; cathedral, 116, 198, 204 and n, 217, 238; students, 193n, 199 and n, 200–1; Illustrations 10
Church, Richard William, 112, 139n, 264
Claughton, Thomas Legh, 100
Clayton, Eliza, 158, 165
Clifden, Nellie, 222, 233
Clough, Arthur Hugh, 103n, 109, 125, 205; F. Nightingale's cousin, 187; admires Arnold, 105; and Newman, 106; bombarded by Ward, 106;

Index 391

rejected by Balliol, 106; suggests the term 'Broad Church', 160
Cockshut, A.O.J., 9–10, 13, 20–1
Colenso, John William, 2, 252 and n, 262, 267; Bishop of Natal, 252–5
Coleridge, John Taylor (*later* Sir), 11
Coleridge, Samuel Taylor, 61, 71, 75, 203; and Bible, 73 and n, 74, 214
Compton, Lord Alwyne Frederick, 327
Conington, John, 209
Conroy, Sir John, 296
Cooper, James Fenimore, 307–8
Coronation, *see* Victoria, Queen
Cotton, George Edward Lynch, 110 and n, 192, 207
Cotton, Richard Lynch, 218 and n
Crawford, Capt. Donald, 32
Crimean War, 35, 185–8, 196, 235, 314, 320
Cromwell, Oliver, 83, 315
Cross, Mary Ann (*née* Evans), *see* Eliot, George

Darwin, Charles, 213
Davidson, Randall Thomas (Archbishop of Canterbury, 1903–28), 210, 313n
Denison, George Anthony, 258, 278 and n
Denison, Sir William, 158
Dickens, Charles, 21, 34, 46, 323; funeral, 269–71
Disraeli, Benjamin (1st Earl of Beaconsfield), 107, 320, 321
Dodgson, Charles Lutwidge, *see* Carroll, L.
Donkin, William Fishburn, 112
Drozdov, Philaret, Metropolitan of Moscow, 196–7 and n, 267

Eddis, Eden, 169 and n
Edinburgh Review, 12, 90n, 159, 164, 213n, 216, 217, 304
Edward ('Bertie', Prince of Wales), 203n, 258, 299, 301, 325, 328; education, 220–2; at Christ Church, 221–2; Clifden affair, 222, 223; tours Egypt and Palestine, 223–8, 229–31; marriage, 232–4, Illustrations 12a; illness, 288–9, 297; attends wedding of Prince Alfred, 290
Elgin, 8th Earl of (James Bruce), 238–9 and n, 306
Eliot, George (Mary Ann Cross, *née* Evans), 214
Elizabeth I, Queen, 245, 268, 315
Elton, Charles, 220
Erdmann, Johann Eduard, 141
Essays and Reviews, 213 and n, 214–17, 218, 246–7, 251, 253, 267, 276, 289, 318; judgment on, 246–7, 251, 287; Illustrations 12c
Ewald, Heinrich, 262–3, 264

Farrar, Frederic William, 207n, 313 and n, 324, 325, 327
Faber, Frederick William, 112, 113
Félix, Elisa-Rachel ('Rachel'), 148 and n
Feodore of Leiningen, Princess, 260 and n, 286
Findlay, William, 179, 180
Fitch, Sir Joshua Girling, 3n
Forster, John, 270
Forster, William Edward, 258, 325 and n
Frederick, Crown Prince of Prussia (*later* Kaiser Frederick III), 284, 285, 290
Freeman, Edward Augustus, 219
Fremantle, William H., 179, 180 and n
Froude, James Anthony, 87 and n
Froude, (Richard) Hurrell, 86–7

Gaisford, Thomas, Dean of Christ Church, 200, 201, 217
Gaskell, Mrs Elizabeth Cleghorn, 33
George III, King, 220
Gibbon, Edward, 25, 58, 80
Gilbert, Ashurst Turner, 102 and n
Girdlestone, Charles, 156–7
Gladstone, William Ewart, at Seaforth, 39, 41; and Oxford University, 76, 162 and n, 164; and Great Exhibition, 165; and death of Disraeli, 321; and death of APS, 325; and APS's successor, 327–8; 170, 251, 258, 261, 264, 277, 301

Goodwin, Charles Wycliffe, 214
Gorham, George Cornelius, 159–60, 216, 252; controversy and judgment, 159–61, 250, 267, 276
Goulburn, Edward Meyrick, 120; Headmaster of Rugby, 118, 174; Dean of Norwich, 174, 280–1
Gray, Robert, Bishop of Cape Town, 253; and Colenso, 253, 255–6
Great Exhibition, 165–6 and n, 175, 177, 247n, Illustrations 7a
Greenhill, William Alexander, 64 and n, 65
Gregory XVI (Pope, 1831–46), 120 and n–121
Greville, Charles Cavendish Fulke, 146 and n
Grosskurth, Phyllis, 208
Grote, George, 258, 269, 271
Grove, George (*later* Sir), 19n, 307 and n, 324

Hall, William, 128
Hampden, Renn Dickson, Regius Professor of Divinity, 11, 89–91, 97, 124, 139, 144; Bishop of Hereford, 144–6, 252; 85, 138, 216, 276; Illustrations 8b
Hansard, Septimus, 213
Hare, Augustus, marries Maria Leycester, 40, 43; recommends Arnold and Rugby, 43, 44; 56; advice on Oxford, 63–4; death, 71; 72
Hare, Augustus J.C. (John Cuthbert), 19 and n, 43, 173, 204; Stanley's adoptive cousin, 26, 71–2, 286n
Hare, Frances, 71
Hare, Julius Charles, 71–2, 74, 75, 82–3, 118, 129, 134, 145, 185 and n, 261, 267; disciple of Coleridge, 71, 214
Hare, Maria (*née* Leycester), 34, 38, 39, 74; marries Augustus Hare, 40, 43; widow, 71; adopts Augustus J. C. Hare, 71–2; death 286
Harper, Dr Gerald, 307, 315, 316, 323, 324
Harrison, Benjamin, canon of Canterbury, 171 and n, 174

Hawkins, Edward, Provost of Oriel, 4, 85 and n, 87, 143
Hawthorne, Nathaniel, 307
Hegel, George Wilhelm Friedrich, 141
Helena, Princess, 236
Henry VII, King, 29, 245, 268 and n–269; his Chapel, *see* Westminster Abbey
Henry VIII, King, 198, 217, 220, 233n, 245
Herbert, Sidney (*later* 1st Baron Herbert of Lea), 185, 186, 187
Hermann, Johann G.J., 140
Herschel, Sir John Frederick William (1st Bart), 269, 271
Heywood, James, 162
Hinds, Samuel, Bishop of Norwich, 156; 163
Holland, Francis, 287
Holland, Sir Henry (1st Bart), 287
Howley, William (Archbishop of Canterbury, 1828–48), 89, 97, 107, 144, 146, 170, 171
Hughes, Thomas, at Rugby, 15, 58, 68–7; *Tom Brown's Schooldays*, 6, 14, 15 and n, 16 and n, 17–18, 45, 46–7, 58, 64, 109, 110n, 136, 208, 210; *Tom Brown at Oxford*, 77, 205
Humphery, Geoffrey, 274
Hussey, Robert, 192–3
Huxley, Thomas Henry, 37, 213 and n

Jackson, Cyril, Dean of Christ Church, 200
Jacobson, William, 146; canon of Christ Church, 201
Jelf, Richard William, canon of Christ Church, 202
Jenkyns, Richard, Master of Balliol, 77, 79, 103–4, 123
Jenner, Sir William (1st Bart), 296, 297, 299, 323
Johnson, Dr Samuel, 3, 13, 134; describes Oxford, 76; *Life*, *see* Boswell, J.
Jones, John, 79
Jowett, Benjamin, described, 93–4; 103 and n, 139, 142, 143, 145, 151, 156, 179, 180 and n, 191, 193, 202, 216,

223, 228, 234, 237, 248, 264, 307; fellow of Balliol, 106; succeeds Tait as tutor, 132; on *Life of Arnold*, 3, 136 and n; tours Germany with APS, 140–1; studies German idealism, 141; visits France with APS, 147–50; relationship with APS, 154–5; his commentary on Pauline epistles, 155 and n, 214; and university reform, 162, 164; and Pusey, *see* Pusey, E.B.; and *Essays and Reviews*, 214–15, 216, 217, 218, 318; his stipend, 217–20, 276; his letter to APS, 316–19; at APS's funeral, 325, 328; praises APS, 328–9; Illustrations 7c

Kant, Immanuel, 141
Keats, John, 311
Keble, John, *Christian Year*, 58, 102, 305; opposes Arnold, 66; APS describes, 82, 102; assize sermon, 86 and n, 170; objects to *Sinai and Palestine*, 190–1; memorial, 268; 89, 91, 111, 202, 219, 247, 267
Kent, Duchess of, 295–6
Keppel, Capt., 224, 225, 276
King, Bryan, 212
Kingsley, Charles, 172, 258, 273 and n
Knox, John, 283

Lachmann, Karl, 141 and n
Lacordaire, Henri, 149
Lake, William Charles, APS's friend at Rugby, 9, 55 and n, 59; and Arnold's teaching, 55, 56; describes APS, 58; praepostor, 59; attracted to Newmanism, 105; fellow of Balliol, 106; and Arnold's death, 127, 128; 74, 75, 93, 103n, 109, 129, 134
Lamartine, Alphonse de, 149, 150
Lear, Edward, 303 and n
Lee, James Prince, 216n
Leopold I (King of the Belgians), 236
Leycester, Osward, 26
Liddell, Alice, 'Alice in Wonderland', 203 and n
Liddell, Henry George, father of 'Alice in Wonderland', 36, 203; at Charterhouse, 36, 203n; preaches at Stanley's ordination, 116n, 161; and *Lexicon*, 155; Oxford commission, 163; chaplain to Prince Albert, 221, 232; Headmaster of Westminster, 237, 244; Dean of Christ Church, 193, 194, 201; vice-chancellor, 280; officiates at APS's wedding, 239; preaches after Augusta's funeral, 301–2; 193, 194, 205, 237, 239, 324–5, 328; Illustrations 8c
Liddell, Lorina (*née* Reeve), 203 and n
Liddon, Henry Parry, 247 and n, 249, 278
Lightfoot, Joseph Barber, 216 and n, 249n
Lind, Johanna Maria ('Jenny'), 258
Livingstone, Dr David, 269, 271
Locker, Lady Charlotte (*née* Bruce), 323
Locker, Frederick, 254n, 258, 323
Lockhart, John Gibson, *Life of Scott*, 134, 135
Longley, Charles (Archbishop of Canterbury, 1862–8), 152n; officiates at wedding of Prince of Wales, 233; summons 1st Lambeth Conference, 255, 266
Lonsdale, James Gylby, 65
Louis Philippe (King of the French), 147, 148, 150, 301n, 315
Lowell, James Russell, 326
Loyson, Père Hyacinthe, 285 and n
Lushington, Stephen, 280 and n, 287
Lyall, William Lowe, Dean of Canterbury, 170, 171, 172, 197
Lyell, Sir Charles (1st Bart), 258, 269, 271

Macaulay, 1st Baron (Thomas Babington), 58
Manning, Henry (*later* Cardinal Archbishop of Westminster), 185 and n, 186
Maria of Hesse-Darmstadt, Tsarina, 291
Marie Alexandrovna (Duchess of Edinburgh), marries Prince Alfred, 289, 290, 291–2
Mary, Queen (Mary Tudor), 245, 268, 315

Maurice, F.D. (Frederick Denison), 72n, 118, 190, 202 and n, 203, 247
Meade, Hon. Robert Henry (*later* Sir), 224, 225, 226
Melbourne, 2nd Viscount (Henry Lamb), 11, 77, 89, 96, 107, 124, 261
Milman, Henry Hart, Dean of St Paul's, 177, 178, 192, 193
Milton, John, 57, 72, 83, 323
Minter, Dr, 224, 225
Mitford, William, 58
Moberly, George, praises Arnold, 46; Rugby examiner, 67; APS's tutor, 80, 81; Headmaster of Winchester, 67, 81; 82
Mohl, Julius, 224n
Mohl, Madame Mary, 224 and n, 235, 258, 296, 305
Montgomery, Henry, 313, 316
Montpensier, Duc de, 301 and n, 315
Morier, Robert Burnett David (*later* Sir), 147 and n
Müller, (Friedrich) Max, 112, 265, 273

Nares, Edward, 124
Neander, August, 141
Nelson, 1st Viscount (Admiral Horatio Nelson), 31n, 169n; *Life, see* Southey, Robert
Nelson, William, canon of Canterbury, 169n
Newman, John Henry (*later* Cardinal and The Blessed), and Arnold, 12, 66, 87, 88, 91, 125–6, 135; his sermons, 87, 88; Newmanism, 93, 103–4, 106, 112, 117; Tract XC, 121–3, 138; converts to Rome, 112, 140, 162, 185, 202, 211, 248; APS visits, 259–60; 21, 86n, 89, 137, 139, 264; Illustrations 6a
Nicolson, Harold, 4–5, 8, 10–11
Niebuhr, Barthold, 61, 118, 189; *History of Rome*, 61n, 112, 263
Nightingale, Florence, 258; and Mary Stanley, 185 and n, 186–8, 304; and Crimean War, 185–8
Nilsson, Christine, 258

Ogilvie, Charles Atmore, canon of Christ Church, 202
Owen, Sir Richard, 258
Oxford (Tractarian) Movement, causes, 86 and n–87, 170; and pull to Rome, 121–2, 185, 211; and Arnold, 124; collapse, 139–40, 142; 124, 162, 171, 202, 211, 276
Oxford University, 76–8; curriculum and examinations, 80–1; royal commission, 161–5, 175, 198, 199, 200; Oxford University Act (1854), 200–1

Paget, George Edward (*later* Sir), 36
Palgrave, Francis Turner, 147 and n
Palmer, Edwin, 328
Palmerston, 3rd Viscount (Henry John Temple), 191, 192, 210, 211, 234; funeral, 261, 269
Parry, Capt. Edward, 36, 40, 41
Parsons, John, Master of Balliol, 79, 80
Pattison, Mark, 99, 108n, 132, 162; and *Essays and Reviews*, 214, 215, 219
Paxton, Sir Joseph, 163
Pearson, Hugh, 19 and n; Stanley's travelling companion, 120, 121, 150; and Vaughan's resignation, 209, 210; 303, 318; and APS's death, 323, 324
Pearson, John Loughborough, 322
Peel, Sir Robert (2nd Bart), 77, 86 and n, 124, 129, 162 and n, 170
Penrhyn, Edward (*formerly* Edward Leycester), 32 and n, 75 and n
Penrose, John, 75–6
Phillips, Thomas, 169
Phillpotts, Henry, Bishop of Exeter, 107, 159n, 252; and Gorham controversy, 159, 160
Pius IX (Pope, 1846–78), 176, 261–2
Plumptre, Edward Hayes, 134
Plumptre, Frederic, Master of University College, Oxford, 109, 143 and n, 169, 179
Powell, Baden, 214n
Pretor, Alfred, 208, 209
Price, Bonamy, 129

Prince Imperial (Prince Napoleon), 188; monument, 315–6, 317
Prince Regent (*later* King George IV), 25
Prothero, Roland (*later* 1st Baron Ernle), *Life and Correspondence of A.P. Stanley*, 20–1, 51, 57, 108, 205, 206n, 210, 263, 271–2, 282
Pusey, Edward Bouverie, and Arnold, 12, 91; sermons, 87, 112; and Jowett, 202, 218, 219, 247–8; and *Essays and Reviews*, 213, 251; 89, 191, 193, 201, 202, 249n, 252, 278, 279

Ranke, Leopold von, 141
Rawson, William, 39 and n, 41, 49
Renan, Ernest, 224 and n, 258, 264, 265
Ritualism, 211–13 and n, 250, 267, 269 and n, 276; commission, 277–8
Robsart, Amy, 243 and n
Ronan, Father William, 186, 187
Routh, Martin Joseph, 202
Roxburgh, Duchess of, 288
Ruskin, John, 21
Russell, 1st Earl (John Russell), ecclesiastical appointments, 97, 144, 146, 156, 157, 169; and Oxford University reform, 162, 164; 165, 169, 177
Russell, Sir Odo William Leopold (*later* 1st Baron Ampthill), 290
Rutherford, Samuel, 283

Salisbury, 3rd Marquess of (Robert Gascoyne-Cecil), 296 and n, 298, 325
Scharf, George, 269
Schlippenbach, Countess, 202
Scott, Sir George Gilbert, 204n, 207, 275, 321–2
Scott, J. Oldrid, 322
Scott, Robert, 155, 249n
Scott, Thomas, 293
Scott, Sir Walter, 29, 298; APS's favourite author, 40, 282, 305; *Life*, *see* Lockhart, J.G.
Sedgwick, Adam, 153
Seeley, John, 264

Shaftesbury, 7th Earl of (Antony Ashley Cooper), 192, 264, 301
Shairp, John Campbell, 122, 298
Shelley, Percy Bysshe, 131 and n, 180
Sheriff, Lawrence, 50
Shuttleworth, Philip Nicholas, 82
Simpkinson, John, 125
Smith, (George) Vance, 248, 249, 284
Smith, Goldwin, 150, 162, 189
Smith, Canon Sydney, 287; praises Catherine Leycester, 26, 312; and public schools, 45, 53
Sophia, Queen of Holland, 260
Southey, Robert, *Life of Nelson*, 134, 135
Sparrow, John, 163
Stanley, Arthur Penrhyn (1815–81), *passim*; *Ancestry*: 28–30; coat of arms, 28, 29; *Childhood*, 1815–28: ch. 1 *passim*; birth, 25, 35; named after Duke of Wellington, 25; fascinated by history, 28; close to his mother, 37–8; character described by his mother, 35, 37, 38, 39, 40; school at Seaforth, 39–41, 43; studious, 40; love of poetry, 40; visit to Pyrenees, 41–3; Arnold and Rugby recommended, 43, 44; *Rugby School*, 1829–34: ch. 2 *passim*; APS's anxiety, 45; unpromising start, 47; nicknames, 47, 50; cleverness, 48–9, 52; examined by Arnold, 48, 50; influenced by Arnold, 5–6, 20, 52, 54, 57, 62, 93, 123, 143, 160, 189, 295, 311, 325; devoted to Arnold, 3, 67; his poetry, 50; sixth form, 7, 52, 54; praepostor, 7, 58; prizes, 50–1, 59–60, 67; books read, 57–8, 134; meets Wordsworth, 61; Balliol scholarship, 64–6; farewell to Arnold, 67; Illustrations 2b; *Balliol College, Oxford*, 1834–7: ch. 3 *passim*; stays with Julius Hare, 71–4; and John Sterling, 72–4; studies Coleridge, 73–4; visits Arnold, 74, 75; arrives in Oxford, 75–6; criticises his teachers, 81, 99; visits Vaughan in Cambridge, 82–3; religious controversies – subscription, 83–5;

Oxford Movement; 86–7; Hampden (1836), 89–91; compares Newman to Arnold, 88; criticises Arnold, 90–91; meets Ward, 92; befriends Jowett, 93; visits Dublin, 94, 98; on Roman Catholics, 94–5; visits Baden-Baden, 95; welcomes father's appointment to Norwich, 97, 98; drafts installation sermon, 98–9; prizes, 100 and n–102; final examinations, 99, 102; snubbed by Balliol, 103–4, 106; *University College, Oxford*, 1838–51: chapters 4, 5 *passim*; agonises over Newmanism, 105–6, 117; fellow and tutor, 108, 109, 111; attends Coronation, 107–8, 166, 177, 233, Appendix I (333–4); prize essays, 111; colleagues, 112; visits German universities, 112, 113, 162; ordination, 113–16; and subscription, 113, 114–16, 117, 170, 276–7; first sermons, 117; tours Continent, 117–121; and Tract XC, 121, 122–3; and Arnold's inaugural lecture, 125; and Arnold's death, 126–8; and Arnold's successor, 129–31; his lectures, 131–2; as tutor, 132–4; *Life of Arnold*, 134–6; and *Ideal of a Christian Church*, 136–9; tours Germany, 140–1; select preacher, 141–4 and n; and Hampden (1842), 144–6; visits France (1848), 147–50, 284; father's death, 151, 153–4; relationship with Jowett, 154–5; and Pauline epistles, 155 and n; and mother, 156, 159; offered deanery of Carlisle, 156; deaths of Owen and Charles, 158–9; and Gorham controversy, 159–61, 267; and Oxford commission, 161–5, 169, 175, 198; attends Great Exhibition, 165–6; appointed canon of Canterbury, 169, portrait, 169, Illustrations 6b; *Canterbury Cathedral*, 1851–8: ch. 6 *passim*; canon, 169, duties, 171, 172, 174–5, 197; his sermons, 172–3; home, 173; visits Italy, 175–7; attends Wellington's funeral, 177–9; tours Egypt and Palestine, 175, 179–84; and Mary's conversion to Rome, 187, 188; visits Paris (1856), 188–9; appointed Regius Professor of Ecclesiastical History, 192–3, 198; his lectures, 193–5; 197; visits Russia, 195–7; Illustrations 9; *Christ Church, Oxford*, 1858–63: ch. 7 *passim*; canon and regius professor, 204; house, 204, 243, 256; his lectures, 205; his sermons 205–6; and Vaughan's resignation, 210–11; and ritualism, 211, 213, 267; and *Essays and Reviews*, 215, 216, 217, 267; and Jowett's stipend, 217–19; lectures Prince of Wales, 221; accompanies Prince of Wales to Egypt and Palestine, 223–8, 229–31, 290; and mother's death, 227–9; and first anniversary of Prince Albert's death, 231–2; attends wedding of Prince of Wales, 232–3; engaged to Augusta Bruce, 236–7; appointed Dean of Westminster, 235, 236, 237; wedding, 239; Illustrations 11; *Westminster Abbey*, 1864–81: chs 8, 9, 10 *passim*; dean, 109, 243, 245, 246, 267; deanery, 256, 257–9; duties, 244, 259; and Pusey, 247–8, 278, 279; and revision of New Testament, 248–9; and Convocation, 248 and n, 249, 250–1, 254–5; and Colenso, 252, 253–5; and Augusta, 256–7; visits Newman, 259–60; and Palmerston's funeral, 261; audience with Pius IX, 261–2; and Biblical criticism, 262–5; and the dead, 268–71, 286–8, 320–1; his sermons, 211–12, 280, 289; and Nonconformists, 272–3, 294; and Athanasian Creed, 276–9; officiates at wedding of Prince Alfred, 289–92; returns to Rugby, 294–5, Appendix IV (342–5); and Augusta's illness and death, 292, 296–301, 302, 303–6, 311, 317; visits USA and Canada, 307–11; and Mary's death, 314; and monument to Prince Imperial,

315–16; letter from Jowett, 316–19; illness, 323 and n–324; death, 324; funeral, 325–6; Illustrations 13b, 14, 15, 16; Books: *Life and Correspondence of T. Arnold* (1844), Introduction *passim*; 207; success of, 3–4, 10, 135, 136n, 144, 308; influenced by, 134–5; influence of, 136, 157; critics, 4–5; impartial, 8–9, 19; death scene, 9–10, 127–8, 223; 12th edn, 322; *Miscellaneous Works of T. Arnold* (ed., 1845), 12n; *Addresses and Charges of E. Stanley* (1851), 154 and n, 312; *Epistles of Paul to the Corinthians* (1855), 155 and n, 214; *Historical Memorials of Canterbury* (1855), 174, 265, 266, Appendix II (335–9); *Sinai and Palestine* (1856), 229; popularity of, 189, 308; Arnold's influence, 189, 263; Keble's objections, 190–1; *Lectures on History of Eastern Church* (1861), 194n; *Sermons in the East* (1863), 230, 231; *Lectures on History of Jewish Church*, 254n, 262–3 and n, 264; vol. i (1863), 236, 262, 303; ii (1865), 263, Appendix III (340–1); iii (1876), 298–9, 303–4; *Historical Memorials of Westminster Abbey* (1868), 265–6, 268; *Essays on Questions of Church and State* (1870), 267, 277, 307n; *Lectures on History of Church in Scotland* (1872), 283; *Addresses and Sermons during visit to US and Canada* (1879), 311–12; *Memoirs of E. and C. Stanley* (1879), 154 and n, 312; *Christian Institutions* (1881), 319–20

Stanley, Lady Augusta (*née* Bruce, APS's wife), 235n, 238, 239, 259, 282, 285, 286, 288, 307, 316; Queen's lady-in-waiting, 21, 227, 232, 235, 292; engaged to APS, 236–7; wedding, 239; assists APS, 244, 256–7, 274–5; 292, 293–4, 298, 304; entertains, 257–9, 272; attends wedding of Prince Alfred, 289–92; illness, 292, 296–7, 298–300, 298–300; edits Duchess of Kent's journals, 295–6; funeral, 301–2, 303; after death, 303–6, 311, 314, 317; Illustrations 12b

Stanley, Catherine ('Kitty', APS's mother), 26, 41, 43, 45, 49, 74, 75, 95, 97, 156, 158, 179, 204, 211, 217, 223; marries Edward Stanley, 26, 34; portrait, 26, Illustrations 1b; character, 26, 34–5, 312; visits Waterloo, 32; describes her children, 35, 37, 38, 39, 40; teaches her children, 34, 38; chooses Arnold and Rugby, 44; admires Arnold's influence, 60, 62; and deaths of Owen and Charles, 159; in Canterbury, 173, Illustrations 1c; death, 227–8, 230, 236, 300, 314

Stanley, Catherine, jnr (APS's sister), 102, 141, 206–7, 307, 324, 326; marriage to C. Vaughan, 326, 159, 185, 209, 211, 229, 305; travels with APS, 141, 158, 314, 315; death, 36

Stanley, Charles ('Charley', APS's brother), 107, 156, 158; at Rugby, 35, 60; army officer, 36, 120, 158; death, 36, 158, 159

Stanley, Edward (APS's father), 30, 41, 47, 48, 51, 60, 102, 124, 157, 158; birth, 26; education, 30–1; naval ambitions, 26, 31 and n; grand tour, 32, 147; visits Waterloo, 32, 284; ordination, 33; rector of Alderley, 26, 27, 31, 33–4; marries Catherine Leycester, 26, 34; visits Seaforth, 41; *Observations on Religion in Ireland*, 94; Bishop of Norwich, 96–9, 150, 151, 152 and n–153, 154, 158, 238, 252, Illustrations 1a; on subscription, 117; consecrates Hampden, 146; death, 151, 159; funeral, 153–4; APS compares to Arnold, 151

Stanley, Edward (*later* 8th Bart and 2nd Baron Stanley of Alderley, APS's cousin), 27, 89, 188, 261

Stanley, Elfrida (APS's cousin), 27

Stanley, Emmeline ('Emmy', APS's cousin), 27

398　　　　　　　　　　　*Index*

Stanley, Lady Henrietta Maria (*née* Dillon, APS's cousin by marriage), 187, 188, 211, 221, 261
Stanley, Isabella (APS's cousin), 36
Stanley, John ('Johnny'), 188, 211
Stanley, Sir John Thomas (6th Bart, APS's grandfather), 30
Stanley, Sir John (7th Bart and 1st Baron Stanley of Alderley, APS's uncle), 25, 26, 27, 30, 33, 157 and n
Stanley, Lucy (APS's cousin), 32, 41 and n
Stanley, Lady Margaret (*née* Owen, APS's grandmother), 30
Stanley, Lady Maria Josepha (*née* Holroyd, APS's aunt), 25, 26, 157, 159, 171, 227
Stanley, Mary ('Mäi', APS's sister), 27, 35, 41, 95, 102, 158, 159, 175, 179, 204, 231; close to APS, 35, 185; and father's death, 151; in Canterbury, 173, 185; meets F. Nightingale, 185; nurses in Crimea, 186–7, 235; clashes with Nightingale, 186–8, converts to Rome, 187, 188, 191, 304; describes Prince of Wales's wedding, 233–4; and APS's marriage, 235; death, 314; Illustrations 1d
Stanley, Owen (APS's brother), 27, 35, 40, 97, 106, 156; 312; character, 37; at Charterhouse, 36, 43, 48; naval ambitions, 36; captains HMS *Rattlesnake*, 158–9; death, 158, 159
Stanley, Sir Thomas (*later* 1st Earl of Derby), 29, 326
Stanley, William (APS's cousin), 27, 188
Sterling, John, 118; J. Hare's curate, 72, 73, 74, 83; idolises Coleridge, 73; death, 74
Stockmar, Christian, Baron von, 220 and n, 222
Strachey, (Giles) Lytton, *Eminent Victorians*, 185n
Stratford de Redcliffe, 1st Viscount (Stratford Canning), 184–5
Strauss, David Friedrich, *Leben Jesu*, 214, 264
Subscription to Articles, 83–85 and n,
89, 93, 107, 117, 138, 217, 277, 279, 280; at APS's ordination, 113, 114–16, 117, 170, 276–7; Clerical Subscription Act (1865), 277
Sumner, John Bird (Archbishop of Canterbury, 1848–62), 146, 216, 234
Sutherland, Duchess of, 234, 277
Symonds, Dr John Addington, 208, 209, 210, 211, 314
Symonds, John Addington, jnr, and Vaughan's resignation, 208–11

Tait, Archibald Campbell (Archbishop of Canterbury, 1868–82), Headmaster of Rugby, 82, 129, 130, 131, 157, 203, 207, Illustrations 7b; Stanley's tutor, 82, 93, 132–3; 91, 94, 103n, 108, 117, 121n, 139, 144, 193, 318, 228; described, 93; disagrees with Ward, 93, 123; visits German universities, 112, 113, 162; opposes Tract XC, 121, 122; Dean of Carlisle, 157, 158; and Oxford commission, 163–5; daughters' deaths, 192 and n, 313; Bishop of London, 191–2, 211, 212, 213, 222, 234, 247, 277; and *Essays and Reviews*, 216, 217; Archbishop, 252, 269, 272, 278, 279, 301, 323, 324; attends APS's funeral, 326
Tait, Catherine, 312n, 313
Tait, Crauford, 312n, 313 and n
Talbot, Revd the Hon. George, 176 and n
Teesdale, Maj. Christopher, Prince of Wales's equerry, 221; tour of Egypt and Palestine, 224–5, 226, 227
Temple, Frederick (Archbishop of Canterbury, 1896–1902), 214n, 247; and *Essays and Reviews*, 214, 215, 216, 217; Headmaster of Rugby, 251; Bishop of Exeter, 251–2, 258, 318, 325
Tennyson, Alfred (*later* 1st Baron) 258
Thackeray, William Makepeace, 36, 270
Thirlwall, Connop, 83, 145, 253n; Bishop of St David's, 260–1, 269n, 278

Thompson, Henry Lewis, 205–6
Thynne, Canon Lord Charles, 170–1
Thynne, Canon Lord John, 244, 322
Tipping, Gartside, 48 and n
Tollemache, Hon. Lionel, 211 and n
Torrigiano, Pietro, 268
Tract XC, 121–3, 136, 138, 139, 276
Trench, Richard Chenevix, Dean of Westminster, 234–5, 236, 247n, 250, 274
Trevelyan, George Macaulay, 86
Trollope Anthony, *Barchester Towers*, 96, 124, 170n; *The Warden*, 145, 159n, 170n; *The Way We Live Now*, 152n
Tulloch, John, 273
Twiss, Travers, 111–12
Tyndall, John, 258

University College, Oxford, chs 4, 5 *passim*; 108–9, 110–11, 131, 142, 162n, 163; Illustrations 5b
Ussher, Archbishop James, 283 and n

Vaughan, Charles John, Stanley's friend at Rugby, 4, 6–7, 51, 54, 59, 129, 206 and n, 210, 294, 314; praepostor, 59; wins scholarship to Trinity, Cambridge, 67; marries Catherine Stanley, 4, 36, 159, 206–7, 210; Headmaster of Harrow, 4, 36, 67, 188, 207, 243; resignation, 206–11; Dean of Llandaff, 314; preaches after Augusta's funeral, 310; preaches before Stanley's funeral, 4, 51, 207, 324, 325, 326; Illustrations 4b; 54, 61, 74, 75, 100, 102, 130, 146, 169n, 305, 313
Vaughan, Henry Halford, 147 and n
Victoria, Queen, 20, 21, 188, 191, 220, 223, 227, 231, 234, 256, 265, 286, 304, 375; Coronation, 107–8, 166, 177, 233, Appendix I (333–4), Illustrations 5a; APS chaplain to, 165, 231; and Great Exhibition, 165, 166; and Prince Albert's death, 232 and n, 288; and Prince of Wales's marriage, 233–4; and Prince of Wales's illness, 289; visits deanery, 258; and marriage of Prince Alfred, 289; and Augusta's illness; 295, 297, 299, 300; and Augusta's death, 301, 302, 306; and Disraeli's death, 321 and n; and APS's death, 325–6; and APS's successor, 327–8
Victoria, Princess Royal ('Vicky', Crown Princess of Prussia), 222, 258–259 and n, 284, 285, 290
Voysey, Charles, 293

Wake, Lady Charlotte, 192
Waller, Edmund, 266
Walrond, Theodore, 19n, 179–80 and n; Stanley's literary executor, 19, 180n; accompanies APS to Egypt and Palestine, 179
Walton, Izaak, *Lives* of poets, 58, 134
Ward, William George, 94, 112, 216; described, 91; visits Arnold, 92; Clough's tutor, 105–6; drawn to Rome, 121, 123; and Tract XC, 123; *Ideal of a Christian Church*, 136–40; degradation, 137, 139, 219, 276; converts to Rome, 139–40
Waterloo, Battle of, 25, 27, 32–3, 284
Waters, Benjamin, 204, 259
Watts, Isaac, 268
Waugh, Evelyn, *Brideshead Revisited*, 230
Wellesley, Gerald, 327
Wellington, 1st Duke of (Arthur Wellesley), 25, 85–6; Stanley named after, 25; praises Charterhouse, 36; chancellor of Oxford University, 84, 95, 163, 179; death, 175; funeral, 175, 177–178 and n, 179, Illustrations 8a
Wesley, Charles, 268
Wesley, John, 268, 311–12, 321
Westbury, 1st Baron (Richard Bethell), 287–8
Westcott, Brooke Foss, 207n, 217, 249n, 325
Westminster Abbey, chs 8, 9, 10 *passim*; 196, 267, 270, 312; history, 245, and nn–246; Jerusalem Chamber, 249, 256, 269, 278; Henry

VII's Chapel, 245, 249, 268, 269n, 301, 305, 315, 326; monuments, 268–9; 274; restoration, 275, 321–2; Illustrations 13a

Westminster, 1st Duke of (Hugh Lupus Grosvenor), 301, 325

Whately, Richard, 92 and n, 138, 234n; *Historic Doubts*, 58; Archbishop of Dublin, 117; on college lectures, 131–2

Whewell, William, 83

White, Gilbert, 31 and n

Wilberforce, Robert Isaac, 87n

Wilberforce, Samuel ('Soapy Sam'), attacks evolution, 13; 145 and n, 146 and n, 226; Bishop of Oxford, 226 and n; and *Essays and Reviews*, 216, 288; chaplain to Prince Albert, 232; Bishop of Winchester, 249, 251; death, 288

Wilberforce, William, 145

Wilhelm (*later* Crown Prince of Prussia and Kaiser Wilhelm II), 234

Williams, Rowland, and *Essays and Reviews*, 214, 217, 246–7, 287

Wilson, Henry Bristow, opposes Tract XC, 122 and n, 214n; and *Essays and Reviews*, 214, 217, 246–7, 287–8

Wolsey, Cardinal Thomas, 198

Wood, Mrs Henry, *East Lynne*, 226

Woolf, Virginia, 4, 47–8

Wordsworth, Christopher, Rugby examiner, 67, 83; Headmaster of Harrow, 67, 207 and n, 243, 252; canon of Westminster, 243–4; Bishop of Lincoln, 248, 258

Wordsworth, Mary (*née* Hutchinson), 61, 62

Wordsworth, William, and French Revolution, 32; Stanley meets, 61–2; 72, 75, 111, 205, 323